Object Oriented Perl

D0597983

Object Oriented Perl

DAMIAN CONWAY

 MANNING

Greenwich
(74° w. long.)

For electronic browsing and ordering of this and other Manning books, visit http://www.manning.com. The publisher offers discounts on this book when ordered in quantity. For more information, please contact:

Special Sales Department
Manning Publications Co.
209 Bruce Park Avenue   Fax: (203) 661-9018
Greenwich, CT 06830   email: orders@manning.com

©2000 by Manning Publications Co. All rights reserved.

No part of this publication may be reproduced, stored in a retrieval system, or transmitted, in any form or by means electronic, mechanical, photocopying, or otherwise, without prior written permission of the publisher.

Many of the designations used by manufacturers and sellers to distinguish their products are claimed as trademarks. Where those designations appear in the book, and Manning Publications was aware of a trademark claim, the designations have been printed in initial caps or all caps.

♾ Recognizing the importance of preserving what has been written, it is Manning's policy to have the books we publish printed on acid-free paper, and we exert our best efforts to that end.

Library of Congress Cataloging-in-Publication Data
Conway, Damian, 1964-
    Object oriented Perl / Damian Conway.
      p. cm.
    includes bibliographical references.
    ISBN 1-884777-79-1 (alk. paper)
    1. Object-oriented programming (Computer science) 2. Perl
(Computer program language) I. Title.
    QA76.64.C639   1999
    005.13'3--dc21   99-27793
                                             CIP

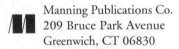 Manning Publications Co.   Copyeditor: Adrianne Harun
209 Bruce Park Avenue   Typesetter: Tony Roberts
Greenwich, CT 06830   Cover designer: Leslie Haimes

Printed in the United States of America
5 6 7 8 9 10 – VHG – 05 04 03 02

For Linda

contents

foreword

I've waited years for the perfect object-oriented Perl book to use for our Stonehenge corporate and open trainings, and the wait is now over. Damian Conway has written a comprehensive guide, organized well for both the casual OO hacker as well as the experienced OO user, including large reusable chunks of code (and that's what OO is all about).

Damian's humor makes the reading light and fast. The depth of coverage from "what's the big fuss about Perl objects?" to "creating a self-tied inheritable overloaded filehandle with auto-loaded accessors" means that this is the first and last book I need to teach Perl objects to my students.

For experienced users, the appendix comparing and contrasting Perl with other popular OO languages is by itself worth the entire price of the book. I've been recommending this book heartily upon seeing the first draft. Thank you, Damian.

RANDAL L. SCHWARTZ

preface

What's this book about?

This book is about the Laziness—on a grand scale.

It's about how to create bigger, more robust applications that require less effort to build, less time to debug, fewer resources to maintain, and less trouble to extend.

Specifically, it's about how to do all that with the object-oriented features of Perl—how those features work and how to make use of the many labor-saving techniques and "tricks" that they make possible. Presenting these new language features requires only a few chapters (specifically, chapters 3 to 6), but the range of programming styles and idioms they make available would fill several books. *This* book concentrates on the most useful and powerful ways to use object-oriented Perl.

This book is also about the tremendous *flexibility* of Perl's approach to object orientation, and how—in Perl—there's almost always more than one object-oriented way to solve a given problem. You'll find that the text revisits a few key examples time and again, extending and re-implementing them in various ways. Sometimes those changes will add extra functionality to a previous example; sometimes they'll merely illustrate an alternative solution with different strengths and limitations.

This book is about helping you to develop new Perl programming skills that *scale*. Perl is a great language for "one-line-stands": ad hoc solutions that are quick, cryptic, and unstructured. But Perl can also be a great language for developing large and complex applications. The only problem is that "quick, cryptic, and unstructured" is cute in a throw-away script, but not so amusing in 5,000 or 50,000 lines of application code. Object-oriented programming techniques are invaluable for building large, maintainable, reusable, and comprehensible systems in Perl.

Finally, this book is about how Perl makes object-oriented programming more enjoyable and how object-oriented programming makes Perl more enjoyable too. Life is too short to endure the cultured bondage-and-discipline of Eiffel programming or wrestle the alligators that lurk in the muddy semantics of C++. Object-oriented Perl gives you all the power of those languages (and more!) with few of their tribulations. And, best of all, like regular Perl, it's fun!

Who's this book for?

This book was written for the whole Perl community. In other words, for an eclectic range of people of wildly differing backgrounds, interests, and levels of experience.

To that end, it starts slowly, assuming only a basic familiarity with the core features of Perl itself: scalars, arrays and hashes, pattern matching, basic I/O, and simple subroutines. If these things sound familiar, this book is definitely for you. If they don't, chapter 2 provides a quick refresher course in everything you'll need to know.

The only other assumption that's made is that you're interested in object orientation. Maybe you've only heard about its many advantages. Maybe you're familiar with the basic concepts (if not, see chapter 1). Maybe you've already had some experience—even a bad one!—in another object-oriented language. If so, you might find appendix B a useful place to start.

If you've already dabbled in object-oriented Perl—perhaps blessed a hash or two—this book is also for you. If you start at chapter 4, you'll find a range of increasingly specialized techniques to expand your repertoire and, maybe, even challenge some of your notions about object-oriented programming.

If you're an experienced object-oriented Perl programmer, this book's for you too. The earlier chapters might contain a few tricks you haven't seen before—blessed a regular expression or a typeglob lately?—and the later chapters may suggest some novel approaches you haven't considered. (The section on generic trees in chapter 12, for example, is worth a look.)

Even if you're a Perl guru, this book's *still* for you. Check out chapter 7, where object methods that don't have a class are called on class objects that don't have a method. Or try chapter 11, where objects are stored as one of their own attributes. Or explore chapter 13, where the entire dispatch mechanism is replaced with one that provides multiply dispatched methods and subroutine overloading.

So what is *object-oriented Perl?*

Object-oriented Perl is a small amount of additional syntax and semantics, added to the existing imperative features of the language. Those extras allow regular Perl packages, variables, and subroutines to behave like classes, objects, and methods.

Object-oriented Perl is also a small number of special variables, packages, and modules, and a large number of new techniques, that together provide inheritance, data encapsulation, operator overloading, automated definition of commonly used methods, generic programming, multiply-dispatched polymorphism, and persistence.

It's an idiosyncratic, no-nonsense, demystified approach to object-oriented programming with a typically Perlish disregard for accepted rules and conventions. Object-oriented Perl draws inspiration, and sometimes syntax, from many different object-oriented predecessors, adapting their ideas to its own needs. It reuses and extends the functionality of existing Perl features and, in the process, throws an entirely new slant on what they mean.

In other words, it's everything that regular Perl is, only object-oriented.

What object-oriented Perl isn't

Perl was not originally designed—or implemented—as an object-oriented language. Its version of object orientation is simple and well integrated, but not fundamental to the language.[1]

---

[1] …as it is in Java, or Eiffel, or Python, for example.

That evolutionary development shows in the few places where object-oriented features of the language are still experimental or incomplete. For example, recent versions of the Perl compiler support weakly typed variables, which provide compile-time checking and optimization for accesses to the data stored in Perl objects. But the current version of the mechanism doesn't actually enforce type safety or proper data encapsulation, nor does it fully support inheritance.

Because Perl wasn't originally designed as an object-oriented language, object-oriented Perl isn't fast. Calling a method through an object is *significantly* slower than calling a regular Perl subroutine. Just how much slower is a matter of some debate, and depends on whether you measure entire software systems or just raw single-call invocation speed.

A single method call is about 30 percent slower than a regular call to the same subroutine (depending on your hardware, your operating system, the phase of the moon, etc.) But though they're individually much slower, method calls are more powerful than regular subroutine calls, due to a feature known as polymorphism (see chapters 1 and 7). In a larger system, that redresses the speed imbalance in a little, but, in general, it's fair to say that an object-oriented implementation of a system in Perl will almost never be faster than the equivalent non-object-oriented implementation, and will usually be somewhere between 20 to 50 percent slower.

Those figures are enough to turn many people away from object-oriented Perl, and that's a pity because then they miss out on the many compensating benefits of object-oriented design and implementation: simpler analysis methods, a domain-oriented approach to design, cleaner and more compact code, more robust implementations, greater code modularity, easier debugging, more comprehensible interfaces to modules (including operator-based interfaces), better abstraction of software components, less namespace pollution, greater code reusability, scalability of software, and better marketability of the final product.[2]

The sad thing is that people get spooked by the numbers (*20 to 50 percent slower!!!*) and forget what that really means (*…just as fast in six months time, when processor speeds have doubled*).

About this book

This book is arranged as a tutorial on the object-oriented features of Perl, and the many techniques developed for using those features.

Chapter 1 provides a quick revision of the fundamentals of object orientation: objects, classes, attributes, methods, inheritance, polymorphism, aggregation, interfaces, genericity, and persistence. Chapter 2 offers a refresher on aspects of the Perl language most relevant to object-oriented Perl: basic data types, subroutines and closures, references, packages and modules, typeglobs, and the CPAN.

Chapter 3 introduces the basic features of Perl's object-oriented mechanisms, concentrating on the most commonly used way of building classes and objects. Chapters 4 and 5 explore numerous other ways of implementing objects in Perl. Chapter 6 introduces Perl's inheritance mechanism and chapter 7 discusses Perl's approach to polymorphism.

---

[2] Not to mention that, according to its more extreme proponents, object-oriented programming apparently builds cardiovascular fitness, reduces weight, lowers cholesterol, makes money fast, promotes world peace, and improves your love life.

Chapter 8 describes two freely available packages that can be used to automate the creation of class methods and attributes. Chapter 9 describes the Perl tie mechanism, which allows objects to be accessed like regular Perl variables or filehandles. This theme is continued in chapter 10 where Perl's operator overloading facilities are introduced.

Chapter 11 looks at the problem of Perl's poor support for encapsulation and suggests three class implementation techniques that can be used to protect attributes within objects. Chapter 12 explains why generic programming techniques are rarely needed in Perl and suggests several useful approaches for the few situations where they are required.

Chapter 13 looks at a generalized form of polymorphism known as multiple dispatch, which allows every argument of a method call to contribute to the invocation process. Chapter 14 examines how persistence techniques can be integrated with an object-oriented system.

Appendix A provides a condensed summary of Perl's object-oriented features, with examples of the syntax for each. Appendix B provides an overview of those same features designed to assist programmers who are already familiar with one of four major object-oriented languages: Smalltalk, C++, Java, and Eiffel. A glossary of important object-oriented terms is also provided.

Throughout the text, each feature and technique is introduced with an example of a common type of programming problem that the feature or technique helps to solve. If you're looking for a specific technique to solve a particular problem, here's a list of the example problems and the chapter and section in which they're discussed. The words *(and following)* indicate a major example that continues in subsequent sections of the same chapter.

- **Bit-strings**
  Chapter 4: *A bit-string class*
  Chapter 6: *The "empty subclass" test*

- **Bugs: storing reports**
  Chapter 3: *Three little rules*
  Chapter 8: *Creating classes* (and following)

- **Case insensitive hashes**
  Chapter 9: *Case-insensitive hashes*

- **CDs: storing catalog information**
  Chapter 3: *A simple class* (and following)
  Chapter 4: *Reimplementing CD::Music* (and following)
  Chapter 6: *Inheriting the CD::Music class*
  Chapter 8: *Automating the CD::Music class* (and following)

- **Chemical vs medical names**
  Chapter 11: *Ambiguous keys in a secure hash*

- **Colours: RGB representation**
  Chapter 11: *Converting to "fast" mode* (and following)

- **Contacts data**
  Chapter 14: *Class specific persistence* (and following)

- **Days of the week**
  Chapter 10: *Fallback operations* (and following)

- Regular expressions: making them more readable
    Chapter 5: *Blessing a regular expression* (and following)

- Roman numerals
    Chapter 10: *A Roman numerals class* (and following)

- Round pegs in square holes
    Chapter 13: *Handling dispatch resolution failure*

- Semaphores: control of a transceiver
    Chapter 4: *Advantages of a pseudo-hash* (and following)
    Chapter 6: *Inheritance and pseudo-hashes*

- Soldiers: dog-tag information
    Chapter 8: *Key-like attributes*
    Chapter 11: *Encapsulation via closures* (and following)

- Stringification: of simple and hierarchical data types
    Chapter 13 *Nonclass types as parameters* (and following)
    Chapter 14: *Encoding/serialization*

- Taxonomies
    Chapter 6: *Constructors and inheritance* (and following)

- Trees: generic binary search trees and heaps
    Chapter 12: *The generic Tree class* (and following)

- Unique IDs: autoincremented scalar variables
    Chapter 9: *A simple example*

Typographical conventions

The following typographical conventions are used throughout this book:

- Technical terms (all of which are explained in the Glossary) are introduced in *italics*.
- Code examples and fragments are set in a `fixed-width font`.
- Comments in code are set in a `fixed-width italic font`.
- Sections of code that are of special significance are set in a **`bold fixed-width font`**. Often these sections represent changes or additions to a previous version of the code.
- All forms of system-level text and anything you might actually type yourself—file names, command-line instructions, program input—are set in a sans-serif font.
- Any kind of program output, including exception and error messages, is set in a **bold sans-serif font**.

acknowledgments

The small number of names on the cover of most books—in this case, just one—is an outright deception. Every book is a collaboration of a large number of dedicated and talented people. In writing this book, I have been guided, helped, and supported by a multitude of generous and wise people. I am especially grateful to…

My beloved Linda, who has borne most of the burdens of our daily life these past six months, and who *still* found time to contribute her wisdom and insight to this book. Every day she sustains me with her extraordinary beauty, grace, and love; she is my inspiration, my joy, and my light.

My parents, James and Sandra, for their faith, love, and very practical support over so many years. They have been the giants on whose shoulders I stood.

My parents-in-law, Corallie and Fred, for their encouragement, their kindness, and their love over the past decade.

Tom Christiansen, for his extraordinary generosity in reviewing the entire manuscript at short notice and in record time. His suggestions have sharpened my prose and my Perl immeasurably.

Nat Torkington, who has been a constant source of wise counsel, practical assistance, and a host of favors far beyond the call of friendship, duty, or even antipodean solidarity.

Randal Schwartz who somehow found time in his insanely busy life to review the entire manuscript, and to suggest many significant improvements.

Bennett Todd, whose excellent advice, unflagging enthusiasm, and endless encouragement, have buoyed me through some very dark hours.

Uri Guttman, whose meticulous last-minute review suggested many subtle changes that greatly enhanced the final manuscript.

Mark-Jason Dominus, whose insight and experience were instrumental in setting the overall structure and direction of my early drafts, and whose guidance I have sorely missed ever since.

The many other reviewers of my manuscripts, who have devoted extraordinary amounts of time, effort, and ability to dissecting my English and my Perl: Ilya Zakharevich, for his expert advice on the care and feeding of operators; Graham Barr, for finding some very subtle bugs—both in my programs and in my writing; Tim Bunce, François Désarménien, Brian Shensky, and Adrian Blakey, for knocking my SQL into shape; Chris Nandor, for a thorough dissection of the toughest five chapters; Gary Ashton-Jones, for highlighting the importance of sequence; Leon Brocard, for keeping the focus where it ought to be; David Cantrell, for his tremendous attention to detail; and John Dlugosz, for making me question so many assumptions.

The eagle-eyed readers of this book, who have gently pointed out typos and other errata. Especially: Mark-Jason Dominus, Brand Hilton, Peter Scott, Mike Stok, and Steven Tolkin.

The many other members of the Perl community who have shared their knowledge and understanding with me and helped to resolve all manner of fine points of Perl lore over the years.

My colleagues at Monash University, for their support and encouragement. In particular: David Abramson, John Crossley, Trevor Dix, Linda McIver, Steve Welsh, and Ingrid Zukerman.

Marjan Bace and the staff of Manning Publications, who have guided and encouraged me at every stage of development with patience, good humor, and very practical support: Brian Riley and Peter Schoenberg, who watched over me; Ted Kennedy, who masterminded the review process, adding his own invaluable suggestions; Ben Kovitz, for his guidance and advice on the material itself and for his inspiring illustrations; Mary Piergies, who turned a raw manuscript into a polished book; Adrianne Harun, who edited away the worst faults of my original copy; and Tony Roberts, who worked typesetting miracles.

And, finally, Larry Wall, for giving us all this wonderful adventure playground called Perl.

author online

Purchase of *Object Oriented Perl* includes free access to a private Internet forum where you can make comments about the book, ask technical questions, and receive help from the author and from other users. To access the forum, point your web browser to http://www.manning.com/ conway. There you will be able to subscribe to the forum. This site also provides information on how to access the forum once you are registered, what kind of help is available, and the rules of conduct on the forum.

All source code for the examples presented in *Object Oriented Perl* is available from the Manning website. The URL http://www.manning.com/conway includes a link to the source code files, and to the inevitable errata.

C H A P T E R   1

What you need to know first

(An object orientation primer)

In order to understand how object orientation works in Perl, we first need to agree what object orientation actually is. And that's surprisingly hard to do. Object-oriented programming has been around for at least three decades now, and in that time many opinions, theories, and even ideologies have been formulated on the subject. Each has purported to definitively characterize object orientation. Most are mutually inconsistent. No two are exactly alike.

Yet the basic ideas of object orientation are simple, obvious, and easy to explain. This chapter provides a quick refresher course in those basic ideas. If you're already familiar with the topic, you may want to skim or skip the following sections. If your object orientation is shaky (or rusty), this chapter should be all you need to firm up your understanding of the concepts underlying object-oriented Perl.

If you're completely new to object orientation, you may find the information here sufficient to bring you up to speed on the essential concepts, or you might prefer to start with one of the excellent introductory texts suggested at the end of this chapter.

1.1 THE ESSENTIALS OF OBJECT ORIENTATION

You really need to remember only five things to understand 90 percent of the theory of object orientation:

- An *object* is anything that provides a way to locate, access, modify, and secure data;
- A *class* is a description of what data is accessible through a particular kind of object, and how that data may be accessed;
- A *method* is the means by which an object's data is accessed, modified, or processed;
- *Inheritance* is the way in which existing classes of object can be upgraded to provide additional data or methods;
- *Polymorphism* is the way that distinct objects can respond differently to the same message, depending on the class to which they belong.

This chapter discusses each of these ideas.

1.1.1 Objects

An object is an access mechanism for data. In most object-oriented languages that means that objects act as containers for data or, at least, containers for pointers to data. But in the more general sense, *anything* that provides access to data—a variable, a subroutine, a file handle—may be thought of as an object.

The data to which an object provides access are known as the object's *attribute values*. The containers storing those attribute values are called *attributes*. Attributes are usually nothing more than variables that have somehow been exclusively associated with a given object.

Objects are more than just collections of variables however. In most languages, objects have an extra property called *encapsulation*. Encapsulation means that the attributes of an object are not directly accessible to the entire program.[1] Instead, they can only be accessed through certain subroutines associated with the object. Those subroutines are called *methods*, and they are usually universally accessible. This layer of indirection means that methods can be used to limit the ways in which an object's attribute values may be accessed or changed. In other words, an object's attribute values can only be retrieved or modified in the ways permitted by that object's methods.

Let's take a real-world example of an object: an automated teller machine (ATM). An ATM is an object because it provides (controlled) access to certain attribute values, such as your account balance, or the bank's supply of cash. Some of those attribute values are stored in attributes within the machine itself—its cash trays—while others are stored elsewhere—in the bank's central accounts computer. From the customer's point of view, it doesn't matter where

---

[1] *Encapsulation* is an awkward term because it has two distinct meanings: "bundling things together" and "isolating things from the outside world." In the literature of object orientation, both senses of the word have been used at different times. Originally, *encapsulation* was used in the "bundling" sense, as a synonym for *aggregation* (see the later section of that name). More recently, *encapsulation* has increasingly been used in the "isolation" sense, as a synonym for *data hiding* (see the later section on *Interface vs implementation*). It is in this more modern sense that the term is used throughout this book and in most of the reference sources suggested at the end of this chapter.

the attribute values actually are, so long as they're accessible via the ATM object. Access to the ATM's attributes is restricted by the *interface* of the machine. That is, the buttons, screens, and slots of the ATM control how encapsulated attribute values—cash, information, and so forth— may be accessed. Those restrictions are designed to ensure that the object maintains a consistent internal state and that any external interactions with its attributes are valid and appropriate.

For example, most banks don't use ATMs consisting of a big basket of loose cash and a note pad on which you record exactly how much you take. Even if the bank could assume that everyone is honest, it can't assume that everyone is infallible. People inevitably end up taking or recording the wrong amount by mistake, even if no one does so deliberately.

The restrictions on access are in the customer's interest too. The machine can provide access to attribute values that are private to a particular client, such as their account balance, and it shouldn't make that information available to just anyone. The account information shouldn't be universally available because, eventually, someone will access and modify the wrong account data by accident.

In object-oriented programming, an object's methods provide the same kinds of protection for data. The question is, *how does an object know which methods to trust?*

1.1.2 Classes

Setting up an association between a particular kind of object and a set of trusted subroutines, or methods, is the job of the object's *class*. A class is a formal specification of the attributes of a particular kind of object and the methods that may be called to access those attributes.

In other words, a class is a blueprint for a given kind of object. Every object belonging to a class has an identical *interface*—a common set of methods that may be called—and *implementation*—the actual code defining those methods and the attributes they access. Objects are said to be *instances* of the class.

When a program is asked to create an object of a particular kind, it consults the appropriate class definition, or blueprint, to determine how to build such an object. Typically, the class definition specifies what attributes the class's objects possess and whether those attributes are stored inside the object, or remotely through a pointer or reference.

When a particular method is called on an object, the program again consults the object's class definition to ensure that the method is "legal" for that object—that is, the method is part of the object's blueprint, and has been called correctly, in line with the definition in the class blueprint.

For example, in software controlling a bank's automated teller network there might be a class called ATM that describes the structure and behavior of objects representing individual ATMs. The ATM class might specify that each ATM object has the attributes cash_remaining, transaction_list, cards_swallowed, and so forth, and methods such as start_up(), withdraw_cash(), list_transactions(), restrict_withdrawal(), chew_cards(), close_down().

Thereafter, when an ATM object receives a request to invoke a method called withdraw_cash_without_debiting_account(), it can check the ATM class blueprint and ascertain that the method cannot be called. Alternatively, if the valid method close_down() is defined to increment a nonexistent attribute called downtime, this coding error can be detected.

1.1.3 Class attributes and methods

So far, we've only considered attributes that are accessed through—or belong to—an individual object. Such attributes are more formally known as *object attributes*. Likewise, we've only talked about methods called on a particular object to manipulate its object attributes. No prizes for guessing that such methods are called *object methods*.

Unfortunately, object attributes and methods don't always provide an appropriate mechanism for controlling data associated with objects of a particular class. In particular, the attributes of an individual object of a class are not usually suitable for encapsulating data that belongs collectively to the complete set of objects of that class.

Let's go back to the ATM example for a moment. At the end of each day, the bank will want to know how much money in toto has been dispensed from all its teller machines. Each of those machines will have a record of how much it has dispensed individually, but no machine will have a record of how much all the bank's machines have dispensed collectively. That information is not a property of a particular ATM. Rather, it's a collective property of the entire set of ATMs.

The most obvious solution is to design another kind of machine—an ATM coordinator—that gathers and stores the collective data of the set of ATMs: total cash dispensed, average number of transactions, funniest hidden video, and so forth. We then create exactly one coordinator machine and arrange for each of the ATMs to feed data to it. Now we can access the accumulated ATM data through the interface of the coordinator machine.

In object-oriented terms, the design of the coordinator machine is the design of a separate class, say, `ATM_Coordinator`, and the construction of such a machine corresponds to the creation of a single `ATM_Coordinator` object. This is certainly a viable solution to the problem of collective data, but it is unattractive in several respects.

For a start, this approach means that every time a class needs to handle collective data, we have to define yet another class and then create a single instance of it. Moreover, we have to be careful not to create more than one instance, to ensure that the collective data is not somehow duplicated or, worse still, fragmented.

Next, we have to provide some mechanism for connecting the collection of individual objects of the original class to the single object of the new collective class. That, in turn, means that the collective object has to be accessible anywhere that any individual object might be created. Consequently, the collective object must be globally accessible, which is generally considered a Bad Thing.

For these reasons, most object-oriented languages don't take this *helper class* approach to regulating collective data. Instead, they allow classes to specify a second kind of attribute, one that is shared by every object of that class, rather than being owned by a single object. Such attributes are, unimaginatively, called *class attributes*.

Of course, to maintain the appropriate protection for this kind of classwide data,[2] a class must also provide *class methods*, through which its class attributes may be safely accessed. A class method differs from an object method in that it is not called on a specific object. That's

---

[2] After all, the bank certainly doesn't want devices outside the ATM network accessing its collective ATM records.

because, unlike an object attribute, a class attribute doesn't belong to a specific object. Instead, a class method is called on the class itself. This usually means that to call a class method we must specify both the class name and the method name. For example, we must instruct our program to *invoke the* `daily_total()` *method for the class* `ATM`.

In some object-oriented languages, class methods provide *strong encapsulation* of a class's class attributes. In other words, there is no way to access a class attribute, except through the appropriate class method. Other languages offer only weak encapsulation of class attributes, which are directly visible to either a class method or an object method. This means that class attributes may be accessed through individual objects as well. As explained in chapter 3, Perl enforces neither of these approaches, but allows us to use either or both.

1.1.4 Inheritance

If you're building an extension to your house, customizing a car, or upgrading your computer, you normally start with an existing blueprint, adding on or replacing certain bits. If your original blueprint is good, it's a waste of time and resources to start from the beginning, separately reconstructing a near replica of an existing structure.

The same thing happens in object-oriented programming. Often you have a class of objects that partially meets your requirements—say, a class that represents a truck—and you want to create a new class that exactly meets your needs—say, a class that represents a fire truck.

To produce a class representing fire trucks, it's not necessary to code that class from scratch, reproducing or maybe cutting-and-pasting the original truck code and adding new methods to implement alarms, ladders, hoses, red braces, and so forth.

Instead, we can just tell the program that the new `FireTruck` class is based on—or *is derived from* or *inherits*—the existing `Truck` class. Then we tell it to add certain extra features —that is, additional attributes and methods—to the `FireTruck` class, over and above those it inherited from the `Truck` class. Any class like `FireTruck` that inherits attributes and methods from another is called a *derived class,* or sometimes, a *child class.* The class from which it inherits, `Truck` in this case, is called its *base class* or its *parent class.*

The relationship between a base class and its derived class is called the *is-a* relationship, because an object of a derived class must necessarily have all the attributes and methods of an object of the base class, and, hence, "is a" base-class object for all practical purposes. This idea corresponds to our inherent sense of the hierarchy of categories: a fire truck *is-a* truck, an automated teller machine *is-a* machine, a hench-person *is-a* person, an unnecessarily long list of analogies *is-a* list of analogies.

The *is-a* relationship is *transitive*, so you can have increasingly general categories over more than two levels: a fire truck *is-a* truck *is-a* vehicle *is-a* device *is-a* thing; a hench-person *is-a* person *is-a* animal *is-a* life-form *is-a* thing.[3]

---

[3] In fact, just about any class of object can be traced back to being a "thing." Of course, that doesn't mean we have to represent all those higher levels of categorization in an actual program. The universal "thingness" of a fire truck, an ATM, or a hench-person is probably completely irrelevant to most applications.

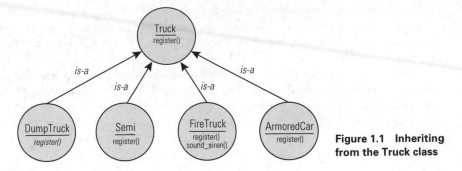

Figure 1.1 Inheriting from the Truck class

The *is-a* relationship is not bidirectional. Though an object of a derived class is always an object of a base class, it's not always or even usually true that an object of a base class *is-a* object of a derived class. That is, although a fire truck always *is-a* truck, it's not the case that a truck always *is-a* fire truck.

Inheritance and abstraction

Naturally, having created a useful base class like `Truck`, we are immediately going to derive from it not just a `FireTruck` class, but also classes representing dump trucks, tow trucks, pickup trucks, armored cars, cement mixers, delivery vans, and so forth. Each of these will separately inherit the same set of characteristics from the original `Truck` class, and each will extend or modify those characteristics uniquely. The relationship between the `Truck` class and its numerous child classes is shown in figure 1.1.

Using inheritance means that we only have to specify how a fire truck or a cement mixer or an armored car differs from a regular truck, rather than constantly needing to restate all the standard features of trucks as well. Assuming we already have the code for a truck, that reduces the amount of code required to define each new type of truck.

More importantly, using inheritance reduces our maintenance load because any change to the behavior of the general `Truck` class, such as modifying its `register()` method in response to some change in transportion regulations, is automatically propagated to all the specific truck classes (`FireTruck`, `DumpTruck`, `ArmoredCar`, etc.) that inherit from `Truck`.

In this way, inheritance also provides a way of capturing the *abstract relationships* between specific classes of objects within a program. Thus, the class of fire trucks is a special case of the more general class of trucks, which, in turn, might be a special case of the even more general class of vehicles. The more abstract classes are generalized blueprints that define the common features of a wide range of objects. The more specialized classes presuppose those common features, then describe the additional attributes and methods unique to their particular kind of object.

Inheritance hierarchies

The relative ease with which we can create and maintain new classes by inheriting from an existing one will almost certainly encourage us to create more complex chains of inheritance. For example, there are many specialized types of fire trucks: ladders, tankers, pumpers, snor-

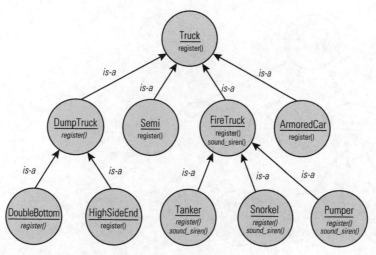

Figure 1.2 Extending the Truck hierarchy

kels, tarmac crash vehicles, and so forth. Likewise, there are many species of dump truck: double bottom, highside end, lowside end, two-axle tractor, three-axle tractor, bob-tail, and so forth.

We may need individual classes for each specific type of truck, perhaps because each of them has unique regulations governing registration and inspection. By deriving such classes from `FireTruck` and `DumpTruck`, we might extend the set of class relationships shown in figure 1.1 to the hierarchy shown in figure 1.2.

Within such a hierarchy, every class offers all the methods offered by any class above it in the hierarchy. Therefore, objects of a particular class can always be treated as if they were objects of a class higher in the inheritance tree.

For example, both a `Tanker` object and a `DoubleBottom` object may be treated as if they were `Truck` objects. That is, you can call their `register()` method, because both of them can trace their ancestry back to the primordial `Truck` class. However, of the two, only the `Tanker` object can be treated as a `FireTruck` object—you could call its `sound_siren()` method—because only the `Tanker` object can trace its ancestry to class `FireTruck`.

Some classes in the `Truck` hierarchy choose to redefine one or more of the methods they inherit. (See the following section on *Polymorphism* for an explanation of why they might want do that.) For example, the `Semi` class redefines the `register()` method it inherits from class `Truck`. We can distinguish a method that has been (re)defined in a class from a method that a class merely inherits from its parent by listing inherited methods in italics.

Multiple inheritance

The inheritance hierarchy shown in figure 1.2 is a branching treelike structure because each class in that hierarchy has at most one parent class even though it may have many child classes. But there is no reason that this has to be the case. We could envisage a situation where a particular class needs to inherit the properties of two or more separate classes.

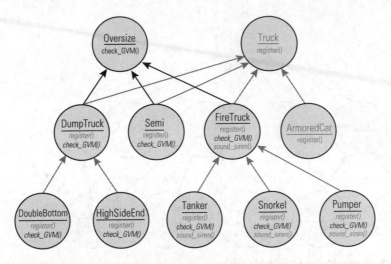

Figure 1.3 Multiple inheritance in the Truck class

Suppose there were special regulations governing "oversize" vehicles. For example, a special license might be required to drive them. We would need extra attributes and methods to implement those additional requirements. Nonetheless, we shouldn't add them to the Truck class because not all trucks are "oversize" (e.g., pickup trucks, armored cars, minivans), and not all oversize vehicles are trucks (e.g., tractors, bulldozers, tanks, oil tankers).

We *could* simply cut-and-paste the same "oversize"-related code into each derived class that needs it but avoiding the maintenance costs and inelegance of doing that was the reason we built the Truck inheritance hierarchy in the first place.

A better solution is simply to create a new Oversize class that provides the necessary attributes (permit_number, turning_circle, gross_vehicle_mass) and methods (renew_permit(), turn(), check_GVM()). We then arrange for the classes representing oversize trucks, such as FireTruck, Semi, DumpTruck, to inherit from class Oversize as well. Adding the Oversize class into the hierarchy shown in figure 1.2 produces figure 1.3.

The ability to have a single class inherit characteristics from two or more parent classes is called *multiple inheritance*. It's a useful feature, because it corresponds to the way most people think about categories (i.e., classes) in the real world. For example, class FireTruck is a special case of the Truck class, but it's also a special case of the EmergencyVehicle class, the TaxpayerFundedMunicipalProperty class, the BigShinyRedThing class, and the WhatIWantToDriveWhenIGrowUp class. Each inheritance relationship may contribute important characteristics to a FireTruck object, even if not all of them are relevant to a particular application.[4]

Designers and users of object-oriented languages are divided over the value of multiple inheritance. Critics point out that multiple inheritance can lead to awkward ambiguities. For

---

[4] A vehicle registration system probably doesn't care that fire trucks are big and shiny and magnetic to small boys; a toy manufacturer certainly *does*.

example, if a Person class inherits from the `Golfer`, `Chef`, and `Ninja` classes, which of the three distinct inherited methods should it invoke in response to a request to `slice`?

Another problem occurs when a class inherits from two parent classes, each of which in turn inherits from a common grandparent class. For example, the `FireTruck` class inherits from `Truck` and `EmergencyVehicle`. It's possible that those two classes each in turn inherited from a common base class, say `Vehicle`. Should the `FireTruck` class receive two distinct copies of the each of `Vehicle`'s attributes because `Truck` and `EmergencyVehicle` each have separate copies? Or should those two separate copies be merged back into one in the `FireTruck` class since they're both really the same attribute from class `Vehicle`? This situation is known as a *diamond inheritance problem* because the inheritance relationships among the four classes form a diamond shape—two arrows out from `FireTruck` to its parents, `Truck` and `EmergencyVehicle`; two arrows in from those parents to `Vehicle`.

Proponents of multiple inheritance point out that there are plenty of ways to resolve such dilemmas and ambiguities. For example, to resolve the problem of inheriting multiple `slice` methods, we can make the compiler detect ambiguous cases and require the programmer to give the offending methods unique aliases in the derived class (`slice_ball`, `slice_carrot`, `slice_throat`). Or the compiler can simply select the `slice` method that was inherited earliest. That is, the compiler can prioritize the inheritance of characteristics from one class ahead of inheritance from any other.

In a similar way, the compiler could detect the duplication of an ancestral attribute under diamond inheritance and either require each inherited copy of attribute to be renamed in the derived class, or else cause the attribute to be inherited through only a single "priority" inheritance path.

Consequently, most modern object-oriented languages, including Perl, allow multiple inheritance, though no two take exactly the same approach. Chapter 6 discusses what Perl's version of multiple inheritance means and how it works.

1.1.5 Polymorphism

If you've ever gone up to someone in a bar or club and introduced yourself, you know that people can respond to the same message—*I'd like to get to know you better*—in very different ways. If we categorize those ways, we can create several classes of person: `ReceptivePerson`, `IndifferentPerson`, `ShyPerson`, `RejectingPerson`, `RejectingWithExtremePrejudicePerson`, `JustPlainWeirdPerson`.

Turning that around, we can observe that the way in which a particular person will respond to your message depends on the class of person they are. A `ReceptivePerson` will respond enthusiastically, a `ShyPerson` will respond tentatively, and a `JustPlainWeirdPerson` will probably respond in iambic pentameter. The original message is always the same; the response depends on the kind of person who receives it.

Language theorists[5] call this type of behavior *polymorphism*. When a method is called on a particular object, the actual method that's involved may depend on the class to which the ob-

---

[5]   …most of whom live at ground-zero in the JustPlainWeirdPerson category…

ject belongs. For instance, if we call an object's `ignite()` method, its response will be different depending on whether it belongs to the `Paper`, `Rocket`, `Passion`, or `FlameWar` class.

Randomly calling an identically named method on objects of different classes is not, of course, a recommended programming technique. However, polymorphic behavior does prove extremely useful when an explicit relationship exists between two or more classes of object, or when an implicit relationship or a common universal property is shared between them. The following subsections discuss each of these cases.

Inheritance polymorphism

Suppose we are creating an object-oriented system for tracking the registration and inspection of trucks. We would almost certainly want to use our `Truck` class and its many descendents to implement the parts of the system that represent individual trucks.

Typically, the objects representing the various trucks are collected in some kind of container, probably a list. Some operations need to be carried out on individual objects (for example, register this particular truck, schedule an inspection for that one, etc.). However, many tasks have to be performed on every truck in the system (for example, send out an annual registration notice for each, print a complete list of recent inspection dates, etc.).

For operations that need to be performed on every truck, the application is likely to walk along the truck list in a loop, calling the appropriate method for each object in turn. For example, the loop might call each object's `print_registration_reminder()` method.

The problem is that the actual procedure to be followed by each object may be different, depending on the actual kind of truck the object represents—that is, the actual class to which it belongs. For instance, the form for registering a semitrailer may be different from the one for a fire truck or an armored car. If that's the case, the processing loop will have to determine the class of each object and then branch to perform a separate method call for each distinct class. That's a pain to code and a bigger pain to re-code every time we add or remove another class of truck.

This situation is the ideal place to use polymorphism. If the ancestral `Truck` class has a `register()` method, then we are guaranteed that every derived class also has a `register()` method, inherited from `Truck`. However, when we specify the derived classes, we may choose to *replace* the inherited `register()` method with one specific to the needs of the derived class.

Having given each class its own unique `register()` method, we can simply step through the list of objects and call `register()` on each. We're sure each can respond to that method call because, at the very least, it will use the `register()` it inherited from the `Truck` class. However, if it has a more specialized way of registering itself, then that more specialized method will be automatically invoked instead. In other words, we can arrange that each object has a `register()` method, but not necessarily the *same* `register()` method.

Although our loop code is very simple:

```
for each object in the list...
   call its register() method
```

the response to those calls is always appropriate to the particular object on which the method is called. Better still, if we subsequently add a new class derived from `Truck`, and put objects of that new class in the list, the old code continues to work without modification. When the loop encounters an object of the new class, it simply calls that object's new `register()` method and executes the new behavior specified by the object's class definition. If the new class doesn't define any new behavior, the old behavior inherited from class `Truck` is used instead.

This kind of polymorphism is known as *inheritance polymorphism* because the objects whose methods are called belong to a hierarchy of classes that are related by inheritance. The presence of the required method in the base class of the hierarchy ensures that objects of any derived class can always respond, if only generically, to a given method call. The ability to re-define individual methods in derived classes allows objects of those classes to respond more specifically to a particular method call if they so wish.

All object-oriented languages support inheritance polymorphism;[6] for some, it's the only form of polymorphism they permit. But inheritance polymorphism certainly isn't the only form that's possible. In fact, there's no need for objects treated polymorphically to have any kind of class relationship at all.

Interface polymorphism

The alternative approach to polymorphism is to allow any object with a suitable method to respond to a call to that method. This is known as *interface polymorphism*, because the only requirement is that a particular object's interface provides a method of the appropriate name.[7]

For example, since there are probably no actual `Truck` objects used in the truck registry application, there's no real need for the `Truck` class at all as far as the polymorphism in the registration loop is concerned. So long as each object in the list belongs to a class that has a `register()` method, the loop doesn't really care what its ancestral class was, whether it's a truck, a trucker, a trucking company, or a truculent. Provided it can respond to a call on its `register()` method, the loop proceeds with serene indifference.

Of course, that's a mighty big proviso. With inheritance polymorphism we could be sure that every object in the list did have a `register()` method, at least the one inherited from `Truck`. There's no such guarantee with interface polymorphism.

Worse still, because the list is almost certainly built at run-time and modified as the program executes, unless we're careful in setting up the logic of our application, we're not likely to know beforehand whether a particular object in the list can respond to a `register()` request. In fact, we're unlikely to find out until the application attempts to invoke the object's `register()` method and finds it doesn't have one.

Consequently, languages that allow interface polymorphism must also provide a run-time mechanism for handling cases where an object is unable to provide a requested method. Typically, this involves providing a means of specifying a fallback subroutine that is called whenever an object cannot respond to a particular method invocation. Alternatively, such languages

---

[6] But that's rather a circular definition, since most language lawyers insist that this form of polymorphism is one of the essential characteristics a language must possess if it's to be considered object-oriented in the first place.

[7] Statically typed object-oriented languages (like Java or Ada) usually also require that the argument list passed in the method call be type-compatible with the parameter list specified by the object's method.

may have some form of exception system. In that case, the language will trigger a well-defined exception if the object cannot respond more appropriately.

Inheritance polymorphism is a special case of interface polymorphism because a common base class guarantees that objects share a specific inherited method. Any language that supports interface polymorphism automatically supports inheritance polymorphism as well. As we shall see in chapter 5, Perl is such a language.

Abstract methods

In the earlier section on *Inheritance and abstraction*, we saw that one purpose of inheritance was to capture abstract relationships between classes and to "factor out" pieces of code (i.e., methods) shared by related classes.

Consequently, it's often the case that a class hierarchy will contain some classes—typically near the top of the hierarchy—that were never intended to be used to build objects directly. In other words, these classes exist only to represent a shared category or provide a single source from which descendent classes can inherit shared methods. Such classes are called *abstract base classes*.

There is one additional role that an abstract base class can fulfill. As described under *Inheritance polymorphism*, any base class, abstract or not, can be used to ensure that every class derived from it has a specific polymorphic method. That's a handy feature because we are then guaranteed that any derived class will be able to respond polymorphically to a specified set of method calls.

Abstract base classes are clearly useful, but in large object-oriented systems two problems can arise. The first is that they may accidentally be used as real classes when someone mistakenly creates an object of their type. Thus, we might find an obscure section of the truck registry code that creates `Truck` objects, rather than `FireTrucks` or `DumpTrucks`, even though `Truck` objects have no proper role in the system and cannot function in meaningful ways. The use of such *abstract objects* is not inherently wrong or bad, but it does indicate a place where the system implementation is almost certainly deviating from the system design.

The second problem is that, although an abstract base class ensures that a derived class has a certain set of methods, it does not require that the derived class redefine any of those methods meaningfully. This can be a problem if many such polymorphic methods are inherited, and we accidentally forget to redefine one of them. The result is that a particular class uses the generic behavior for a polymorphic function, instead of its own appropriate class-specific behavior. Misimplementations of this kind can be annoyingly hard to discover.

Many object-oriented programming languages solve these two problems by introducing the concept of an *abstract method*.[8] An abstract method is a method in an abstract base class that has no valid implementation and exists only to indicate a necessary part of each derived class's interface. It is a kind of placeholder in the interface, indicating the need for a certain functionality, but not actually providing it.

---

[8] ...which is also known as a *pure virtual function,* or a *deferred feature*. In other languages, abstract interface specifications—such as *interfaces* in Java and Modula-3 or the Smalltalk *protocol*—serve a similar purpose.

Suppose, for example, the register() method of the Truck class had been declared as an abstract method (i.e., defined but not implemented). Now, because that ancestral register() method doesn't provide a working implementation, whenever a Truck object is created, and its register() method is called, an error will be flagged. This immediately solves the general problem of incorrect use of objects belonging to an abstract base class.

Better still, it also solves the problem of forgetting to redefine a method in a derived class. For example, if the person coding the FireTruck class neglects to implement a suitable registration method for that class, then the register() method inherited from Truck will be called instead. Rather than performing some inadequate default registration process, the inherited abstract method will immediately signal an error, indicating that the implementation is incorrect.

Most object-oriented languages provide some mechanism for declaring abstract methods. Chapter 6 describes how to do so in Perl.

1.2 OTHER OBJECT-ORIENTED CONCEPTS

None of the remaining ideas of object orientation is any harder to understand than those described so far. In this section, we'll look at some extra concepts particularly relevant to object-oriented programming in Perl:

- Interfaces hide messy and changeable details from the world at large.
- You can build more complicated objects by collecting together simpler ones.
- It's sometimes useful to generalize the syntactic structure of code rather than its semantics.
- Objects can live beyond the program that creates them.

1.2.1 Interface vs. implementation

Thinking back to the ATM example mentioned earlier, we can see another useful feature of objects: The *interface* with which you interact is distinct from the internal *implementation* that makes everything happen.

Each ATM in the late Cretaceous era[9] had a trained octopus inside. Nowadays, cephalopods are considered unreliable and have largely been replaced by mechanical cash dispensers and computer chips. In the future, we can expect that ATMs will be controlled by isolinear gel-packs and will distribute cash via matter transporter.

The point is, as long as the ATM designers continue to use the same interface—the now-familiar keypad, instruction screen, and slots—the customer doesn't care what goes on inside the ATM object. Whether its innards are squishy or solid-state has no bearing on the way customers interact with the machine. Customers only care whether the ATM behaves in a predictable and consistent manner.

It's the same with automobiles. Electric cars still have a steering wheel, an accelerator, a brake pedal, and a speedometer. Under the hood, everything is completely different—batteries instead of a fuel tank, electric motors instead of an engine, a flywheel instead of brake pads—but the everyday user interface is essentially the same as that of a fossil fueled car.

---

[9]   …at least, those around the town of Bedrock…

In the same way, object-oriented programming languages provide an important separation between how data is used externally—the methods that can be called on an object—and how that data is represented and manipulated internally—the way its attribute values are stored, and its methods are coded. So long as the interface remains stable, the implementation can be changed as necessary—optimized, extended, parallelized, distributed, and so forth.

Localizing implementation details within an object's methods provides an important *decoupling* of different parts of the program. For example, if the storage mechanism for a particular attribute has to be changed, say, from a fixed-length array to a linked list, we need only alter the internals of the methods through which that attribute is accessed. The rest of the program that uses those methods shouldn't have to change at all.

Of course, there's nothing revolutionary about this idea of encapsulating implementation details inside a subroutine. Good procedural programmers have been doing that for decades. The evolutionary aspect of object-oriented programming is that those encapsulating subroutines (methods) are now explicitly associated with only a single class of object. This ensures that the subroutines themselves cannot "accidentally" be applied to the wrong data.

1.2.2 Aggregation

One of the most useful properties of a subroutine is that it can call other subroutines to do part of its job. For example, if you're writing a subroutine that calculates the initial velocity needed to throw a ball a certain horizontal distance,[10] then you want to call the `sqrt` and `sin` functions to compute parts of the answer. In this way, larger and more complicated subroutines can be built up out of simpler components: a process known as *aggregation*.

In an object-oriented system, it's usually the objects that are aggregated together, to produce larger and more complicated objects.

This process of constructing larger objects by bringing together and jointly encapsulating smaller ones is certainly not a new idea. Single-celled organisms have been doing it for over a billion years, collecting mitochondria, reticula, centrioles, ribosomes, vacuoles, and a nucleus, inside a cytoplasmic membrane. That membrane provides an interface that protects the attributes of the cell from outside attack, while allowing important nutrients in.

More recently—a mere 800 million years ago—a diverse collection of single-celled organisms started working together inside the shelter of another layer of encapsulation (i.e., skins, coats, shells, etc.), and the first multicellular creatures, the sponges, arose. Within the last half a billion years, multicellular creatures have evolved to cooperate in so-called "colony organisms," the earliest being coral polyps. Such colonies typically build themselves yet another layer of encapsulation, such as the calcium carbonate endoskeletons of coral, the mounds of termites, or the office buildings of multinational corporations.

Software objects can be built up in the same way. Small, simple objects representing the behaviors and state of an individual employee can be used to implement the attributes of larger, more complex ones, representing the entire employee. The employee object can then be aggregated with other asset objects to construct an object representing a corporation.

---

[10] $velocity = \sqrt{\dfrac{distance \times gravitation}{\sin(2 \times launch\_angle)}}$

Why aggregate?

Let's consider the attributes of the ATM class (cash_remaining, transaction_list, cards_swallowed). These attributes might be raw variables, or they might instead be implemented using objects of other classes. The cash_remaining attribute, for example, might be an object of the MoneyAmount class.

That class might have methods such as debit() and credit(), which we would call whenever it was necessary to change the value of the cash_remaining attribute of an ATM object. That means that when someone invokes an ATM object's withdraw_cash() method, that method, in turn, invokes the debit() method of the object's cash_remaining attribute.

Why arrange all this apparent complexity? Why not just make the cash_remaining attribute an integer variable (i.e., how many dollars left) and avoid the multiple method calls? One advantage of making the cash_remaining attribute a nested object is that we then have better control over how its data is modified. For example, the debit() method might check that a debit operation does not reduce the amount to less than zero. Or it might send a message to the bank ("Send more cash!") when the machine's cash reserves drop below a certain threshold.

The point is that the ATM object's withdraw_cash() method doesn't need to concern itself with any of these "side-effects." They're encapsulated inside the methods of the MoneyAmount class, so if the requirements change—for example, if we now also need to ensure that the debited amount does not exceed a predetermined limit—the basic withdraw_cash() algorithm doesn't have to be modified. Instead, we put the new code in the MoneyAmount class's debit() method.

Likewise, if the bank decides it also wants to dispense coins from its ATMs, then representing a machine's cash reserves as an integer number of dollars won't work any more. Either the representation will have to change to a pair of integers—one for dollars, one for cents—or else we'll have to change units—to an integer number of cents. If the cash_remaining attribute is an unencapsulated integer, we will have to recode every ATM method that relies on that representation—probably most of them. On the other hand, if the cash_remaining attribute is a MoneyAmount object, then we can just alter the representation specified inside that class, adjust the debit() and credit() methods to compensate, and none of the ATM methods need be altered at all.

Objects are useful precisely because they *decouple* the public interface of data from its private implementation, and thereby reduce the costly flow-on effects of changes in representation or in local behavior. There is no reason why the methods of a class shouldn't also benefit from the protection offered by object encapsulation. Using simple objects to implement the attributes of more complicated ones makes that possible.

1.2.3 Genericity

Class hierarchies provide a useful means of reusing common fragments of code, by allowing derived classes to inherit them. Inheritance does, however, imply a type relationship between any classes that inherit that common code. Sometimes that's just not appropriate because the only aspects of the common code that *aren't* reusable are the types involved.

Consider, for example, the design of a class implementing a binary search tree. The mechanics of such a class are straightforward: each node has up to two subtrees; each subtree contains only nodes less than or not less than its parent node; the tree can be traversed recursively by visiting the less than subtree, then the current node, then the not less than subtree; and so forth.

The same general structure can be used to store any kind of data for which a "less than" relationship can be defined. Structurally speaking, the only difference between a binary search tree of logical expressions and a binary search tree of the sayings of Dan Quayle is the type of data that is stored in each node (i.e., Boolean versus character string).

And, because it's the data (i.e., the attributes) that differ in each type of tree, inheritance isn't a good solution. In most object-oriented languages, inheritance allows derived classes to redefine the behavior of inherited methods, but not to change the types of inherited attributes.

What we actually want is something much *less* sophisticated, less "polymorphize the semantics of the hierarchy," and more "fill in the blanks in the syntax." In other words, we'd like to be able to create a class blueprint with certain features, such as the type of data stored in a node, left unspecified. Such a blueprint becomes a pattern that can be used to generate a range of distinct (and unrelated!) classes, simply by filling in the missing information (e.g., stating what kind of data is to be stored in the nodes of a particular kind of search tree).

In a similar way, we might wish to specify a generic method for finding the largest element in a list:

```
assume the first <whatever> is the largest <whatever>

for the remaining <whatever>s…
   if the next <whatever> is larger than the current largest <whatever>…
      replace the current largest <whatever> with the next <whatever>


return the current largest <whatever>
```

To generate a specific method for a list of integers, we replace `<whatever>` with `Integer`; to generate a specific method for lists of character strings, we replace `<whatever>` with `String`; to generate a specific method for lists of egos, we replace `<whatever>` with `Ego`.

Of course, this scheme only works if the *is-larger* operator is polymorphic. That is, we need to be sure that, when *is-larger* is applied to two `Ego` objects, the behavior is appropriate, and different from the behavior that results when the operator is applied to two `Integer` objects.

Generic classes and methods are less important in languages where type information is dynamic—that is, a property of the data, not its container. Perl is such a language. However, even in dynamically typed languages generic techniques can still be useful in reducing the overall coding required. Chapter 12 presents some approaches to generic programming in object-oriented Perl.

1.2.4 Persistence

In object-oriented terms, *persistence* is the ability of objects to retain their attribute values, their association with a class, and their individual identity, between separate executions of a program. In other words, persistent objects are those that, next time you start running the program, are still there.

Persistence requires more than just dumping an object's attribute values into a file or a database when the program terminates, and then creating a new object, and reloading the saved data next time the program executes. The essence of persistence is that when the program next executes, a persistent object will have been *identifiably* reconstructed, either with the same name, the same location in memory, or another way of accessing it that is consistent between executions.

Moreover, the reconstruction ought to be as fully automated as possible. Ideally, the programmer should only have to somehow mark an object as persistent, and thereafter it will automagically reappear every time the program executes. In practice, very few languages can achieve that level of transparency.[11]

More often, to create a persistent object it is necessary to create a special-purpose class, perhaps by deriving it from the object's original class. This, in turn, requires the programmer to create some custom code to translate internal representations of the object—the bit patterns representing it in the program—to external representations—the bit patterns in a file or database.

This translation process is called *encoding* or *serialization* and is difficult to implement in the general case. It's particularly hard if some attributes of a persistent object store pointers or references to other data. In such cases, it may also be necessary to also encode the data being referred to, as well as the abstract relationship between the persistent objects involved. In an inherently persistent language, this requirement must be met for an arbitrary number of attributes storing arbitrary interrelationships between arbitrary objects of arbitrary classes. Not surprisingly, few languages fully support both object orientation and automatic persistence.

Another important issue is the granularity of the persistence conferred upon objects. Some languages, such as HyperTalk, offer fine-grained persistence, in which every change in the attributes of an object is immediately recorded externally. Most, however, offer only coarse-grained persistence, where the attributes of an object are recorded only at the very end of a program's execution.

Coarse-grained persistence is almost always a more efficient alternative since it minimizes the amount of disk access a program performs. Fine-grained persistence, on the other hand, is clearly the safer alternative since it ensures that an object's state can always be reconstructed in a subsequent execution of the program, even if a previous execution terminated prematurely.

Of course, in practice, not even the finest of fine-grained persistence offers any real guarantee of data integrity. Even if an object is updated every time it is modified, the program might still crash in the middle of the update process itself, or, in crashing at some other point, it might somehow trash the file system on which the object was recorded. However, these problems also apply to coarse-grained persistence, which is far more likely to lose data due to an inopportune termination since, in general, nothing at all will have been recorded prior to the crash.

In many respects, persistence is the evil half-brother of object orientation: misunderstood, troublesome, unreliable, hard to coexist with, yet occasionally essential to the plot. Consequently, many definitions of object orientation don't include persistence as one of their re-

---

[11] Perl, fortunately, is one of them.

quired features, and most object-oriented languages don't directly support persistence, though it *can* be grafted on to almost all of them.

Chapter 14 looks at a range of techniques for adding either fine- or coarse-grained persistence to Perl objects.

1.3 TERMINOLOGY: A FEW (TOO MANY) WORDS

The systematic study of object orientation is a relatively young science.[12] Nowhere is this more evident than in the mishmash of mutually contradictory jargon that besets it. In the literature on object-oriented programming, standard concepts pass by many strange aliases. It sometimes seems that every object-oriented language designer deliberately invents a completely new set of names for the same fundamental ideas.

To help makes sense of this cacophony of jargon, table 1.1 summarizes the most common alternatives to the terms used in this book. The glossary at the end of this book may also be of assistance.

Table 1.1   Other names for standard object oriented concepts

Concept...	Also known as...
object	class instance, instance variable
class	user-defined type, object template, meta-object, package, module
object attribute	field, slot, instance variable, member object, data member
class attribute	class variable, class field, static field, static data member, shared attribute, class datum
object method	instance method, selector, handler, message handler, feature, member function, operation, package operation
class method	static method, static member function, shared method
method invocation	method call, method activation, message, event
interface	protocol, feature set
inheritance	subclassing, class specialization, derivation
encapsulation	data hiding, data privacy
generic class	template, parameterized class, generic package, generic module
polymorphic method	virtual function, generic:method, overridden operation, method
abstract method	pure virtual function, deferred feature
superclass	parent class, base class
subclass	child class, derived class

1.4 WHERE TO FIND OUT MORE

The world is awash with textbooks, tutorials, and other resources dedicated to object-oriented programming. Your local bookstore probably stocks several dozen titles, and your local techni-

---

[12] It's older than quantum computing, but not as old as quantum physics.

cal bookstore, several hundred. In early 1999, a naive search of the web on the term "object-oriented" returned 840,000 matches. This section distils that bounty to four books, two websites, and two newsgroups.

1.4.1 Books

Most books on the subject are linked to a particular language—most often C++ or Java, but sometimes Eiffel, Smalltalk, Ada, or Visual Basic. That connection isn't necessarily a bad thing, provided you're careful not to let your first object-oriented language warp your view of object orientation in general.

The classic text on object orientation is *Object-Oriented Software Construction* by Bertrand Meyer. Although its concepts and examples are slanted toward Meyer's own programming language, Eiffel, the explanation of object-oriented concepts is sufficiently general that the text forms a useful introduction to the entire field.[13]

Another excellent introductory text is *Object-Oriented Design with Applications* by Grady Booch. The first edition introduced object orientation by taking examples from five different languages: Smalltalk, Object Pascal, C++, CLOS, and Ada.[14] The second edition, retitled *Object-Oriented Analysis and Design with Applications*, confines itself to C++.

For a practical and highly detailed guide to actually *doing* object-oriented software development, Trygve Reenskaug's *Working With Objects* offers the fruits of more than twenty years of experience by one of the pioneers of object orientation.

If you find these references too technical or too caught-up in specific languages, you might like to consider *Object Technology: A Manager's Guide* by David A. Taylor. Don't let the title put you off; this is an excellent language-independent introduction to the fundamental concepts of object orientation.

See the bibliography for full details of each of these books and others mentioned in later chapters.

1.4.2 Websites

While it's not surprising that object-oriented programming is so profusely represented on the web, it's also no surprise that much of the material available is of dubious value at best. Rather than attempt to pick the most suitable sites, this section lists two that provide broad entry points into the vast array of on-line resources.

Cetus Links, at http://www.cetus-links.org/, is probably the most extensive list of resources and links related to object orientation and the related area of component-based programming. Currently, it offers over 13,000 links, categorized in every way imaginable. The page http://www.cetus-links.org/oo_infos.html is a good place to start.

The other exceptionally comprehensive starting point is the Object FAQ site at http://www.cyberdyne-object-sys.com/oofaq2/. It provides a somewhat smaller and more technically oriented resource than Cetus Links, but is exceptionally accurate and conveniently arranged.

---

[13] If you are familiar with Eiffel you may find it useful to consult appendix B, which presents a comparison of object-oriented Perl with that language.

[14] Appendix B also provides a comparison of Perl with Smalltalk and C++.

1.4.3 Newsgroups

The principal newsgroups for discussions of object-oriented programming are comp.object and comp.object.moderated. As usual, the unmoderated group has much greater level of traffic and more noise, while the moderated group drifts into deep and theoretical discussions at times. However, both groups have high signal-to-noise ratios and are relatively novice-friendly.

1.5 SUMMARY

- Objects are mechanisms that provide controlled access to collections of data (attributes) and allow them to be manipulated in predefined ways.
- This access and manipulation is provided by methods, which are subroutines specifically associated with a particular class of objects.
- A class defines the attributes and methods that a certain type of object provides.
- Inheritance allows new classes of objects to be created by extending or altering the behavior of an existing class. A derived class has all the attributes and methods of the classes it inherits and typically adds new ones as well.
- The way an object responds to a standard method call often depends on the kind of object it is. This is known as polymorphism.
- The main advantage of object orientation is that it separates the interface to data from the implementation of that data and of the operations defined on it.
- Object attributes may also be objects of simpler classes. Building larger objects by joining together smaller ones is known as aggregation.
- Sometimes it's useful to generalize the syntactic structure of a set of similar classes, rather than their semantics. Such structural generalizations produce generic classes or methods.

CHAPTER 2

What you need to know second
(A Perl refresher)

Object orientation in Perl is achieved using standard features of the language—hashes, packages, subroutines, and references—held together with a surprisingly small amount of new glue.[1] To understand how that extra adhesive works, you first need to be comfortable with the standard Perl features it's connecting.

As with the previous chapter, if you're already confident with this material, you'll probably want to skip ahead and get straight down to business. Alternatively, if you're completely new to the language, you might prefer to seek refuge in the introductory Perl texts suggested at the end of this chapter.

2.1 ESSENTIAL PERL

2.1.1 Scalars

A scalar variable is able to store a single value of any standard Perl type: a number, a character string, or a reference (see section 2.1.5). The value of a scalar variable can be accessed or assigned by giving its name, preceded by a dollar sign:

---

[1] Much less, for example, than C++ adds to C.

21

```
$unit = "meters";
$earth_diameter = 12756000;
$height = 1.80;
$horizon_distance = sqrt($height * $earth_diameter);
```

The name can be up to 251 characters long and can only be composed of alphabetical characters (in upper or lower case), digits, and underscores. In addition, the name can't start with a digit.

Scalar variables have no fixed or static type associated with them. Instead, they can be thought of as dynamically taking on the type of the value that they are currently storing (number, character string, etc.).

It's not necessary to predeclare a scalar variable—or an array or a hash for that matter—before using it, though it is possible to do so with a my qualifier (see the section on *Lexical variables* below) or a use vars statement:

```
use vars qw($unit $earth_diameter $height $horizon_distance);
```

2.1.2 Arrays

An array variable is able to store a series of values, with each value uniquely identified by an integer known as its *index*. The contents of an array can be accessed collectively by giving the array's name, preceded by an "at sign" (@):

```
@dwarfs= ("Happy", "Sleepy", "Grumpy", "Dopey", "Sneezy", "Bashful", "Doc");
@deadly_sins= ("Gluttony", "Sloth", "Anger", "Envy", "Lust", "Greed", "Pride");

print "@dwarfs never commit @deadly_sins\n";
```

Individual values stored in the array can be accessed by giving the array's name, preceded by a dollar sign[2] and followed by a numeric value—the index—in square brackets:

```
foreach $i (0..5)
{
   print $dwarfs[$i], " was accused of ", $deadly_sins[$i], "\n";
}
print "and ", $dwarfs[6], " was accused of ", $deadly_sins[6], "\n";
```

The index of the first element is zero, not one, because the index indicates how far the element is from the start of the array, not its ordinal position.

Elements can also be individually assigned to, and will automatically be created if they do not already exist:

```
$dwarfs[7] = "Funky";
$deadly_sins[11] = "Incompetence";
```

Because array elements are always consecutive, assigning a value to $deadly_sins[11] causes the @deadly_sins array to grow to a length of twelve elements—elements 0 through 11. The extra three elements—$deadly_sins[8], $deadly_sins[9], and $deadly_sins[10]—that are also created are initalized to the special undefined value undef.

---

[2] …because each element of an array is itself a (nameless) scalar variable, and accesses to scalars always start with a dollar sign.

CHAPTER 2 WHAT YOU NEED TO KNOW SECOND

There are two ways of obtaining information about the length of an array, depending on whether we want to access the last element or to count the number of elements. The variable $#array_name always stores the last index of the array @array_name. Therefore

```
print $deadly_sins[$#deadly_sins];
```

always prints the last deadly sin, no matter how many are in the array.

Another way to access the end of an array is to use a negative index. In Perl, negative indices count backward from the end of the array, with −1 being the last element, −2 the second last, etc:

```
print $deadly_sins[-1];     # also prints value of last element
```

The value of $#array_name is always one less than the number of elements in the array because indices start from zero, but counting starts from one. If a complete array is referred to somewhere that a scalar value was expected—this is called a *scalar context* (see *Calling context* below)—then the resulting scalar value is the number of elements in the array. For example

```
$sin_count = @deadly_sins; # equivalent to: $sin_count = 7
while ($n < @dwarfs)       # equivalent to: while ($n < 7)
{
   print $dwarfs[$n++], "\n";
}
```

In the first example, the assignment to a scalar variable ($sin_count) means that a scalar value is expected to the right of the = operator. The @deadly_sins array has been used in a scalar context, so the number of elements it contains is returned. In the second example, both operands of the < operator are expected to be numeric (scalar) values, so @dwarfs is also in a scalar context.

Arrays and lists

Arrays are closely related to (but not the same as) lists. A Perl list is a sequence of comma separated values usually in a set of parentheses. A Perl array is a *container for* a sequence of values (that is, a container for a list). As shown in the examples in the previous section, lists are commonly used to initialize arrays. Assigning a list to an array places each item in the list in a consecutive element of the array.

Lists may also be used to extract values from arrays. If an array is assigned to a list of scalar variables, the value of each element of the array is copied into consecutive variables in the list. For example

```
($dw1, $dw2, $dw3, $dw4, $dw5, $dw6, $leader) = @dwarfs;
```

assigns $dwarf[0] to $dw1, $dwarf[1] to $dw2, $dwarf[2] to $dw3, and so forth.

If there are more variables in the list than elements in the array, the extra variables are assigned the undefined value (undef). If there are fewer variables than array elements, the extra elements are ignored. For example, in the following assignments

```
($dw1, $dw2, $dw3, $dw4, $dw5, $dw6, $leader, $dw8) = @dwarfs;
($mad, $bad, $dangerous_to_know) = @deadly_sins;
```

the variables $dw1 through $dw6 and $leader are assigned the seven names stored in @dwarf, while $dw8 is assigned undef. In the second assignment, the three variables are assigned only the first three sins in @deadly_sins. The rest would be ignored.

You can also assign lists of values to lists of variables:

```
($sanguine, $saline, $doleful) = ("blood", "sweat", "tears");
```

which is particularly useful for swapping the value of two variables:

```
($friend, $foe) = ($foe, $friend);
```

Lists of literal character strings like ("blood", "sweat", "tears") can be annoying to type in and difficult to read. Perl provides a special operator (qw) that can be used to specify a list of single words, where each "word" is a character string that don't contain a whitespace character:

```
($sanguine, $saline, $doleful) = qw(blood sweat tears);
```

Whenever you put a qw before the listifying parentheses, you can omit the quotation marks and the commas. In fact, you *must* omit them since they're valid non-white space characters and will simply be treated as part of whatever whitespace-delimited word to which they're connected.

List flattening

Contrary to what you might expect, if a list contains another nested list:

```
@virtues = ( "faith", "hope", ("love", "charity") );
```

then this *doesn't* produce a hierarchical list of three elements, where the third element is itself a two-element list. That's because each element of a list must be a scalar, not another list.

What happens instead is that the entire nested list is flattened by the removal of all internal bracketing. Therefore, the previous example is actually equivalent to

```
@virtues = ( "faith", "hope", "love", "charity" );
```

Any arrays that appear in a list are also expanded in this way. Therefore,

```
@virtues = ( "faith", "hope", @deadly_sins );
```

puts nine elements (not three) into @virtues.

It *is* possible to build hierarchical lists in Perl, but you need to use references to arrays (see *References* below).

Arrays as stacks and queues

Perl provides support for using arrays to implement stacks and queues, via the built-in functions push, pop, shift, and unshift.

The push function takes an array and a list of elements to append to it. It then appends them and returns the new length of the array. The pop function removes the last element of an array and returns that element. If the array is empty, it returns undef. For example

```
$stack_height = push @stack, $next;
$stack_height = push @stack, ($item1, $item2, $item3);
```

```
print "$next\n"
  while $next = pop @stack;    # assume no undef elements in stack
```

The unshift and shift functions work just like push and pop respectively, except that they add elements to the start of an array instead of to the end.

The combination of pushing elements onto the end of an array and shifting them off the start of it produces a queue:

```
push @menu, qw(appetizer soup entree main dessert coffee mints);
print "the next course is $next_course\n"
  while $next_course = shift @menu;
```

The push, pop, shift, and unshift functions are all special cases of a more general function called splice, which changes the elements of an array. The splice function takes four arguments: the array to be modified; the index at which it's to be modified; the number of elements to be removed (starting at the index specified in the previous argument), and a list of extra elements to be inserted at the index (after the previous elements are removed). The function returns a list of the elements removed from the array being modified.

So, for example, to replace Deadly Sins 3 and 4 with the four Virtues, we would write

```
@ex_sins = splice @deadly_sins, 3, 2, @virtues;
```

In other words, take the @deadly_sins array, go to index 3, remove two elements (i.e., elements 3 and 4), and replace them with the elements in @virtues. The two elements removed are returned by splice and saved in the @ex_sins array.

Slicing an array

Sometimes it's useful to be able to extract or assign to only part of an array. For example, we might want to print out elements 3 through 5 of a particular array:

```
print $tragedy[3], $tragedy[4], $tragedy[5];
```

or perhaps reassign them

```
($tragedy[3], $tragedy[4], $tragedy[5])
      = ("Macburger", "King Leer", "Hamlet, A Pig in the City");
```

This kind of thing happens so often that Perl provides a special syntax to simplify it. If the contents of a trailing pair of square brackets are a list of comma-separated values, rather than a single value, Perl produces an *array slice*, instead of a single array element:

```
print @tragedy[3,4,5];       # same as previously, but less cluttered
```

That slice is a list (hence, the @ prefix) that acts just like a subset of the original array. In other words, rather than just being copies, the elements of that temporary array are the same scalars as in the original array. Thus, assigning to an array slice assigns to the original elements:

```
@tragedy[3,4,5] = ("Macburger", "King Leer", "Hamlet, A Pig in the City");
                             # same as previously, but much less cluttered
```

The list of indices in the square brackets need not be comma-separated, explicit, or even sequential. For example:

```
@sqr[1..4]= (1, 4, 9, 16);                 # range of indices
@sqrt[1,49,9,16,4]= (1, 7, 3, 4, 2);       # non-sequential indices
@inverse[@sqr]= (1, 0.25, 0.1111, 0.0625); # indices stored in
                                           # another array
```

2.1.3 Hashes

A hash[3] is best thought of as a two-column table, where the left column stores keys and the right column stores their associated scalar values. It's called a hash because a hashing algorithm is used to map each key string to an internal index into the table.

A hash variable is prefixed with a percent sign and initialized with a list:

```
%sound = ("cat", "meow", "dog", "woof", "goldfish", undef);
```

The initializer list consists of an alternating sequence of keys and their associated values. Therefore, in the hash %sound, the key "cat" is associated with the value "meow," the key "dog" with the value "woof", and the key "goldfish" with the value undef.

In a long list of such key/value pairs, it can be easy to lose track of which elements are keys and which are values. To improve the readability of such hash initializers, Perl provides a special operator (=>) that may be used instead of a comma:

```
%sound = ("cat"=>"meow", "dog"=>"woof", "goldfish"=>undef);
```

The => operator is exactly equivalent to a comma except that it has a useful extra property. It treats any potential identifier—that is, a string of alphanumerics and/or underscores—to its immediate left as if it were a quoted character string. That allows us to write

```
%sound = (cat=>"meow", dog=>"woof", goldfish=>undef);
```

The value after the => still requires quotation marks if it's a character string.

The individual values stored in a hash (called *entries*) are accessed in much the same way as the individual elements of an array. The only difference is that, instead of specifying an index in square brackets, we specify a key in curly braces. For example:

```
print "The cat replied: ", $sound{"cat"};

$sound{"cat"} = "purr";
print "The cat replied: ", $sound{"cat"};

$animal = "cat";
print "The $animal replied: ", $sound{$animal};
```

As with the array elements, a hash entry such as $sound{"cat"} is the cat entry of the hash %sound, and has nothing whatsoever to do with the scalar variable $sound.

Like the left-hand side of a => operator, the interior of the curly braces of a hash entry will automatically interpret an identifier as a quoted string. Consequently, we could simply write:

---

[3] Back when dinosaurs rule the Earth, hashes were known as *associative arrays*, because each stored value is associated with (and accessed through) its key, rather than having some positional index as in a normal array. However the term is now archaic and calling a hash an associative array will see you shunned by polite Perl society.

```
print "The cat replied: ", $sound{cat};
$sound{cat} = "purr";
# etc.
```

This is only true, however, if the contents are an unbroken sequence of alphanumerics or underscores. That is, we can't write:

```
$sound{homo sapiens vendax} = "have a nice day";      # Wrong!
```

if we mean:[4]

```
$sound{"homo sapiens vendax"} = "have a nice day";
```

Iterating a hash

Unlike arrays, where the elements are ordered by their sequential indices, entries in a hash are not stored in any obvious or useful order.[5] In particular, entries are not stored alphabetically, nor are they stored in the order in which they were added to the hash. Therefore, stepping through each entry in a hash isn't quite as simple as in an array.

Perl provides three built-in functions that assist in iterating a hash: keys, values, and each. The keys function takes a hash as its argument and returns a list of its keys, in an apparently random order. Likewise, the values function returns a list of the values of its hash argument in the same apparently random order.[6] Thus, to print out all the key/value pairs in a hash, we could write:

```
foreach $key (keys %sound)
{
   print "The key $key has the value $sound{$key} \n";
}
```

Or, if we just wanted the values without the keys, we could write:

```
foreach $val (values %sound)
{
   print $val, "\n";
}
```

Alternatively, we could use the built-in function each. The each function takes a hash and returns one distinct key from that hash every time it's called. When successive calls to each have returned every possible key from the hash, the next call returns undef, after which the cycle repeats. Consequently, each is used like so:

---

[4] Without the quotes, the hash access $sound{homo sapiens vendax} would be interpreted as a call to the subroutine vendax with no arguments, then a call to the subroutine sapiens passing it the value returned from vendax, then a call to the subroutine homo passing it the return value of sapiens. The final return value would then be used as a key into %sound. See the section on *Subroutines*.

[5] Of course, they *are* stored internally in a specific order—the order of the integers to which their keys are hashed—but that order is certainly not obvious or useful from the point of view of most programmers.

[6] That is, the nth element of keys %hash is always the key of the entry whose value is returned as the nth element of values %hash.

```
while (defined($nextkey = each %sound))     # get next key until undef
{
    print "The key $nextkey has the value $sound{$nextkey} \n"
}
```

If each is called in a *list context*—for example, if its return value is assigned to a list, array, or hash—it returns a two-element list containing the next key and its associated value. After all keys have been returned by successive calls, each returns an empty array (which would cause a while loop to fail). For example:

```
while ( ($nextkey,$nextval) = each %sound )
{
    print "The key $nextkey has the value $nextval \n";
}
```

Slicing a hash

The values function returns values in an apparently random order, so to create a list of values from a hash with a specific order, we have to write something like this:

```
print ($sound{cat}, $sound{goldfish}, $sound{dog}, $sound{dolphin})
```

That's a tedious solution to a common problem, so Perl provides some shorthand for it:

```
print @sound{"cat", "goldfish", "dog", "dolphin"};
```

This is called a *hash slice*, and it's analogous to the array slice notation described earlier. Instead of putting a single key in the curly braces, a list of keys is specified.[7] The slice's prefix is @, not $ or %, because the result is a list, not a single scalar or a hash.

As with an array slice, the list produced by a hash slice may be the target of an assignment:

```
@sound{"mouse", "bird"} = ("arriba!", "itortitawapuddytat");
```

This causes the "mouse" and "bird" entries in the original hash to be assigned the corresponding elements of the list or array.

2.1.4 Subroutines

A *subroutine* is a small, user-defined, self-contained subprogram. Like Perl's built-in functions, a subroutine is invoked by name and may have arguments passed to it. A subroutine may return a scalar or list value.

Subroutines are defined using the sub keyword, followed by the subroutine code in curly braces:

```
sub dictionary_order
{
    @ordered = sort @_;
    return @ordered;
}
```

---

[7] Because the list of keys is not a single identifier, the keys are not automatically stringified within the curly braces. Instead, they must be explicitly quoted, often with the qw operator:
`@sound{ qw(cat goldfish dog dolphin) }`

The arguments passed to the subroutine are available within its code block via the special `@_` array. The built-in function `return` causes execution of the subroutine to finish immediately and the value specified after the `return` to be returned as the result. Using a `return` is optional in a subroutine. If none is specified, the subroutine automatically returns the value of the last statement it actually executed.

Subroutines are called by specifying their name, followed by a list of arguments:

```
@sorted = dictionary_order ("eat", "at", "Joes");
@sorted = dictionary_order (@unsorted);
@sorted = dictionary_order (@sheep, @goats, "shepherd", $goatherd);
```

Just like any other list, if the argument list has nested lists or arrays, they are "flattened." Therefore, at the start of the third call to `dictionary_order`, `@_` would contain the contents of the array `@sheep`, followed by the contents of `@goats`, the value `"shepherd"`, and, finally, the scalar value stored in `$goatherd`. It *is* possible to pass two or more arrays to a subroutine and keep them "unflattened" (see *Passing subroutine arguments as explicit references* later in this chapter). If the subroutine does not require arguments, it can be called with an empty argument list. The list can also be omitted completely as long as Perl already knows it's a subroutine:

```
sub get_next { return <> }

prompt();                    # always okay
$next = get_next();          # always okay

prompt;                      # error: hasn't seen definition yet
$next = get_next;            # okay: get_next definition already seen

sub prompt { print "next> " }
```

Like variables, subroutines have a leading symbol that indicates what they are. The "formal" name of a subroutine has an ampersand (`&`) prefix, which may be used when calling it

```
@sorted = &dictionary_order("eat", "at", "Joes");
```

and must be used in certain other contexts (see *References* below). However, it *can't* be used when defining the subroutine:

```
sub &dictionary_order     # Fatal compile-time error!
{
    return sort @_;
}
```

Because a subroutine's arguments are passed to it in the special array `@_`, and because all arrays in Perl are dynamically sized, any subroutine may be passed any number of arguments.[8] Hence, the `dictionary_order` subroutine shown above can be given as many arguments as required. Similarly, we could write a generic maximum function for numeric values:

---

[8] Subroutine prototypes can be used to limit the number of arguments that can be passed to a subroutine. See the section on *Prototypes* below.

```
sub max
{
    $max = shift @_;               # assume the first arg is the largest
    foreach $candidate ( @_ )      # for the rest...
    {
        $max = $candidate          #   replace the current largest
            if $max < $candidate;  #   if some other is bigger
    }
    return $max;
}
```

Other ways to call a subroutine

Subroutines that have been defined earlier in a program may also be called without parentheses around the argument list:

```
sub make_sequence    # args: (from, to, step_size)
{
    @list = ();
    for ($n = $_[0]; $n < $_[1]; $n+=$_[2])
    {
        push @list, $n;
    }
    return @list
}


# then later...


@stepped_sequence = make_sequence $min, $max, $step_size;
```

Another way to call a subroutine is to use its & prefix but provide no argument list. Such a subroutine call has the contents of the current @_ array passed to it instead. This is most often used to call subroutines from within other subroutines. To surround an existing subroutine—for example, one called inverse—with pre- and post-conditions, we could write the following:

```
sub checked_inverse
{
    die "can't invert 0" if $_[0] == 0;       # pre-condition
    $inv = &inverse;                          # call &inverse with same args
    die "inversion failed" unless $inv*$_[0]==1;   # post-condition
    return $inv;
}
```

This means there is a subtle difference between

```
&checked_inverse;        # means checked_inverse(@_);
```

and:

```
checked_inverse;         # means checked_inverse();
```

A final variation on calling a subroutine also uses the & prefix, but invokes the subroutine with a goto as well:

```
goto &inverse;
```

But this version acts like the previous no-argument `inverse` call in that it automatically passes the current contents of @_ to the invoked subroutine. But this version differs in that it doesn't call the `inverse` subroutine and then return to the next statement after the call. Instead, `goto &inverse` *replaces* the call to the current subroutine with a call to `inverse`. For example, if we only wanted a precondition on `inverse`, we could write:

```
sub checked_inverse
{
    die "can't invert 0" if $_[0] == 0;   # pre-condition
    goto &inverse;                         # become a call to &inverse
                                           # (using the current arg list)
}
```

This special form of subroutine call is used mainly in autoloaded subroutines (see section 2.2.2).

Named arguments

Suppose we want to implement a subroutine called `listdir` that provides the functionality of our operating system's directory listing command (i.e., dir or ls). Such a subroutine might take arguments specifying which files to list, what type of files to consider, whether to list hidden files, what details of each file should be reported, whether files and directories should be listed separately, how to sort the listing, whether directories should be listed recursively, how many columns to use, and whether the output should be paged or just dumped.

But we certainly don't want to have to specify every one of those nine parameters every time we call `listdir`:

```
listdir("*", "any", 1, 1, 0, 0, "alpha", 4, 1);
```

Even if we arranged things so that specifying an undefined value for an argument selects a default behavior for that argument, the call is no easier to code and no more readable:

```
listdir(undef, undef, 1, 1, undef, undef, undef, 4, 1);
```

Some programming languages provide a mechanism for naming the arguments passed to a subroutine. This facility is especially useful when implementing a subroutine like `listdir`, where there are many potential parameters, but only a few of them may be needed for a particular call.

Perl supports named arguments in a cunning way. If we pretend that a particular subroutine takes a hash, rather than a list, we can use the => operator to associate a name with each argument. For example

```
listdir(cols=>4, page=>1, hidden=>1, sep_dirs=>1);
```

Inside the subroutine, we simply initialize a hash with the resulting contents of the @_ array. We can access the arguments by name, using each name as the key to an entry in the hash. For example, we can define `listdir` like so:

```
sub listdir
{
    %arg = @_;  # Convert argument list to hash

    # Use defaults for missing arguments…
```

```
$arg{match} = "*" unless exists $arg{match};
$arg{cols}  = 1  unless exists $arg{cols};
# etc.

# Use arguments to control behaviour...
@files = get_files( $arg{match} );
push @files, get_hidden_files() if $arg{hidden};
# etc.
}
```

Apart from documenting the call better, this approach has another important advantage. Since the entries of a hash can be initialized in any convenient order, we no longer need to remember the order of the nine potential arguments, as long as we remember their names.

In addition, because hashes are flattened inside lists, if we have several calls that require the same subset of arguments, we can store that subset in a separate hash and reuse it:

```
%std_listing = (cols=>2, page=>1, sort_by=>"date");

listdir(file=>"*.txt", %std_listing);
listdir(file=>"*.log", %std_listing);
listdir(file=>"*.dat", %std_listing);
```

We can even override specific elements of the standard set of arguments, by placing an explicit version *after* the standard set. Then the explicit version will reinitialize (i.e., overwrite) the corresponding entry in the hash:

```
listdir(file=>"*.exe", %std_listing, sort_by=>"size");
```

This idea of a standard argument set, overridden by explicitly specified arguments, can also be used *within* the subroutine to simplify the handling of default values. For example:

```
sub listdir
{
   %defaults = (match=>"*", cols=>1, sort_by=>"name");
   %arg = (%defaults, @_);

   # Use arguments to control behaviour...
   # etc.
}
```

In this version, the default values are stored in the %defaults hash, and are then flattened into the list used to initialize the %arg hash. The default values appear first in the initializer list. Any entry of the same name passed in via @_ will therefore overwrite the corresponding entry in %arg, replacing the default value with the user-specified one. As a final optimization, the default hash could be moved outside listdir, so that it need only be initialized once, before the program runs, rather than each time listdir is called:

```
%defaults = (match=>"*", cols=>1, sort_by=>"name");

sub listdir
{
   %arg = (%defaults, @_);
   # etc.
}
```

Aliasing of parameters

Elements of the @_ array are special in that they are *not* copies of the actual arguments of the function call. Rather they are *aliases* for those arguments. That means that if values are assigned to $_[0], $_[1], $_[2], etc., each value is actually assigned to the corresponding argument with which the current subroutine was invoked. For example, the following subroutine increments its first argument each time it's called, but keeps the result less than 10 at all times.

```
sub cyclic_incr
{
    $_[0] = ($_[0]+1) % 10;
}
```

It would be called like this:

```
$next_digit = 8;
print $next_digit;          # prints: 8

cyclic_incr($next_digit);
print $next_digit;          # prints: 9

cyclic_incr($next_digit);
print $next_digit;          # prints: 0
```

Attempting to call such a subroutine with an unmodifiable value:

```
cyclic_incr(7);
```

would provoke a fatal run-time error.

This aliasing behavior is useful when you need it, but can introduce subtle bugs if you trip it unintentionally. Therefore, if you don't intend to change the values of the original arguments, it's usually a good idea to explicitly copy the @_array into a set of variables, to avoid "accidents":

```
sub next_cyclic
{
    ($number,$modulus) = @_;
    $number = ($number+1) % $modulus;
    return $number;
}
```

Apart from protecting the original arguments from unintended modification, this approach has an added advantage: Provided the variable names are well-chosen, they document the number and purpose of the expected arguments and make the code of the subroutine more readable as well.

Of course, this approach can lead to other unexpected side effects, since the variables $number and $modulus used above are global variables. A safer approach is to use the my keyword to restrict the variables to the subroutine (see *Lexical variables* below).

Calling context

When a subroutine is called, it's possible to detect whether it was expected to return a scalar value, or a list, or nothing at all. These possibilities define three *contexts* in which a subroutine may be called. For example:

```
listdir(@files);              # void context: no return value expected

$listed = listdir(@files);    # scalar context: scalar return value expected

@missing = listdir(@files);   # list context: list return value expected
($f1,$f2) = listdir(@files);  # list context: list return value expected
print( listdir(@files) );     # list context: list return value expected
```

This information may be obtained via a call to the built-in wantarray function. This function returns:

- undef (i.e., false and undefined) if the current subroutine was not expected to return a value,
- " " (i.e., false but defined) if it was expected to return a scalar,
- 1 (i.e., true and defined) if it was expected to return a list.

We could use this information to select the appropriate form of return statement (and perhaps optimize for cases where the return value would not be used). For example

```
sub listdir
{
   # Do file listing, and then:

   return @missing_files if wantarray();
   return $listed_count if defined(wantarray());
}
```

When it's time to return, the listdir subroutine first checks to see if the value returned by wantarray is true, indicating that a list of values is required. If so, it returns the contents of a particular array. Otherwise, the subroutine checks whether the false value returned by wantarray is nevertheless defined, indicating a scalar value is required. If so, it returns the contents of a scalar variable. If neither of those cases is true, the value returned by wantarray must have been undef, so the subroutine allows itself to return without a value, by reaching the end of its block. If the subroutine is *always* supposed to return a value, we could issue a warning whenever that return value is ignored:

use Carp;

```
sub listdir
{
   # Do file listing, and then:

   return @missing_files if wantarray;
   return $listed_count if defined(wantarray);
   carp "subroutine &listdir was called in void context";
}
```

We use Carp::carp subroutine, instead of the built-in warn function, so that the warning reports the location of the call to listdir, instead of the location within listdir at which the error was actually detected.

Determining a subroutine's caller

The Carp module is useful because it reports the location of a subroutine's caller, rather than the location of the subroutine's code. Sometimes, it can also be useful to have access to that sort of information within a program. For example, to improve debugging, we might wish to track where particular data was initialized (see chapter 9). Or to enhance modularity, we might want to allow access to certain data only to code from a single source file (see chapter 11).

Unlike most languages, Perl makes it easy to determine where a subroutine was called. The built-in `caller` function returns a list of values[9] indicating:

[0] the package (see *Packages* below) from which the current subroutine was called,

[1] the name of the file containing the code that called the current subroutine,

[2] the line in that file from which the current subroutine was called.

If `caller` is called in a scalar context (i.e., `$calling_package = caller()`), then only the first element is returned.

Therefore, when initializing some simulation data, we could determine the file and line at which the initialization subroutine was actually called and record that as part of the data:

```
sub initial_sample
{
    ($reaction_rate, $temperature, $pressure) = @_;
    ($package, $file, $line) = caller();
    %state = (
                rate  => $reaction_rate,
                temp  => $temperature,
                pres  => $pressure,
                _trail=> "init ($file:$line)",
            );
}
```

The `"_trail"` entry in the hash has nothing to do with the thermodynamics of the simulation, but is included so that, if something goes wrong, we can easily track down where the errant data originated. Other subroutines that modify the data might update the `"_trail"` entry, so that a full bit-trail is always available. For example

```
sub catalyse
{
    ($catalyst, $rate_multiplier) = @_;
    ($package, $file, $line) = caller();
    $state{rate} *= $rate_multiplier;
    $state{catalyst} = $catalyst;
    $state{_trail} .= ", catalysed ($file:$line)";
}
```

If `caller` is called in a list context with an integer argument, then it returns some additional information:

---

[9] The numbers indicate the index at which each datum is returned in the list.

[3] the name of the subroutine,

[4] whether the subroutine was passed arguments,

[5] the context in which the subroutine was called (the value returned by `wantarray`),

[6] the actual source code that called the subroutine (but only if the call was part of an `eval TEXT` statement),

[7] whether the subroutine was called as part of a `require` or `use` statement.

The above descriptions deliberately don't say "...the *current* subroutine...", because the integer argument passed to `caller` determines which particular subroutine is reported on. If the argument is zero, then the information returned refers to the current subroutine (i.e., which file and line it was called from, its name, whether it was passed arguments, etc.) If the argument is 1, then the immediate caller of the current subroutine is reported on (i.e., what was the caller of the caller of the current subroutine). If the argument was 2, then the caller of the caller of the caller of the current subroutine is reported; and so on up the hierarchy of calls for ever larger integer arguments.[10]

Chapter 11 illustrates another use for the information returned by `caller`, namely to enable the `Tie::SecureHash` module to enforce the encapsulation of attributes within certain packages and source files.

Prototypes

Subroutines can also be declared with a *prototype*, which is a series of specifiers that tells the compiler to restrict the type and number of arguments with which the subroutine may be invoked. For example, in the subroutine definition

```
sub insensitive_less_than ($$)
{
    return lc($_[0]) lt lc($_[1]);
}
```

the prototype is `($$)` and specifies that the subroutine `insensitive_less_than` can only be called with exactly two arguments, each of which will be treated as a scalar—even if it's actually an array![11] The full range of specifiers allowed in a prototype, and their various meanings, are described in the perlsub documentation.

Prototypes are only enforced when a subroutine is called using the *name(args)* syntax. Prototypes are not enforced when a subroutine is called with a leading & or through a subroutine reference (see *References and referents* below). Chapter 3 explains why they are also ignored when an object method is called.

---

[10] If you try to look too far up the hierarchy, beyond the primordial subroutine call at the top level of the program, `caller` just returns an empty list.

[11] In other words, a $ prototype causes the corresponding argument to be evaluated in a scalar context. That means, for example, that a call like `insensitive_less_than(@a, @b)` will treat @a and @b as scalars. The two values passed to `insensitive_less_than` will be the lengths of @a and @b respectively, not their contents. This kind of introduced subtlety is a good reason to avoid using a prototype, unless you're very confident that you know its full consequences.

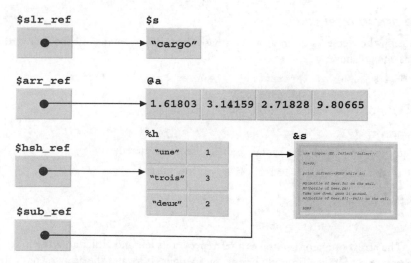

Figure 2.1   References and referents

2.1.5   References and referents

Sometimes, it's important to be able to indirectly access a variable, a subroutine, or a value. That is, occasionally, it's important to be able to refer to something in a general way, rather than directly using its name.

To this end, Perl provides a special scalar datatype called a *reference*. A reference is like the traditional Zen idea of the "finger pointing at the moon." The finger (reference) isn't the moon (the variable, function, or value), merely a means of locating it.

To create a reference to an existing variable or value we use the unary \ operator, which takes a variable or value and returns a reference to it. The original variable or value is then known as the *referent* to which the reference refers.

For example, if $s is a scalar variable, then \$s is a reference to that scalar variable—or a finger pointing at it. Likewise, if &s is a subroutine, \&s is a reference to that subroutine. You can also take references to array, hashes, and typeglobs (see *Typeglobs* below).

Any of these types of references can be stored in a scalar variable. For example:

```
$slr_ref = \$s; # scalar $slr_ref now stores a reference to scalar $s
$arr_ref = \@a; # scalar $arr_ref now stores a reference to array @a
$hsh_ref = \%h; # scalar $hsh_ref now stores a reference to hash %h
$sub_ref = \&s; # scalar $sub_ref now stores a reference to subroutine &s
```

Figure 2.1 shows the relationships produced by those assignments.

Once we have a reference, we can get back to the original thing it refers to by simply prefixing the reference (optionally in curly braces) with the appropriate symbol. So, to refer to $s, we write ${\$s} or $$slr_ref or ${$slr_ref}. Likewise, we can access @a as @{$arr_ref}, %h as %{$hsh_ref}, or &s as &$sub_ref. If we attempt to prefix a reference with the wrong symbol—for example: @{$sub_ref}—Perl produces a fatal run-time error.

The arrow operator

Accessing the elements of an array or a hash through a reference can be awkward using the syntax shown above:

```
$a[0] = ${$hsh_ref}{"first"};       # i.e. $a[0] = $h{"first"}

# or...

${$arr_ref}[0] = $h{"first"};       # i.e. $a[0] = $h{"first"}
```

so Perl provides a little extra syntax to make life less cluttered:

```
$a[0] = $hsh_ref->{"first"};        # i.e. $a[0] = $h{"first"}

# or...

$arr_ref->[0] = $h{"first"};        # i.e. $a[0] = $h{"first"}
```

The arrow operator (->) takes a reference on its left and either an array index (in square brackets) or a hash key (in curly braces) on its right. It locates the array or hash that the reference refers to, and then accesses the appropriate element of it.

The arrow operator can also be applied to subroutine references, so instead of writing:

```
&{$sub_ref}($arg1, $arg2, $etc);    #i.e. s($args1, $arg2, $etc)
```

we can write

```
$sub_ref->($arg1, $arg2, $etc);     #i.e. s($args1, $arg2, $etc)
```

Identifying a referent

Because a scalar variable can store a reference to any kind of data, and dereferencing a reference with the wrong prefix leads to fatal errors, it's sometimes convenient to be able to determine the type of referent to which a specific reference refers. Perl provides a built-in function called `ref` that takes a scalar, such as `$slr_ref`, and returns a description of the kind of reference it contains. Table 2.1 summarizes the string that is returned for each type of reference.

Table 2.1 What `ref` returns

If `$slr_ref` contains...	then `ref($slr_ref)` returns...
a scalar value	`undef`
a reference to a scalar	`"SCALAR"`
a reference to an array	`"ARRAY"`
a reference to a hash	`"HASH"`
a reference to a subroutine	`"CODE"`
a reference to a filehandle	`"IO"` or `"IO::Handle"`
a reference to a typeglob	`"GLOB"`
a reference to a precompiled pattern	`"Regexp"`
a reference to another reference	`"REF"`

The `ref` function can be used to improve error messages,

```perl
die "Expected scalar reference" unless ref($slr_ref) eq "SCALAR";
```

or to allow a subroutine to automatically dereference any arguments that might be references:

```perl
sub trace
{
  ($prefix, @args) = @_;
  foreach $arg ( @args )
  {
    if (ref($arg) eq 'SCALAR')    { print $prefix, ${$arg} }
    elsif (ref($arg) eq 'ARRAY')  { print $prefix, @{$arg} }
    elsif (ref($arg) eq 'HASH')   { print $prefix, %{$arg} }
    else                          { print $prefix, $arg }
  }
}
```

If a reference is used in a context where a string is expected, then the `ref` function is called automatically to produce a string, and a unique hexadecimal value representing the internal memory address of the referent is appended. That means that printing out a reference

```perl
print $hsh_ref, "\n";
```

produces something like:

HASH(0x10027588)

since each element of `print`'s argument list is stringified before printing.

The `ref` function has a vital additional role in object-oriented Perl, where it can be used to identify the class to which a particular object belongs (see chapter 3).

References and anonymous arrays

References are particularly useful in creating multidimensional data structures. As we saw earlier, nested lists are automatically flattened, so trying to build a list of lists doesn't work:

```perl
@table = (
          ( 1, 2, 3),
          ( 2, 4, 6),
          ( 3, 6, 9),
        );
```

This fails to have the desired effect because flattening makes the above equivalent to:

```perl
@table = (1,2,3,2,4,6,3,6,9);
```

Fortunately, each element in a Perl array can store any kind of scalar value. Since a reference is just a special kind of scalar, it's possible to write:

```perl
@row1 = ( 1, 2, 3);
@row2 = ( 2, 4, 6);
@row3 = ( 3, 6, 9);

@cols = (\@row1,\@row2,\@row3);

$table = \@cols;
```

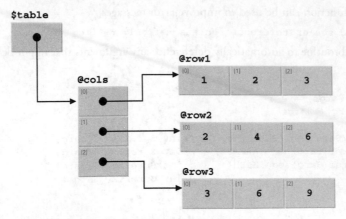

Figure 2.2   Internal structure of a 2D table

Figure 2.2 illustrates the structure that has been set up.

Now, elements in the "row" arrays can be accessed using the arrow notation:

```
print "2 x 3 is ", $table->[1]->[2];
```

The $table->[1] bit means: *find the array referred to by the reference in* $table *(i.e.,* @cols), *then get the element at index 1.* That element stores another reference (a reference to @row2). The final ->[2] bit means: *find the array referred to by* $table->[1] *(i.e.,* @row2), *then get the element at index 2.* Figure 2.3 illustrates the full path taken through the data structure.

Of course, tables like this are very popular, so Perl provides some syntactic assistance. If we specify a list of values in square brackets instead of parentheses, the result is not a list, but a reference to a nameless (or anonymous) array. That array is automatically initialized to the specified values. Using this syntax we can replace the table set-up code with the following:

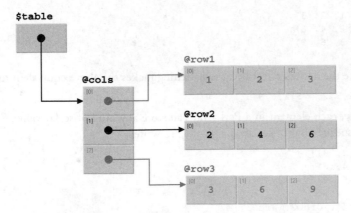

Figure 2.3   Traversing the internal structure of a 2D table

```
$row1_ref = [ 1, 2, 3];
$row2_ref = [ 2, 4, 6];
$row3_ref = [ 3, 6, 9];

$table = [$row1_ref, $row2_ref, $row3_ref];
```

Better still, we can eliminate the $row... variables entirely, by nesting sets of square brackets:

```
my $table =
[
  [ 1, 2, 3],
  [ 2, 4, 6],
  [ 3, 6, 9],
];
```

This results in the data structure shown in figure 2.4. That data structure is identical to the structure shown in figure 2.2 except that the various arrays are now nameless and, therefore, only accessible via the reference in $table.

As a final piece of syntactic assistance, in any expression like:

```
print $table->[$x]->[$y];
```

each arrow between a closing square or curly bracket and an opening square or curly bracket is optional. So we can write:

```
print $table->[$x][$y];
```

References and anonymous hashes

It's also possible to create references to anonymous hashes by replacing the parentheses of a hash-like list:

```
%association = ( cat=>"nap", dog=>"gone", mouse=>"ball" );
```

with curly braces:

```
$association = { cat=>"nap", dog=>"gone", mouse=>"ball" };
```

Like the [...] array constructor, the {...} hash constructor returns a reference, which must be assigned to a scalar variable ($association), not to a hash (%association).

Access to the resulting anonymous hash is only possible through the returned reference:

```
print "When I say 'cat', you say...", $association->{cat};
```

We can even create multilevel hashes, by nesting anonymous hash references:

```
$behaviour =
{
  cat   => { nap => "lap", eat => "meat" },
  dog   => { prowl => "growl", pool => "drool" },
  mouse => { nibble => "kibble" },
};
```

Here again, accessing the data requires a chain of arrow operators:

```
print "A cat eats ", $behaviour->{cat}->{eat};
```

And, as with multidimensional arrays, any arrows after the first can be omitted:

```
print "A mouse nibbles ", $behaviour->{mouse}{nibble};
```

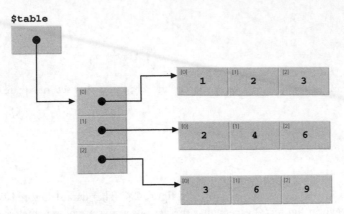

Figure 2.4   The internal structure of another 2D table

Anonymous subroutine references

In addition to anonymous arrays and hashes, anonymous subroutines can be created by using the sub keyword without giving a subroutine name:

```
sub { print "Heeeeeeeeere's $_[0]!\n" };
```

Of course, by itself such a declaration is useless, since there's no way of actually calling such a nameless subroutine. Fortunately, when sub is used in this way, it returns a reference to the anonymous subroutine it just created. If we cache that reference in a scalar:

```
$sub_ref = sub { print "Heeeeeeeeere's $_[0]!\n" };
```

we can then use it to call the original subroutine, via the arrow notation:

```
$sub_ref->("looking at you, kid");
```

The need for anonymous subroutines doesn't crop up very often in regular Perl programming, but they are surprisingly useful in object-oriented Perl. The section on *Closures* below explains their relationship with the object-oriented concept of encapsulation. Chapters 5 and 11 explain how anonymous subroutines can be used as the basis for special types of objects.

Passing subroutine arguments as explicit references

References also provide a means of passing unflattened arrays or hashes into subroutines. Suppose we want to write a subroutine called insert, to insert a value into a sorted array of values, so that the ordering of the array is preserved. We can't call this subroutine in the obvious way:

```
insert(@ordered, $next_val);
```

because normal list flattening will squash the contents of @ordered and the value of $newval into a single list (i.e., @_). Then there would be no way within the subroutine to access @ordered itself in order to insert the new element.[12]

Instead, we could set up insert so that it expected a *reference* to the array as its first argument:

```
sub insert
{
   ($arr_ref, $new_val) = @_;
   @{$arr_ref} = sort {$a<=>$b} (@{$arr_ref}, $new_val); # numerical sort
}
```

We could then call it like so:

```
insert(\@ordered, $next_val);
```

Now, within insert, we can dereference the array reference (@{$arr_ref}), to direct-ly access the original array that $arr_ref refers to (e.g., @ordered). Consequently, any changes made to @{$arr_ref} will change that original array.

2.1.6 Packages

In the cult movie *The Adventures of Buckaroo Banzai across the 8th Dimension,*[13] the alien Lec-troids don't quite understand the human concept of names. Consequently, every one of them is called John. The same problem arises when programming: we'd all like to use the "popular" variable and subroutine names such as $file, @options, &create, $John, %John, &John, and so forth. But, if we did, there would be no way to reuse other people's code, since they'd be using those variable names too, almost certainly for incompatible purposes.

The Lectroids solved the problem by given everyone a unique family name: John Whor-fin, John Bigboote, John Yaya, John Emdall, John Parker, and so forth. Perl solves the problem in exactly the same way. Each named variable[14] and each named subroutine belongs to a par-ticular family, known as a *package*. Each package maintains its own distinct symbol table, or *namespace*. Two different packages may each have distinct variables or subroutines of the same name in their respective namespaces.

By default, Perl assumes that code is written in the namespace of the main package, but you can change that default at any time using the package keyword. A package declaration changes the namespace until another package declaration is encountered, or until the end of the current enclosing block, eval, subroutine, or file. For example, the following code:

```
sub call
{
   ($sub_ref, @args) = @_;
   $sub_ref->(@args);
}


package Telephone;
sub call
{
   if (dial()) { talk(); }
}
```

---

[12] The normal aliasing of @_ to the subroutine's arguments doesn't help in this case. Each scalar element of the @ordered array *is* aliased to the corresponding element in @_, but the @ordered array itself isn't aliased to anything.

[13] Vestron Video, 1984.

[14] Except variables that are declared "lexical" (see below).

```
package Poker;

sub call
{
   $pot += $_[0];
   compare_hands();
}
```

declares three completely distinct subroutines named call. The first call is defined in the main namespace, the second in the namespace Telephone, and the last in the Poker namespace. If we then returned to the main namespace and wrote:

```
package main;

call($callback_sub);
```

the first version of call would be invoked, since it's the one that belongs to the current package at the point of invocation. If we meant to invoke the call subroutine defined in the Telephone package, we'd either have to switch back to that package

```
package Telephone;

call("1-800-BLAQ-LECTROID");
```

or prefix the subroutine name with the name of its package, separating the two with a double colon (::):

```
package main;

Telephone::call("1800-BLAQ-LECTROID");  # i.e. &call in package Telephone

Poker::call(0.50);                      # i.e. &call in package Poker

main::call($timeout_sub);               # i.e. &call in package main
call($timeout_sub);                     # i.e. &call in current package
```

This second solution is like referring to someone who is not present by their full name, to distinguish them from someone with the same name who's currently in the room: "Tell me John, did you ever meet John Glenn or John Kennedy?"

Package names can have multiple parts, as surnames sometimes do, with each part separated by a double colon:

```
package Telephone::Mobile;

sub call
{
   if ( signal() && dial() ) { talk() }
}

package Poker::Saloon::Traditional;
sub call
{
   &Poker::call;     # Call &Poker::call with same args
   accuse();
   draw();
```

```
    shoot();
    die;
}
```

The fact that the packages `Telephone` and `Telephone::Mobile` share the initial part of their names doesn't imply any hierarchical connection between them. In particular, `Telephone::Mobile` is not, in any important sense,[15] a "subpackage of..." or "located inside..." the `Telephone` package.[16]

Package variables

Perl variables come in two flavors: *package variables* and *lexical variables*. They look and act much the same, but there are fundamental differences between them.

As the name suggests, each package variable belongs to a package—normally, the current one. Package variables are the ones that casual Perl programmers use most of the time. They're the standard, no-preparation-necessary, ready-to-serve, instant variables frequently used in small throw-away programs:

```
for ($i=0; $i<100; $i++)
{
    $time = localtime();
    print "$i at $time\n";
}
print "last time was: $time\n";
print "last index was: $ i\n";
```

Here, the variables `$time` and `$i` are both package variables. They are created automatically the first time they're referred to and continue to exist until the end of the program. They belong to the current package.

Whenever it's necessary to make a package variable's ownership explicit, its "personal" name can be prefixed with the name of its package, just as subroutine names were in the previous section.

Package variables belonging to packages other than the current package are not accessible unless you use their fully qualified name. For example, this code:

```
package main;

for ($i=0; $i<100; $i++)
{
    $Other_package::time = localtime();
    print "$i at $Other_package::time\n";
}
```

---

[15] In a purely technical sense, there *is* a reference to the symbol table of Telephone::Mobile inside the symbol table of Telephone, but if that sense ever becomes important to you, you'll be far beyond such minor semantic quibbles.

[16] Mark-Jason Dominus gave the clearest explanation of this *nonnesting* of packages in his "Just the FAQs" column in issue #12 of *The Perl Journal*, when he pointed out that Sir Isaac Newton (`Newton::Isaac`) is not related to Olivia Newton-John (`Newton::John::Olivia`).

```
```

```
package Other_package;
print "last time was: $time\n";
print "last index was: $main::i\n";
```

uses the package variable $time belonging to the package called Other_package, and the package variable $i belonging to the main package. Within their home packages, they can be referred to directly; elsewhere, you have to give their package name as well.

The package name prefix always comes *after* the leading symbol. That is, you write $Other_package::time, not Other_package::$time.

Lexical variables

The other type of variable is a lexical variable. Unlike package variables, lexicals have to be explicitly declared, using the my keyword:

```
package main;

my $i;
for ($i=0; $i<100; $i++)
{
  my $time = localtime();
  print "$i at $time\n";
}
```

Lexical variables differ from package variables in three important respects:

- They don't belong to any package, so you can't prefix them with a package name.
- They are only directly accessible within the physical boundaries of the code block or file scope in which they're declared. In the code above, $time is only accessible to code physically located inside the for loop and not to code called during or after that loop.
- They usually cease to exist each time the program leaves the code block in which they were declared. In the code above, the variable $time ceases to exist at the end of each iteration of the for loop (and is recreated at the beginning of the next iteration).

It may help to think of the two types of variables—package and lexical—in the way the Ancient Greeks thought of their gods. Ancient Greece had big general-purpose gods like Uranus, Zeus, Aphrodite, and Atropos, who existed for all time and could appear anywhere without warning. These are analogous to package variables.[17]

Then there were the small, specialized gods like the spirits of trees, or doorsteps, or hearths. These gods were restricted to a well-defined domain—a tree, a building, the fireplace—and existed only for a specific period—the life of the tree, the occupation of the building, the duration of a fire. These are like lexical variables: localized and transient.

Generally speaking, package variables are fine for very short programs, but cause problems in larger code. Because package variables are accessible throughout the program source, changes made at one point in the code can unexpectedly affect the program's behavior elsewhere. The typical example is something like this:

---

[17] The big Greek gods even came in "packages": $Titans::Uranus, $Olympians::Zeus, $Olympians::Aphrodite, $Fates::Atropos.

```
package Recipe;

sub print_recipes
{
   for ($i=0; $i<@_; $i++)
   {
      print_ingredients($_[$i]);
      print_directions($_[$i]);
   }
}

sub print_ingredients
{
   for ($i=0; $i<$#recipes; $i++)
   {
      print $_[0]->{ingredients}[$i], "\n";
   }
}
```

The problem is that $i is a package variable, since it's not predeclared as a lexical with a my. That means that the subroutines Recipe::print_recipes and Recipe::print_ingredients both use the same package variable, $Recipe::i, in their respective for loops. So after Recipe::print_ingredients has been called from within Recipe::print_recipe, $Recipe::i will no longer contain the index of the current recipe. Instead, it will contain a number one greater than the number of ingredients of the current recipe, since that's the value left in it by the for loop in Recipe::print_ingredients.

If we'd use lexical variables instead:

```
package Recipe;
sub print_recipes
{
   for (my $i=0; $i<@_; $i++)
   {
      print_ingredients($_[$i]);
      print_directions($_[$i]);
   }
}

sub print_ingredients
{
   for (my $i=0; $i<@_; $i++)
   {
      print $_[0]->{ingredients}[$i], "\n";
   }
}
```

there would be no unexpected interaction between the two subroutines.[18] Each lexical $i is distinct, unrelated to any other lexical $i or to the package variable $Recipe::i, for that matter. Most importantly, each lexical is confined to the body of the for loop in which it's declared.

---

[18] An interaction of this kind between subroutines is known as *coupling*, and just as in real life, it can cause no end of difficulties.

The only problem is that, in Perl, lexical variables and package variables look the same, and since package variables can be conjured into existence just by mentioning them, this similarity can lead to subtle difficulties. For example, if we added an extra statement to the end of the loop timer shown earlier:

```
package main;

my $i;
for ($i=0; $i<100; $i++)
{
  my $time = localtime();
  print "$i at $time\n";
}
print "last time was: [$time]\n";
```

we'd find that the last line printed was

last time was: []

Because the lexical variable $time exists only inside the for loop, Perl assumes that when we referred to $time outside the loop, we meant the (undefined) package variable $main::time. This problem doesn't arise if you always put a use strict at the start of your code, because use strict requires that all package variables be fully qualified (to avoid just this kind of confusion).

Reference counting

Lexical variables normally cease to exist at the end of the block or file in which they're declared, but not always. The rule is that a lexical is destroyed at the end of its block unless some other part of the program still has a reference to it. In that case it continues to exist until that reference disappears.

For example, consider a subroutine that returns a reference to a lexical array:

```
sub make_array_ref
{
  my @array = @_;
  return \@array;
}

# and later...

$arr_ref = make_array_ref(1,2,3,4,5);
```

Normally, the lexical @array would be destroyed when the make_array_ref subroutine ended, but, in this case, the code that called make_array_ref receives a reference to that lexical. Because the lexical array variable is now accessible through $arr_ref, Perl arranges for the lexical to "survive" the end of its original scope.[19] Indeed, the lexical continues to survive until no more references to it exist anywhere in the program.

---

[19] Perl's behavior in this regard is very different from that of many statically typed OO languages (e.g., Ada or C++), where returning a reference, or pointer, to a variable declared within a subroutine is a Very Bad Thing.

For example, if we were to subsequently reassign $arr_ref:

```
$arr_ref = "something else";
```

then the reference to @array is replaced, causing the last reference to @array to be lost. When that happens, Perl finally destroys that lexical variable.

This behavior is called *reference counting* because each lexical has a count associated with it, telling Perl how many references to it exist. Each time another reference to the lexical is created, the count goes up; each time a reference disappears, the count goes down. Each time the count goes down, Perl checks to see if it hit zero, in which case the variable is destroyed.

You may have noticed that the make_array_ref subroutine shown above is a hand-built equivalent of the standard Perl anonymous array constructor. That is:

```
$arr_ref = make_array_ref(1,2,3,4,5);
```

is exactly the same as:

```
$arr_ref = [1,2,3,4,5];
```

It's probably no surprise therefore that anonymous arrays and hashes are also subject to reference counting and, like lexicals, will vanish automatically when the last reference to them ceases to exist.

Localized variables

Just to muddy the waters a little more, Perl has another way of imposing a limited scope on a variable.

The local function takes package variables—but not lexicals—and temporarily replaces their value. Thereafter, any reference to that package variable anywhere in the program accesses that new temporary value. The original value (that is, the value before the call to local) is only restored when execution reaches the end of the block in which the replacement was originally made. Figure 2.5 illustrates the idea.

For example, if we write:

```
package main;

$myname = "Damian";
print $myname;

if (secret_identity())
{
    local $myname = "OOP-erman";
    print $myname;

    protect_innocent_attributes();
    dispatch_evil_methods();
}

print $myname;
```

then:

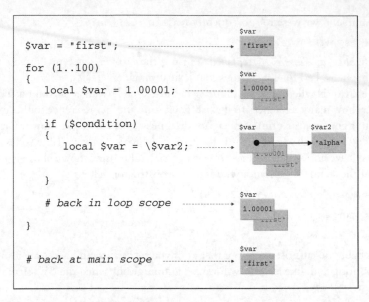

```
$var = "first";  ------------------------->    $var
                                               "first"

for (1..100)
{
    local $var = 1.00001;  ------------->      $var
                                               1.00001
                                               first

    if ($condition)
    {
        local $var = \$var2;  --------->       $var       $var2
                                               ●  ------> "alpha"
                                               1.00001
                                               first
    }

    # back in loop scope  -------------->      $var
                                               1.00001
                                               first
}

# back at main scope  ----------------->      $var
                                               "first"
```

Figure 2.5   Localizing a package variable

- The first `print` statement would print "**Damian**" (since that's the value assigned to the package variable `$main::myname` at the time),
- The second `print` would produce "**OOP-erman**" (since the call to `local` temporarily replaces the value of `$main::myname` within the `if` block),
- The third `print` would output "**Damian**" again (since the temporary replacement caused by `local` ceases at the end of the block containing the call to `local`).

In addition, if either of the subroutines `protect_innocent_attributes` or `dispatch_evil_methods` ever refers to the package variable `$myname`, perhaps as `$main::myname`, the subroutine will access the replacement value, not the original value. That's because, when the subroutine is called, the temporary replacement of `$main::myname` is still in effect. Execution hasn't yet reached the end of the `if` block from which the subroutine was called.

It's important to be clear about the difference between `my` and `local`. The `my` qualifier *creates* a new lexical variable, accessible by name only in the current block and not directly accessible in any subroutines called by the current block. Using `local` *temporarily replaces* an existing package variable, still accessible by name anywhere, including in subroutines called by the current block.

In other words, lexical variables are restricted to the spatial (syntactic) boundaries of the block in which their `my` is specified, while `local`ized package variables are restricted to the temporal (execution) boundaries of the block in which their `local` is called.

If you want a variable with a limited scope—and no nasty surprises when distant and unrelated code messes with its value—you want `my`. If you want to temporarily change the value of a package variable until the end of the current block, you want `local`. In practice, you almost always want `my`.

2.2 NONESSENTIAL (BUT VERY USEFUL) PERL

Although you can create Perl classes with just the standard data types, subroutines, references, and packages, to realize the full power and beauty of object-oriented Perl, you really need to take advantage of Perl's more advanced features. In particular, you need an understanding of modules, autoloading, closures, and typeglobs.

2.2.1 Modules

When you've created some usable code, the last thing you want to do is cut-and-paste that same code into other applications. It's inefficient and inelegant. It also creates a maintenance nightmare every time you find a bug. Fortunately, Perl provides a simple module system that allows us to put packaged code into a separate file, put that file in a well-defined place, and thereafter have the compiler add the file into other programs semiautomatically. The standard `perlmod` and `perlmodlib` documentation explains the concept in detail, and it's worth taking the time to read them carefully. Meanwhile, this section provides a minimal survival guide.

What is a module?

A Perl module is simply a text file (with a .pm suffix) containing some Perl code. The file is placed in one of several standard directories where the compiler knows to look for it. Whenever the compiler encounters a `use` statement in a program, it searches through these standard directories, locates the matching file, and evaluates the code inside it.[20] That evaluation makes the code in the file available to the rest of the program.

Within a Perl program, module names look just like package names. Frequently, there is a one-to-one correspondence, with each module storing one package. The module name is also related to the actual name of the text file. To determine the file name, take the module name and replace each `::` with the local directory path separator, then append .pm. The resulting path is the location of the file, relative to one of the standard directories in Perl's current "include" path.

So what does that mean, exactly? Well, suppose a program includes the following `use` statement:

```
use Database::Access::Control;
```

On encountering the `use` statement, the compiler translates each `::` into a file path separator, yielding:

- Database/Access/Control.pm under Unix or Linux or OS/2
- Database\Access\Control.pm under Windows

---

[20] It also handles compilation errors, prevents multiple or circular loading of modules, enforces a separate lexical scope on the module's code, and automatically calls the module's `import` subroutine. See the `perlmod` documentation for gory details.

- Database:Access:Control.pm under MacOS
- [Database.Access]Control.pm under VMS

The compiler then starts searching through its list of standard and user-defined library directories, looking for a file matching that relative path. That list of directories is available within a Perl program as the global array variable @INC. You can even change the contents of @INC to change the search path for modules (see below).

The Perl compiler opens the first matching file it finds, and eval's the text inside it. If the eval fails, compilation is terminated with an error message. That can happen if the file is inaccessible, the code it contains is invalid, or the code doesn't produce a true value when executed.

Otherwise, the compiler looks through the module's code for a subroutine named import, and if it finds one, calls it (see *Importing from a module* below). When the module's import subroutine returns, compilation continues back in the original file, from the line after the use statement.

Setting up a module

To place your own code in a separate module that you can subsequently use, you need to do the following:

1 **Choose the standard library directory under which you want the module to reside.** You may have to create such a directory if this is your first personal module. Typically, such a directory lives under your home directory. For example, on UNIX, you might create a subdirectory called ~/lib/perl5. Under MacOS you might set up the folder Users:Applications:MacPerl ƒ:lib:my modules. For Windows, you might use the directory C:\USERS\DAMIAN\PERLLIB.

2 **Tell Perl of the existence of your directory.** If you want to permanently inform Perl of the new module directory, you can add the path name to the colon-separated list stored in the shell variable PERL5LIB:

```
% PERL5LIB="${PERL5LIB}:/users/damian/lib/perl5"          # UNIX sh shell
% export PERL5LIB
```

(assuming you're working on an operating system that has such things), or add the path to the appropriate list in the Perl application's preferences (when using MacPerl, for example), or you can invoke Perl with the -I<pathname> option.

On the other hand, if you only want to add the directory for a particular program, you can push a string containing the full path onto the array @INC (in a BEGIN block at the start of your program):

```
#! /usr/local/bin/perl -w

BEGIN { push @INC, "/users/damian/lib/perl5" }
```

Better still, use the use lib directive:

```
#! /usr/local/bin/perl -w

use lib "/users/damian/lib/perl5";
```

3 **Create nested subdirectories under that standard directory for each component of the module name, except the last.**[21] If the module is going to be called W::X::Y::Z, then you need to create the subdirectories W, W/X, and W/X/Y, or whatever the local translation of those are on your operating system, inside your chosen library directory.

4 **Create a text file in the bottom subdirectory.** The file must have the same (case-sensitive) name as the last component of the module name, plus a .pm suffix, in this case Z.pm.

5 **Insert your code into the text file.**

6 **Add an extra statement that evaluates to true, to the end of the text file.** The usual choice is simple to place a line consisting of

```
1;
```

at the end of the file.

So, for example, under the sh shell on Unix,[22] you could use the following sequence of commands to set up a module containing the Database::Access::Control source code:

```
% cd ~/lib                # go to your personal lib directory
% mkdir perl5             # create a perl5 subdirectory...
% cd perl5                # ...and descend into it
% mkdir Database          # create a Database subdirectory...
% cd Database             # ...and descend into it
% mkdir Access            # create a Access subdirectory...
% cd Access               # ...and descend into it
% vi Control.pm           # create the module file, then copy your
                          # code into it, and append a 1; at the end
% PERL5LIB= "${PERL5LIB}:${HOME}/lib/perl5"
                          # add the name of the root include directory
                          # into the PERL5LIB environment variable
% export PER5LIB          # ...and export it to other programs (i.e. perl)
```

You'll probably want to put those last two commands in your .profile file,[23] so the PERL5LIB environment variable is correctly set up every time you log in.

Once your new module is in place, any Perl program can access it by including the statement use Database::Access::Control.

---

[21] Alternatively, you can combine steps three and four by using the h2xs application that comes standard with Perl. If you use the -Axn flag, h2xs will set up a nice skeleton package for you (see the h2xs documentation for details).

[22] If you're of the "other" persuasion, Ron Savage has a full example of setting up a new module under Windows 95/NT at: http://savage.net.au/Perl-tutorials/tutorial1.html

[23] or put the appropriate equivalents in your .login file, or wherever else your particular system allows you to define environment variables for an interactive session.

Version control in modules

The `use` statement also allows a program to specify that a module must be at least a certain version number. For example, if we need to be sure we're using version 1.20 or later of the Database::Access::Control module, we would write

```
use Database::Access::Control 1.20;
```

If a `use` statement includes a version number like this, then, when the module has been loaded, its VERSION subroutine is automatically called with the requested version number. The default VERSION subroutine[24] checks to make sure that the requested version is less than or equal to the value of the $VERSION variable belonging to the named package. In other words, specifying a version number as in the above `use` statement causes the compiler to verify that `1.20 <= $Database::Access::Control::VERSION`. If the condition isn't true, the default VERSION subroutine dies with an appropriate error message.

You could provide your own VERSION subroutine if you really wanted to, but it's almost never a good idea, since other programmers who use your module will expect the standard behavior from it.

All you need to do to ensure that your module supports regular Perl version control is to define a variable called $VERSION within the appropriate package:

```
package Database::Access::Control;
$VERSION = 1.00;
use strict;
# ...etc.
```

$VERSION must be a package variable, so don't put a `my` in front of it. It's easiest to define $VERSION *before* any `use strict` comes into effect. Otherwise, you have to fully qualify it:

```
package Database::Access::Control;
use strict;
$Database::Access::Control::VERSION = 1.00;
```

Or you can placate `use strict` with a `use vars` statement:

```
package Database::Access::Control;
use strict;
use vars '$VERSION';
$VERSION = 1.00;
```

Export control in modules

Whenever a module is successfully located and compiled into a Perl program, the subroutine `import` belonging to that module is called. The default behavior of `import`[25] is to do nothing, but you can change that behavior by creating your own `import` subroutine in the module.

When it is called, the `import` subroutine is passed the name of the module being used as its first argument, followed by any argument list that appears at the end of the `use` statement. For example, if a program included the line

---

[24] ...which is lives in the UNIVERSAL package. See chapter 6.

[25] ...once again, defined in the UNIVERSAL package...

```
use Database::Access::Control ("my.db");
```

then, after the Database::Access::Control module had been located and compiled, the subroutine `Database::Access::Control::import` would automatically be called:

```
Database::Access::Control::import("Database::Access::Control","my.db");
```

Very few people ever write their own `import` subroutine (although we'll see how to do so in chapter 12). Instead, they generally use the Exporter module, which is part of the Perl standard distribution. Exporter makes it easy to take care of the typical tasks for which `import` is used, namely, importing package variables and subroutines from the module's name space to the caller's.

We won't discuss the use of Exporter here. See, instead, the documentation that comes with the module. Though important in regular Perl, the Exporter module and the `import` subroutine are hardly ever used in object-oriented Perl, since exporting variables or subroutines from classes goes against the encapsulation principle of object orientation.

2.2.2 Autoloading

In most programming languages, if you call a subroutine that doesn't exist, you get an immediate and fatal error, and there's nothing you can do about it. But that behavior implies that every subroutine must be defined before the program runs, and that's not always what we want.

Perl gives us a way of creating a catchall subroutine for each package, which will be called instead when a requested subroutine doesn't exist. That catch-all is called AUTOLOAD.

For example, if the subroutine `Robot::move_arm` is invoked:

```
Robot::move_arm(left=>100);
```

but the Robot package doesn't have a subroutine named `move_arm`, then, before it issues a fatal error, Perl also tries to call `Robot::AUTOLOAD`.

A package's AUTOLOAD subroutine is always invoked with the argument list that was intended for the missing subroutine. In the above example, `Robot::AUTOLOAD` would be invoked with the argument list: `("left", 100)`.

Usually, it's also important for the catch-all subroutine to know exactly which subroutine was actually requested. So, whenever an AUTOLOAD is invoked, the package variable $AUTOLOAD is automatically assigned the fully qualified name of the missing subroutine, in this case: `Robot::move_arm`.

For example, we could set up the Robot package's catch-all to politely point out that the requested action isn't implemented:

```
package Robot;

sub AUTOLOAD
{
   print"Sorry $AUTOLOAD isn't defined.\n",
       "(I'll just pretend, shall I?)\n";
}
```

Any attempt to call an unimplemented subroutine in the Robot package now gets a similar message:

```
package Robot;

wash_floor();                    # Sorry, Robot::wash_floor isn't defined…"
empty_trash("all");              # Sorry, Robot::empty_trash isn't defined…"

package main;

Robot::barada_nikto("Klaatu"); # Sorry, Robot::barada_nikto isn't defined…"
```

Of course, polite error messages aren't particularly useful, except during software development.[26] A more interesting application of autoloading is to have the AUTOLOAD subroutine work out what to do, and then actually do it. For example:

```
sub AUTOLOAD
{
    $AUTOLOAD =~ s/.*:://;       # Strip leading package name
    return `$AUTOLOAD @_`;       # Execute in a shell
}

# and later…

$files = dir();
del('DATA.TMP');
$help = type("HELP.TXT");
```

In this example, the AUTOLOAD subroutine first strips off any leading package name from the full subroutine name in $AUTOLOAD. It executes the resulting short name as a DOS command, using backquotes to capture the resulting output. Consequently, with a two line AUTOLOAD, you can instantly do DOS programming directly in Perl.[27]

In chapter 3, we'll look at extra features of autoloading that come into play when methods are invoked. We'll also see how a class-specific AUTOLOAD can be used to simplify the creation of object methods, particularly those used to access and modify attributes.

2.2.3 Closures

To hear some people talking about closures, you'd think they were discussing quantum physics, brain surgery, or VCR programming. In reality, the idea of closures is incredibly simple and obvious, once the technical jargon has been stripped from it.

In Perl, a closure is just a subroutine that refers to one or more lexical variables declared outside the subroutine itself. For example

```
my $name = "Damian";

sub print_my_name
{
    print $name, "\n";
}
```

---

[26] …when it's sometimes convenient to use autoloading to implement a set of placeholder subroutines, known as "stubs".

[27] The standard Shell module that comes with Perl is a vastly more robust, portable, and sophisticated version of this idea.

The subroutine `print_my_name` accesses the lexical variable `$name`, which is declared outside the code block of the subroutine, so `print_my_name` is a closure. The subroutine is perfectly within its rights to access `$name`, because that variable's scope extends from the point at which it is declared to the end of the surrounding block.[28]

The interesting bit is that lexical variables usually cease to exist once execution reaches the end of the scope in which they are declared. That is, in a piece of code like this

```
{
    my $name = "Damian";
}
```

```
# $name not accessible out here
```

the `$name` variable would become inaccessible and cease to exist[29] at the end of the block. However, if we define a closure within the block

```
{
    my $name = "Damian";

    sub print_my_name { print $name, "\n" }
}
```

```
# $name not accessible out here (except through &print_my_name)
```

then the definition of that subroutine confers eternal life on the otherwise-doomed variable `$name`. In other words, as long as the `print_my_name` subroutine continues to exist (i.e., for the rest of the program), Perl will make sure that the lexical variable stays available for the subroutine's use.

The tricky bit is that, apart from this special relationship with `print_my_name`, the normal rules of accessibility still apply to the lexical variable. That is, at the end of the block, `$name` will become inaccessible to the rest of the program, except for `print_my_name`. Therefore, after the block ends, the *only* way to access `$name` is by calling that subroutine.

That's all there is to a closure: a subroutine that preserves any lexical variables it's using, even after they become invisible everywhere else.

Anonymous subroutines and closures

Of course using closures can get a great deal more complicated than the previous examples, especially when closures are built using anonymous (unnamed) subroutines.

For example, here is a generator subroutine, which creates an anonymous closure that can be used to skip along an array by a fixed step size:

```
sub hop_along
{
    my ($from, $to, $step) = @_;        # Unpack args
    my $next = $from-$step;             # Initialize counter
    my $closure_ref =                   # Build closure
            sub                         # that does the following…
```

---

[28] …or to the end of the current file, if the lexical wasn't declared inside a block.

[29] The two aren't the same, as we'll see in a moment.

```
        {
            $next+=$step;              # Take a step
            return if $next > $to;     # undef if out of range
            $_[0] = $next;             # Otherwise set new value
            return 1;                  # and succeed
        };
    return $closure_ref;               # Return closure
}
```

When the `hop_along` subroutine is called, it copies its three arguments into lexical variables, sets up another lexical (i.e., `$next`) as a counter, and then creates an anonymous subroutine that uses the values in those variables. The anonymous subroutine increments `$next` by `$step` each time the subroutine is called, until the result is greater than `$to`. A reference to the newly created anonymous subroutine is then returned.

The generator would be used like this:

```
$iterator = hop_along 1, 100, 7;      # Create closure
while ($iterator->($next))            # Call closure
{
    print $next;
}
```

in this case skipping from 1 to 99 in steps of 7.

Normally, the lexical variables inside the call to `hop_along` (i.e., `$from`, `$to`, `$step`, `$next`) would cease to exist when `hop_along` returned. But, because the anonymous subroutine still needs access to them, Perl arranges for them to live on in seclusion, accessible only by the anonymous subroutine itself.

It's important to realize that the next time `hop_along` is called:

```
$iterator2 = hop_along -1000000, +1000000, 0.000001;
```

it creates an entirely new set of lexical variables and sets up a completely separate anonymous subroutine with access to those new variables. For example, we could set up two closures at once, each with its own range and step size:

```
$row = hop_along 1, 1024, 1;
while ($row->($r))
{
    $col = hop_along 1, 768, 2;
    while ($col->($c))
    {
        draw_pixel($r, $c, $video_buffer->[$r][$c]);
    }
}
```

Closures are a means of giving a subroutine its own private memory— variables that persist between calls to that subroutine and are accessible only to it.

Even more interestingly, two or more closures can *share* the same private memory or *state*:

```
{
    my $locked;

    sub lock   { return 0 if $locked; $locked=1; }
    sub unlock { $locked=0 }
```

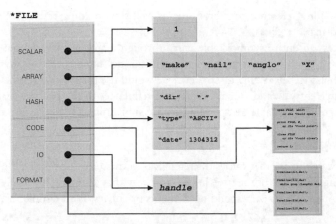

Figure 2.6   An entry (typeglob) in a package's symbol table

```
}

# and later

lock() or die "Resource already in use";
# Do critical stuff...
unlock();
```

In this case, the two subroutines `lock` and `unlock` share access to the lexical `$locked` variable, even after it becomes generally inaccessible—and would normally have ceased to exist—outside the block they share.

This ability of closures to provide restricted access to certain variables is an excellent, if unusual, example of the object-oriented concept of encapsulation. Indeed, we will see how closures can be used to implement encapsulation for Perl classes in chapter 11.

2.2.4   Typeglobs

Typeglobs are among the most poorly understood features of Perl, right up there with closures, in fact. But, like closures, they're actually easy to understand and use once you unravel their mysterious syntax and their polymorphic behavior.

As was mentioned in the earlier section on packages, Perl maintains separate namespaces for each package and each type of named construct within a package. Therefore, within a given package you can have the variables `$FILE`, `@FILE`, and `%FILE`, as well as the subroutine `&FILE`. Best of all, you can use them all at the same time.

Unlike many other languages, where an identifier must be associated with exactly one thing in the symbol table, in Perl there's no confusion. Each identifier has a unique prefix symbol indicating its type. In fact, they all live together in the very same entry of their package's symbol table, as figure 2.6 illustrates.

Each Perl symbol table entry is like a sampler box of chocolates. You get one slot for each type of Perl reference: one for a scalar reference; one for an array reference; one for a hash reference; and one for a reference to subroutine (as well slots holding references to one file-handle and one format).

You can access an entire symbol table entry through a special piece of syntax called a *typeglob*:[30] `*symbol_name`. To refer to the complete symbol table entry for anything that's called "FILE", such as `$FILE`, `%FILE`, `&FILE`, etc., we would use the typeglob `*FILE`. The slots in that symbol table entry would contain individual references to the package scalar variable `$FILE`, the package array variable `@FILE`, the package subroutine `&FILE`, and so forth.

Typeglob assignment

Assigning one typeglob to another causes the references in the second symbol table entry to be assigned to the matching slots of the first, in the same way that assigning one array to another or one hash to another assigns corresponding elements or entries. For example

```
*FILE = *SOURCE;
```

means "assign the references stored in the various slots of the symbol table entry for `'SOURCE'` to the corresponding slots of the symbol table entry from `'FILE'`." So now, as figure 2.7 illustrates, the scalar variable referred to by the "SCALAR" slot in `*FILE` is actually the same one referred to by the "SCALAR" slot in `*SOURCE` (i.e., `$SOURCE`).

That means, whenever Perl goes to look up the package variable `$FILE`, and checks in the symbol table, it will go to the symbol table entry `*FILE`, follow the reference in its "SCALAR" slot, and arrive at `$SOURCE`. In the same way, when looking for the subroutine `&FILE`, Perl will follow the reference in the "CODE" slot of `*FILE` and will end up at `&SOURCE` instead. In other words, assigning `*SOURCE` to `*FILE` makes `$FILE` another name for `$SOURCE`, `&FILE` another name for `&SOURCE`, `@FILE` another name for `@SOURCE`, and so forth.

The simplest use of such a typeglob assignment is to shorten the name of an unwieldy set of variables:

```
*rules = *the_Marquis_of_Queensbury_rules;

$rules = rules(@rules);

# instead of
# $the_Marquis_of_Queensberry_rules =
#   the_Marquis_of_Queensberry_rules(@the_Marquis_of_Queensberry_rules);
```

or to import things from another package:[31]

```
*rules = *Open::Software::rules;
```

However, typeglobs have another important trick up their sleeve: they can be *selectively* assigned to. If a typeglob is assigned a reference of any kind

```
*SOURCE = \$SOURCE1;
*args = \@ARGV;
*do_it = sub { print "doin' it!\n" };
```

---

[30] ...because it "globs" (generically matches) any type of variable with the correct name.

[31] ...typically as part of the `import` subroutine of a module. See *Export control in modules*.

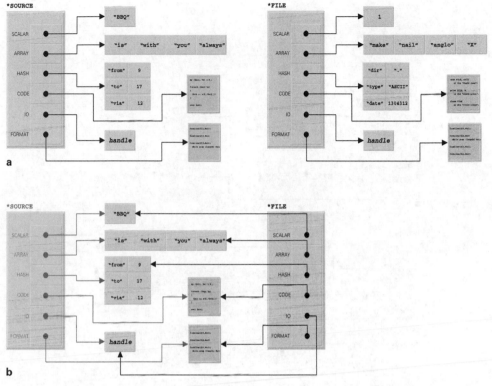

Figure 2.7 The effect of a typeglob-to-typeglob assignment
a   Before *FILE = *SOURCE;
b   After *FILE = *SOURCE;

then only the typeglob slot of the corresponding kind is replaced. In other words, given the above three assignments, $SOURCE will now be another name for $SOURCE1, while @SOURCE, %SOURCE, &SOURCE, and so forth. will be unaffected. Likewise @args will now be another name for @ARGV and &do_it will be another name for the anonymous subroutine. Figure 2.8 illustrates the effect of the *SOURCE = \$SOURCE1 assignment.

This assignment behavior is an example of polymorphism. The stimulus—an assignment—is always the same, but the response—which bit of the typeglob actually gets altered—depends on the type of value being assigned.

Creating references to typeglobs

Typeglobs are just another container data type in Perl, like arrays or hashes. They are more specialized in their storage ability—"one of each" rather than "many of any"—and more sophisticated in their assignment semantics. Otherwise, typeglobs are quite similar to other container datatypes. For example, it's perfectly possible to take a reference to a typeglob:

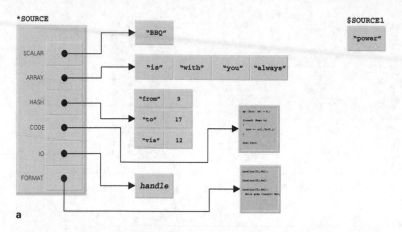

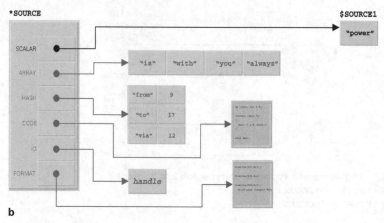

Figure 2.8 The effect of a reference-to-typeglob assignment
a Before `*SOURCE = \$SOURCE1;`
b After `*SOURCE = \$SOURCE1;`

```
$var = 'this is $var';
%var = (v=>"very", a=>"active", r=>"rodent");
sub var { print "this is &var\n" }

$typeglob_ref = \*var;
```

Now, `$typeglob_ref` holds a reference to the symbol table entry for everything called "var" (as shown in figure 2.9). Only three of the symbol's slots are filled, indicating that there is no @var array, var filehandle, nor associated format.

We can access the individual elements of that symbol table entry through the reference, but it's a two-step operation. First, we have to retrieve the typeglob itself, which we do by prefixing the reference, `$typeglob_ref`, with the usual typeglob prefix: `*$typeglob_ref`.

If we want to get to the corresponding scalar variable (i.e., `$var`), we need to prefix the resulting typeglob with a dollar-sign: `${*$typeglob_ref}`. The curly braces are required

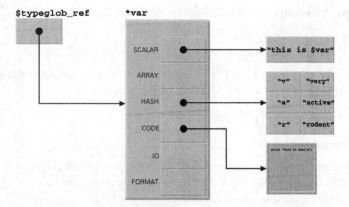

Figure 2.9   A reference to a typeglob

here to prevent Perl from treating the leading "$*" of $*$typeglob_ref as the name of the special variable $*.

If we want access to the corresponding hash %var instead, we have to use a percent sign as the prefix: %{*$typeglob_ref}. If we want to call the subroutine component var(), we prefix with an ampersand and add the argument list in parentheses at the end: &{*$typeglob_ref}().

Typeglob references are an obscure way of accessing a variable or subroutine, but they are often the only reasonable means of accessing a filehandle. Chapter 5 demonstrates the use of typeglob references in accessing filehandles in an object-oriented manner.

Accessing the references within typeglobs

As the previous sections indicate, the slots of a typeglob don't directly store the scalar, array, hash, subroutine, and filehandle that belong to the symbol represented by the typeglob. Instead, they store references to each of those things.

To allow us access to those references, Perl provides what is known as the *foo{THING} syntax. If we take a typeglob (like *foo) and append a hash-like key selector (like {THING}), Perl returns the reference in the corresponding slot of the typeglob. The keys are the names returned by Perl's built-in ref function (see table 2.1):

```
$slr_ref = *var{SCALAR};    # same as: $slr_ref = \$var
$arr_ref = *var{ARRAY};     # same as: $arr_ref = \@var
$hsh_ref = *var{HASH};      # same as: $hsh_ref = \%var
$sub_ref = *var{CODE};      # same as: $sub_ref = \&var
```

In addition, you can use the *foo{THING} syntax to get references to the file handle or directory handle slot of a typeglob, which are otherwise unreachable:

```
$hdl_ref = *var{IO};        # reference to IO handle named var
```

Apart from being arguably more readable, the *foo{THING} syntax is particularly handy if you have a reference to a typeglob, say $typeglob_ref, and you want a reference to one of its components, for example, its hash. Without the `*foo{THING}` syntax, you'd have to write:

```
$hsh_ref = \%{*$typeglob_ref};
```

which (quite appropriately) looks more like you're cursing. With the `*foo{THING}` syntax the same operation becomes slightly more readable and self-documenting:

```
$hsh_ref = *$typeglob_ref{HASH};
```

Symbolic references

There's yet another way to access variables and subroutines via the symbol table: via a *symbolic reference*. A symbolic reference is simply a character string containing the name of a variable or subroutine in a particular package's symbol table.

When Perl encounters such a string anywhere that it was expecting to find an ordinary reference, it simply looks up the corresponding name in the current symbol table and replaces it with a reference to the appropriate type of thing (scalar, array, subroutine, etc.) For example

```
package main;

$name = "data";

print ${$name};          # equivalent to: print $main::data
push @{$name}, $next;     # equivalent to: push @main::data, $next
&{$name}();               # equivalent to: &main::data()
```

If the string looks like a fully qualified name, then the appropriate symbol table is used instead of the current one:

```
$name = "Remote::Sensing::data";
print ${$name};               # equivalent to: print $Remote::Sensing::data

$name = "Lt::Commander::data";
push @{$name}, $next_gen; # equivalent to: push @Lt::Commander::data, $next_gen

$name = "data";
&{"Meta::".$name}();      # equivalent to: &Meta::data()
```

A regular reference can appear as the first argument of the arrow operator (`->`), so Perl allows symbolic references in that position too:

```
$symref = "set";

$symref->{type} = "discrete"; # equivalent to: $set{type} = "discrete"

$elem_1 = $symref->[0];       # equivalent to: $elem_1 = $set[0]

$symref->("jello");           # equivalent to: set("jello")
```

Incidentally, provided you know what type of thing you want to refer to, it's always possible to convert a symbolic reference into a regular reference. For example, if `$symref` contains the name of a scalar package variable, we can create a normal reference (`$ref`) to that same variable as follows:

```
$ref = \${$symref};          # create an "unsymbolic" reference to a scalar
```

Likewise, for the other common data types:

```
$ref = \@{$symref};          # create an "unsymbolic" reference to an array
$ref = \%{$symref};          # create an "unsymbolic" reference to a hash
$ref = \&{$symref};          # create an "unsymbolic" reference to a subrou-
tine
```

It's important to remember that, because symbolic references always consult a symbol table, they cannot be used to access lexical variables. For example:

```
package main;

my $grain = "headache";

${"grain"} = "rye";

print $grain;
```

prints **headache**, not **rye**. That's because, although the lexical variable $grain does hide the package variable $main::grain from any code that follows,[32] Perl looks only at the package symbol table when resolving a symbolic reference like ${"grain"}. So, ${"grain"} refers to $main::grain, which is then duly assigned the value "rye". This leaves the lexical $grain with its original value, which is subsequently printed.

We can even use symbolic references to access the symbol table itself. For example, if we had a scalar variable $symbol_name, which contained the name of a particular typeglob we were interested in

```
$symbol_name = "data";
```

then we could access that typeglob as *{$symbol_name}, rather than as *{data}. This seemingly esoteric capability to avoid hard-coded symbol names is actually extremely useful in certain types of generic programming, as we shall see in chapter 12.

The subtleties of symbolic references can be a genuine headache when invoked accidentally, so the use strict directive (or, more specifically, use strict "refs") makes them illegal. This is a handy safety feature and no real imposition, since you can always add a no strict "refs" directive to any block where you're deliberately using a symbolic reference.

Symbolic references are not widely used in regular Perl and are even rarer in object-oriented Perl. However, chapter 14 illustrates how symbolic references can be used to help add persistence to Perl objects.

2.3 THE CPAN

Perhaps the two best features of Perl are its broad and diverse community of devotees and the extraordinary wealth of the resources they so freely share with one another. Over the years, hundreds of people have contributed to the Perl language by making available free source code—for the language itself, and for many modules and example scripts—as well as binary

---

[32] As far as print is concerned, $grain refers to the lexical variable of that name, not the package variable.

distributions, documentation, FAQs, and information shared through Perl newsgroups. All to make everyone's Perl programming life easier.

That vast wealth of information and tools (over 750 MB of it) is archived in the Comprehensive Perl Archive Network, universally known as the CPAN (pronounced "see pan"). The brainchild of Jarkko Hietaniemi and Andreas König, the CPAN describes itself as "the collected wisdom of the Perl community," and it fulfils that role admirably. If it's related to Perl and it's worth knowing about or having, it's almost certainly accessible from the CPAN.

2.3.1 How to access the CPAN

How you access the CPAN depends on what you want to achieve. The usual way to begin is to explore it "on foot" via the web, starting at the introductory page at http://www.perl.com/CPAN/index.html.

When you go to this page, or any page starting http://www.perl.com/CPAN/..., you are automatically redirected to a mirror of the CPAN, one that is almost certainly not actually stored at the www.perl.com site.

The CPAN is an archive network, which means that it is distributed throughout the Internet on a large number of mirror sites (close to 100). Every site contains the complete CPAN archive, and, with so many spread around the world, you usually don't have to endure interminable download delays from a distant centralized site.

Of course, it's still convenient to access the CPAN as if it *were* centrally located. That way there's only one URL to remember. Therefore, www.perl.com helpfully redirects all CPAN requests to a site closer to you, using the mystical CPAN multiplex dispatcher. Better still, if you don't like the site that's automatically chosen for you, you can visit the Multiplexer itself, at http://www.perl.com/CPAN (note: no trailing slash!). There can choose an alternative site, which the multiplexer will remember for next time.

Once you're at the introductory page, you can discover the ways in which the resources of the CPAN can be accessed. Specifically, the page directs you to the top-level entries of the archive—a list of categories under which the CPAN's contents are indexed.

It's worth taking a little time to poke around the regions of the CPAN. Think of it as a game of rogue or hack: roaming around a labyrinth, looking for unexpected treasure. Later, when you have a particular dragon to slay, that familiarity with the layout of the CPAN will help you quickly locate the right weapon and reward you many times over in saved development time.

2.3.2 How to search the CPAN

Of course, you may have better things to do with your brain than using it to carry around a mental map of the CPAN on the off-chance you'll someday need it to locate a particular resource. The alternative is to make use of either WAIT–The Great CPAN Search Engine, or the CPAN Search website.

WAIT is a sophisticated search engine developed by Norbert Gövert and Ulrich Pfeifer, based on their Wais search engine module. It provides exact, inexact, and even phonetic searching of a subset of the CPAN. Modules and documentation may be located according to a range of criteria, including module name, author's name, synopsis, bugs, description, or examples.

It also provides Boolean search operators that allow you to specify searches on two or more criteria, or to exclude certain criteria. For example: *find any module whose description contains "class," but not "multimethod," and whose author is named Damian.* The WAIT is available at http://ls6-www.cs.uni-dortmund.de/ir/projects/SFgate/CPAN/. There's also the CPAN:: WAIT module (available from http://www.perl.com/CPAN/authors/id/ULPFR/), which grafts the WAIT functionality on to the CPAN module.

CPAN Search is a search engine maintained by Randy Kobes. It can search the entire CPAN archive, using exact and prefix-only pattern-matching on a range of criteria including archive file name; module, script, or package name; module or script description; contents of module documentation; or author's name or ID. Like the WAIT, CPAN Search has a forms-based interface that makes specifying your search criteria easy. It's available at http://theory.uwinnipeg.ca/search/cpan-search.html.

2.3.3 How to install modules from the CPAN

Finding the module you need is usually only a small skirmish, a prelude to the main battle of installing it on your local system.

Using the CPAN.pm module

By far the easiest way to locate, download, and install modules from the CPAN is to use the CPAN.pm module. If you're using Unix, Linux, Solaris, or MacOS, and if you're fortunate, someone may already have installed the module on your system, in which case it's just a matter of firing it up:

```
% perl -MCPAN -e shell
```

and downloading whatever you need. The CPAN module comes with quite extensive documentation, and is relatively easy to use once you're set up. If you know the name of the module you want, say Text::Balanced, the entire installation process is often as easy as typing

```
cpan> install Text::Balanced
```

The CPAN.pm module does the rest.

If you're using another operating system, or if you try to run the module and get an error along the lines of

Can't locate CPAN.pm in @INC...

then you're going to have to install the CPAN.pm module—or else just install the actual module you wanted—yourself (see the next section).

The first time you run the module's interactive shell—that's what the command perl -MCPAN -e shell actually does—you will be taken through a configuration process that sets the necessary defaults to allow the module to automatically download, unpack, build, test, and install modules for you.

It's safe to ignore most of the questions you'll be asked in this configuration process, and just go with the module's suggested configuration. The one question you really *do* want to answer yourself is the one asking if there are any parameters you want passed to the perl Makefile.PL command. At very least, you need to tell CPAN.pm to add a PREFIX=*some/directory* parameter, so that downloaded modules are installed in your personal module library, rather than in the global one.[33]

The *some/directory* bit should be replaced with the full path name of the directory containing your personal modules directory (see *Setting up a module*). For example, if you keep your own Perl modules in a directory called /users/staff/damian/lib/perl5, then you should tell the CPAN configuration to add the parameter PREFIX=/users/staff/damian whenever it calls perl Makefile.PL. To do that, you need to answer the relevant question as follows (but with your home directory):

Every Makefile.PL is run by perl in a separate process. Likewise we run 'make' and 'make install' in processes. If you have any parameters (e.g. PREFIX, INSTALLPRIVLIB, UNINST or the like) you want to pass to the calls, please specify them here.

If you don't understand this question, just press ENTER.

> PREFIX=/users/staff/damian

Doing it yourself

Compared with using the CPAN.pm module, downloading and installing modules by hand is complex and tedious. But, if you don't have access to CPAN.pm, or a friendly sysadmin to install it for you, you're going to have to do things by hand.

The general procedure for doing this is always the same:

- Download the file from the CPAN using your favorite browser or ftp program
- Decompress the file and unpack it into a directory
- Build the file
- Test the module
- Install it in your local module library

The problem is that the details of every one of these of these steps vary considerably depending on which operating system you're using. Fortunately, recent releases of Perl come with Jon Orwant's invaluable perlmodinstall documentation (also available from http://www.perl.com/CPAN/doc/manual/html/pod/perlmodinstall.html).

This document takes you, step-by-step, through the module installation procedure under Unix, MacOS, Windows 95, Windows NT, DOS, OS/2, VMS, or MVS. Even if you decide to use CPAN.pm, it's worth reading through the perlmodinstall document, to better understand what the module is doing for (or occasionally, to) you.

2.4 WHERE TO FIND OUT MORE

A single chapter such as this can only hope to touch briefly on a relevant subset of the Perl. Fortunately, there are a multitude of excellent sources of information about Perl, many of them freely available. The following are some of the most useful.

---

[33] ...to which you usually won't have write access.

2.4.1 Essential books

There is now a wide range of books related to Perl, but the three most generally useful are undoubtedly *Learning Perl*, *Programming Perl*, and the *Perl Cookbook* (see the bibliography for full details on each).

Learning Perl, 2nd Edition, by Randal Schwartz and Tom Christiansen, is an excellent introduction to Perl for those with a programming background. It covers the basic features of the language, but not advanced concepts such as references, closures, or typeglobs.

If you're a nonprogrammer (or the "none-too-recently" programmer), you may find Andrew Johnson's new book, *The Elements of Programming with Perl*, a kinder, gentler introduction, both to programming and to Perl.

Programming Perl, 2nd Edition, by Larry Wall, Tom Christiansen, and Randal Schwartz, is the "Perl bible." Co-authored by the inventor of the language, it's a reference book covering almost all of Perl's features and many of its idioms. It's comprehensive, technically accurate, authoritative, and entertaining, but it's aimed at people who are already moderately experienced programmers.

Perl Cookbook, by Tom Christiansen and Nathan Torkington, is a large collection of practical, but mercifully bite-sized, examples of Perl programming. It covers almost all the common programming tasks for which the language is used and demonstrates how to solve problems in native Perl as opposed to transliterating a solution from some other language. This is not the book from which to learn Perl-the-language; rather it's the book from which to learn Perl-the-mindset.

2.4.2 Useful books

The other books recommended here are more specifically targeted at certain areas of Perl much as this book is focused on its object-oriented features.

Advanced Perl Programming, by Sriram Srinivasan, is a thorough exploration of the deeper, darker recesses of the Perl language. It covers many important aspects of Perl that are relevant to advanced object-oriented programming, including references and nested data structures, typeglobs and symbol tables, closures, modules and packages, ties, and persistence. It even has a couple of chapters on object orientation itself (though, naturally, not as many or as varied as this book).

Effective Perl Programming, by Joseph Hall and Randal Schwartz, is a collection of sixty practical tips and techniques that will improve your understanding and command of idiomatic Perl. It includes useful advice on object-oriented programming, references, packages, and modules, as well as an invaluable coverage of Perl's built-in debugger.

Mastering Regular Expressions, by Jeffrey Friedl, covers exactly that: the nitty-gritty of using regular expressions in Perl (and elsewhere). Though regular expressions are not directly related to object orientation,[34] it's difficult to write useful Perl without a good understanding of the power and the limitations of Perl's pattern matching features.

MacPerl: Power and Ease, by Vicki Brown and Chris Nandor, and *Learning Perl on Win32 Systems*, by Randal Schwartz, Erik Olson, and Tom Christiansen, provide excellent introduc-

---

[34] ...except in chapter 5 of this book where they actually *become* objects...

tions to Perl on non-Unix platforms. Although Perl is largely platform independent,[35] most books and other resources default to the Unix-centric view. These books redress that bias for the benefit of those of us who worship at many altars. Further down that same track is *Cross-Platform Perl*, by Eric F. Johnson, which bravely sets out to introduce Perl from a multiplatform perspective (Unix and Windows) and succeeds admirably.

2.4.3 The Perl documentation

Perl is a remarkable language in many respects, but perhaps its most underappreciated facet is the extraordinary amount of high-quality free documentation that comes with it.

If Perl has been properly installed on your system, you should be able to access the standard documentation via man or perldoc under Unix, perldoc or your favorite HTML browser under Windows, or the shuck application on a Mac. Even if they're not available locally, you can always find them on the CPAN.

The sections of the documentation most important to understand before embarking on object-oriented Perl are shown in table 2.2. Each of them is well worth studying, even after you've read this book.

Table 2.2   Important Perl documentation

Document	Description
perldata:	summarizes the basic data types in Perl.
perlsub:	describes the various features of Perl subroutines.
perlmod and **perlmodlib:**	explain Perl's module system, as well as the use of packages, symbol tables, and typeglobs.
perlmodinstall:	explains how to download and install modules from the CPAN.
perlref and **perlreftut:**	cover references and symbolic references and the various ways of creating them (i.e., the backslash operator, the anonymous array and anonymous hash constructors, sub, etc.)
perldsc and **perllol:**	discuss the creation and use of hierarchical data structures in Perl: arrays of arrays, hashes of hashes, arrays of hashes of arrays, etc.
perltoot:	provides a brief but gentle tutorial introduction to object-oriented programming in Perl.
perlobj:	is the reference manual for Perl's object-oriented features
perlbot:	offers a "cookbook" of several programming techniques specific to Perl's unique version of object orientation.

2.4.4 The Perl Journal

The Perl Journal is a quarterly publication, edited by Jon Orwant, devoted entirely to Perl programming. Every issue is full of well-written, entertaining, and enlightening articles reflecting the enormous range of programming techniques and applications areas that Perl encompasses.

The journal also features regular columns in which leading Perl experts explain the fundamentals of the Perl language. Particularly relevant articles in recent back issues include:

---

[35] ...and far more so than purportedly platform-independent languages like Java ...

"Coping with Scoping" by Mark-Jason Dominus (Issue #12), "Threads" by Dan Sugalski (Issue #10), "Understand References Today" by Mark-Jason Dominus (Issue #10), "The Auto-Loader" by Randy Ray (Issue #6), "Understanding Regular Expressions" by Jeffrey Friedl (Issues #2, #3, #4), and "Data Hiding" by Jon Orwant (Issue #3).

You can find out more about *The Perl Journal* at its website: http://www.tpj.com/.

2.4.5 Websites

The main website for Perl is the PERL.COM site (http://www.perl.com/). This site provides links to just about anything online even tenuously related to Perl: from book reviews to the latest Perl news, tutorials to mailing lists, where to find commercial support to a litany of Perl success stories that may help you convince your local Powers-That-Be to let you use Perl in your next project.

This book also has its own page on the http://www.manning.com/ website. There you will find the complete source code to every example in the text, as well as an interactive discussion forum on object-oriented Perl, a query line, and any updates or errata.

2.4.6 Newsgroups

There are four useful Perl-related newsgroups:

- comp.lang.perl.misc: A general-purpose unmoderated newsgroup in which to ask novice questions (after carefully reading the Perl documentation and FAQs, of course).
- comp.lang.perl.moderated: Another general-purpose group, but moderated and hence less prone to irrelevance, inanity, or incendiaries. Whether that's a good thing is, of course, purely a matter of personal taste. One important advantage of this group is that the moderators tend to ensure that information posted to it is correct.
- comp.lang.perl.modules: An unmoderated newsgroup devoted to the discussion of the hundreds of publicly available modules for Perl. When you've written your own Perl module this is where you can announce it and have it discussed. If you're using a particular module (from the CPAN or elsewhere) this is where you can ask curly questions about it.
- comp.lang.perl.announce: A very low traffic, tightly moderated newsgroup dedicated to announcements of new modules, new source code releases, and the occasional message regarding Perl-related events in the Real World.

The Perl groups provide an extraordinary amount of useful information and feedback, and an exceptional opportunity to interact with the designers and implementers of the Perl language. They are frequented by a large cross-section of the worldwide Perl community from raw novices to supreme gurus.

It's particularly important, therefore, to be aware of the culture and customs of the various groups before attempting to post. If nothing else, be sure to read the relevant introductory messages (e.g., "Welcome - read this first" in comp.lang.perl.moderated). Better still, lurk around the various groups a little before you post. Read the messages and get a feel for what's appropriate.

2.5 SUMMARY

- Scalars store single values (numbers, strings, or references). Arrays store lists of values. Hashes store a set of key/value pairs.
- Subroutines are declared with a `sub` statement. They take any number of arguments, passed as aliases in the `@_` array. Subroutines act like closures, preserving the local context (i.e., lexical variables) at the point of their declaration.
- A reference represents the location of another variable or value, which is known as the referent. A symbolic reference represents the name of a package variable. The `ref` function can be used to determine the type of referent to which a nonsymbolic reference refers.
- Anonymous arrays are created using the `[...]` notation. Anonymous hashes are created using the `{...}` notation. Anonymous subroutines are created using the `sub` keyword without a subroutine name. All three return a reference to the newly created anonymous referent.
- The arrow notation may be used to access elements of arrays (`$arr_ref->[$index]`) or entries of hashes (`$hsh_ref->{$key}`) via a suitable reference. They may also be used to call subroutines (`$sub_ref->(@args)`).
- Packages provide separate nonhierarchical namespaces. Package variables are universally accessible, and live in a package's symbol table. Package variables may be made `local`, which temporarily replaces their value in nested scopes until execution reaches the end of the current scope.
- Lexical variables are declared with a `my` qualifier. Direct access to lexical variables is restricted to the lexical scope of block in which they're declared.
- A typeglob is a symbol table entry. It contains a slot for one instance of each Perl datatype. When a typeglob is assigned to another, every slot is reassigned. When a reference is assigned to a typeglob, only the appropriate slot is reassigned.

C H A P T E R   3

Getting Started

If you've ever used another object-oriented programming language, or been traumatized by some prior exposure to object orientation, you're probably dreading tackling object orientation in Perl—more syntax, more semantics, more rules, more complexity. On the other hand, if you're entirely new to object orientation, you're likely to be equally nervous about all those unfamiliar concepts, and how you're going to keep them all straight in your head while you learn the specific Perl syntax and semantics.

Relax!

Object-oriented Perl isn't like that at all. To do real, useful, production-strength, object-oriented programming in Perl you only need to learn about one extra function, one straight-forward piece of additional syntax, and three very simple rules.[1]

3.1 THREE LITTLE RULES

Let's start with the rules...

---

[1]   The three rules were originally formulated by Larry Wall, and appear in a slightly different form in the perlobj documentation.

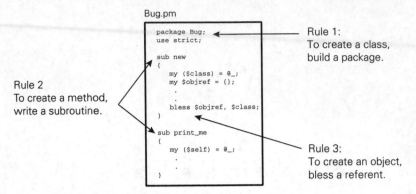

Figure 3.1   Three little rules

3.1.1   Rule 1: To create a class, build a package

Perl packages already have a number of classlike features:

- They collect related code together;
- They distinguish that code from unrelated code;
- They provide a separate namespace within the program, which keeps subroutine names from clashing with those in other packages;
- They have a name, which can be used to identify data and subroutines defined in the package.

In Perl, those features are sufficient to allow a package to act like a class.

Suppose we wanted to build an application to track faults in a system. Here's how to declare a class named Bug in Perl:

```
package Bug;
```

That's it! Of course, such a class isn't very interesting or useful, since it has no attributes or behavior. And that brings us to the second rule...

3.1.2   Rule 2: To create a method, write a subroutine

Methods are just subroutines, associated with a particular class, that exist specifically to operate on objects that are instances of that class.

Happily, in Perl, a subroutine that is declared in a particular package *is* associated with that package. So to write a Perl method, we just write a subroutine within the package acting as our class.

For example, here's how we provide an object method to print our Bug objects:

```
package Bug;

sub print_me
{
    # The code needed to print the Bug goes here
}
```

Again, that's it. The subroutine `print_me` is now associated with the package Bug, so whenever we treat Bug as a class, Perl automatically treats `Bug::print_me` as a method.

Calling the `Bug::print_me` method involves that one extra piece of syntax—an extension to the existing Perl "arrow" notation. If you have a reference to an object of class Bug (we'll see how to get such a reference in a moment), you can access any method of that object by using a -> symbol, followed by the name of the method.

For example, if the variable `$nextbug` holds a reference to a Bug object, you could call `Bug::print_me` on that object by writing:

```perl
package main;

# set $nextbug to refer to a Bug object, somehow, and then…

$nextbug->print_me();
```

Calling a method through an arrow should be familiar to any C++ programmers; for the rest of us, it's at least consistent with other Perl usages:

```perl
$hsh_ref->{"key"};        # Access the hash referred to by $hashref
$arr_ref->[$index];       # Access the array referred to by $arrayref
$sub_ref->(@args);        # Access the sub referred to by $subref
$obj_ref->method(@args);  # Access the object referred to by $objref
```

The only difference with the last case is that the thing referred to by `$objref` has many ways of being accessed, namely, its various methods. So, when we want to access an object, we have to specify which particular way, or method, should be used.

Just to be a little more flexible, Perl doesn't actually require that we hard-code the method name in the call. It is also possible to specify the method name as a scalar variable containing a string matching the name (i.e., a symbolic reference) or as a scalar variable containing a real reference to the subroutine in question. For example, instead of:

```perl
$nextbug->print_me();
```

we could write:

```perl
$method_name = "print_me";    # i.e. "symbolic reference" to some &print_me
$nextbug->$method_name();     # Method call via symbolic reference
```

or:

```perl
$method_ref = \&Bug::print_me;  # i.e. reference to &Bug::print_me
$nextbug->$method_ref();        # Method call via hard reference
```

In practice, the method name is almost always hard-coded.

When a method like `Bug::print_me` is called, the argument list that it receives begins with the object reference through which it was called,[2] followed by any arguments that were explicitly given to the method. That means that calling `Bug::print_me("logfile")` is *not* the same as calling `$nextbug->print_me("logfile")`. In the first case, `print_me` is treated as a regular subroutine so the argument list passed to `Bug::print_me` is equivalent to:

---

[2] The object on which the method is called is known as the *invoking object* or, sometimes, the *message target*. It is the reference to this object that is passed as the first argument of any method invoked using the -> notation.

```
( "logfile" )
```

In the second case, `print_me` is treated as a method so the argument list is equivalent to:

```
( $objref, "logfile" )
```

Having a reference to the object passed as the first parameter is vital, because it means that the method then has access to the object on which it's supposed to operate[3]. Hence you'll find that most methods in Perl start with something equivalent to this:

```
package Bug;

sub print_me
{
  my ($self) = shift;
  # The @_ array now stores the explicit argument list passed to &Bug::print_me
  # The rest of the &print_me method uses the data referred to by $self and
  # the explicit arguments (still in @_)
}
```

or, better still:

```
package Bug;

sub print_me
{
  my ($self, @args) = @_;
  # The @args array now stores the explicit argument list passed to &Bug::print_me
  # The rest of the &print_me method uses the data referred to by $self and
  # the explicit arguments (now in @args)
}
```

This second version is better because it provides a lexically scoped copy of the argument list (`@args`). Remember that the `@_` array is magical in that changing any element of it actually changes the caller's version of the corresponding argument. Copying argument values to a lexical array like `@args` prevents nasty surprises of this kind and improves the internal documentation of the subroutine (especially if a more meaningful name than `@args` is chosen).

The only remaining question is: *how do we create the invoking object in the first place?*

3.1.3 Rule 3: To create an object, bless a referent

Unlike other object-oriented languages, Perl doesn't require that an object be a special kind of recordlike data structure. In fact, you can use *any* existing type of Perl variable—a scalar, an array, a hash—as an object in Perl.[4]

Hence, the issue isn't so much how to *create* the object—you create an object exactly as you would any other Perl variable— but rather how to tell Perl that such an object *belongs* to

---

[3] There are similar automatic features in all object-oriented languages. C ++ member functions have a pointer called `this`; Java member functions have a reference called `this`; Smalltalk methods have the `self` pseudo-object; and Python's methods, like Perl's, receive the invoking object as their first argument.

[4] You can also bless other things, such as subroutines, regular expressions, and typeglobs, but we'll leave that for chapter 5.

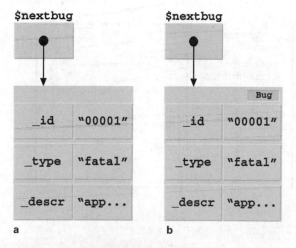

Figure 3.2 What changes when an object is blessed
a Before `bless($nextbug, "Bug")`
b After `bless($nextbug, "Bug")`

a particular class. That brings us to one extra built-in Perl function you need to know. It's called `bless`, and its only job is to mark a variable as belonging to a particular class.

The `bless` function takes two arguments: a reference to the variable to be marked and a string containing the name of the class. It then sets an internal flag on the variable, indicating that it now belongs to the class.[5]

For example, suppose that `$nextbug` actually stores a reference to an anonymous hash:

```
$nextbug = {
                _id        => "00001",
                _type      => "fatal",
                _descr     => "application does not compile",
           };
```

To turn that anonymous hash into an object of class Bug we write:

```
bless $nextbug, "Bug";
```

And, once again, that's it! The anonymous hash referred to by `$nextbug` is now marked as being an object of class Bug. The variable `$nextbug` itself hasn't been altered in any way. We didn't bless the *reference*; we blessed the *referent*. The scalar didn't change—only the name-less hash it refers to has been marked. Figure 3.2 illustrates where the new class membership flag is set.

You can check that the blessing succeeded by applying the built-in `ref` function to `$nextbug`. Normally, when `ref` is applied to a reference, it returns the type of that reference.

---

[5] Actually, the second argument is optional, and defaults to the name of the current package. However, as we'll see in chapter 6, although omitting the second argument may occasionally be convenient, it's never a good idea. It's better to think of both arguments as being morally required, even if legally they're not.

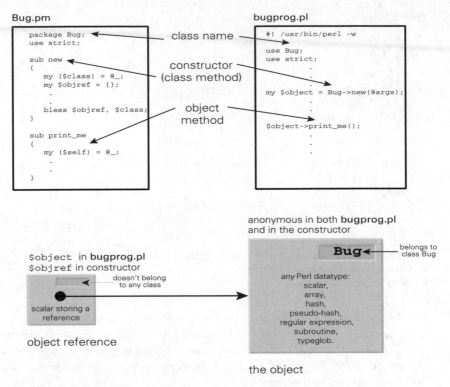

Figure 3.3 Object basics

Hence, before `$nextbug` was blessed, `ref($nextbug)` would have returned the string `'HASH'`.

Once an object is blessed, `ref` returns the name of its class instead. So, after the blessing, `ref($nextbug)` will return `'Bug'`. Of course the object itself still *is* a hash, but now it's a hash that *belongs* to the Bug class.

The entries of the hash become the attributes of the newly created Bug object. Note that in the above example each key begins with an underscore. This is the Perl convention for indicating that something is internal to a package, or, in this case, to a class. Here it's used to suggest that attributes and methods that are to be treated as not for public use.[6]

Given that we're likely to want to create many such Bug objects, it would be more useful if we had a subroutine that took the necessary information, wrapped it in an anonymous hash, blessed the hash, and gave us back a reference to the resulting object. And, of course, we might as well put such a subroutine in the Bug package itself and call it something that indicates its role. Such a subroutine is called a *constructor* and generally looks like this:

---

[6] Mind you, it's only a suggestion. Unlike other object-oriented languages, Perl doesn't enforce the encapsulation of attributes. More on that point shortly.

```
package Bug;

sub new
{
    my $class = $_[0];
    my $objref = {
                    _id      => $_[1],
                    _type    => $_[2],
                    _descr   => $_[3],
                 };
    bless $objref, $class;
    return $objref;
}
```

When we call `Bug::new`, we pass the name of the class into which the new object should be blessed (`"Bug"`), followed by the ID, type, and description of the bug. Of course, we can always hard-code the class name into the call to `bless`, but that loses us some important flexibility that we'll need later when we start inheriting from classes in chapter 6.

The `bless` function makes writing constructors like this a little easier by returning the reference passed as its first argument—that is, the reference to whatever it just blessed into objecthood. Since Perl subroutines automatically return the value of their last evaluated statement, that means we can condense the definition of `Bug::new` to:

```
sub Bug::new
{
    bless { _id => $_[1], _type => $_[2], _descr => $_[3] }, $_[0];
}
```

This version has exactly the same effects: slot the data into an anonymous hash, bless the hash into the class specified first argument, and return a reference to the hash.

Regardless of which version we use, whenever we want to create a Bug object, we can just call:

```
$nextbug = Bug::new("Bug", $id, $type, $description);
```

That's a little redundant, since we have to type "Bug" twice. Fortunately, there's another feature of the arrow method-call syntax that solves this problem. If the operand to the left of the arrow is the name of a class—rather than an object reference—the appropriate class method of that class is called. More importantly, if the arrow notation is used, the first argument passed to the method is automatically a string containing the class name. That means that we can rewrite the previous call to `Bug::new` like this:

```
package main;

$nextbug = Bug->new($id, $type, $description);
```

There are other benefits to this notation when your class uses inheritance (chapter 6), so you should always call constructors and other class methods this way.

Apart from encapsulating the messy details of object creation within the class itself, using a class method like this to create objects has another big advantage. If we abide by the convention of only creating new Bug objects by calling `Bug::new`, we're guaranteed that all such objects will always be hashes. Of course, there's nothing to prevent us from manually blessing arrays, scalars, file handles, and so forth, as Bug objects, but life is *much* easier if we stick to blessing one type of object into each class.

For example, if we can be confident that any Bug object is going to be a blessed hash, we can finally fill in the missing code in the `Bug::print_me` method:

```
package Bug;

sub print_me
{
  my ($self) = @_;
  print "ID: $self->{_id}\n";
  print "$self->{_descr}\n";
  print "(Note: problem is fatal)\n"
     if $self->{_type} eq "fatal";
}
```

3.2 A SIMPLE PERL CLASS

Now, let's take the three rules explained above, plus `bless`, plus the arrow notation, and use them to build a simple, but usable, Perl class. We'll create a class that can be used to store information regarding a particular music CD (its name, the artist, publisher, ISBN, number of tracks, where it's stored in your extensive collection, etc.)

3.2.1 The code

The basic class is defined in listing 3.1. Take a few moments and puzzle through the code, keeping in mind the three rules given above.

Okay, now let's examine the entire class definition to see what's going on and, more importantly, why the class is strucured as it is.

Declaring the class

The first line is a straightforward application of the first rule. We want a new class to store information on music CDs, so we create a package called CD::Music. We could have called it something else, such as Music::CD, but the choice depends on what other related classes we expect to develop later. We might, for example, expect to create other classes for other types of CDs (CD::ROM, CD::WORM, CD::DVD, CD::Shiny::Beer::Mat). The common feature here is the "CD-ishness" of each type of object, and so we make that the more general term in the package name.

In contrast, if we had intended to develop classes for representing other types of music, we might have made Music:: the top level of the package name and had Music::CD, Music::LP, Music::Internet, Music::Of::The::Spheres, and so on.

Providing a constructor

Having successfully named the class, we ask Perl to be strict with us, which is *always* a good idea, no matter what kind of Perl programming we're doing. (See section 3.3.)

Listing 3.1 The CD::Music Class

```perl
package CD::Music;
use strict;

sub new
{
  my ($class) = @_;
  bless {
            _name      => $_[1],
            _artist    => $_[2],
            _publisher => $_[3],
            _ISBN      => $_[4],
            _tracks    => $_[5],
            _room      => $_[6],
            _shelf     => $_[7],
            _rating    => $_[8],
        }, $class;
}

sub name      { $_[0]->{_name}      }
sub artist    { $_[0]->{_artist}    }
sub publisher { $_[0]->{_publisher} }
sub ISBN      { $_[0]->{_ISBN}      }
sub tracks    { $_[0]->{_tracks}    }

sub location
{
  my ($self, $shelf, $room) = @_;
  $self->{_room} = $room   if $room;
  $self->{_shelf}= $shelf  if $shelf;
  return ($self->{_room}, $self->{_shelf});
}

sub rating
{
  my ($self, $rating) = @_;
  $self->{_rating} = $rating if defined $rating;
  return $self->{_rating};
}
```

We next provide a method for creating CD::Music objects. Note that the overall structure is very similar to the previous Bug::new example. We create an anonymous hash, fill in the relevant items, bless the hash, and return a reference to it.

The choice of a hash as the basis of both the Bug class and this one is no coincidence. Hashes are the usual basis for objects in Perl. That's because, unlike a scalar, a hash allows us to store multiple values of various types in the same object. And, unlike an array, a hash allows us to give each of those values a meaningful tag (i.e., its key).

Occasionally, for performance or other special reasons, it may be better to implement objects as something other than hashes. More importantly, Perl 5.005 introduced a new general purpose data type—the pseudo-hash—which is specially designed for implementing objects.

In the next two chapters, we'll look in detail at the pseudo-hash, as well as cases where other data types make more suitable bases for a class. For now, though, we'll stick with hashes.

Accessing an object's read-only data

The CD::Music class declares five methods: `CD::Music::name`, `CD::Music::artist`, `CD::Music::publisher`, `CD::Music::ISBN`, and `CD::Music::tracks`. Each method simply takes the blessed hash reference, looks up the corresponding attribute in the invoking object—that is, the appropriate entry in the hash—and returns its value. Such methods are called *accessors* because their whole purpose is to provide access to attributes

These methods provide a means of *reading* the different entries of the hash, but not of *overwriting* them. That restriction makes sense in this example, because the title, artist, publisher, ISBN, and number of tracks on a standard audio CD never change.

You might wonder why we would bother to declare these methods, expecting users of the class to write `$cdref->name()` when they already have a reference to the hash itself—`$cdref`—and can just use the normal Perl arrow syntax for accessing a particular entry: `$cdref->{_name}`.

The reason we don't want to encourage direct access is that those hash entries are collectively implementing the internal data of each object in the class, and one of the cardinal rules of object orientation is this: *Thou shalt not access thy encapsulated data directly, lest thou screwe it up*. You should look back at section 1.2.1 in chapter 1 if you're not sure why this is an important rule to honor.

Of course, unlike most other object-oriented languages, which *enforce* this kind of encapsulation, Perl will quite happily allow you to directly access the hash elements if you choose. But then you're not playing by the rules, and, when Bad Things happen, you'll only have yourself to blame.

If this philosophy of encapsulation by good manners strikes you as unnervingly insecure, take heart. Later in the chapter, and more extensively in chapter 11, we'll explore techniques for ensuring that your encapsulated data is truly unmolestable.

Accessing read-write data

The remaining two methods—`CD::Music::location` and `CD::Music::rating`—are slightly more complex. They still return the value of the appropriate hash entries, but, before that, they check their parameter lists to see if any new values have been specified for those elements.

For example, if `CD::Music::location` is called like so

```
$cdref->location(12)
```

then it:

- Sets the internal data `$cdref->{_shelf}` to 12, then
- Leaves the data in `$cdref->{_room}` unchanged (since no new value was provided), and finally
- Returns a list of the resulting room and shelf numbers.

Such methods are called *mutators* because they can change the internal state of an object.

The two methods can still be called without any argument (just like the other five accessor methods), in which case they just return the current value(s) of the relevant object data.

Catching attempts to change read-only attributes

Of course, because users of the CD::Music class can change the location or ratings information by passing new values to those two methods, they may well expect to do the same with CD::Music::title, CD::Music::artist, and so forth. This incorrect generalization could lead to subtle logical errors in the program, since those read-only methods will simply ignore any extra parameters they are given.

There are several ways to address this potential source of errors. The most obvious solution is to resort to brute force, and simply kill any program that attempts to call a read-only method with arguments. For example:

```
package CD::Music;
use strict;
use Carp;

sub read_only
{
    croak "Can't change value of read-only attribute " . (caller 1)[3]
        if @_ > 1;
}

sub name      { &read_only; $_[0]->{_name}      }
sub artist    { &read_only; $_[0]->{_artist}    }
sub publisher { &read_only; $_[0]->{_publisher} }
sub ISBN      { &read_only; $_[0]->{_ISBN}      }
sub tracks    { &read_only; $_[0]->{_tracks}    }
```

Here, each read-only access method calls the subroutine CD::Music::read_only, passing its original argument list (by using the old-style call syntax—a leading & and no parentheses). The read_only subroutine checks for extra arguments and throws an informative exception if it finds any. Of course, there will always be at least one argument to any method, namely the object reference through which the method was originally called.

Think of this technique as a form of Pavlovian conditioning for programmers: every time their code actually attempts to assign to a read-only attribute of your class, their program dies. Bad programmer!

As enjoyable as it may be to mess with people's minds in this way, this approach does have a drawback; it imposes an extra cost on each attempt to access a read-only attribute. Moreover, it isn't proactive in preventing users from making this type of mistake; it only trains them not to repeat it after the fact.

Besides, psychology has a much more subtle tool to offer us, in the form of a technique known as *affordances*.[7] Affordances are features of a user interface that make it physically or psy-

---

[7] The concept of affordances comes from the work of user-interface guru Donald Norman . His landmark book *The Psychology of Everyday Things* (later renamed *The Design of Everyday Things*) is essential reading for anyone who creates interfaces of any kind, including interfaces to classes. See the bibliography for details.

chologically easy to do the right thing. For example, good designers don't put handles on un-latched doors that can only be pushed. Instead, they put a flat plate where the handle would otherwise be. Just about the only thing you can do with a plate is to push on it, so the physical structure of the plate helps you to operate the door correctly. In contrast, if you approach a door with a fixed handle, your natural tendency is to pull, which usually proves to be the right course of action.

Affordances work well in programming too. In this case, we want to make any attempt to change read-only object data psychologically awkward. The best way to do that is to avoid raising the expectation that overwriting this data is even possible.

For instance, we could change the names of the read-only methods to "get_…" and separate the two functions of each read-write accessor into distinct "get…" and "set…" methods:

```
package CD::Music;
use strict;

sub new
{
    # as before
}
sub get_name        { $_[0]->{_name}}
sub get_artist      { $_[0]->{_artist}}
sub get_publisher   { $_[0]->{_publisher}}
sub get_ISBN        { $_[0]->{_ISBN}}
sub get_tracks      { $_[0]->{_tracks}}
sub get_rating      { $_[0]->{_rating}}
sub get_location    { ($_[0]->{_room}, $_[0]->{_shelf}) }
sub set_location
{
    my ($self, $shelf, $room) = @_;
    $self->{_room}      = $room  if $room;
    $self->{_shelf}     = $shelf if $shelf;
}
sub set_rating
{
    my ($self, $rating) = @_;
    $self->{_rating} = $rating if $rating;
}
```

Now, the user of our class has no incentive to pass arguments to the read-only methods, because it doesn't make sense to do so. And, because no set_name, set_artist, and so on exist, it's obvious that these attributes can't be changed.

Method prototypes

You might be tempted to think that we could have avoided all this psychological manipulation by giving each method a prototype and letting the Perl compiler catch cases where the wrong number of arguments are passed to a method:

```
package CD::Music;

sub name();
sub rating(;$);
sub location(;$$);
# ...etc.
```

Unfortunately, this idea doesn't actually work, because Perl doesn't check prototypes when a package subroutine is called as a method, using the `$objref->method(@args)` syntax).

There are good reasons why Perl ignores the prototypes of a method but, as they have to do with inheritance and polymorphism, we'll defer discussion of them until chapter 6.[8] For the moment, it's sufficient to remember not to rely on prototypes to safeguard your methods. Because they won't.

Accessing class data

So far, apart from constructors, we've only looked at the attributes and methods belonging to individual objects of a class. We may also need to implement attributes and methods shared by the class as a whole. These class attributes and class methods are typically provided to access and manipulate information that is not tied to a particular object.

For example, when using the CD::Music class, we might wish at some point to ascertain the total number of CD::Music objects created.[9] So far, that information is a collective property of the class, and so it won't be stored in any particular object.

Instead, we could modify the class as follows:

```
package CD::Music;
use strict;

{
    my $_count = 0;
    sub get_count     { $_count }
    sub _incr_count   { ++$_count }
}
sub new
{
    my ($class,@arg) = @_;
    $class->_incr_count();
    bless       {
                        _name=> $arg[0],
                        _artist=> $arg[1],
                        _publisher=> $arg[2],
                        _ISBN=> $arg[3],
```

---

[8] Oh, all right. The compiler can't check the prototypes because all Perl methods are polymorphic so, in general, it's not possible to know until run time which subroutine will actually be invoked in response to a particular method call.

[9] That's not the necessarily the same thing as the number of CD::Music objects *currently* in existence, since some objects may have ceased to exist in the interim. We'll explore that point further in the later section on *Destructors*.

```
                              _tracks=> $arg[4],
                              _room=> $arg[5],
                              _shelf=> $arg[6],
                              _rating=> $arg[7],
                      }, $class;
        }
```

The extra block just after use strict provides a nested lexical scope within the class. Within that scope, we declare a lexical variable (my $_count) and initialize it to zero. The my means that it is only visible within the scope of the current block (i.e., the nested scope). In object-oriented terms, it's encapsulated within the block and, therefore, within the CD::Music class.

Two methods—CD::Music::get_count and CD::Music::_incr_count—are also defined in the same block. They have access to this variable, though no other methods or subroutines defined anywhere else, including the other methods of CD::Music, are able to access the variable directly. Access to the methods themselves is not confined to the nested scope. Like all named Perl subroutines, they are not restricted to the scope in which they are defined but are globally accessible.

Normally, when we reach the end of a block, any lexical variables declared within it cease to exist. However, in this case, $_count avoids that end-of-scope annihilation because there are still two valid references to it outside the block, namely those within the bodies of CD::Music::get_count and CD::Music::_incr_count. See the section on *Closures* in chapter 2 if it's not clear why $_count goes out of scope, but not out of existence.

In any case, the result is that the CD::Music class now has two extra methods, and those methods provide the only general access to the variable $_count. The methods themselves are straightforward: CD::Music::get_count can be used to access the current value of the hidden $_count variable, while CD::Music::_incr_count can be used to increment the same variable. Note that _incr_count's name starts with an underscore, which is the standard Perl convention for indicating that it's intended to be used only within the current package. Although, as usual, Perl in no way enforces that restriction. We'll come back to that point shortly.

The only other change required is to add a single command to the constructor to increment the global count every time a new CD::Music object is created. Now, whenever we need to know how many CD::Music objects have been created, we can call the class method to find out:

```
package main;

# Create and use some CD::Music objects, and then…

print "There have been ", CD::Music->get_count(), " CDs created\n";
```

The more bitterly experienced reader will already be protesting that there is no guarantee that the number returned by CD::Music::get_count bears *any* relationship to the actual number of CD::Music objects created, since the CD::Music::_incr_count method allows us to manipulate the count to our own nefarious ends:

```
package main;

# Create 100 CD::Music objects, and then…
for $i (1..100)
{
   push @cds, CD::Music->new($data[$i]);
}

# double our productivity!
for (1..100)
{
   CD::Music->_incr_count();
}
```

```
print "There have been ", CD::Music->get_count, " CDs created\n";
```

There are two answers to that. The simplest response is that calling a subroutine with a leading underscore that clearly marks it for internal use only just isn't playing by the rules. Programmers who do so thoroughly deserve the grief that inevitably results.

A more pragmatic answer is that it's not difficult to extend the nested scope and use a lexical subroutine reference to remove the dangerous subroutine from public accessibility:

```
package CD::Music;
{
    my $_count = 0;
    sub get_count { $_count }
    my $_incr_count  = sub { ++$_count };

    sub new
    {
        $_incr_count->();
        # etc. as before
    }

    # Other methods that need to adjust the
    # count value, via $_incr_count, go here
}

# Methods that don't need to adjust
# the count value go here
```

In this version, the counter increment subroutine is anonymous and only accessible via a reference stored in the lexical variable $_incr_count. That variable is, in turn, only accessible within the block that starts just after the package declaration, so CD::Music::new has access to the counter adjustment subroutine, but no code outside the block does. Problem solved.

Other readers might feel that this level of security is un-Perl-like, and possibly bordering on the paranoid, especially when we could get the same effect without all that barbed wire:

```
package CD::Music;
{
    my $_count = 0;
    sub get_count { $_count }

    sub new
    {
        ++$_count;
        # etc. as before
    }

    # Other methods that need to directly
    # access $_count value go here
}

# Methods that don't need to directly
# access $_count go here
```

This simpler solution may be satisfactory in a small application, but, even there, the decision to directly access class attributes is likely to come back and bite you as your code develops. In general, you are far more likely to future-proof your code if you consistently wrap *all* attribute accesses in subroutines. In chapter 6, for example, we will see how things can go horribly wrong with directly accessible class attributes when classes are inherited.

3.2.2 Using the CD::Music class

Once the class is written, we could go about using it like this:

```
package main;
# Create an object storing a CD's details
my $cd = CD::Music->new(   "Canon in D", "Pachelbel",
                           "Boering Mußak GmbH", "1729-67836847-1",
                           1,
                           8,8,
                           5.0);
# What's the CD called?
print $cd->name, "\n";
# Where would we find it?
printf "Room %s, shelf %s\n", $cd->location;
# Move it to room 5, shelf 3
$cd->location(5,3);
# How many CDs in the entire collection?
print CD::Music->get_count, "\n";
```

Just as with ordinary Perl subroutines, if a call to a method doesn't require arguments, we can omit the trailing empty parentheses after the method name. That is, we can write `$cd->name` and `CD::Music->get_count`, rather than `$cd->name()` and `CD::Music->get_count()`. However, unlike regular Perl subroutines, if a method *does* take arguments, you have to put them in parentheses. For example, you can't treat a method as an operator and write something like: `$cd->location 5, 3;`

It's also worth noting that method calls that return lists—for example, `$cd->loca-tion`—start with a `$`, not a `@`. This may seem inconsistent at first, but it really isn't. Only arrays and slices must be prefixed with a `@`. Actual lists, such as `(1,2,3)`, and subroutine calls that return lists, such as `caller()`, never have such a prefix.

3.3 MAKING LIFE EASIER

We can make the process of creating and using classes much easier in several ways. Putting them into separate modules is a good start, since it provides an extra level of encapsulation and a great deal more reusability than cutting-and-pasting. Turning on all the debugging features is another obvious way to reduce the unexpected. Finally, there's a useful shortcut that alleviates the repetitive task of setting up accessor methods.

3.3.1 Class modules

Once we have a usable class, the obvious thing to do is to put it into a module, so that its functionality is available to any code that might require it. If you're already familiar with writing modules, then you'll be used to the following procedure, as it's described in chapter 2:

- Create an appropriately named .pm file in an appropriately named subdirectory;
- Put your code in it and make sure the last statement evaluates to true;
- Arrange to import the module's interface—typically one or more subroutines—into the package that's going to use it.

To set up a module containing object-oriented code, the first two steps are exactly the same: put the code implementing the class into a suitable file and add a `1;` after it. Normally, we'd then set up a list of subroutine names to be exported, either by using the Exporter module or writing our own `import` subroutine. The question is: *what subroutines should we export from an object-oriented module?*

And the answer is, *absolutely none!*

The entire point of building a class is to encapsulate attributes and methods within the namespace of that class to ensure that they're accessed in a controlled manner. Exporting a class's attributes would compromise that encapsulation, so there's no reason to export any variables from an object-oriented module.

Exporting the methods of a class usually doesn't make much sense either, since methods are always supposed to be called through an invoking object, or through the package itself. In either case, Perl will automatically look for the method in the namespace of the class package, not the namespace to which subroutines are exported.

For the moment, just remember that you don't need to export anything from an object-oriented module (but see chapter 14 for some interesting exceptions).

3.3.2 use strict and the -w flag

Using `use strict` and the `-w` flag in serious code should be second nature. Perl's range of diagnostics is exceptionally comprehensive, and the compiler is remarkably adept in identifying even the most arcane of semantic mistakes. Even when it guesses wrong, the error messages it generates will still tell you that something is amiss. By turning on those facilities, you will save yourself hours of time puzzling over the unexpected behavior of your code.

In object-oriented code, use strict will pick up nasty little traps such as this:[10]

```perl
package CD::Music;

# WARNING: BAD CODE AHEAD...

sub set_location
{
    my ($self, @loc) = @_;
    $self{_room} ||= $loc->[0];
    $self{_shelf}||= $loc->[1];
    return;
}
```

Occasionally the -w flag will nag about things that you know are okay in your particular code. Rather than switching off all warnings, you can temporarily switch off warnings by localizing the $^W variable:

```perl
# This code may generate a warning if "more" is unavailable,
# but it's okay to ignore it...
sub print_paged
{
    my ($self) = @_;
    local $^W;                               # Locally reset warning switch
    local *STDOUT;
    open STDOUT, "|more" or open STDOUT, ">-"; # Might generate warning
    $self->print_me;
}
# Warnings are active again from this point in the execution
```

Be careful, however, since the localized $^W variable propagates into any subroutine called from CD::Music::print_paged (for example, into CD::Music::print_me). This could mask other problems elsewhere in your code.

Some people are also reluctant to give up the syntactic liberties that use strict denies them. Indeed, the documentation on the use strict pragma suggests that, in its full glory, it is too stringent for casual programming. But, whatever casual programming may be, it is almost never object-oriented programming, so it's a wise move always to include a use strict at the top of any object-oriented code you create.

Remember, though, that a use strict pragma only affects code that *follows* it in the same scope, so put it near the top of your module. You should also be aware that, although use strict respects block scopes, it ignores package boundaries. So if you give one package a use strict, it may also apply to any packages that appear later in the file.

---

[10] If it's not immediately obvious what's wrong in the code, you *definitely* need to use strict! The problem is that $self{_room} is accessing an entry in the package variable %CD::Music::self, not the one in the hash referred to by my $self. Likewise $loc->[0] is attempting to access the first element of the array referred to by the scalar package variable $CD::Music::loc, not the first element of my @loc.

3.3.3 Automating data member access

Previously, we saw how to create accessor methods to provide access to an object's data in a controlled manner. For example, class CD::Music defined the following read-only data accessors:

```
package CD::Music;

sub get_name       { $_[0]->{_name}       }
sub get_artist     { $_[0]->{_artist}     }
sub get_publisher  { $_[0]->{_publisher}  }
sub get_ISBN       { $_[0]->{_isbn}       }
sub get_tracks     { $_[0]->{_tracks}     }
sub get_rating     { $_[0]->{_rating}     }
sub get_location   { ($_[0]->{_room}, $_[0]->{_shelf}) }
```

Even such simple accessors quickly become tedious to write, especially if there are many of them. Apart from the tedium, it's easy to be mesmerized into making a mistake, as we just did with the get_ISBN method above. (It should access $_[0]->{_ISBN}, not $_[0]->{_isbn}.) Mistakes such as this can be hard to track since the compiler gives no warning of them, even (alas!) under use strict and -w.

Sometimes a better solution is to provide a single catchall method that can be called in response to any attempt to call an accessor. Packages already provide the ability to define such a catchall by defining a subroutine called AUTOLOAD. Since a Perl class is just a package with delusions of grandeur, it should come as no surprise that we can use AUTOLOAD as a catchall for methods as well.

For example, we can replace the series of "get_…" methods with the following:

```
package CD::Music;
use strict;
use vars '$AUTOLOAD';                          # keep 'use strict' happy

sub AUTOLOAD
{
  my ($self) = @_;
  $AUTOLOAD =~ /.*::get(_\w+)/                  # extract attribute name
    or croak "No such method: $AUTOLOAD";
  exists $self->{$1}                            # locate attribute
    or croak "No such attribute: $1";
  return $self->{$1}                            # return attribute
}

sub get_location { ($_[0]->{_room}, $_[0]->{_shelf}) }

# But don't define the other get_… methods
```

Now, whenever Perl fails to find a method for an object of class CD::Music, the CD::Music::AUTOLOAD method is invoked instead. The AUTOLOAD method itself is simple. It's invoked just like the methods it replaces; that is, with a reference to an object passed as its first argument. The name of the method actually requested is provided in the $AUTOLOAD package variable.

Therefore, if the original method call was: `$cdref->get_artist()`, then the catchall method `CD::Music::AUTOLOAD` is called with one argument—the object reference stored in `$cdref`—and the package variable `$CD::Music::AUTOLOAD` contains the string `"CD::Music::get_artist"`.

The CD::Music class's `AUTOLOAD` first uses a regular expression to locate and extract (as `$1`) the name of the actual object attribute being requested. It checks that the requested attribute is in fact present in the object and then it returns the corresponding value.

If that extract-and-lookup process fails for any reason—either because the method name didn't have a `get_` prefix, or because the corresponding entry didn't exist in the object hash—`CD::Music::AUTOLOAD` gives up and throws an appropriate exception.

We still need to provide an explicit definition for `get_location` since it doesn't fit into the common structural pattern that `AUTOLOAD` simulates. Since the `AUTOLOAD` method for a class is only called if normal method lookup fails, the explicit version of `get_location` is found and called before `AUTOLOAD` is considered.

Problems still arise with the above version of `AUTOLOAD` if the CD::Music class also uses hash entries to implement nonpublic attributes of an object. For example, if an entry with the key `'_read_count'` is used to track how often each object has been read-accessed, then the previous `AUTOLOAD` allows that internal data to be accessed via a call to the accessor `$cdref->get__read_count()`. We can provide better control by making `AUTOLOAD` a little smarter:

```perl
package CD::Music;
use strict;
use vars '$AUTOLOAD';   # Keep 'use strict' happy

{
    my %_attrs =
      ( _name          => undef,
        _artist         => undef,
        _publisher      => undef,
        _ISBN           => undef,
        _tracks         => undef,
        _rating         => undef,
        _room           => undef,
        _shelf          => undef,
      );

    sub _accessible { exists $_attrs{$_[1]} }
}

sub AUTOLOAD
{
    my ($self) = @_;
    $AUTOLOAD =~ /.*::get(_\w+)/
        or croak "No such method: $AUTOLOAD";
    $self->_accessible($1)
        or croak "No such attribute: $1";
    $self->{_read_count}++;
    return $self->{$1};
}
```

In this version, AUTOLOAD checks the requested attribute name against a predefined list of publicly accessible attributes, rather than simply checking for existence in the object. The keys of the encapsulated hash %_attrs enumerate the attributes to which AUTOLOAD is allowed to provide access. Notice that we use the nested scope trick again to encapsulate the internal data and provide controlled access to it via a method.

In the above example, the values of the %_attrs hash convey no useful information. But they could. For instance, we can arrange for AUTOLOAD to handle the "set_..." methods of the class as well. The values of %_attrs can then be used to indicate whether a particular attribute is read-only or writable as well. That requires further modifications to the above code, as shown in listing 3.2.

The tests are a little more "Perlified," but the only significant difference in this version is that the class method CD::Music::_accessible now checks whether the specified attribute is accessible in the required mode (i.e., 'read' or 'write').

The use of an encapsulated hash to specify the valid attributes of a class and other related information is a technique commonly used in object-oriented Perl. We'll see variations on this approach at the end of this chapter and in chapter 4.

Reducing the cost of autoloading

The convenience of having accessor methods conjured up for us whenever they're needed comes at a price. In order to determine that autoloading is required, Perl must first attempt to locate a suitable method in the current class and fail to do so, invoking the AUTOLOAD instead. That's more expensive than just finding the method and calling it. As we'll see in chapter 6, if the class also inherits from another class, the search for the correct method becomes even more expensive, as does locating the appropriate AUTOLOAD method.

Even when the AUTOLOAD method is eventually invoked, it's less efficient than a hard-coded method would be. In the CD::Music class, for example, it has to identify the method with one or two pattern matches, determine whether the method is callable (with another method call to accessible), and, finally, simulate the method itself. By comparison, a hard-coded method could simply do its job immediately without any identification or verification phases.

Worst of all, the CD::Music class never learns from the experience of resorting to auto-loading. The next time the same method is called, AUTLOAD will be forced to go through the same expensive lookup–identify–verify sequence all over again.

Fortunately, because Perl provides direct run-time access to a package's symbol table, it's easy to extend an AUTOLOAD method so that all those extra costs are incurred only the first time that AUTOLOAD is required to implement a particular method. In other words, with surprisingly little extra effort, we can arrange for AUTOLOAD to teach its class a new method whenever one is needed:

```
sub CD::Music::AUTOLOAD
{
  no strict "refs";
  my ($self, $newval) = @_;

  # Was it a get_... method?
```

```perl
    if ($AUTOLOAD =~ /.*::get(_\w+)/ && $self->_accessible($1,'read'))
    {
        my $attr_name = $1;
        *{$AUTOLOAD} = sub { return $_[0]->{$attr_name} };
        return $self->{$attr_name}
    }

    # Was it a set_... method?
    if ($AUTOLOAD =~ /.*::set(_\w+)/ && $self->_accessible($1,'write'))
    {
        my $attr_name = $1;
        *{$AUTOLOAD} = sub { $_[0]->{$attr_name} = $_[1]; return };
        $self->{$1} = $newval;
        return
    }

    # Must have been a mistake then...
    croak "No such method: $AUTOLOAD";
}
```

Note how similar this version is to the one shown in figure 3.2. The difference is that here, when AUTOLOAD determines that a valid get_... or set_... accessor has been called, it *creates* an optimized version of that accessor (as an anonymous subroutine) and then installs that accessor in the appropriate symbol table.[11]

The anonymous subroutine that AUTOLOAD creates is a closure, so it remembers the value of the lexical $attr_name variable even after that variable goes out of scope. That way, each subroutine generated by AUTOLOAD is specific to whichever attribute is required for the get or set operation that AUTOLOAD is currently handling.

By installing the anonymous subroutine in the package's symbol table in response to a method call, we have effectively created a new method of the same name within the class. Next time that method is called, the look-up mechanism will find an entry for it in the symbol table and immediately call the corresponding subroutine. AUTOLOAD will no longer be required to handle calls to that particular method, which will now be executed much more quickly.

3.3.4 Documenting a class

Having written the code, the task of building a class is approximately half done. If the class is to be anything more than a one-off, throw-away convenience, it needs to be documented.

Perl makes documenting code particularly easy. You can embed documentation written in the POD markup language right in your module, even interspersing it through the code if you wish. The perlpod documentation that comes with Perl explains how to document your code. This section provides a guide on *what* to document.

When documenting a class, you need to provide users with at least the following information:

---

[11] ...by assigning it to the typeglob *{$AUTOLOAD}. Since $AUTOLOAD holds the full name of the required method, it can be used as a symbolic reference into the symbol table. See the section on *Symbolic references* in chapter 2.

Listing 3.2   A smart AUTOLOAD method for the CD::Music class

```perl
package CD::Music;
use strict;
use vars '$AUTOLOAD';      # Keep 'use strict' happy

# constructor and destructor, as before…
# and then…

{
    my %_attrs =
        ( _name      => 'read',
          _artist    => 'read',
          _publisher => 'read',
          _ISBN      => 'read',
          _tracks    => 'read',
          _rating    => 'read/write,
          _room      => 'read/write',
          _shelf     => 'read/write',
        );

    sub _accessible
    {
        my ($self, $attr, $mode) = @_;
        $_attrs{$attr} =~ /$mode/
    }
}
sub AUTOLOAD
{
    my ($self, $newval) = @_;

    # Was it a get_… method?
    $AUTOLOAD =~ /.*::get(_\w+)/
        and $self->_accessible($1,'read')
        and return $self->{$1};

    # Was it a set_… method?
    $AUTOLOAD =~ /.*::set(_\w+)/
        and $self->_accessible($1,'write')
        and do { $self->{$1} = $newval; return }

    # Must have been a mistake then…
    croak "No such method: $AUTOLOAD";
}
```

- The name and purpose of the class.
- The version of the class which the documentation documents.
- A brief synopsis of how the class is used.
- A more extensive description of how the class is used. This should include specific documentation on how to create objects of the class, what methods those objects provide, what class methods are available, and any special features or limitations of the class.
- A complete list of diagnostics that the class is likely to generate (whether they be exceptions thrown, special values returned, or warning messages generated), plus a description of likely error conditions that the class will not be able to diagnose itself.
- Any environment variables or files that can—or must—be used.
- Any other modules that the class relies on, and how to obtain them if they're not available on the CPAN.
- A list of any known bugs, with suggested workarounds.
- Cross-references to any other relevant documentation.
- A copyright notice.
- The name and contact details of the author or authors.

Listing 3.3 provides a POD skeleton of suitable documentation for a class.

3.4 *The creation and destruction of objects*

The object-oriented features of Perl have been around long enough for many conventions and *idioms* to have evolved. We've already discussed a number of those that relate to methods and attributes. In this section, we'll look at a few conventions that users of your Perl classes will expect you to observe in regard to the creation and removal of objects.

However, as with many aspects of Perl programming, these matters are customs, not graven in stone. You are free to ignore any or all of them, though that may get your code talked about.[12]

3.4.1 Constructors

By convention, each Perl class provides a class method that can be called to produce new objects of the class. That method is called a constructor (as it is in C++ or Java) and, just as in the examples above, it is usually called `new`. Of course, it's perfectly legitimate to call your constructor `create`, `make`, `conjure_forth_from_the_Eternal_Void_I_adjure_thee`, or anything else that's appropriate for your application, but `new` has the three distinct advantages of being short, accurate, and predictable.

Some object-oriented programmers prefer to completely separate the process of object creation from the process of initialization, and so provide two methods: `new` to create the object, and `init` to set up its internal data. This type of fastidiousness makes sense in other languages where the process of construction may fail, often with fatal and hard-to-detect consequences, but it's usually misplaced and excessively paranoid in Perl. Besides, such behavior has the overwhelming disadvantage of making it inevitable that someone will create an ob-

---

[12] ...or worse still, ignored.

Listing 3.3 Class documentation template

```
=head1 NAME

Full::Class::Name - One line summary of purpose of class

=head1 VERSION

This document refers to version N.NN of Full::Class::Name,
released MMMM DD, YYYY.

=head1 SYNOPSIS

   # Short examples of Perl code that illustrate the use of the class

=head1 DESCRIPTION

=head2 Overview

=head2 Constructor and initialization

=head2 Class and object methods

=head2 Any other information that's important

=head1 ENVIRONMENT

List of environment variables and other O/S related information
on which the class relies

=head1 DIAGNOSTICS

=over 4

=item "error message that may appear"

Explanation of error message

=item "another error message that may appear"

Explanation of another error message

etc…

=back

=head1 BUGS

Description of known bugs (and any work-arounds).
Usually also includes an invitation to send the author bug reports.

=head1 FILES

List of any files or other Perl modules needed by the class and a brief
explanation why.

=head1 SEE ALSO

Cross-references to any other relevant documentation.

=head1 AUTHOR(S)

Name(s)
(email address(s))

=head1 COPYRIGHT

Copyright (c) YYYY(s), Author(s). All Rights Reserved.
This module is free software. It may be used, redistributed
and/or modified under the same terms as Perl itself.
```

ject and fail to initialize it. Better to put all your object initialization in a single constructor method.

That's not to say that you shouldn't separate the two processes *within* the constructor. If your initialization sequence is even moderately complex, you should consider putting it in a separate method, like so:

```perl
package CD::Music;
use strict;

sub new
{
    my $self = {};
    bless $self, shift;
    $self->_incr_count();
    $self->_init(@_);
    return $self;
}

{
    my @_init_mems =
        qw( _name _artist _publisher _ISBN _tracks _room _shelf _rating );

    sub _init
    {
        my ($self,@args) = @_;
        my %inits;
        @inits{@_init_mems} = @args;
        %$self = %inits;
    }
}
```

In this version, CD::Music::new performs only the actions associated with object creation: incrementing the global object count, creating the anonymous hash that implements the object, blessing that hash into the class. Then the CD::Music::_init method is called to populate the hash with appropriate values before CD::Music::new returns a reference to the new object. Note that _init is underscored to indicate that it's nonpublic. As always, nothing enforces this distinction except the goodwill of any client code.

The way in which CD::Music::_init goes about populating the hash is interesting. It first creates a temporary hash (%inits) and immediately generates a "slice" of it (@inits{@_init_mems}). This slice is then assigned the various arguments _init was passed. Finally, the now-initialized temporary hash is assigned back to the blessed object being initialized.

This approach offers the advantage that adding another data member to the class is now simply a matter of adding another element to the secret @_init_mems array—and remembering to pass the correct argument list.

Another way to call a constructor

Perl provides a second syntax for calling a constructor, or any other method belonging to a class. It's known as the indirect object syntax, and it's already familiar to you. We'll discuss it here, and then you should tear out this page and eat it, so that you'll never be tempted to use the syntax. You'll see why shortly.

The general forms of the syntax are:

```
methodname OBJECTREF ARGLIST
methodname CLASSNAME ARGLIST
methodname BLOCK ARGLIST
```

In other words, it's exactly like the standard print-to-a-file handle syntax:

```
print STDERR "arg", "u", "mentl", "ist";
```

So what does that have to do with constructors? Well, the same indirect syntax that we use for printing is available to call any method. So you can call a constructor like this

```
my $cd = new CD::Music (  "Toccata and Fugue", "J.S.Bach",
                          "Classic Records", "1456-432443424-2",
                          6, 2,7, 9.5);
```

Many programmers prefer this indirect object syntax, at least for constructor calls, since it's less densely punctuated and more reminiscent of constructor invocation in several other object-oriented languages.

The indirect object syntax does, however, suffer from the same type of ambiguity problems that sometime befuddles print. Provided Perl has already seen the class name before it reaches the indirect object call, there's no problem as long as you always use a bareword class name or a scalar variable as the *CLASSNAME* element:

```
use CD::Music;


$CDM = 'CD::Music';

my $cd1 = new CD::Music (@data);          # okay
my $cd2 = new $CDM (@data);               # okay too
```

Things don't go so well if you use a function call in that position:

```
my $cd3 = new get_classname() (@data);    #Compilation error!
```

So what, (you're thinking) *when am I* ever *going to do something arcane like that?* Well, you'd be surprised how easy it is. Suppose you were trying to follow good software engineering practice and factor out a widely used explicit string into a predefined constant:

```
package main;
use constant CLASS => "CD::Music";

# and later…

new CLASS (@data);
```

Oops! The constant.pm module works by defining a tiny subroutine called main::CLASS, like this:

```
sub main::CLASS() { return "CD::Music" }
```

Now you *do* have a function call in the *CLASSNAME* slot, and the compiler gets confused. In fact, because it's looking for a parameter list straight after the function name, the compiler thinks that you're trying to call main::CLASS with the argument list (@data), and use the result as the argument list to a normal subroutine (main::new). In other words, what was intended to be a CD::Music constructor call is parsed as if it were

```
main::new( main::CLASS(@data) );
```

Of course, since the empty prototype for `main::CLASS` forbids it to take any arguments, and the main package probably doesn't have a `new` subroutine, the compiler rejects the entire expression (with an obscure error message complaining that **unquoted string new may clash with future reserved word...**).

You *can* use a predeclared pseudo-constant like CLASS, but, to do so, you have to use the third form the indirect object syntax and put the function call in its own block:

```
new {CLASS} (@data);
```

This doesn't seem all that much clearer than an explicit method call (`CLASS->new(@data)`). It's probably safer to stick with the direct call syntax, which doesn't have any special cases.

An even better reason not to use the indirect object syntax is that another inherent ambiguity exists when a method is called without arguments. For example, consider a call intended for the `CD::Music::get_name` method:

```
package main;

print(get_name $cd);
```

Now, because the indirect object notation can be used with any method, that should be identical to

```
package main;

print($cd->get_name);
```

And it usually is. The only problem occurs if `main` happens to have its own subroutine called `get_name`. In that case, the compiler assumes you are calling `main::get_name` *without* parentheses around its arguments, as if you'd meant

```
package main;

print( main::get_name($cd) );
```

Even if you use a bareword, as is commonly the case when calling a constructor, things can go horribly wrong if the class you want is declared too late in the program. For example

```
package SeenFirst;
sub new { print "called &SeenFirst::new('$_[0]')\n" }

package main;
sub new { print "called &main::new('$_[0]')\n" }

SeenFirst->new();
new SeenFirst;

SeenLater->new();
new SeenLater;

package SeenLater;
sub new { print "called &SeenLater::new('$_[0]')\n" }
```

The four (supposed) constructor calls actually produce the following output:

```
called &SeenFirst::new('SeenFirst')
called &SeenFirst::new('SeenFirst')
called &SeenLater::new('SeenLater')
called &main::new('SeenLater)
```

because, at the point where it executes the statement new SeenLater, Perl doesn't yet know that SeenLater is a class name. Consequently, Perl doesn't realize that the call is supposed to be to an indirect object method, rather than a regular subroutine.

All in all, the seductive intuitiveness of the indirect object syntax probably isn't worth either the burden of remembering when it's safe to use or the pain of tracking down obscure bugs like these when it isn't. Stick with the arrow syntax for all methods, including constructors and class methods.

Constructor argument lists

One of the most pleasant features of object-oriented programming is that method calls don't generally involve passing a long list of arguments. That's because most of the data a method needs is typically already stored in the object on which the method is called.

Constructors are frequently an exception to this rule, because they exist to convey data to an object, rather than extract an object's data or internally manipulate it. For example, the constructor for the CD::Music class takes eight arguments, whereas no other method of that class takes more than two, and the majority take none.

Such argument-laden methods are painful to call because it's easy to get the argument order wrong or forget an argument. An alternative and safer way to pass data to a constructor is to pass the argument list as though it were a hash (see *Named arguments* in chapter 2).

For example we could rewrite CD::Music::new as follows:

```
package CD::Music;
use strict;

sub new
{
    my ($class, %arg) = @_;
    $class->_incr_count();
    bless {
            _name        => $arg{name},
            _artist      => $arg{artist},
            _publisher   => $arg{publisher},
            _ISBN        => $arg{ISBN},
            _tracks      => $arg{tracks},
            _room        => $arg{room},
            _shelf       => $arg{shelf},
            _rating      => $arg{rating},
        }, $class;
}
```

Now, the creation of a new CD::Music object is self-documenting, and the data can be specified in any convenient order:

```
my $cd = CD::Music->new(  name      => "Piano Concerto 20",
                          artist    => "Mozart",
                          rating    => 10,
                          room      => 5,
                          shelf     => 1,
                          publisher => "Salieri Intl.",
                          ISBN      => "1426-43235624-2",
                        );
```

The use of named arguments is certainly not a universally applied convention, and is occasionally a topic of minor philosophical debate, but the greater verbosity of named arguments more than pays for itself every time code has to be maintained. As a rule of thumb, if your constructor takes more than two or three arguments, it will be far easier to use if those arguments are named.

Constructor default values

Did you notice in the previous example that we neglected to specify how many tracks there were? Of course, even with named parameters, if an argument is accidentally omitted when a constructor is called, the corresponding internal data will be undefined. That may be a reasonable default value, especially if it's a conscious choice, or it may be better to provide explicit defaults for any missing value:

```
package CD::Music;
use strict;

sub new
{
    my ($class, %arg) = @_;
    $class->_incr_count();
    bless {
            _name      => $arg{name}      || croak("missing name"),
            _artist    => $arg{artist}    || "???",
            _publisher => $arg{publisher} || "???",
            _ISBN      => $arg{ISBN}       || "???",
            _tracks    => $arg{tracks}     || "???",
            _room      => $arg{room}       || "uncataloged",
            _shelf     => $arg{shelf}      || "",
            _rating    => $arg{rating}     || ask_rating($arg{name}),
          }, $class;
}

sub ask_rating { print "What is your rating for $_[0]? "; scalar <> }
```

The defaults specified in this way may be explicit values, or a particular action (such as throwing an exception, or prompting for missing data).

The use of the || operator—a common Perl idiom—means that no argument can have the value 0, since the left-hand side of the operation would then be false, so the default on the right-hand side would used. If valid values of 0 and other false values like "0", or "" are required, the above code would have to be uglified with the ternary operator instead:

```
bless{
        _name=> defined($arg{name}) ? $arg{name} : croak("missing name"),
        _artist=> defined($arg{artist}) ? $arg{artist} : "???",

        # etc.

    }, $class;
```

Constructors as object duplicators

We can get even more sophisticated. For example, we can arrange that, whenever the constructor is called as an object method (with no arguments), the values for the newly created object are taken from the existing object through which the constructor was called. In other words, the constructor can also act like a copy operation.

Note that a constructor call is required. Simple object-to-object assignment won't do the trick for several reasons:

- A simple assignment of object references ($objref1 = $objref2) doesn't copy the referent. Both variables will end up pointing to the same object.
- A simple assignment of the underlying objects (%$objref1 = %$objref2) won't assign the blessing of the original object to the new one, nor will it adjust a class attribute that keeps count of objects.
- Even if we *could* assign the objects with their blessings, *and* have the count correctly updated, if any of the original object's attributes themselves contained references, we'd have the same problem all over again, only at the next level down.

Thus, Perl's shallow copy semantics frustrates our desire to use simple assignment as a copying mechanism.

The way the constructor was previously set up, to copy an object we'd first have to determine its type (using the built-in ref function). We could then create an object of the same type by calling new via the resulting class name. Finally, we could initialize the newly created object with a simple hash-to-hash assignment. Like this:

```
%{$objref2 = ref($objref1)->new()} = %{$objref1};
```

Provided the object doesn't contain any nested references, this works quite well. But it's not obvious to code, nor easy to understand once coded. Laziness is a cardinal virtue in Perl, so a custom has developed that when users of a class call a class's constructor as an object method, the defaults that the constructor uses are taken from the original object. This means that the copy operation can be accomplished just by writing

```
$objref2 = $objref1->new();
```

To implement that behavior we need one extra tweak in the CD::Music constructor:

```
package CD::Music;

{
    my $_class_defaults =
    { _name       => "???",
      _artist     => "???",
```

```
        _publisher    => "???",
        _ISBN         => "???",
        _tracks       => "???",
        _room         => "uncataloged",
        _shelf        => "",
        _rating       => -1,
    };

    sub _class_defaults     { $_class_defaults }
    sub _class_default_keys { map { s/^_//; $_ } keys %$_class_defaults}
}
sub new
{
    my ($caller, %arg) = @_;
    my $class = ref($caller);
    my $defaults = $class ? $caller : $caller->_class_defaults();
    $class ||= $caller;
    $class->_incr_count();
    my $self = bless {}, $class;
    foreach my $attrname ( $class->_class_default_keys )
    {
        if (exists $arg{$attrname})
            { $self->{"_$attrname"} = $arg{$attrname} }
        else
            { $self->{"_$attrname"} = $defaults->{"_$attrname"} }
    }
    return $self;
}
```

In this version, CD::Music::new first determines if $caller is an object, in which case ref($caller) returns a class name. In that case, the default values for the initialization should come from that object, so $defaults is made to refer to the object, $caller, itself. If ref($caller) returns an empty string instead, then $caller itself must have stored a class name. That is, the constructor must have been called as a class method: CD::Music-> new(@data). In that case, the default values are taken from the class itself—$caller->_ class_defaults()—and $class is reassigned the value of $caller (i.e., the class name).

After that point, we are guaranteed that $class stores the class name into which the object is to be blessed, and $defaults stores a reference to a hash with entries suitable for use as default values. That hash may be another object, or it may be the hash referred to by $_ class_defaults, but we no longer care which.

Having blessed an empty hash into the class, all that is required is to initialize that object by stepping through each valid internal datum—conveniently specified by the keys of the class defaults. For each key, we strip the leading underscore to generate the external name, $attr- name, that would have been used to label the corresponding argument to CD::Music::new. We assign either the argument passed to the constructor, $arg{$attrname}, or, if no suitable argument was passed, the default value from the hash referred to by $caller, $caller->{"_ $attrname"}.

With a constructor like this, we can now copy an existing object:

```
my $cdref2 = $cdref1->new();
```

Or we can copy and modify an object in one step:

```
my $cdref2 = $cdref1->new(  name   => "Also Sprach Zarathustra",
                            artist => "Strauss");
```

Or just use the standard defaults

```
my $cdref2 = ref($cdref1)->new();
```

This last constructor call *doesn't* use the values in the object referred to be `$cdref1`, because `ref($cdref1)` is the name of the object's class, not a reference to the object itself.

A separate clone method

While many experts view the overloading of constructors as object copiers to be a natural extension of their functionality, others consider the technique unintuitive, too subtle, and more likely to produce obscure and hard-to-maintain code. Whether or not that's the case, it certainly *is* true that the code for the constructors themselves is considerably more complicated.

The alternative is to provide a completely separate method for duplicating objects. Such a method is typically called `clone` or `copy` and would be implemented like this:

```
package CD::Music;

# constructor as in earlier versions

sub clone
{
    my ($self) = @_;
    my $class = ref($self);
    $class->_incr_count();
    bless { %{$self} }, $class;
}
```

The new `clone` method reproduces the essential behavior of the CD::Music constructor—incrementing the object count, then blessing a hash as the new object—but requires much less initialization code, since it can simply copy the contents of the existing object, `%{$self}`, on the assumption that it's already correctly structured.

However, this approach is not always sufficient, particularly if some of a class's attributes are implemented as references. In such cases we need to copy each reference attribute from the `$self` object separately. For example, if the `"_artist"` and `"_ISBN"` attributes were actually references to objects of the classes Artist and ISBN (each with its own `clone` method), then we would have to implement the CD::Music::clone method like this:

```
sub clone
{
    my ($self) = @_;
    my $class = ref($self);
    $class->_incr_count();
    my $newobj = bless { %{$self} }, $class;
    $newobj->{_artist} = $self->{_artist}->clone();
    $newobj->{_ISBN}   = $self->{_ISBN}->clone();
    return $newobj;
}
```

Whether you decide to provide object cloning facilities implicitly (as part of a standard constructor), or explicitly (as a separate method), depends on the nature of the application you're building, and—more importantly—on the expectations and conventions of those who may use your code. If you have a choice, it's probably better to code a separate `clone` method. Apart from keeping your individual methods simpler and less prone to bugs, the method's name will force client code to be more clearly self-documenting.

3.4.2 Destructors

Most object-oriented languages provide the ability to specify methods that are called automatically when an object ceases to exist. Such methods are usually called *destructors* and are used to undo any side-effects caused by the previous existence of an object, including:

- Deallocating related memory (although, in Perl, that's almost never necessary since reference counting usually takes care of it for you);
- Closing file or directory handles stored in the object;
- Closing pipes to other processes;
- Closing databases used by the object;
- Updating classwide information;
- Anything else that the object should do before it ceases to exist (such as logging the fact of its own demise, or storing its data away to provide persistence, etc.).

In Perl, you can set up a destructor for a class by defining an object method called DE-STROY. The method is automatically called on an object just before that object's memory is reclaimed. That happens either as soon as the program loses its last reference to the object—that is, when the object's reference count reaches zero—or when the interpreter thread in which the object was created shuts down. Typically, the destructor is called when the last variable holding a reference to the object goes out of scope or has another value assigned to it.

For example, we could provide a destructor for the CD::Music class like this:

```
package CD::Music;

sub DESTROY
{
   my ($self) = @_;
   print "<<here lies the noble '", $self->name(), "'>>\n";
}
```

Now, every time an object of class CD::Music is about to cease to exist, that object will automatically have its DESTROY method called, which will print an epitaph for the object. For example, the following script

```
package main;
use CD::Music;

open CDDATA, "CD.dat" or die "Couldn't find CD data";
while (<CDDATA>)
{
    my @data = split ',', $_;
    my $cd = CD::Music->new(@data);
```

```
    print "Title: ", $cd->name, "\n";
}
print "(end of list)\n";
```

prints out something like the following

Title: Canon in D
<<here lies the noble 'Canon in D' >>
Title: Toccata and Fugue
<<here lies the noble 'Toccata and Fugue' >>
Title: Concerto in D
<<here lies the noble 'Concerto in D' >>
Title: The Four Seasons'
<<here lies the noble 'The Four Seasons' >>
(end of list)

That's because, at the end of each iteration of the while loop, the variable $cd goes out of scope, taking with it the only reference to the CD::Music object created earlier in the same loop. That object's reference count immediately becomes zero, and, because it was blessed, the corresponding DESTROY method, CD::Music::DESTROY, is automatically called on the object, printing out the "here lies..." message.

Of course, in a real program you want your destructor to bury your CDs, not to praise them. Rather than printing a valedictory, we could do some useful work in the destructor and, for example, remedy the bug in the class attribute that keeps track of the number of CD::Music objects.

The problem is that the CD count keeps merrily incrementing every time CD::Music::new is called, but the count is never decremented, even when CD::Music objects cease to exist. Technically, it's a count of how many objects have ever existed, not how many currently exist.

Up to this point we've had no way of ensuring that the shared count is decreased whenever an object vanishes, but now it's easy:

```
package CD::Music;
use strict;

{
  my $_count = 0;

  sub get_count { $_count }
  sub _incr_count { ++$_count }
  sub _decr_count { --$_count }
}

sub new
{
  my $class = ref($_[0]) || $_[0];
  $class->_incr_count();
  # etc. as before
}
```

```
sub DESTROY
{
  my ($self) = @_;
  $self->_decr_count();
}
```

We are now guaranteed that the collective object count is correctly updated each time a CD::Music object is destroyed.

Destructors and circular data structures

Apart from manipulating global attributes like the object count, destructors are rarely needed in object-oriented Perl. By and large, Perl cleans up after itself so effectively that there's usually nothing left for a destructor to do. There is one situation, however, where a destructor *is* required to help clean up after objects: reclaiming circular data structures.

Let's consider a class that represents a network of some kind (i.e., a set of nodes connected by one-way links). Such a class might be needed for email routing, or traffic monitoring software, or in a LAN configuration program, or the finite state machine of a parser, or to implement a neural net. The Network class would probably look something like this:

```
package Network;
use strict;

sub new
{
  my ($class) = @_;
  bless { _nodes => [] }, $class;
}

sub node
{
  my ($self, $index) = @_;
  return $self->{_nodes}->[$index];
}

sub add_node
{
  my ($self) = @_;
  push @{$self->{_nodes}}, Node->new();
}
```

Notice that it makes use of another class, Node. The Node class looks like this:

```
package Node;
use strict;

{
  my $_nodecount=0;
  sub _nextid { return ++$_nodecount }
}
```

```perl
sub new
{
  my ($class) = @_;
  bless { _id => _nextid(), _outlinks => [] }, $class;
}

sub add_link_to
{
  my ($self, $target) = @_;
  push @{$self->{_outlinks}}, Link->new($target)
}
```

The Node class in turn relies on another class, Link, whose objects represent a single uni-directional link to another Node. The Link class looks like this:

```perl
package Link;
use strict;

{
  my $_linkcount=0;
  sub _nextid { return ++$_linkcount }
}

sub new
{
  my ($class) = @_;
  bless { _id => _nextid(),
          _to => $_[1],
        }, $class;
}
```

Therefore, a Network consists of zero or more Node objects, each of which has an ID number and a list of references to zero or more outward-going Link objects. Each Link in turn has an ID number and a reference to the Node at which it terminates. Links act as connectors between Nodes, Nodes act as end-points of Links, and the Network object acts as a container for the lot. Figure 3.4(a) illustrates these relationships for a simple three-node network implemented by the following code:

```perl
use Network;

my $network = Network->new();

foreach (0..2) { $network->add_node(); }

$network->node(0)->add_link_to($network->node(1));
$network->node(0)->add_link_to($network->node(2));
$network->node(1)->add_link_to($network->node(2));
$network->node(2)->add_link_to($network->node(1));
```

This kind of interaction among several classes illustrates one of the most important features of object-oriented programming: the construction of classes out of the interactions of other simpler classes. Unfortunately, in this case, it's in those interactions that the problem arises.

Suppose that three-node network were created in some nested lexical scope, say, in a subroutine:

```
use Network;

sub analyse_network
{
    my $network = Network->new();

    foreach (0..2) { $network->add_node(); }

    $network->node(0)->add_link_to($network->node(1));
    $network->node(0)->add_link_to($network->node(2));
    $network->node(1)->add_link_to($network->node(2));
    $network->node(2)->add_link_to($network->node(1));


    # Do analysis here
}
```

Everything works fine, until we reach the end of `analyse_network`, and the lexical variable `$network` goes out of scope. At that point, the Network object being referred to by `$net-work` has no other references to it, so it also ceases to exist. That, in turn, means that each of the Node objects in the Network object's node list has its reference count decremented. We might assume that those counts go to zero and the Nodes are also removed, but that isn't the case, as figure 3.4 illustrates.

The first Node object in the list, `$network->node(1)`, does indeed end up with a zero reference count and is correctly reclaimed. That decrements the reference counts of the first two Link objects, causing them to disappear as well. Each of those links has a reference to one of the remaining Node objects, so their reference counts also decrement. Those counts only reduce to 1, because each of the two remaining Link objects still contains a reference to a Node object. At that point, the cascade of destructor calls ceases, since all the remaining objects have nonzero reference counts.

There's the problem. From the point-of-view of the rest of the program, the two remaining Nodes and their interconnecting Links are inaccessible, since the rest of the program has no reference to them. And the memory they occupy will never be reclaimed because their reference counts are nonzero.

The stubborn Nodes and Links form a cycle, in which each object stores a reference to some other, which stores a reference to some other, which stores a reference to some other, which stores a reference back to the first. Such chains of references are self-sustaining, because even if no other reference exists to any of the objects, every one of them is referred to at least once. Consequently, their reference counts can never be zero and they can never be reclaimed.[13]

To avoid this leakage of memory, we need to be able to break the sequence of mutual references before losing access to the offending Nodes and Links; in other words, before `$net-work` ceases to exist. We can ensure such a break occurs by providing the Network class with a destructor that explicitly removes the Links between Nodes at the appropriate time:

```
package Network;

# as before
```

---

[13] At least, not until the end of the current interpreter thread.

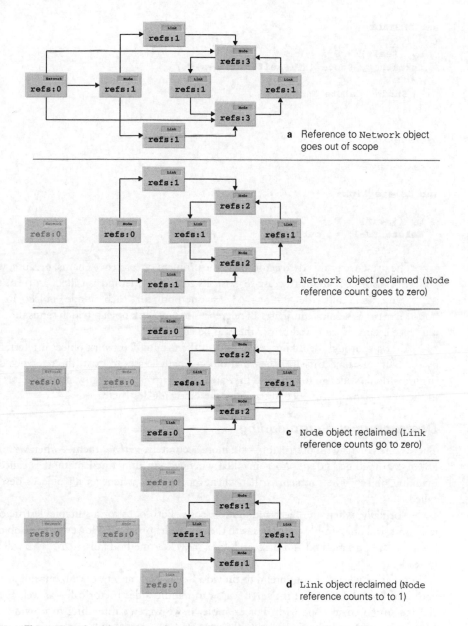

a Reference to Network object goes out of scope

b Network object reclaimed (Node reference count goes to zero)

c Node object reclaimed (Link reference counts go to zero)

d Link object reclaimed (Node reference counts to to 1)

Figure 3.4   Leaking network caused by circular references

```
sub DESTROY
{
  my ($self) = @_;
  foreach my $node ( @{$self->{_nodes}} )
  {
      $node->delete_links();
  }
}

package Node;

# as before

sub delete_links
{
  my ($self) = @_;
  delete $self->{_outlinks};
}
```

The presence of this destructor solves the problem of reference chains, because, whenever a Network object is about to cease to exist, its DESTROY method is called. In turn, that DE-STROY method calls the delete_links method for each Node object in its list. Node::delete_links eliminates all references to any Link object, which sends those objects' reference counts to zero and causes them to be collected.

After a thorough delinking, each node in the original Network object is referred to only by the Network object itself. When that object finally ceases to exist, the reference counts of the individual Nodes go to zero, and they are cleaned up as well. Figure 3.5 illustrates the steps in the new clean-up sequence initiated by the Network destructor.

Destructors and autoloading

There's one gotcha with destructors—or, more accurately, *without* them—when we're using an AUTOLOAD method. AUTOLOAD is invoked whenever an undefined method is called for the invoking object. The problem is that whenever includes whenever an object's destructor is called.

Normally, when an object goes out of scope, Perl looks for a suitable destructor and, if it doesn't find one, simply continues with the rest of the program. However, if the object's class has an AUTOLOAD method and the search for a DESTROY method fails, AUTOLOAD will be called instead.

So, at very least, if you intend to provide a class with an AUTOLOAD but not a DESTROY, you need to make sure that the AUTOLOAD can handle a destructor call—as well as anything else it's supposed to cope with. For example, if we weren't intending to provide CD::Music::DESTROY, we'd need to modify the CD::Music::AUTOLOAD method in Figure 3.5 like this:

```
sub CD::Music::AUTOLOAD
{
  my ($self, $newval) = @_;

  # Was it a destructor call?
```

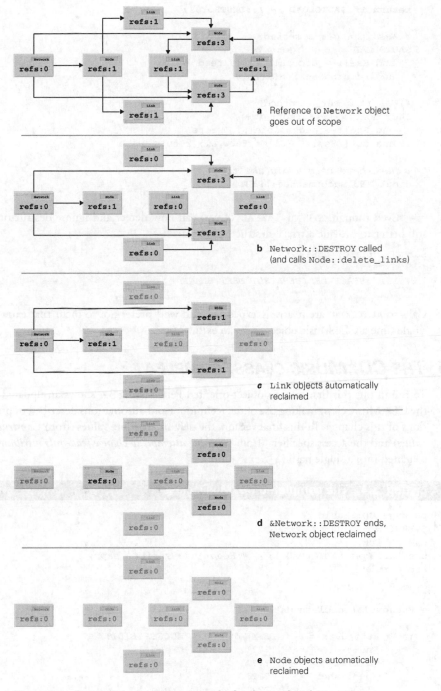

Figure 3.5   Network leakage overcome by implementing destructor

```
    return if $AUTOLOAD =~ /::DESTROY$/;

    # Was it a get_… method?
    $AUTOLOAD =~ /.*::get(_\w+)/
        and $self->_accessible($1,'read')
        and return $self->{$1};

    # Was it a set_… method?
    $AUTOLOAD =~ /.*::set(_\w+)/
        and $self->_accessible($1,'write')
        and do { $self->{$1} = $newval; return };

    # Must have been a mistake then…
    croak "No such method: $AUTOLOAD";
}
```

Even though `CD::Music::AUTOLOAD` can now detect and ignore destructor calls, it is still better to provide a trivial destructor instead:

```
sub CD::Music::DESTROY
{
    # THIS SPACE DELIBERATELY LEFT BLANK
}
```

Calls to AUTOLOAD are relatively expensive, and we'd prefer not to incur that extra cost every single time a CD::Music object ceases to exist.

3.5 THE CD::MUSIC CLASS, COMPLEAT

To round out this first taste to object-oriented Perl, Listing 3.4 shows an updated version of the CD::Music class, making use of the techniques and automations described in previous sections of this chapter. In this final version, the default attribute values (from *Constructor default values*) and the access specifiers (from *Catching attempts to change read-only attributes*) are consolidated into a single hash (`%_attr_data`).

Listing 3.4   The completed CD::Music class

```
package CD::Music;
$VERSION = 1.00;
use strict;
use vars qw( $AUTOLOAD );    # Keep 'use strict' happy
use Carp;

{
# Encapsulated class data

    my %_attr_data = #    DEFAULT         ACCESSIBILITY
        ( _name      => [ '???',          'read'],
          _artist    => [ '???',          'read'],
          _publisher => [ '???',          'read'],
          _ISBN      => [ '???',          'read'],
          _tracks    => [ '???',          'read'],
```

```
        _rating    => [ -1,              'read/write'],
        _room      => [ 'uncataloged', 'read/write'],
        _shelf     => [ "",             'read/write'],
    );

    my $_count = 0;
# Class methods, to operate on encapsulated class data

    # Is a specified object attribute accessible in a given mode
    sub _accessible
    {
        my ($self, $attr, $mode) = @_;
        $_attr_data{$attr}[1] =~ /$mode/
    }


    # Classwide default value for a specified object attribute
    sub _default_for
    {
        my ($self, $attr) = @_;
        $_attr_data{$attr}[0];
    }


    # List of names of all specified object attributes
    sub _standard_keys
    {
        keys %_attr_data;
    }


    # Retrieve object count
    sub get_count
    {
        $_count;
    }


    # Private count increment/decrement methods
    sub _incr_count { ++$_count }
    sub _decr_count { --$_count }


}
# Constructor may be called as a class method
# (in which case it uses the class's default values),
# or an object method
# (in which case it gets defaults from the existing object)

sub new
{
    my ($caller, %arg) = @_;
    my $caller_is_obj = ref($caller);
    my $class = $caller_is_obj || $caller;
    my $self = bless {}, $class;
    foreach my $attrname ( $self->_standard_keys() )
    {
```

```perl
    my ($argname) = ($attrname =~ /^_(.*)/);
    if (exists $arg{$argname})
       { $self->{$attrname} = $arg{$argname} }
    elsif ($caller_is_obj)
       { $self->{$attrname} = $caller->{$attrname} }
    else
       { $self->{$attrname} = $self->_default_for($attrname) }
  }
  $self->_incr_count();
  return $self;
}


# Destructor adjusts class count
sub DESTROY
{
  $_[0]->_decr_count();
}

# get or set room&shelf together

sub get_location  { ($_[0]->get_room(), $_[0]->get_shelf()) }
sub set_location
{
    my ($self, $room, $shelf) = @_;
    $self->set_room($room) if $room;
    $self->set_shelf($shelf) if $shelf;
    return;
}


# Implement other get_... and set_... methods (create as necessary)

sub AUTOLOAD
{
    no strict "refs";
    my ($self, $newval) = @_;

    # Was it a get_... method?
    if ($AUTOLOAD =~ /.*::get(_\w+)/ && $self->_accessible($1,'read'))
    {
       my $attr_name = $1;
       *{$AUTOLOAD} = sub { return $_[0]->{$attr_name} };
       return $self->{$attr_name}
    }

    # Was it a set_... method?
    if ($AUTOLOAD =~ /.*::set(_\w+)/ && $self->_accessible($1,'write'))
    {
       my $attr_name = $1;
       *{$AUTOLOAD} = sub { $_[0]->{$attr_name} = $_[1]; return };
       $self->{$1} = $newval;
       return
    }
```

```
        # Must have been a mistake then...
        croak "No such method: $AUTOLOAD";
}

1;  # Ensure that the module can be successfully use'd
```

3.6 SUMMARY

- A Perl class is just a package containing subroutines that implement methods.
- Any of Perl's standard data types—hash, array, scalar, typeglob, subroutine, regex—may be used as an object.
- To convert something to an object, we use the `bless` function to associate the thing with the appropriate package. Always use the two-argument form of `bless`.
- A constructor is just a method that blesses an object, initializes it, and returns a reference to it.
- A destructor is a special method called DESTROY that is automatically called when an object is about to be garbage-collected. Destructors are rarely needed in Perl, except when circular data structures are involved.
- Accessors are methods that provide read or write access to an attribute. It is much safer to encapsulate attributes in accessors than to access them directly.
- To create class attributes, use a lexical variable declared in some nested block within the package. Define accessors for the variable within the same nested block.
- An AUTOLOAD method can provide a "catchall" or generic method for a class. Alternatively, AUTOLOAD may create and install a suitable method at run time. When using autoloaded methods, it's a good idea to provide a destructor, even if it doesn't do anything.

C H A P T E R   4

Blessing arrays and scalars

As the last chapter illustrated, you can build objects in Perl with little more than a hash and a blessing. But one of Perl's defining characteristics is flexibility, and in keeping with its unofficial motto—*There's more than one way to do it*—you can just as easily bless any other Perl data type into objecthood. This chapter examines cases where blessing something other than a hash may be appropriate.

4.1 WHAT'S WRONG WITH A HASH?

Hashes are well suited to act as the basis for objects. They can store multiple values of differing types, they give each value a descriptive label, they can be expanded to store additional items at need,[1] and they can be made hierarchical (by storing references to other anonymous hashes in an entry).

Hashes are usually a good choice for implementing class objects, but they're by no means perfect. For a start, they are a comparatively expensive way to store collections of data, occupying more space than an equivalent array, and providing slower access as well. Often those small overheads are insignificant, but, occasionally (such as when large numbers of objects are involved, or when a much simpler data structure would do just as well), the difference in performance or style matters.

---

[1] This will come in handy in chapter 6 when we look at class inheritance.

A more serious problem with hashes has to do with an otherwise convenient feature they possess called *autovivification*. Autovivification is the name for what happens when you attempt to assign a nonexistent entry of a hash. Rather than complaining, Perl automatically creates the missing hash entry for the key you specified.

And that's the problem. If you have a reference to a hash-based object, say, $objref, and you're using an attribute such as $objref->{_weirdness_factor}, then chances are that somewhere in the heat of coding, you'll accidentally write something like $objref-> {_wierdness_factor}++.

The first time that code is executed, Perl won't complain about the spelling mistake or the fact that it causes your code to access a nonexistent entry. Instead, it will try to be helpful: autovivifying the new hash entry, then silently converting its undef value to zero, then incrementing it to 1. Thereafter, you'll spend about a week trying to work out why that increment operator seems to increase the real world's weirdness factor, but not $objref's.

4.2 BLESSING AN ARRAY

Let's start with the obvious first candidate for an alternative to hashes. Arrays provide almost all the advantages of hashes and then throw in a few more. Just like hashes they can store multiple values of differing types. They also can be hierarchical and expanded as necessary. And arrays have a distinct performance advantage, both in using less memory and providing faster access to elements.

Just about the only drawbacks to using arrays instead of hashes are that they still autovivify (we'll see a solution to that problem in the next section), and you lose the readable object attributes labels provided by the keys of a hash. For example, it's much harder to pick the bug in:

```
sub Projectile::get_velocity
{
  my ($self) = @_;
  return $self->[2]/$self->[11];
}
```

than in the equivalent hash-based method:

```
sub Projectile::get_velocity
{
  my ($self) = @_;
  return $self->{_flight_time}/$self->{_flight_distance};
}
```

Using names instead of numbers makes it obvious that we're calculating delay (in seconds/foot), instead of velocity (in feet/second). Of course, it's relatively straightforward to avoid the pitfalls of such meaningless index numbers, by predefining some appropriate constants—and fixing the bug, of course:

```
package Projectile;
use strict;

use constant FLIGHT_TIME     => 2;
use constant FLIGHT_DISTANCE => 11;
```

```
sub get_velocity
{
    my ($self) = @_;
    return $self->[FLIGHT_DISTANCE]/$self->[FLIGHT_TIME];
}
```

Reimplementing CD::Music

Figure 4.1 shows an array-based reimplementation of the CD::Music class from chapter 3.

After the usual preliminaries—package, version, strictness—the eight object attributes of the class are associated with eight consecutive array indices via use constant statements. This actually creates eight tiny functions in the CD::Music namespace, but Perl's optimizer is smart enough to replace all future calls to any of them with the constant value they return. In accordance with the standard Perl conventions, the constants are all upper-case.

Listing 4.1 The CD::Music class implemented via arrays

```
package CD::Music;
$VERSION = 1.10;
use strict;
use Carp;

use constant NAME      => 0;
use constant ARTIST    => 1;
use constant PUBLISHER => 2;
use constant ISBN      => 3;
use constant TRACKS    => 4;
use constant ROOM      => 5;
use constant SHELF     => 6;
use constant RATING    => 7;

# Create a mapping from previous hash keys to array indices
# (this is needed to provide hash-like arguments for new)
my %_index_for;
@_index_for{  qw(name artist publisher ISBN tracks rating room shelf)}
             = (NAME,ARTIST,PUBLISHER,ISBN,TRACKS,RATING,ROOM,SHELF);

# Set up the default data (same as in the hash version, but more concise)
my @_default_data;
@_default_data[ NAME,ARTIST,PUBLISHER,ISBN,TRACKS,RATING, ROOM,SHELF ]
    = ('???','???','???',0,'???',-1,"uncataloged","" );

{
    # Private class attribute, as in the hash version
    my $_count = 0;

    # Retrieve object count
    sub get_count { $_count; }

    # Private count increment/decrement methods
    sub _incr_count { ++$_count }
```

```perl
        sub _decr_count { --$_count }

}

# Constructor may be called as a class method

sub new
{
    my ($caller, %arg) = @_;
    my $caller_is_obj = ref($caller);
    my $class = $caller_is_obj || $caller;
    no strict "refs";
    my $self = bless [\%{"${class}::FIELDS"}], $class;

    foreach my $member ( keys %_index_for )
    {
        my $index = $_index_for{$member};
        if (exists $arg{$member})
            { $self->[$index] = $arg{$member} }
        elsif ($caller_is_obj)
            { $self->[$index] = $caller->[$index] }
        else
            { $self->[$index] = $_default_data[$index] }
    }
    $self->_incr_count();
    return $self;
}

# Destructor adjusts class count
sub DESTROY
{
    $_[0]->_decr_count();
}

# get or set room&shelf in one method

sub get_location { ($_[0]->get_room(), $_[0]->get_shelf()) }

sub set_location
{
    my ($self, $room, $shelf) = @_;
    $self->set_room($room) if $room;
    $self->set_shelf($shelf) if $shelf;
    return;
}

# Implement all the other get_... and set_... methods,

sub get_name      { return $_[0]->[NAME]}
sub get_artist    { return $_[0]->[ARTIST]}
sub get_publisher { return $_[0]->[PUBLISHER]}
sub get_ISBN      { return $_[0]->[ISBN]}
sub get_tracks    { return $_[0]->[TRACKS]}
```

```
sub get_room       { return $_[0]->[ROOM] }
sub get_shelf      { return $_[0]->[SHELF] }
sub get_rating     { return $_[0]->[RATING] }

sub set_room       { $_[0]->[ROOM] = $_[1] }
sub set_shelf      { $_[0]->[SHELF] = $_[1] }
sub set_rating     { $_[0]->[RATING] = $_[1] }
```

Apart from ensuring that access speed to an array element is not compromised, these functions can promote better user respect for encapsulation, because they must be fully qualified if used outside the CD::Music class. For example, code like:

```
package main;
use CD::Music;

# and later...

$cd->[TRACKS]++;
```

will almost certainly cause an exception to be thrown.[2]

Of course, there's nothing to stop the miscreant from writing:

```
$cd->[CD::Music::TRACKS]++;
```

or just:

```
$cd->[4]++;
```

The added security, therefore, relies entirely on Laziness, which is very poor security indeed.

The constructor of the array-based version is also a little different. As with the previous hash-based version, we'd like it to take a hash-like argument list, provide default values for uninitialized attributes, and also be usable as an object method for copying.

To enable hash-like arguments to be used, we need to provide a mapping from the keys to the corresponding array indices. That's the purpose of the lexical %_index_for hash. For compactness, we initialize %_index_for via a hash slice (@_index_for{...}).

Because the default data will be used to initialize an array-based object, it's more efficient to store that data in an array (@_default_data). Again, to provide compactness without loss of readability, we initialize using a slice—an array slice this time. The same effect could have been achieved in a single line:

```
my @_default_data = (('unknown') x 5, -1, 'uncataloged', '');
```

but the two lines saved don't justify the serious loss of clarity and maintainability.

The constructor itself is identical in structure to that of the hash-based version. It still steps through each attribute name and assigns to that attribute either the corresponding value in the %arg hash, or the corresponding attribute from the invoking object, or the default value.

The only other change needed is to reimplement most of the attribute accessor methods, so that they use array accesses instead of hash lookups. Note, however, that the get_location and set_locations methods are unchanged, since they rely on the public interface of the class (which, of course, is why they were implemented that way in the first place).

---

[2] Unless there's also a subroutine &main::TRACKS defined, in which case *anything* might happen.

The accessor methods are each coded explicitly, rather than defining a single AUTOLOAD function to handle them all. The reason is performance. The whole point of reimplementing CD::Music objects as arrays was to improve their access speed. Using AUTOLOAD would compromise that objective. To see why, let's implement the AUTOLOAD version and examine its performance:

```
my $_readable = 'name|artist|publisher|ISBN|tracks|rating|room|shelf';
my $_writable = 'rating|room|shelf';

sub AUTOLOAD
{
    my ($self, $newval) = @_;
    if ($AUTOLOAD =~ /.*::get_($_readable)/o)
    {
        return $self->[$_index_for{$1}];
    }
    elsif ($AUTOLOAD =~ /.*::set_($_writable)/o)
    {
        $self->[$_index_for{$1}] = $newval;
        return;
    }
    croak "No such method: $AUTOLOAD";
}
```

Even this heavily optimized version will require on average 1.5 pattern matches, a hash lookup, and an array access. That's much more expensive than the single array access of the explicitly coded accessors.

4.2.1 An array-specific example—iterators

The decision to reimplement CD::Music using arrays was based entirely on the desire to improve space efficiency and speed of access. Sometimes, however, the actual purpose of a class naturally suggests an array implementation.

For example, consider the problem of iterating through a Perl hash. In most cases, of course, there is no problem. You just use the built-in each function:

```
%desc = (blue => "moon", green => "egg", red => "Baron" );

while ( ($key,$value) = each %desc )
{
    print "$value is $key\n";
}
```

The problem appears when you want to nest iterations of the same hash:

```
while ( ($key1,$value1) = each %desc )
{
    while ( ($key2,$value2) = each %desc )
    {
        print "$value2 is not $key1\n"
            unless $key1 eq key2;
    }
}
print "(finished)\n";
```

This isn't going to behave in the way you might expect, because the each function relies on the hash it's iterating to keep track of the next available key. That means that the two nested calls to each are both incrementing the same cursor stored inside %desc.

The outer loop starts with each returning the "blue"=>"moon" pair. The inner loop iterates through the remaining two pairs, before returning an empty list that halts the inner loop. When each returns that empty list, it also resets the cursor inside %desc, so next time through the outer loop, each finds itself back at the "blue"=>"moon" pair. Thus the entire process repeats…and repeats…and repeats…

An object-oriented solution to this problem would be to replace the calls to each with methods calls on special iterator objects:

```
$iter1 = Iterator->new(%desc);
while ( ($key1,$value1) = $iter1->each() )
{
    $iter2 = Iterator->new(%desc);
    while ( ($key2,$value2) = $iter2->each() )
    {
        print "$value2 is not $key1\n"
            unless $key1 eq key2;
    }
}
```

The implementation of the Iterator class is simple enough that it can be done quite informally:

```
package Iterator;
$VERSION = 1.00;
use strict;

sub new
{
    my ($class,@data) = @_;
    @data = @$class if !@data && ref($class);
    bless [ @data ], ref($class)||$class;
}

sub each
{
    my ($self) = @_;
    my @next = splice @$self, 0, 2;
    return wantarray? @next : $next[0];
}
```

The class consists of only two methods: a constructor and an iteration method. The constructor takes the contents of a hash, which have been flattened into the @_ array, and copies them into a new anonymous array object, which is then blessed into the Iterator class.

The iteration method extracts the first two elements in the array object using a splice.[3] Since the built-in each function returns different values in list and scalar contexts, Iterator::each consults the wantarray function to determine whether it has been called in a list

---

[3] …which is more efficient than my @next = (shift @$self, shift @$self)

or nonlist context. If it was called in a list context, Iterator::each returns the pair of elements—key and value—it extracted from the list. In a scalar context, it returns only the key.

The constructor's blessing uses ref($class)||$class as the class name. This allows the constructor to be called as either a class method (Iterator->new(%hash)) or an object method ($iter->new(%hash)).

More interestingly, if the constructor is called as an object method and no hash entries are passed to it, Iterator::new uses the current contents of the existing Iterator object (@$class) as the set of values the new Iterator object is to iterate over. That would allow us, for example, to generate all two-entry permutations of a multientry hash:

```perl
sub permute_pairs
{
  $entry1 = Iterator->new(@_);          # iterate entire hash
  while (@entry1 = $entry1->each)
  {
    $entry2 = $entry1->new();           # iterate what's left of $entry1
    while (@entry2 = $entry2->each)
    {
      push @permutations, { @entry1, @entry2 };
    }
  }
  return @permutations
}
```

Of course, even in the case of the Iterator class, which lends itself so readily to an array implementation, nothing exists to prevent us from using a hash except efficiency considerations:

```perl
package Iterator;
$VERSION = 2.00;
use strict;

sub new
{
  my $class = shift;
  @_ = %$class if !@_ && ref($class);
  bless { @_ }, ref($class)||$class;
}

sub each
{
  my ($self) = @_;
  each %$self;
}
```

In this case we're effectively duplicating each hash we wish to iterate (in new) and then iterating it in the normal way (in each).

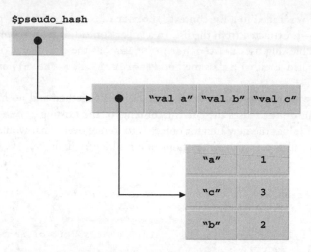

Figure 4.1   The structure of a pseudo-hash

4.2.2   Where to find out more

The constant.pm module is part of the standard Perl distribution and includes its own documentation. Autovivification is described in the perlref documentation (under "Using references") and also mentioned in perlfaq4.

4.3   BLESSING A PSEUDO-HASH

Neither a hash nor an array seems to provide the ideal basis for a Perl object. Hash entries are accessed by comprehensible keys, but hashes are big and slow. Arrays are compact and fast, but the use of integer indices can lead to obscure code. Both approaches are prone to autovivification-induced bugs. Ideally, we'd like the best of both worlds—fast access, compact storage, readable tags, and no autovivification.

4.3.1   A pseudo what???

As of Perl release 5.005, that wish has been granted in the form of a new and experimental[4] data structure called a *pseudo-hash*, which is really just an array reference pretending to be a hash reference.

To maintain the pretense, the array actually being referred to must have a reference to a real hash as its first element. That real hash is used to map key names onto array indices. In other words, a pseudo-hash has a structure like that shown in figure 4.1 and is declared like this:

```
my $pseudo_hash = [ {a=>1,b=>2,c=>3}, "val a", "val b", "val c" ];
```

---

[4]   Hence, if you're currently using a later version of Perl, you may need to check in the perlref documentation to see whether the details presented in this section are still correct.

Such an array can still be accessed as an array, by specifying a numeric index in square brackets:

```
$pseudo_hash->[1];
```

It can also be accessed as if it were a hash by using one of the specified keys in curly braces:

```
$pseudo_hash->{"a"};
```

Whenever Perl encounters an array reference being used as a hash reference in this way, it translates the expression to something equivalent to the following:

```
$pseudo_hash->[$pseudo_hash->[0]->{"a"}];
```

In other words, it first retrieves the hash reference stored in element zero of the array ($pseudo_hash->[0]). It then uses that hash to look up the index corresponding to the specified key ($pseudo_hash->[0]->**{"a"}**), and finally it uses that index to access the appropriate element in the original array (**$pseudo_hash->[**$pseudo_hash->[0]-> {"a"}**]**).

Limitations of a pseudo-hash

If the first element of a pseudo-hash array isn't a hash reference:

```
my $pseudo_hash = [ "not a hash ref", "val a", "val b", "val c" ];

# and later…

$pseudo_hash->{"a") = $newval;
```

the program throws an exception with the message: **can't coerce array into hash**. If the first element *is* a hash reference, but the corresponding hash doesn't contain the given key

```
my $pseudo_hash = [ {a=>1,b=>2,c=>3}, "val a", "val b", "val c" ];

# and later…

$pseudo_hash->{"z") = $newval;
```

the program throws an exception with the message: **no such array field**.[5] In other words, unlike a real hash, pseudo-hash entries aren't autovivifying; they don't spring into existence the first time you attempt to access them.

You *can* add new entries to a pseudo-hash, but it's a two-step procedure (see figure 4.2). First, you add a new key-to-index mapping:

```
$pseudo_hash->[0]->{"z"} = @{$pseudo_hash};
```

which maps the key "z" onto the first unused index in the pseudo-hash array. After that, you can access the new entry directly, to assign it a value:

```
$pseudo_hash->{"z"} = "value z";
```

Of course, if your stomach is strong enough, you can do those two steps in a single statement:

---

[5] The reason it refers to a field instead of an entry will become clear in a moment.

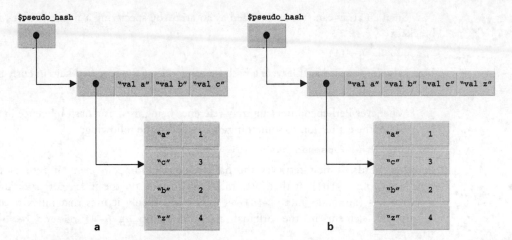

Figure 4.2   Extending a pseudo-hash
a   The pseudo-hash's mapping extended
b   The pseudo-hash's data extended

```
$pseudo_hash->[$pseudo_hash->[0]->{"z"} = @{$pseudo_hash}] = "value z";
```

4.3.2   Advantages of a pseudo-hash

The awkwardness of having to manually add new keys to a pseudo-hash is actually a useful property, because it helps to prevent hard-to-detect bugs that can easily find their way into classes built on ordinary hashes. Consider the Transceiver class defined in listing 4.2. The class provides sentinel methods (start_transmit and end_transmit, start_receive and end_receive) that may be used to ensure that transmission and reception do not overlap.

The problem is that the Transceiver::transmit method has accidentally been coded to check the status of the hash entry $self->{recieve}, instead of $self->{receive}. The first time it does so, this nonexistent entry will produce a value of undef. Hence, the un-less test will *never* fail and transmission will always be allowed, no matter what the current state of reception is.

If we implement Transceiver objects as pseudo-hashes instead:

```
package Transceiver;
use strict;

sub Transceiver::new
{
  my $class = ref($_[0])||$_[0];
  my $self = [ {receive=>1, transmit=>2} ];
  $self->{transmit} = 0;
  $self->{receive} = 0;
  bless $self, $class;
}

# etc. as before
```

Listing 4.2 A simple hash-based transceiver class

```perl
package Transceiver;
$VERSION = 1.00;
use strict;

sub new
{
   my $class = ref($_[0])||$_[0];
   my $self = { receive=>0, transmit=>0 };
   bless $self, $class;
}

sub start_transmit
{
   my ($self) = @_;
   ++$self->{transmit} unless $self->{recieve};
   return $self->{transmit};
}

sub end_transmit
{
   my ($self) = @_;
   --$self->{transmit};
}

sub start_receive
{
   my ($self) = @_;
   ++$self->{receive} unless $self->{transmit};
   return $self->{receive};
}

sub end_receive
{
   my ($self) = @_;
   --$self->{receive};
}
```

then the first time `Transceiver::transmit` is called, we get an exception indicating **No such array field...**, which will eventually lead us to the misspelled key.

4.3.3 The worst of both worlds?

That's all very useful, but when you first read that:

```perl
$pseudo_hash->{"a"};
```

is equivalent to:

```perl
$pseudo_hash->[$pseudo_hash->[0]->{"a"}];
```

you may notice a slight flaw in the pseudo-hash concept. Sure, it enables you to use an array like a hash, but to do so requires that you use a real hash *as well*. Worse still, to access a pseudo-hash entry requires both a hash lookup *and* an array lookup. So now we're using more than twice as much overhead[6]—an array + a hash + a reference—to access elements less than half as fast—an array access + a hash access + another array access. Rather than the best of both worlds, don't we have the worst?

If that were all there was to pseudo-hashes, you'd be quite correct. Fortunately, Perl provides a standard module called fields.pm that, along with some compile-time support, rescues the whole pseudo-hash concept.

4.3.4 Compile-time support for run-time performance

Like pseudo-hashes, the fields.pm module was introduced in Perl 5.005 as an experimental feature. When you import it into a class, via a use `fields` statement, you must also provide a list of the names of the object attributes (or fields) that you're going to use in that class:

```
use fields qw( field names here );
```

This procedure:

- Informs the Perl compiler that those are the only valid names that may be accessed in objects of the class.
- Creates a package hash named %FIELDS with an entry for each named field. The entries have consecutive integer values, starting at 1.
- Causes the Perl compiler to translate any pseudo-hash accesses (i.e., to any of the named fields) into direct array accesses.

For example, adding the statement

```
package Transceiver;
use strict;
use fields qw( receive  transmit );
```

does the following:

- Informs the Perl compiler that only `receive` and `transmit` are valid hash keys for Transceiver objects and enforces that constraint at compile-time by throwing an exception if access to any other key is attempted.
- Creates the hash %Transceiver::FIELDS and initializes it to (receive=>1, transmit=>2), or possibly vice versa.
- Causes the Perl compiler to identify and replace any access to a pseudo-hash of the form $transceiver_ref->{receive} with the direct array access $transceiver_ref->[1]. Likewise, $transceiver_ref->{transmit} is replaced with the direct array access $transceiver_ref->[2]

---

[6] Of course, it's only the internal overheads of storage that increase. Whether or not these increased overheads represent a significant extra cost will depend on the size of the actual data, which is only stored once.

That neatly solves the performance problem. All pseudo-hash accesses can be coded with the readability of hash accesses, but are now executed with the performance of array accesses. It also improves on the solution to misspelled attribute names, since they are now caught at compile time, rather than run time. The `%Transceiver::FIELDS` hash even makes it more efficient to implement the pseudo-hashes for `Transceiver` objects. Every `Transceiver` pseudo-hash can now use a reference to that single hash as its first element:

```
sub Transceiver::new
{
  my $class = ref($_[0])||$_[0];
  no strict "refs";
  my $fields_ref = \%{"${class}::FIELDS"};
  my $self = [ $fields_ref ];
  $self->{transmit} = 0;
  $self->{receive} = 0;
  bless $self, $class;
}
```

`Transceiver::new` has to contort a little to get the full name of the `%FIELDS` array (i.e., the array belonging to the class into which it's blessing the new object).

We could *probably* get away with saying

```
  my $fields_ref = \%FIELDS;
```

but that short cut would come back to torment us if we ever decided to inherit from Transceiver (see chapter 6).

Having set up the blessed pseudo-hash, only one question remains: *just how does Perl know at compile time that a particular variable is referring to a Transceiver object, when the variable isn't assigned a value until run time?*

4.3.5 Typed lexicals

Glad you asked. The answer is that you have to tell Perl as part of the declaration of the variable. Perl 5.005 introduced an extension to the lexical variable declaration syntax for that purpose.[7]

The new syntax has the forms:

```
my Classname $variable_name;
my Classname ($variable_name1, $variable_name2, $etc);
```

In other words, the new syntax is exactly like the regular lexical syntax, except you put a class name straight after the my. The class name can be the name of any package that Perl knows about at that point, but not one that's first mentioned later in the program.

Variables declared using this new my syntax are known as *typed lexicals*, as opposed to the usual untyped lexicals created by the standard my statement. Of course, they are not typed in the sense that variables in statically typed languages, such as C++ or Modula-3, are typed. You can still assign regular Perl strings to them, or numbers, or unblessed hash references, or

---

[7] Note, however, that there's no equivalent mechanism for package variables, not even local ones.

references to objects of other types, or anything else you like. They'd be more accurately described as classified lexicals, since the new my syntax associates them with a particular class.

Declaring a typed lexical variable, such as my `Transceiver $t`, merely informs Perl that the variable is *supposed* to be used to refer to pseudo-hash-based objects of the specified class. With that information, the compiler can watch for hash-like accesses through that variable, for example `$t->{transmit}` or `$t->{receive}`.

When it finds such an access, the compiler looks for the requested field name in the %FIELDS package hash of the same class—for example, it looks in `%Transceiver::FIELDS` for any accesses via `$t`. If the key is not present in the %FIELDS hash, the compiler immediately throws a **No such field...** exception. If the key is found, the compiler converts the pseudo-hash access to a direct array access. For example, `$t->{transmit}` is converted to `$t->[2]`.

So, if we intend to use pseudo-hashes and want compile-time checking, we need to "type" the my variables we use to refer to objects. Listing 4.3 shows the Transceiver class, modified accordingly.

Of course, all this sexy compile-time optimization and checking only occurs if you use the "typed" my syntax. If you leave out the class name, the code still works, but there's no optimization of pseudo-hash accesses, and the field name checking occurs only at run-time:

```
my Transceiver $t1 = Transceiver->new();
my $t2 = Transceiver->new();

print $t1->{receive}; # optimized and checked at compile-time
print $t2->{receive}; # unoptimized, checked at run-time
```

Hence, although using pseudo-hashes and the fields.pm module engenders a warm feeling of code reliability, that assurance depends entirely on the consistent use of typed lexicals. In other words, it's still a matter of programmer discipline. More secure approaches to attribute access control are presented in chapter 11.

4.3.6 Yet another version of CD::Music

Listing 4.4 presents still another version of the CD::Music class, this time implemented using pseudo-hashes and the fields.pm module. In keeping with the hybrid nature of the pseudo-hash, it reads like an amalgam of the hash-based and array-based solutions presented in listing 3.4 and listing 4.1 respectively.

The pseudo-hash version declares its eight fields at the beginning of the class. This implicitly sets up the `%CD::Music::FIELDS` hash with an appropriate mapping of these field names to array indices.

The constructor creates the pseudo-hash-based object by blessing an anonymous array containing only a reference to the %FIELDS hash. The actual fields of this pseudo-hash are initialized by copying either the caller pseudo-hash (if there was one) or the hash of default values. The constructor's hash-like arguments are then processed one at a time. The availability of the %FIELDS hash makes validity checking of argument tags considerably easier than in previous versions of the class.

Listing 4.3 A pseudo-hash-based transceiver class with compile-time checking

```perl
package Transceiver;
$VERSION = 2.00;
use strict;
use fields qw( transmit receive );

sub new
{
  my $class = ref($_[0])||$_[0];
  no strict "refs";
  my Transceiver $self = [ \%{"${class}::FIELDS"} ];
  $self->{transmit} = 0;
  $self->{receive} = 0;
  bless $self, $class;
}
sub start_transmit
{
  my Transceiver ($self) = @_;
  ++$self->{transmit} unless $self->{receive};
  return $self->{transmit};
}

sub end_transmit
{
  my Transceiver ($self) = @_;
  --$self->{transmit};
}

sub start_receive
{
  my Transceiver ($self) = @_;
  ++$self->{receive} unless $self->{transmit};
  return $self->{receive};
}

sub end_receive
{
  my Transceiver ($self) = @_;
  --$self->{receive};
}
```

The only other notable difference from earlier versions is that each accessor method is explicitly coded, and accesses the pseudo-hash object through a typed lexical. This allows Perl to check and optimize the accesses at compile time.

Listing 4.4   The CD::Music class implemented via pseudo-hashes

```perl
package CD::Music;
$VERSION = 1.20;
use strict;
use Carp;

use fields qw(_name _artist _publisher _ISBN _tracks _room _shelf _rating );
use vars qw( %FIELDS );

my %_default_data;
@_default_data{qw(_name _artist _publisher _ISBN _tracks _rating _room _shelf )}
    = ('???','???','???',0,'???',-1,"uncataloged","");

{
   # Private class attribute
   my $_count = 0;

   # Retrieve object count
   sub count { $_count; }

   # Private count increment/decrement methods
   sub _incr_count { ++$_count }
   sub _decr_count { --$_count }

}

# Constructor may be called as a class method or an object method

   sub new
   {
      my ($caller, %arg) = @_;
      my CD::Music $caller_is_obj = ref($caller);
      my $class = $caller_is_obj || $caller;
      my CD::Music $self = bless [\%FIELDS], $class;

      my %defs = $caller_is_obj ? %$caller_is_obj : %_default_data;
      @$self{keys %defs} = values %defs;

      my ($field,$value);
      while (($field,$value) = each %arg)
      {
       croak "Invalid argument to &CD::Music::new: $field"
         unless (exists $FIELDS{"_$field"});
       $self->{"_$field"} = $value;
      }

      $self->_incr_count();
      return $self;
   }

# Destructor adjusts class count
   sub DESTROY
   {
```

```
        $_[0]->_decr_count();
    }

# get or set room&shelf together

    sub get_location { ($_[0]->get_room(), $_[0]->get_shelf()) }

sub set_location
{
    my ($self, $room, $shelf) = @_;
    $self->set_room($room) if $room;
    $self->set_shelf($shelf) if $shelf;
    return;
}

# Implement all the other get_... and set_... methods,

sub get_name     { my CD::Music $self = $_[0]; return $self->{_name}     }
sub get_artist   { my CD::Music $self = $_[0]; return $self->{_artist}   }
sub get_publisher{ my CD::Music $self = $_[0]; return $self->{_publisher}}
sub get_ISBN     { my CD::Music $self = $_[0]; return $self->{_ISBN}     }
sub get_tracks   { my CD::Music $self = $_[0]; return $self->{_tracks}   }
sub get_room     { my CD::Music $self = $_[0]; return $self->{_room}     }
sub get_shelf    { my CD::Music $self = $_[0]; return $self->{_shelf}    }
sub get_rating   { my CD::Music $self = $_[0]; return $self->{_rating}   }

sub set_room     { my CD::Music $self = $_[0]; $self->{_room} = $_[1]    }
sub set_shelf    { my CD::Music $self = $_[0]; $self->{_shelf} = $_[1]   }
sub set_rating   { my CD::Music $self = $_[0]; $self->{_rating} = $_[1]  }

1;   # Ensure that the module can be successfully use'd
```

4.3.7 Where to find out more

Pseudo-hashes are described briefly in the perlref documentation (under *Pseudo-hashes: Using an array as a hash*). Their use as the basis for classes is also described in the documentation for the standard fields.pm module.

For other, more robust approaches to the encapsulation and existence checking of object attributes, see chapter 11.

4.4 BLESSING A SCALAR

You almost never see a Perl class based on a blessed scalar value. Although there are several good reasons for that, a scalar can occasionally prove to be the best choice for implementing an object. This section looks at two such cases.

4.4.1 Why not bless a scalar?

The main reason that a scalar so rarely forms the basis of a Perl class is that classes rarely store only a single piece of information. One of the main reasons for building a class is to bind together a set of related attribute values and provide controlled access to them. If the data is really only a single datum, then building an object-oriented shell around it usually seems like serious overkill.

In Perl, we can't even use the excuse that data ought to be encapsulated, since Perl's encapsulation is almost entirely voluntary. If we have blessed a scalar and are passing around a reference to it (as $sref), there's absolutely nothing to prevent any part of the program from ignoring the lovely controlled object-oriented interface we provided and manipulating the underlying scalar directly:

```
$$sref = undef;     # Bwah-ha-ha-ha!!!
```

What's more, in those few cases where an object *does* possess a single value, it's just as easy to go with a more familiar hash-based implementation, using only a single entry. Allocating an entire hash to store a single value may be considerably less efficient, both in terms of memory usage and access speed, but it has the advantages of:

- *Familiarity to the implementer.* The selection of a hash as the underlying object representation is often the automatic choice and, frequently, not even a conscious one.
- *Familiarity to others.* A better reason for choosing a hash when a scalar would suffice is that the hash-based implementation is also likely to be far more familiar to anyone else attempting to understand or modify the code.
- *Readability.* If nothing else, storing the single value as a hash entry means that the value has to be given a meaningful key, which ought to improve the code's readability.
- *Extensibility in subclasses.* As we shall see in the next chapter, a class cannot usually assume that an internal representation sufficient to its own needs will serve derived classes equally well.

4.4.2 An object-oriented password

Despite all those factors against the practice, there's nothing immoral or illegal about blessing a scalar. In most cases, it's even slimming.[8] For example, listing 4.5 illustrates the simple case of a class that implements an encrypted password as a single scalar string.

The only tricky part about using scalars as objects is creating one in the first place. Unlike arrays and hashes, scalars are not provided with a special syntax for creating anonymous instances. There's no scalar syntax corresponding to [...], which creates anonymous arrays, or to {...}, which creates anonymous hashes. Instead, we have to hijack a lexical variable, for example, $pw in the Password constructor.

The constructor takes a text string as its argument, randomly creates a salt value,[9] encrypts the string with a call to the built-in crypt function, assigns the encrypted version to a lexical variable $pw, and blesses $pw into the class.

The important point to understand is that, even though $pw is a lexical, it does not cease to exist at the end of the call to Password::new. That's because bless returns a reference to $pw, and that reference is then returned as the result of new.

---

[8] "Reads faster, less memory!"

[9] The crypt function implements a family of related one-way encryption schemes. The actual scheme crypt uses is determined by a two-character "salt" string passed as its second argument.

Listing 4.5   A scalar-based password class

```
package Password;
$VERSION = 1.00;
use strict;

my @salt = ("A".."Z","a".."z","0".."9","/",".");

sub new
{
  my ($class, $cleartext) = @_;
  my $salt = $salt[rand @salt].$salt[rand @salt];
  my $pw = crypt($cleartext,$salt);
  return bless \$pw, ref($class)||$class;
}

sub verify
{
  my ($self, $candidate) = @_;
  my $salt = substr($$self,0,2);
  return crypt($candidate,$salt) eq $$self;
}
```

Assuming the reference is immediately assigned to a variable in some outer scope

```
my $password = Password->new("fermat");
```

then the number of live references to the scalar remains greater than zero, and the blessed lexical scalar escapes destruction at the end of the scope in which it was declared.

The verify method is equally straightforward. It encrypts the candidate string and compares the result to the password string (i.e., to the invoking object itself). This process takes advantage of the fact that the first two letters of a crypt'ed string are identical to the salt with which the original call to crypt was seasoned.

Accessing the object's data is slightly different when the object is a scalar. We can't use the arrow notation to access an entry or an element as we do with references to hashes or arrays. With a scalar-based object, we need to explicitly dereference the scalar reference. Thus, the single value stored in the object referred to by $self is always accessed as $$self.

The class could be used like so:

```
use Password;

print "Enter password: ";
my $password = Password->new(scalar <>);

# and later…

while (<>)
{
  last if $password->verify($_);
  print "Sorry. Try again: ";
}
```

Listing 4.6 A scalar-based Password package

```perl
package NonOO::Password;
$VERSION = 1.00;
use strict;

my @salt = ("A".."Z","a".."z","0".."9","/",".");

sub new
{
 my ($cleartext) = @_;
 my $salt = $salt[rand @salt].$salt[rand @salt];
 my $pw = crypt($cleartext,$salt);
 return $pw;
}

sub verify
{
 my ($password, $candidate) = @_;
 my $salt = substr($password,0,2);
 return crypt($candidate,$salt) eq $password;
}
```

It could reasonably be argued that the use of object orientation in this implementation is needlessly ostentatious. However, good software engineering practice suggests that the mechanics of password creation and verification *should* be encapsulated in subroutines. Suppose, for example, that we later decide that the crypt algorithm is insufficiently secure and that MD5 or PGP or SHA must be used instead? Clearly, we don't want raw calls to crypt spread throughout the code to be hunted down and changed one at a time.

It is interesting to reflect that the code required to package password creation and verification routines in a non-object-oriented manner (see listing 4.6) is almost indistinguishable from the object-oriented version. Often, the decision to package simple functionality like this, as either a class or as a set of distinct subroutines, will be based on cultural considerations or personal preferences. In particular, if the rest of the system is object-oriented, then the password verification component ought to be as well, even if the purists on either side sneer.

4.4.3 A bit-string class

Occasionally, objects of a class need to store multiple data, but a scalar implementation is *still* the best choice. Consider the Bit::String class shown in listing 4.7.

Bit sets are optimally stored at a density of 1 byte per 8 bits. In comparison, an array implementation of a bit set is appallingly wasteful at 4 bytes or more per bit. The solution is to pack the bits away into a character string using Perl's built-in pack and vec functions. As the name suggests, the pack function loads an array of values tightly into a single multibyte string. The vec function can then be used to treat such a string as a vector of unsigned integers, each of a certain width. By setting that width to 1, the individual bits of consecutive bytes of a string can be directly addressed.

Listing 4.7 A simple bit-string class

```perl
package Bit::String;
$VERSION = 1.00;
use strict;

sub new
{
  my $class = ref($_[0])||$_[0];
  my $initbits = join '', map {$_?1:0} @_[1..$#_];
  my $bs = pack 'b*', $initbits;
  bless \$bs, $class;
}

sub get
{
  my ($self, $bitnum) = @_;
  return vec($$self,$bitnum,1);
}

sub set
{
  my ($self, $bitnum, $newval) = @_;
  vec($$self,$bitnum,1) = $newval?1:0;
}

sub bitcount
{
  8 * length ${$_[0]};
}

sub complement
{
  my ($self) = @_;
  my $complement = ~$$self;
  bless \$complement, ref($self);
}

sub print_me
{
  my ($self) = @_;
  for (my $i=0; $i < $self->bitcount(); $i++)
  {
    print $self->get($i);
    print ' ' unless ($i+1)%8;
    print "\n" unless ($i+1)%64;
  }
  print "\n";
}
```

The constructor for the Bit::String class builds a bit-string in a lexical scalar ($bs), by mapping its arguments onto a list of 1's and 0's (i.e., map {$_?1:0} @_[1..$#_]). It then joins those binary values into a single string ($initbits) and, finally, packs that string into the bits of the scalar string $bs. That packed string is blessed as the Bit::String object, and a reference to it returned from the constructor.

For example, suppose we create a Bit::String like this:

```
my $is_lucky = Bit::String->new(0,"yes",0,1,undef,'',"0","lucky 7","",0);
```

The map operation will convert this haphazard series of arguments into the standardized list of Boolean values (0,1,0,1,0,0,0,1,0,0). The join converts this to a single string: "0101000100", which pack finally reduces to two bytes: "\212\000".[10]

Once the bit-string is packed and blessed, both accessor methods use the vec function to access the individual bits. As with the Password objects discussed in the previous section, the value of scalar bit-string is retrieved by directly dereferencing the object reference in $self—that is, accessing $$self—rather than via the arrow operator.

The Bit::String::get method passes this dereferenced value to vec, along with the requested bit number, and a third argument of 1, indicating that the bit-string is to be interpreted as a series of one-bit values. The result vec returns is the value of the corresponding bit, zero-padded out to the native integer format. It's also important to remember (and document) that bit indices start at zero:

```
print $is_lucky->get(12);       # Is the number 13 lucky?
```

Bit::String::set converts the value it is given to a standardized bit value (1 or 0) and assigns that value to the appropriate bit within the string:[11]

```
$is_lucky->set(6,0);            # Make 7 unlucky
```

The conversion of values to a standard 1-or-0 format is critical, since the call to vec examines only the lowest bit of the numeric value assigned to it.[12] That means that true values that are even (2, "2", etc.) are treated as a zero bit. Worse still, true values that are nonnumeric, such as true, add insult to injury by producing an **Argument "true" isn't numeric...** warning[13] before defaulting to zero.

Using the vec function to control bit-level access into the bit-string is not only highly efficient, it's extremely robust. In particular, if we attempt to access a bit that's outside the range of bits stored in the string—that is, a bit index greater than $self->bitcount()-1— vec will automatically grow the string to the required length, padding each new byte with

---

[10] You may have noticed that the octal value 212 actually corresponds to the sequence of bits 010001010, which is the reverse of the original sequence. That's because pack 'b*' packs individual bytes "most-significant-bit-first" (i.e., right-to-left), but packs successive bytes like characters of a string (i.e., left-to-right). Fortunately, this odd packing scheme is exactly what the vec function expects, so, in the best traditions of object-orientation, we can completely ignore the idiosyncrasies of this internal representation, as long as we use the standard interface (i.e., vec).

[11] The vec function is magical in the same way as the more familiar substr. Assignments to a call to vec actually change part of the original string passed to vec.

[12] In general, an assignment vec($str, $elemnum, $bitwidth) = $value converts $value to a numeric value and then assigns the bottom $bitwidth bits of that value to the appropriate place in $str.

[13] Unless, of course, you elected to fly blind and didn't use the -w flag.

zeroes. This useful behavior works both on read accesses and assignments, and substantially decreases the complexity of the Bit::String accessor functions.

The `Bit::String::bitcount` method again dereferences the object reference through which it is invoked. Note the use of curly braces in this case, since an unbracketed `$$_[0]` would be misinterpreted as `($$_)[0]`, which certainly isn't the object referred to by the first argument. The bit count is easy to compute, since each character in the bit-string holds 8 bits.

The `Bit::String::print_me` method is useful for debugging. It prints out the entire bit-string, with bits grouped in eight 8-bit bytes per line. In good object-oriented style, it reuses the public interface of the class, thereby isolating itself from any subsequent changes in implementation. Such I/O methods are usually good candidates for the insulated approach, since their execution is typically constrained by the performance to the I/O pipeline, which swamps the extra cost of the additional method calls.

The Bit::String class also provides a method for generating the complement of a bit-string, which is returned as a separate Bit::String object. The `Bit::String::complement` method takes advantage of the smart semantics of Perl's complement operator (~), which performs a bit-wise complement on each byte when applied to a character string.

The scalar Bit::String object created by `Bit::String::complement` is obtained by declaring a lexical scalar variable, `$complement`, within the scope of the method. Because the `complement` method returns a blessed Bit::String object, we can chain method calls as follows:

```
print "$n is unlucky\n" if $is_lucky->complement()->get($n);
```

This works because -> is a left-associative binary operator, so the `if` condition is equivalent to

```
( $is_lucky->complement() )->get($n)
```

Since `Bit::String::complement` returns reference to a Bit::String object, that return value can in turn have any Bit::String method called through it. In contrast, using Perl's complement operator directly

```
my $isnt_lucky = ~$$is_lucky;
print $isnt_lucky->get(7);
```

doesn't work, and complains: **Can't call method "get" on unblessed reference**.... In this case, even though the scalar referred to by `$isnt_lucky` contains a string with the right bit pattern, that scalar hasn't been blessed into the Bit::String class.

Of course, it's not unreasonable to expect to be able to apply the complement operator directly to a Bit::String object. In fact, we'd like to be able to apply all the bit-wise operators directly to the Bit::String references, like so:

```
my $is_prime = Bit::String->new(2,3,5,7,11);
my $isnt_lucky = ~$is_lucky;
my $unlucky_prime = $isnt_lucky & $is_prime;
my $unlucky_composite = ~($is_prime | $is_lucky);
```

Chapter 10 explains exactly how to achieve this.

4.4.4 Where to find out more

The `crypt`, `pack`, and `vec` functions are all described in the perlfunc documentation.

For more information on various one-way encryption schemes such as `crypt`, MD5, PGP and SHA (also known in cryptography circles as message digests or hashes) see http://dir.yahoo.com/Computers_And_Internet/Security_And_Encryption/Cryptography/.

4.5 SUMMARY

- Hashes are the usual basis of objects. When in doubt, use a hash.
- Arrays generally provide better access speed. Use constants to give attributes logical names.
- Arrays may also be a better choice if the objects being implemented have a fundamentally listlike structure or function.
- Pseudo-hashes provide the convenience of hash-like access with the performance of array-like access, but only if we use typed lexicals to access them.
- Occasionally, an object may be most efficiently implemented as a blessed scalar.

CHAPTER 5

Blessing other things

Although they're the usual choice, variables—hashes, arrays, and scalars—aren't the only things that can be used as the basis of objects in Perl. In this chapter, we'll see how to build objects from things as improbable as regular expressions, anonymous subroutines, and raw symbol table entries.

5.1 BLESSING A REGULAR EXPRESSION

Perl 5.005 introduced a new mechanism that enables precompiled regular expressions to be created. These regular expressions are just as blessable as any other Perl data type and can be used to give Perl's powerful pattern matching features an object-oriented slant.

5.1.1 The qr operator

One of the most useful features of Perl regular expressions is that, like double-quoted strings, they're interpolated at run time. This means that it's possible to set up loops like this:

```
@patterns = (
            '(\w*(cat))',
            '(\w*(dog))',
            '(\w*(fish))',
          );
```

```
while (<>)                                  # Get a word...
{
   foreach $pattern ( @patterns )           # Then try each pattern...
   {
         if (/$pattern/)                     # If it matches...
         {
            print "a $1 is a kind of $2\n";  # Say so...
            last;                            # ...and go on to next word
         }
   }
}
```

In the inner loop, each pattern string in @patterns gets sequentially converted into a regular expression and matched against the current input line. When a large number of patterns is involved, this approach is a definite win in maintainability, since the actual matching code is kept small no matter how many patterns are eventually added to the @patterns array.

But the price for this ease of maintenance is high. Every time round the foreach loop, the current value of $pattern is reinterpolated into the regular expression. So, for every iteration, the current contents of $pattern has to be re-parsed to determine the components of the regular expression, re-checked to ensure that the regular expression is valid, and re-converted into Perl's internal "table-driven" representation for regular expressions.

That takes time, and makes the loop much slower than if a separate match for each pattern had been separately coded:

```
while (<>)
{
   /(\w*(cat))/  and print "a $1 is a kind of $2\n" and next;
   /(\w*(dog))/  and print "a $1 is a kind of $2\n" and next;
   /(\w*(fish))/ and print "a $1 is a kind of $2\n" and next;
}
```

In this hard-coded version, each pattern would only be parsed, checked, and converted once—at compile time—no matter how many times each match is attempted. That makes it about six times faster than the version with interpolated patterns.

There are clever tricks that allow a table of patterns to be matched efficiently, but as of Perl 5.005, it's possible to have the convenience of the interpolated solution with (almost) the speed of the hard-coded alternative. The feature that makes this possible is a new quote-like operator: qr.

Just as the qq{...} operator converts its single argument into an interpolated string literal, so the qr{...} operator takes its single argument and converts it into a Perl regular expression. That is, qr{...} acts like just the initial stages of an m{...} matching operator, in that it *compiles* a regular expression, but doesn't actually *match* it against anything.

Instead, it returns a reference to the compiled regular expression. So a statement like:

```
$rxref = qr{[A-Za-z_][A-Za-z0-9_]*};
```

causes $rxref to contain a reference to a regular expression that will match any Perl identifier. The reference in $rxref can then be interpolated into pattern matches and substitutions just like a string, except that when it is interpolated, the regular expression doesn't need to be reparsed, rechecked, or recompiled:

```
$pattern_string = qq{[A-Za-z_]\w*}; # Make a pattern string
$regex_reference= qr{[A-Za-z_]\w*}; # Make a regex reference

$str =~ m/$pattern_string/;# Interpolate string, recompile regex, then match
$str =~ m/$regex_reference/;# Interpolate precompiled regex, then match
```

That means we could rewrite the earlier example like this:

```
@regexes = (
                qr /(\w*(cat))/,  # Note: as with q or qq,
                qr {(\w*(dog))},  # you can use any
                qr |(\w*(fish))|, # delimiters for qr
                );

while (<>)
{
   foreach $regex ( @regexes )
   {
      /$regex/ and print "a $1 is a kind of $2\n" and last;
   }
}
```

This version is nearly 70 percent as fast as the hard-coded one, but much easier to maintain for large numbers of regular expressions.

5.1.2 Why an object-oriented regular expression class?

At first glance, there would seem to be little justification for wrapping the wolf of regular expressions in the sheep's clothing of a class. Pattern matching is such an integral part of Perl, it seems odd to want to encapsulate and abstract it.

The obvious response is that, although regular expressions are at the heart of Perl's charm, they are also largely responsible for its reputation as a language built from line-noise. The combination of the terse and symbol-ridden syntax for patterns, the standard choice of /.../ delimiters, and the unfamiliarity of the =~ and !~ operators, can make a raw pattern match look obscure. Much can be said for replacing something that looks like comic-book profanity:[1]

```
($tmp=$@)=~s/,(.*),//s and $_.="$tmp:$1" for (@_);
```

with a more readable object-oriented syntax:

```
use English;
use Regexp;

my $middle = Regexp->new(',(.*),',SINGLE_LINE);
foreach (@ARGS)
{
   $middle->substitute($tmp=$EVAL_ERROR,"") and
      $ARG .= "$tmp:".$middle->backref(1);
}
```

---

[1] It actually says: *for each element of the current subroutine's argument list, take a copy of the last error message, locate anything between two commas, and, if something suitable is found, move the bit between the commas to the end of the copy of the error message and append the result to the original argument.*

Sure it's longer to type, but it's also much less cryptic to read. And good code is always read *far* more frequently than it's written.

The Regexp module actually exists; you can download it from the CPAN. It provides just such an object-oriented interface to Perl regular expressions, although, as of release 0.004, the Regexp module doesn't provide a `Regexp::substitute` method like the one used above.

Fortunately, that's no real problem in object-oriented Perl, since we can easily install one ourselves:

```perl
package Regexp;        # Reopen the class...

sub substitute        # ...and add in a substitute method
{
   my ($self, $string, $substitution) = @_;
   $self->match($string) or return;
   $_[1] = $self->prematch . $substitution . $self->postmatch;
   return $_[1];
}
```

The new method returns `undef` or an empty list if the substitution fails. Otherwise, it replaces the matched substring of the original string with the specified substitution text. The newly added member is careful to respect the public interface of the Regexp class and doesn't try to access the `$self` object's private attributes directly. That way, when version 0.005 of the Regexp module appears, `Regexp::substitute` will still work.[2]

A slight variation on the theme could also provide the standard /g global substitution behavior:

```perl
sub Regexp::substitute_all
{
   my ($self, $string, $substitution) = @_;
   $self->match($string) or return;
   my $newstring = "";
   while ($self->match($string))
   {
      $newstring .= $self->prematch . $substitution;
      $string = $self->postmatch;
      last unless $string;
   }
   return $_[1] = $newstring . $string;
}
```

5.1.3 Designing a different regular expressions mechanism

Whether or not you're convinced by the maintenance advantages of an object-oriented syntax for pattern matching, a much better reason exists for creating an object-oriented regular expression class: who says that such a class must have the same semantics as Perl's built-in operations?

---

[2] Provided, of course, that Nick, Ilya, and Graham (who wrote the Regex module) play by the rules and don't change its public interface!

The design of Perl's pattern matching semantics makes certain tradeoffs and compromises that make some things easy to do with regular expressions and other things more difficult. The design of a regular expression class could easily incorporate different choices and provide a different feature set.

For example, standard Perl pattern matching has the following features and tradeoffs:

- Matches and substitutions are operations;
- Substitutions change the contents of the variable being substituted (so it's more complicated to create a substituted string without changing the original);
- Substrings that match parenthesized subpatterns are returned in the read-only variables: $1, $2, etc;
- Substrings that match the full pattern and its preceding and following text are also returned in variables: $&, $`, and $';
- Indices of the substring that matched the full pattern are difficult to obtain—the start of the matching substring of $string is at index length($`); the end is at index pos($string)-1 or length($`.$&)-1).

Listing 5.1 shows a class that changes every one of these behaviors. The AltRegex class is based on a blessed regular expression, and its methods return references to objects of another class, AltRegex::Match (see listing 5.2).

Using the AltRegex class:

- Matches and substitutions are now method calls;
- Substitutions do not affect the contents of the variable being substituted;
- Substrings that match parenthesized subpatterns are returned as attributes of an AltRegex::Match object;
- Substrings that match the full pattern and its preceding and following text are also returned as attributes of a AltRegex::Match;
- Indices of the substring that matched the full pattern are easily obtained via method calls.

This is a different approach to pattern matching. For example, the line-noise example

```
($tmp=$@)=~s/,(.*),//s and $_="$tmp:$1" for (@_);
```

would now be implemented as

```
use English;
use AltRegex;

my $middle = AltRegex->new(',(.*),');
foreach (@ARGS)
{
  $match = $middle->substitute($EVAL_ERROR) and
     $ARG .= $match->result.":".$middle->subpatterns(0);
}
```

There's now no need for a temporary variable to shield $EVAL_ERROR from the effects of the substitution.

Listing 5.1 A regular expression class with alternative semantics

```perl
package AltRegex;
$VERSION = 1.00;
use strict;
use AltRegex::Match;

sub new
{
   my ($class, $pattern) = @_;
   eval { bless qr/$pattern/, ref($class)||$class };
}

sub match
{
   my ($self, $str) = @_;
   my @subpatterns = ($str =~ $self) or return;
   return AltRegex::Match->new(@subpatterns,$`,$&,$',$str);
}

sub substitute
{
   my ($self, $str, $subs) = @_;
   my @subpatterns = ($str =~ $self) or return;
   $str =~ s/$self/$subs/;
   return AltRegex::Match->new(@subpatterns,$`,$&,$',$str);
}

sub substitute_all
{
   my ($self, $str, $subs) = @_;
   $str =~ s/$self/$subs/g;
   return AltRegex::Match->new($`,$&,$',$str);
}
```

Better still, because each AltRegex object is just a blessed qr/.../ regular expression, such objects can still be used with standard Perl pattern matching semantics. For example

```perl
my $regex = AltRegex->new("cie");

$corrected = $regex->substitute($original, "cei")->result; # new semantics

($corrected = $original) =~ s/$regex/cei/;                  # old semantics
```

5.1.4 A closer look at the two classes

Using the qr operator, the AltRegex constructor converts the pattern passed to it into a pre-compiled regular expression. That regular expression is immediately blessed as an object of the class, and a reference to it is returned. The eval around bless is necessary because the string passed to the constructor might not be a valid Perl pattern. In that case, the qr operator

Listing 5.2   The AltRegex::Match helper class

```
package AltRegex::Match;
$VERSION = 1.00;
use strict;

sub new
{
  my $class = shift;
  my ($pre, $match, $post, $result) = splice @_, -4;
  bless {   _result        => $result,
            _match         => $match,
            _pre           => $pre,
            _post          => $post,
            _subpatterns   => [@_],
          }, ref($class)||$class;
}
sub result{ return $_[0]->{_result}}
sub match { return $_[0]->{_match}}
sub prematch{ return $_[0]->{_pre}}
sub postmatch{ return $_[0]->{_post}}

sub from
{
  my ($self) = @_;
  $self->{_from} = length($_[0]->{_pre})
    unless defined $self->{_from};
  return $self->{_from}
}

sub to
{
  my ($self) = @_;
  $self->{_to} = $self->from + length($self->{_match}) - 1
    unless defined $self->{_to};
  return $self->{_to}
}

sub subpatterns
{
  my ($self, $index) = @_;
  return $self->{_subpatterns}[$index] if defined $index;
  return @{$self->{_subpatterns}};
}
```

throws an exception. The eval catches that exception and converts it to a (less aggressive) undef, which is the normal return value used to indicate a constructor has failed. We can then test for success like this:

```
my $regex;
print "Enter a pattern: ";
print "Try again: " until $regex = AltRegex->new(scalar <>);
```

The remaining methods of the class implement the standard operations on a regular expression: matching, single substitution, and multiple substitution. The single substitution method captures the set of bracketed subpatterns ($1, $2, etc.), which the normal Perl s/// operator does not.

For each matching operation, if the operation fails, undef is immediately returned. If the operation succeeds, information derived from the match is packed into an AltRegex::Match object and returned.

The AltRegex::Match class collects information provided to it inside a standard hash-based object. That information is then available through the methods of the class. Classes like AltRegex::Match are often called *helper classes* because they exist solely to support the operations of another class. The AltRegex:: prefix provides a handy hint about the subordinate status of the class, as well as a useful way of conserving namespace.

The AltRegex::Match::from and AltRegex::Match::to methods are interesting to consider. They are examples of what is known as a *memoized computed attribute*. When an AltRegex::Match object is initially constructed, it doesn't store explicit values for these two attributes. Their values are computed only if they are requested, via a call to the corresponding method. However, once computed, they are subsequently stored—or *memoized*—in the object, so that the computation need never be repeated.

It's also worth noting that deferring the computation of such values until they are needed and then storing them may not actually result in better performance. In fact, deferring the computation is only a win if there's a good chance the attribute will *never* be accessed. Likewise, memoizing the computed value only makes sense if the cost of computation is greater than the cost of checking whether the value is already known.

The implementation of the AltRegex::Match::subpatterns method is also instructive. If the method is called with an argument, it returns just the text that matched the specified subpattern:

```
print $regex->match($string)->subpatterns(0);     # just print $1
```

In other words, it takes the role of $1, $2, etc., except that the indices start at zero. On the other hand, when the method is called without any arguments, it returns the complete list of all the parenthesized subpatterns from the match it represents:

```
$match = $regex->match($string);
foreach $subpattern ($match->subpatterns)
{
   print "matched ($subpattern)\n";
}
```

Whether this overloading of functionality is considered elegant or obscure is largely be a matter of personal taste. The alternative is to provide separate methods for each task perhaps get_subpattern and get_all_subpatterns.

The obvious choices for naming these two methods—subpattern and subpatterns— are not appropriate, as it is inevitable that some clever person will immediately go and write

```
$match = $regex->match($string);
print "matched ($_)\n"
    foreach ($match->subpattern);
```

and, for want of a single letter, will miss most of the data. That's because the call to $match->subpattern is equivalent to $match->subpattern(undef), and the undef is silently converted to zero when used as an array index inside subpattern. Consequently only the first matched substring is returned.

5.1.5 On the separation of Search and State

The class-plus-helper approach provides a uniform interface to all matching operations and a clean separation between the matching processes and the results of those processes. Notice how small and focussed each class is. That makes them easier to build, debug, and maintain.

For example, the separation means that we could add extra matching methods to Alt-Regex (say, AltRegex::conditional_match or AltRegex::substitute_last), without affecting the retrieval of matching information from AltRegex::Match. Likewise, if we wished to provide AltRegex::Match with additional methods for retrieving matching information (for example, AltRegex::Match::pre_and_post or AltRegex::Match::match_len), there would be no need to alter the matching mechanisms in AltRegex.

More importantly, the separation of *process* (AltRegex) and *result* (AltRegex::Match) means that, when either is modified, the amount of client code that also needs to be changed is kept to a minimum.

5.1.6 Where to find out more

You can read about the new qr operator in the standard perlop documentation (under *Quote and Quote-like Operators*).

Helper classes are described in most good texts on object-oriented programming techniques (*Design Patterns* or *Object-Oriented Software Design*, for example).

For a deeper discussion of many aspects of pattern matching see *Mastering Regular Expressions* by Jeffrey Friedl.

5.2 BLESSING A SUBROUTINE

Using a subroutine as an object may seem contradictory or, at best, arcane. Surely, the subroutine is the natural enemy of the object? A subroutine isn't even a thing in the usual sense. It's certainly not data like a hash, or an array, or even a precompiled regular expression.

5.2.1 So, how can a subroutine be an object?

It's easiest to see how we can treat a subroutine like an object by considering an example. Take the hash iterator class described in chapter 4. Here's a version pared to its essentials:

```
package Iterator;
$VERSION = 2.01;
use strict;
```

```
sub new
{
  my ($class, %data) = @_;              # get class name and copy hash
  my $hashref = \%data;                 # get reference to copy of hash
  bless $hashref, ref($class)||$class;  # Bless the copy
}

sub each
{
  my ($self) = @_;
  each %$self;                          # Iterate the copy
}
```

In this simplifed version, the constructor builds an anonymous hash containing a copy of the original hash's data and blesses that anonymous hash as the new Iterator object. Then the `Iterator::each` method provides a means to iterate through the blessed hash.

Now, let's turn the Iterator class inside-out:

```
package Iterator;
$VERSION = 3.00;
use strict;

sub new
{
  my ($class, %data) = @_;              # get class name and copy hash
  my $subref = sub { each %data };      # Wrap a sub around the copy
  bless $subref, ref($class)||$class;   # Bless the sub
}

sub each
{
  my ($self) = @_;
  $self->();                            # Call the sub
}
```

In the new version, the constructor still builds a lexical copy, `%data`, of the original hash's data, but now it creates an anonymous subroutine that can iterate through that lexical hash. It is this subroutine, not the data itself, that is blessed to become the Iterator object. Now, when `Iterator::each` needs to iterate the data, it merely calls the anonymous subroutine. This works because the anonymous subroutine is a closure and has ongoing access to any lexical variables, such as `%data`, that existed when the subroutine was created.

Both versions of the Iterator class provide the same functionality through the same interface.[3] The only difference is that, in the second version, the object is a subroutine with access to the data, rather than a copy of the data itself.

And *that's* why a subroutine can be an object—because an object *isn't* data, it's something that provides *access to data*. Normally, we use a hash or an array as an object and that access is provided by the `->{...}` or `->[...]` syntax. But, in Perl, subroutines can also provide access

---

[3] That's the whole point of the object-oriented approach.

to data; specifically, to any lexical that was in scope when the subroutine was created. Therefore, subroutines can be used as objects.

5.2.2 Why objectify a subroutine?

Okay, so a subroutine can act like an object. Why would we ever bother with something so obscure? To answer that entirely reasonable question, let's consider a larger and more realistic example.

Suppose we wished to build a class to represent the *lexical analyzer* (or *lexer*) in an input parsing system. A lexical analyzer is normally just a subroutine that takes an input string and breaks it up into a sequence of *tokens*. A token is simply a substring of the original input with an associated label indicating what role it plays in the string. For example, given the string `"That which does not kill us, makes us stronger"`, a lexer might return the following list:

```
(
    "That"     =>    DEM_PRONOUN,
    "which"    =>    REL_PRONOUN,
    "does"     =>    AUXILIARY_VERB,
    "not"      =>    NEGATION,
    "kill"     =>    VERB,
    "us"       =>    PERS_PRONOUN,
    ","        =>    COMMA,
    "makes"    =>    VERB,
    "us"       =>    PERS_PRONOUN,
    "stronger" =>    ADJECTIVE,
)
```

In other words, a lexer breaks up some input text and identifies the parts, so that they can be interpreted by a program. Another typical use of a lexer would be in identifying which parts of an HTML document are content, and which are mark-up tags.

In some situations, it may be useful, or necessary, to provide a number of distinct lexers for the same parser. For example, a compiler like gcc, which handles several different languages, may need to label the parts of a program differently depending on which language is used. For instance: `"class"` is a reserved word in C++, part of a compiler directive in Objective C, and an ordinary identifier in C, and gcc has to deal with all three cases correctly. The easiest way to do so is to provide separate lexers for each language and select the correct one for the particular source code.

In such cases, turning each lexer into an object is a good idea because, instead of passing numerous subroutine references about, we can pass objects instead. This is good psychology, since most programmers will find objects far more familiar and comprehensible than references to anonymous subroutines.

More importantly, turning a lexing subroutine into an object enables us to provide a range of ways to call that subroutine (i.e., different methods of the object). For example, at different points in the parsing process the lexer may be asked to

• Determine the next single token in the input string, remove it from that string, and return it (*token extraction*);

- Determine the next single token in the input string, and return it *without* removing it from the input string (*look ahead*);
- Extract successive tokens from the input string and throw them away, until a certain token is encountered (*resynchronization*);
- Extract the next line of text from the input string, split it into a list of tokens, and return all of them at once (*line tokenization*);
- Split the entire input string into a list of tokens and return all of them at once (*full tokenization*).

An object-oriented lexer could provide a separate method corresponding to each of these tasks.

5.2.3 A lexer object

Listing 5.3 shows a Lexer class built along the lines described above.

Listing 5.3 An object-oriented lexer class

```
package Lexer;
$VERSION = 1.00;
use strict;
use Carp;

sub new
{
  my ($class, @token_defs) = @_;
  my $code = '';
  while (my ($pattern, $token) = splice @token_defs, 0, 2 )
    {
      $code .= '$_[0] =~ s/\A\s*?('.$pattern.')// ';
      $code .= ' and return ("$1", '.'"'$token');\n";
    }
  $code .= '$_[0] =~ s/\A\s*(\S)// and return ("$1",""); ';
  $code .= 'return;';

  my $sub = eval "sub { $code }" or _croak_cleanly($@);
  bless $sub, ref($class)||$class;
}

sub _croak_cleanly
{
  $_[0] =~ m{/\\A\\s\*\((.*)\)/(.*) at .*}s;
  croak "/$1/$2";
}

sub extract_next
{
  $_[0]->($_[1]);
}

sub lookahead
```

```
{
  my ($self, $str) = @_;
  my @next = $self->($str);
  return wantarray ? @next : $next[0];
}


sub extract_to
{
  my ($self) = @_;
  my @tokens = ();
  while (my @token_and_type = $self->($_[1]))
  {
    push @tokens, @token_and_type;
    last if defined($_[2]) && $token_and_type[1] eq $_[2];
  }
  return @tokens;
}

sub resync_after
{
  $_[0]->extract_to($_[1], $_[2]);
  return;
}

sub extract_all
{
  $_[0]->extract_to($_[1],undef);
}
```

The constructor takes a list of alternating patterns and token types, all specified as strings, and builds a string ($code) containing Perl statements. These statements define an anonymous subroutine that uses those tokens to parse input.

For example, if a Lexer object was created like this:

```
my $lexer = Lexer->new ( '\n'          => 'NL',
                         '\d+'         => 'DIGITS',
                         '\w+'         => 'WORD',
                         ';'           => 'SEMICOLON',
                         '[^\d\w]+'    => 'OTHER',
                       );
```

then the constructor would assemble the following string in $code:

```
'sub
{
  $_[0] =~ s/\A\s*?(\n)//        and return ("$1", 'NL');
  $_[0] =~ s/\A\s*?(\d+)//       and return ("$1", 'DIGITS');
  $_[0] =~ s/\A\s*?(\w+)//       and return ("$1", 'WORD');
  $_[0] =~ s/\A\s*?(;)//         and return ("$1", 'SEMICOLON');
  $_[0] =~ s/\A\s*?([^\d\w]+)//  and return ("$1", 'OTHER');

  $_[0] =~ s/\A\s*(\S)//         and return ("$1", "");  #default case
```

```
   return;
 }'
```

which is close to what you might write yourself if you were building the lexer by hand.

Each of the patterns has the smallest possible amount of leading white space removed during matching (`\A\s*?`...), so it's still possible to specify tokens that explicitly match white space characters. If a pattern matches, the matching text is returned, along with a string indicating which token succeeded.

The default case in the second last line is added automatically. It matches any single non-space character if no other token seems appropriate. The final `return` is there to catch the special case where the string is empty.

Having built this code text, the constructor `eval`'s it into a real live Perl subroutine. If the `eval` fails, it must be because one of the patterns is invalid. In that case the constructor calls the utility subroutine `Lexer::_croak_cleanly`, which tidies up the error message in `$@` before throwing an exception.

If all patterns *are* valid, the `eval` will succeed, and `$sub` will contain a reference to an anonymous lexing subroutine like the one shown above. The constructor then takes this subroutine and blesses it, thereby making it a Lexer object.

The remaining methods of the class use the subroutine object (i.e., `$self`) to implement the different lexing behaviors described in the previous section. The simplest behavior is to extract the next token from a given string. `Lexer::extract_next` implements this behavior by calling the blessed subroutine with the argument it is given. Therefore, a call to

```
($token, $type) = $lexer->extract_next($data);
```

invokes the lexing subroutine on the string `$data`, to extract the next token and return it (and its type). If the subroutine fails to find a matching token in the data, it returns an empty array, so the code can also be used in a loop:

```
while ( ($token, $type) = $lexer->extract_next($data) )
{
   # Do something with $token according to its $type
}
```

The `Lexer::lookahead` method also invokes the blessed subroutine, but passes it a temporary copy of the input string, instead of the string itself. This means that the next token is extracted from the copy, and so the original input string is unchanged:

```
if ( ($lexer->lookahead($data))[1] eq 'NL' )
{
   # Do something that should happen just before an end of line
}
```

Instead of extracting one token at a time, we might prefer to process the contents of `$data` line-by-line or statement-by-statement. The `Lexer::extract_to` method supports this approach. It takes the string to be lexed, followed by the name of a token type, and returns a list of (*token, type*) pairs, up to and including the first token whose type matches the second argument. For example

```
# process first three lines line-by-line...
for (1..3)
{
  my @tokens_and_types = $lexer->extract_to($data, 'NL');
  process_line(@tokens_and_types);
}

# process remaining lines statement-by-statement...
while ($data)
{
  my @tokens_and_types = $lexer->extract_to($data, 'SEMICOLON');
  process_statement(@tokens_and_types);
}
```

Lexer::resync_after provides a handy way of skipping past errors. It behaves exactly like extract_to, except that it throws away the tokens it extracts. A typical use might be

```
unless ( process_line($lexer->extract_to($data, 'NL')) )
{
  warn "Error near " . ($lexer->lookahead($data))[0];
  $lexer->resync_after($data,'SEMICOLON');
}
```

Finally, Lexer::extract_all, provides a way to tokenize an entire string in one step. Both Lexer::resync_after and Lexer::extract_all make use of Lexer::extract_to, which simplifies them and isolates potential bugs to that one method.

5.2.4   Example: A simple pretty-printer

Listing 5.4 shows a typical application of the Lexer class—a pretty-printer for a (very small) subset of Perl. The code itself is simple and almost declarative in style, which makes it easy to add extra tokens and their associated printing rules.

The Lexer object is set up, as before, by passing a list of pattern=>type pairs to Lexer::new. The program sucks up all of the text on STDIN, and sets the indentation level to zero. Finally, the pretty-printing code iterates through each token that the lexer extracts from the input data, determines the token's type, and prints out the token with the appropriate formatting.

The specified formatting causes semicolons and newlines to insert a newline and reapply the current level of indentation (i.e. "\t" x $indent). Curly braces insert newlines and indentation too, but they also increment or decrement the indentation level appropriately. Any "#" encountered is treated as a comment introducer, and the remainder of the same line is skipped with a call to the resync_after method. Other tokens are printed as is with only minimal white space between them.

5.2.5   Where to find out more

Chapter 7 develops a more sophisticated version of the Lexer class, with polymorphic tokens.

Perl's anonymous subroutines are explained in chapter 2. They are also described in the standard perlsub and perlref documentation. The closure behavior of subroutines is explained in detail in chapter 4 of *Advanced Perl Programming*.

Listing 5.4 A simple pretty-printer

```
package main;
use Lexer 1.00;

# What symbols are understood...

my $lexer = Lexer->new ( '\d+'    => 'NUMBER',
                         '\$\w+'  => 'VARIABLE',
                         '\w+'    => 'IDENTIFIER',
                         '=|<'    => 'OPERATOR',
                         '\('     => 'LB',
                         '\)'     => 'RB',
                         '\{'     => 'LCB',
                         '\}'     => 'RCB',
                         ','      => 'COMMA',
                         ';'      => 'SEMICOLON',
                         '\n'     => 'NL',
                       );

# The pretty-printer itself...

my $indent = 0;
my $input = join '', <>;
my $token;
while ( ($token, $_) = $lexer->extract_next($input) )
{
    if (/SEMICOLON/)  {print ";\n", "\t" x $indent }
    elsif (/NL/)      {print "\n", "\t" x $indent }
    elsif (/LCB/)     {print "\n", "\t" x $indent++, "{\n", "\t" x $indent}
    elsif (/RCB/)     {print "\n", "\t" x --$indent, "}\n", "\t" x $indent}
    elsif (/HASH/)    { print "\n", "\t" x $indent;
                        $lexer->resync_after($input,'NL') }
    else              {print "$token " }
}
```

A similar, but simpler and non-object-oriented, approach to building processors for sets of regular expressions is described in perlfaq6 and, in more depth, in chapter 6 of *Perl Cookbook*. If you're interested in more general lexing and parsing, especially of the object-oriented variety, you may want to look at the Parse::RecDescent, Parse::Yapp, byacc-perl, and Parse::Lex packages, all available from the CPAN.

The perltoot tutorial describes (in a section titled *Closures as Objects*) an entirely different use for blessed subroutines, namely to implement a strong form of encapsulation. This powerful and elegant technique is explained in detail in chapter 11.

5.3 BLESSING A TYPEGLOB

By this point, the rules of the game should be clear: if you can take a reference to it, you can bless it into a class. As a final variation on this theme, we'll bless a typeglob to create an object that acts like a paged filehandle. Actually, far from being an arcane anomaly, blessing a typeglob is a common operation in Perl. Every time you use any of the IO:: modules (IO::Handle, IO::File, IO::Pipe, etc.), you're doing exactly that. An IO::File object, for instance, is just a typeglob that has been blessed into the IO::File package.

It's enlightening to read through the IO:: modules to see how they go about wrapping Perl's endearingly messy I/O features in tidy objects.

5.3.1 Paging STDOUT

It's common to want to "page" the output of a program so that it appears a screenful at a time. For example, if a program is printing help information, we'd like that information to appear gradually (and under our control), instead of in a scrolling blur.

It's relatively easy to set up STDOUT so that it pages correctly:

```
{
    local *STDOUT;
    open STDOUT, "|more" or die "Can't connect to pager (more)";

    # Any print to STDOUT in the rest of the block will be paged.
    # For example:
    foreach my $i (1..100)
    {
        print "$i\n";# Each line is paged through more(1)
    }
}
print "done\n";   # Unpaged
```

Some subtleties here are worth mentioning. Firstly, the localization of STDOUT ensures that the paging doesn't permanently interfere with the standard output filehandle. We could, of course, simply use a different global filehandle name, but, in a large system, it might be difficult to be sure that we're not trampling on someone else's I/O.

More importantly, if we used another filehandle, we would have to remember to close it explicitly:

```
open PAGER, "|more" or die "Can't connect to pager (more)";

# Any print to PAGER in the rest of the block will be paged
# For example:
foreach my $i (1..100)
{
    print PAGER "$i\n";# Each line is paged through more(1)
}

close PAGER;

print "done\n";   # Unpaged
```

The close sends an end-of-file message to the paging program—which is running as a child process—and ensures that the main program waits for the pager to finish. Without that implicit `wait`, the main program terminates after completing the `print` operations, causing all its child processes, including the pager, to finish prematurely.[4]

If instead we choose to localize `STDOUT`, it's important to embed the paged I/O in a block, so that the normal `STDOUT` will be restored after the paging is complete. The nested scope also ensures that the pipe between the main program and the pager is `closed` properly at the end of the block when the local filehandle is cleaned up. Otherwise, we would again have to remember to issue an explicit `close`.

5.3.2 A multiprocess pager class

Of course, even if you can remember and cater for all of these issues, if the nominated pager program isn't available—if you're not running on a Unix-ish system—the program will die a horrible death without printing anything useful.[5] To avoid this nonportability, we can build a class that encapsulates a paging filehandle, but doesn't rely on external paging programs at all. Listing 5.5 shows the complete IO::Pager class suitable for any system that implements the built-in `fork` function.

Listing 5.5 The pager class

```
package IO::Pager;
$VERSION = 1.00;
use strict;
use Carp;
use Symbol;

sub new
{
    my $class = shift;
    my %args = (lines=>23, prompt=>"--More--", endprompt=>"--No more--", @_);
    my ($self, $KEYBOARD) = ( gensym, gensym );
    open $KEYBOARD, "<&STDIN" or croak "lost contact with keyboard";
    my $pid = open $self, "|-";
    croak "Could not create pager" unless defined $pid;
    _page($KEYBOARD,%args) unless $pid;
    return bless $self, $class;
}

sub _page
{
    my ($KEYBOARD,%args) = @_;
    $| = 1;
    while (<>)
    {
```

---

[4] This can be a trap even for experienced programmers, who may be tempted to insert an explicit `wait` to ensure that the pager gets a chance to finish. That doesn't work because, without the end-of-file sent by `close`, the pager waits for more input from the main program, while the main program waits for the pager to terminate.

[5] Hmmm, that *is* similar to the standard help behavior on certain systems.

```
        print;
        _prompt($args{prompt},$KEYBOARD) || last
                unless $. % $args{lines};
    }
    _prompt($args{endprompt}, $KEYBOARD);
    exit;
}

sub _prompt
{
    print $_[0];
    return (readline(*{$_[1]}) !~ /^q/i); # Return false if user types 'q'
}

sub close
{
    close $_[0];
}

sub print
{
    my ($self) = @_;
    print $self (@_);
}

sub DESTROY
{
    $_[0]->close;
}

1;
```

The constructor does most of the work required to set up the paging mechanism. It first parses the argument list, extracting the class name and the configuration arguments. The arguments are passed as a hash-like list of tags and values. These tags/value pairs are

- `lines => $num`, which specifies how many lines should be shown per page before pausing and prompting to continue;
- `prompt => $str`, which specifies the string to be printed at each pause;
- `endprompt => $str`, which specifies a separate string to be printed once all the data has been paged out.

The defaults are interpolated into the `%args` hash before the constructor arguments, so that the arguments take precedence. The default values are the standard ones for more. Consequently, the following produces a more-ish paging filehandle:

```
my $PAGER = IO::Pager->new();
```

In contrast, this constructor call:

```
my $PAGER = IO::Pager->new(prompt=>": ", endprompt=>"(END)");
```

creates a pager that mimicks less.

Having determined the style of paging required, the constructor creates two local typeglobs:

```
my ($self, $KEYBOARD) = (gensym, gensym);
```

The `Symbol::gensym` subroutine is a handy utility subroutine that returns a reference to anonymous typeglob.

Once the two new typeglobs have been created, they are both immediately used, although in very different ways. The filehandle in the `$KEYBOARD` typeglob is connected to the same input stream as `STDIN`, via an `open $KEYBOARD, "<&STDIN"`. This filehandle will be used to provide the paging process with access to the original input stream, so that it can receive replies to its paging prompts.

This will be necessary because the paging process is created—in the very next statement—by opening the filehandle in `$self`'s typeglob with the magical `"|-"` output pipe. This `open` causes the main program to fork and create a pipe to the new child process. That child process has its input stream (i.e. `STDIN`) connected to one end of the pipe, and the filehandle inside `$self` is connected to the other. Hence, anything written to the `$self` filehandle will appear on the standard input of the child process. The child process needs its own copy of the original `STDIN` (inside `$KEYBOARD`), since its own `STDIN` has been taken over by the inter-process pipe.

The forking `open` returns zero to the new process and nonzero to the original one. In the child process—where the condition `unless $pid` is true—the `IO::Pager::_page` subroutine is called to begin the paging process. In the parent process, the `unless $pid` condition is false, so control skips to the last line of the constructor where the writable end of the inter-process pipe (stored in `$self`'s typeglob) is blessed as an object of the class, and returned.

The upshot of all that fancy footwork is that the original process that calls `IO::Pager::new` receives a reference to a blessed typeglob containing a filehandle. That filehandle is connected to a pipe that leads to the `STDIN` of another process currently executing the `IO::Pager::_page` subroutine. Figure 5.1 illustrates that long chain of connections.

Perl's built-in `print` function is quite smart and knows that, if we give it a typeglob reference (blessed or not), it should send its output to the filehandle inside that typeglob. Now we can write

```
my $PAGER = IO::Pager->new();
print $PAGER ($long, $text, $to, @be_paged_out);
```

and `print` sends the output text to the filehandle referred to by `$PAGER`. That filehandle routes the text through the pipe and into the `STDIN` of the child process. All then required is to arrange for the child process to grab that incoming data and page it out.

Recall that the constructor left the child process executing the `IO::Pager::_page` subroutine. Not surprisingly, that subroutine does nothing but read lines from its `STDIN`, print them to its `STDOUT`, and prompt whenever the line count reaches a multiple of a screenful (that is, when `$. % $args{lines}` is zero).

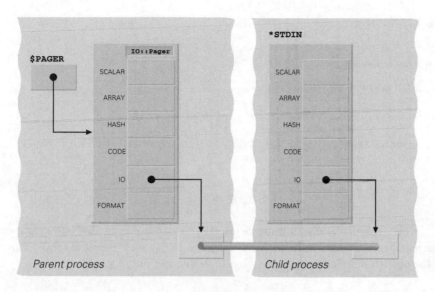

Figure 5.1   The internal structure of an IO::Pager object

The helper subroutine IO::Pager::_prompt uses the filehandle in $KEYBOARD to collect feedback. Reading from STDIN would not have the desired effect, since it's now connected to the interprocess pipe, not the keyboard.

The _prompt subroutine also returns a Boolean value indicating whether the user typed q (or Q) in response to the paging prompt. This is caught in _page's while loop, allowing paging to terminate early if a quit is requested. It's easy to imagine _prompt and _page handling a much richer set of interactive commands (*back-up, save, find,* etc.) in a similar manner.

The IO::Pager::print and IO::Pager::close methods exist only to provide an object-oriented interface for these two standard activities. Their presence makes the following pairs of statements equivalent:

```
print $PAGER @data;
$PAGER->print(@data);

close $PAGER;
$PAGER->close();
```

The first version of each of these pairs is *not* an indirect object method call, but rather a normal call to Perl's built-in print or close function. In this case, of course, the effect is identical, but it illustrates once again why the indirect object syntax is best avoided.

Finally, the class destructor (IO::Pager::DESTROY) ensures that the filehandle in the blessed typeglob is properly closed before it is finally relinquished. As explained above, the implicit wait that this close performs prevents the main process from terminating prematurely and killing the pager process before all the output has been paged.

Using the IO::Pager class, the earlier paging example now becomes

```
use IO::Pager;

{
   my $PAGER = IO::Pager->new();

   # Any print to $PAGER in the rest of the block will be paged
   # For example:
   foreach my $i (1..100)
   {
      print $PAGER "$i\n";   # Each line is paged through &IO::Pager::_page
   }

}
print "done\n";            # Unpaged
```

Note in particular that, because the paging typeglob is now blessed into a class with a destructor, there is no need to remember the vital call to `close`. It is now automatically invoked by the object's destructor when the reference finally goes out of scope.

5.3.3 A threaded pager class

With a little more effort, the IO::Pager class could use Perl's built-in threads,[6] rather than separate O/S processes. Figure 5.6 illustrates the variation. Naturally, this version of the class provides exactly the same interface as the nonthreaded version.

Listing 5.6 The Pager class (threaded)

```
package IO::Pager;
$VERSION = 2.00;
use strict;
use Carp;
use Symbol;
use Thread 'async';

sub new
{
   my $class = shift;
   my %args = (lines=>23, prompt=>"--More--", endprompt=>"--No more--", @_);
   my ($READHANDLE, $WRITEHANDLE) = (gensym, gensym );
   pipe $READHANDLE, $WRITEHANDLE or die;
   my $self = bless $WRITEHANDLE, $class;
   my $thread_ref = async { _page($READHANDLE,%args) };
   *$self = \$thread_ref;
   return $self;
}

sub _page
```

---

[6] Perl's thread facilities are still experimental. The thread-specific details in this section may have changed if you're using a version of Perl later than 5.005.

```
    {
        my ($input,%args) = @_;
        while (readline *$input)
        {
            print;
            _prompt($args{prompt}) || last
              unless $. % $args{lines};
        }
        _prompt($args{endprompt});
    }

sub _prompt
{
    print $_[0];
    return (<> !~ /^q/i);   # Return false if user types 'q'
}

sub close
{
    close $_[0];
    ${*{$_[0]}}->join;
}

sub print
{
    my ($self) = @_;
    print $self (@_);
}

sub DESTROY
{
    $_[0]->close;
}


1;
```

The overall structure and operation of the threaded IO::Pager class is unchanged from the multiprocess version. It still connects the two parallel flows of control, the main program and the pager, with a pipe, but now the pipe is explicitly created by calling the built-in pipe function on two anonymous typeglobs.

The typeglob storing the writable end of the pipe is immediately blessed as the pager object. The readable end of the pipe is passed to _page, which is invoked in a separate thread via the Thread::async subroutine. Thread::async returns a reference to a Thread object, temporarily stored in the lexical $thread_ref.

This Thread object will be needed later, so we need to keep it warm and dry in the interim. The SCALAR slot of the now-blessed typeglob, $self, is the ideal place. The assignment that accomplishes this, *$self = \$thread_ref, may look arcane, but it's just a standard typeglob assignment, placing a reference into a scalar to the appropriate slot of the typeglob referred to by $self.

Both the writable end of the interthread pipe and the reference to the pager thread itself are now stored in the one blessed typeglob, which is finally returned to the main program.

Meanwhile the _page subroutine is running in a separate thread, waiting to read lines from the readable end of the pipe (note: *not* from STDIN in this version). Once again it prints batches of lines and issues a prompt. Because the paging thread takes its input directly from the pipe, STDIN is still attached to the keyboard, so the threaded version of _prompt can obtain feedback with a simple diamond operation (<>).

The only other difference in the threaded version is in the IO::Pager::close method. It still performs a built-in close on the pipe, thereby sending the pager thread the necessary end-of-file. However, because the pager is no longer running in a child process, the close doesn't issue an implicit wait to allow the pager to finish.

Instead, we need to tell the main thread to pause until the pager thread finishes. This is done by calling the Thread::join method on the Thread object representing the pager thread. Fortunately, the constructor cached a reference to that Thread object in the scalar slot of the blessed typeglob. All we need to do is access that reference and call join through it.

Accessing the reference is a little ugly, as we have to write: ${*{$_[0]}}. This means: take the first argument, **$_[0]**, dereference it to a typeglob, ***{$_[0]}**, and select the scalar slot, **${*{$_[0]}}**. The curly braces are required because, without them, $*$_[0] would be interpreted as $* $_[0], which is both invalid (**missing operator before $_[0]**), and deplorable (**use of $* variable is deprecated**). Fortunately, since the visually offensive, but syntactically acceptable, version is hidden away in a method, no one else need ever know our shame.

5.3.4 Where to find out more

Typeglobs and their filehandles are challenging to understand, but are discussed at length in chapter 2. They are also widely mentioned in the standard Perl documentation in the files: perldata (*Typeglobs and Filehandles*), perlmod (*Symbol Tables*), perlop (*I/O Operators*), perlref (*Making References*), and perlsub (*Passing Symbol Table Entries*). For an excellent tutorial on typeglobs, see chapter 3 of *Advanced Perl Programming*.

Threads are a recent and still experimental addition to Perl. The standard perl documentation perlthrtut provides an good overview. The specifics of their use are described in the documentation of the Thread.pm module.

5.4 SUMMARY

- The qr operator builds a precompiled regular expression. Such regular expressions may be blessed as objects.
- Blessing a regular expression makes it possible to build efficient object-oriented pattern matchers, possibly with different semantics from Perl's built-in regular expressions.

- A subroutine may also be blessed as an object. Such subroutines will typically be eval'd into existence according to a predefined template.
- Alternatively, blessed subroutines may be created as anonymous closures, to restrict access to lexical variables.
- A typeglob is really just a special type of container, and may also be blessed. Typically, this is done so that the filehandle within the typeglob can be used as an object.

CHAPTER 6

Inheritance

As the previous three chapters illustrate, you can build complex and useful classes without ever venturing into the darker waters of inheritance. However, Perl does provide good support for this important object-oriented programming technique. In this chapter, we'll explore how to build classes and class hierarchies that take advantage of the power that inheritance offers.

6.1 HOW PERL HANDLES INHERITANCE

Perl's approach to inheritance is typically low-key and uncomplicated. Packages acting as classes simply announce their allegiance to another class and dynamically inherit that class's methods. Perl also provides standard methods that all classes inherit and a small dose of syntactic sugar to make rewriting inherited methods easier. Let's start with the pledge of allegiance...

6.1.1 The @ISA array

A class informs Perl that it wishes to inherit from another class by adding the name of that other class to its @ISA package variable. For example, the class PerlGuru could specify that it wishes to inherit from class PerlHacker as follows:

```
package PerlGuru;
@ISA = ( "PerlHacker" );
```

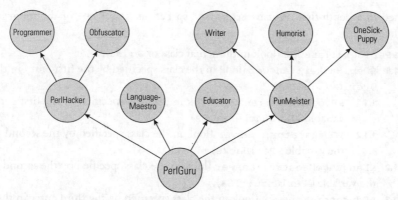

Figure 6.1   PerlGuru's inheritance hierarchy

That's it. From that point on, whenever Perl needs to determine if PerlGuru has any inherited methods, it checks the contents of the array @PerlGuru::ISA. Any package whose name appears in that array is considered to be a parent class of PerlGuru. Of course, since it's an array, we can have many class names in @PerlGuru::ISA, allowing the class to inherit methods from more than one parent:

```
package PerlGuru;
@ISA = qw( PerlHacker LanguageMaestro Educator PunMeister );
```

And, of course, if those four parent classes also inherited from other classes:

```
package PerlHacker;
@ISA = qw( Programmer Obfuscator );

package PunMeister;
@ISA = qw( Writer Humorist OneSickPuppy );
```

then PerlGuru would also inherit methods from those grandparents. All this inheritance creates the hierarchy shown in figure 6.1.

6.1.2   What inheritance means in Perl

Inheritance in Perl is a much more casual affair than in other object-oriented languages. In essence, inheritance means nothing more than: *if you can't find the method requested in an object's blessed class, look for it in the classes that the blessed class inherits from.*

In other words, if we call:

```
my $guru = PerlGuru->new();

# and later…

my $question = <>;
print $guru->answer($question);
```

then, if class PerlGuru doesn't provide a PerlGuru::answer method, Perl searches the parent classes (as specified by the current value of the @PerlGuru::ISA array). The parents are searched in a depth-first recursive sequence,[1] so Perl looks for one of the following (in this order):

1 `&PerlGuru::answer` (look in the actual class of `$guru`),

   1.1 `&PerlHacker::answer` (look in the class specified by the first entry in the variable `@PerlGuru::ISA`),

      1.1.1 `&Programmer::answer` (look in the class specified by the first entry in the variable `@PerlHacker::ISA`)

      1.1.2 `&Obfuscator::answer` (look in the class specified by the second entry in the variable `@PerlHacker::ISA`),

   1.2 `&LanguageMaestro::answer` (look in the class specified by the second entry in the variable `@PerlGuru::ISA`),

   1.3 `&Educator::answer` (look in the class specified by the third entry in the variable `@PerlGuru::ISA`),

   1.4 `&PunMeister::answer` (look in the class specified by the fourth entry in the variable `@PerlGuru::ISA`),

      1.4.1 `&Writer::answer` (look in the class specified by the first entry in the variable `@PunMeister::ISA`),

      1.4.2 `&Humorist::answer` (look in the class specified by the second entry in the variable in `@PunMeister::ISA`),

      1.4.3 `&OneSickPuppy::answer` (look in the class specified by the third entry in the variable `@PunMeister::ISA`).

If any of these methods is defined, the search terminates at once and that method is immediately called.[2] This process of searching for the right method to call is known as *method dispatch*.

If you're used to the complicated inheritance semantics in another object-oriented language, it's important to realize that inheritance in Perl is merely a way of specifying where to look for a method *and nothing else!* There is no direct inheritance of attributes—unless you arrange for it—nor any hierarchical calling of constructors or destructors—unless you explicitly write those methods that way—nor any compile-time consistency checks of the interface or implementation of derived classes.

This process of finding the correct method to call also explains why Perl ignores any prototype associated with a method (see chapter 3), and why you can't use prototypes to constrain the number of arguments given to a method. The prototype check occurs when the code is being compiled, but, at that point, the compiler has no idea which of the many potential answer

---

[1] Sean M. Burke's Class::ISA module, available from the CPAN, allows you to extract the exact sequence in which a class's parent's are searched as a list of class names.

[2] When looking in a parent class, Perl checks the left-most parent first, and then the left-most parent of that class, and the left-most parent of that class and so forth. Hence, if a class's left-most great-great-great-grandparent has a method of the right name (e.g., `answer`), that method will be called, even if another of the object's direct parents also has a suitable method. In other words, you don't necessarily get the method that is "closest" up the inheritance hierarchy; you get the method that was inherited through the left-most inheritance chain. This is known as "left-most ancestor wins."

subroutines will actually be called since the choice will depend on the contents of the various @ISA arrays at the time the method is actually called. So the compiler has no way of determining which subroutine's prototype to check the argument list against.

6.1.3   Where the call goes

The exact semantics of where, and in what order, Perl looks for a method are relatively straightforward, but warrant a brief discussion.

The rules for handling a call such as `$obj->method()` can be summarized as follows:

1. If the class into which `$obj`'s referent is blessed (say, MyClass) has a subroutine `method`, call that.

2. Otherwise, if MyClass has an @ISA array, step through each parent class in that array and apply steps 1 and 2 to it; that is, recursively search in depth-first, left-to-right order up the hierarchy. If a suitable `method` subroutine is found in any package in the hierarchy, call that.

3. Otherwise, if the UNIVERSAL[3] class has a subroutine `method`, call that.

4. Otherwise, if MyClass has an `AUTOLOAD` method, call that.

5. Otherwise, if one of the ancestral classes of `$obj`'s referent—once again searched in depth-first, left-to-right order—has an `AUTOLOAD` method, call that.

6. Otherwise, if the UNIVERSAL class has an `AUTOLOAD` method, call that.

7. Otherwise, give up and throw an exception: **Can't locate object method "method" via package "MyClass"**.

Once a suitable method has been found for an object of a particular class, a reference to it is cached within the class. Thereafter, any subsequent call to the same method through objects of the same class doesn't need to repeat the search. Instead, it uses the cached reference to go directly to the appropriate method.

If the class's @ISA array, or that of any of its ancestors, is modified, or if new methods are defined somewhere in the hierarchy, the cached method may no longer be correct. In such cases, the cache is automatically cleared. The next method call simply does a new search and, recaches the resulting subroutine reference.

6.1.4   Constructors and inheritance

Because constructors for Perl classes are regular methods, they are inherited in the way described above. That is, if a class doesn't provide a constructor itself, then attempting to call its constructor will send Perl searching up its inheritance hierarchy, looking for a suitably named method in an ancestor class. The first, and only the first, matching method in any inherited class will be called.

For example, given the following code:

---

[3]   …which is described in section 6.2.

```
package PerlHacker;
@ISA = qw( Programmer Obfuscator );

sub new
{
   my ($class, %args) = @_;
   bless{ _name     => $args{name},
          _alias    => $args{moniker},
          _langs    => $args{languages}
        }, ref($class)||$class;
}


package PunMeister;
@ISA = qw( Writer Humorist OneSickPuppy );

sub new
{
   my ($class, %args) = @_;
   bless{ _name      => $args{name},
          _pun_gent  => $args{pun}
        }, ref($class)||$class;
}
package PerlGuru;
@ISA = qw( PerlHacker PunMeister );
```

then an attempt to create a new PerlGuru object

```
my $guru = PerlGuru->new(name        =>"Tom",
                         languages  =>["English","Latin","Greek"],
                         pun_gent   =>"Metaclassical tools");
```

searches for `PerlGuru::new` and, failing to find it, looks next for `PerlHacker::new`. Since this method exists, it is immediately called. As usual, the first argument is the name of the class through which it was *called* (not the class to which the method *actually belongs*). Hence, the `$class` variable is initialized with the string `"PerlGuru"`, not `"PerlHacker"`.

This is different from the constructor behavior of most other object-oriented languages, where the constructor of *every* ancestral class is called when an object is created.

More importantly, we finally see why it's essential to always use the two-argument form of `bless`. If the PerlHacker class had used the one-argument form

```
sub new
{
   my ($class, %args) = @_;
   bless{ _name => $args{name},
          _alias=> $args{moniker},
          _langs=> $args{languages}
        };
}
```

then the object returned by `PerlGuru->new(@args)` would have been a PerlHacker object, instead of a PerlGuru. The one-argument form always blesses into the current package, not the package through which the constructor was called.

Fortunately, we *did* use the two-argument `bless`, so the call to `PerlHacker::new` creates an anonymous hash and correctly blesses it into the class specified by the first argument (that is, into the PerlGuru class).

Of course, in creating that object, `PerlHacker::new` only initialized entries for `"_name"`, `"_alias"`, and `"_langs"`. The entries for `"_pun_gent"` (needed by the methods inherited from class PunMeister) or any other attributes that the PerlGuru class might itself require remain undefined.

To solve this problem it's necessary to plan ahead in setting up the ancestral classes. The typical solution, which works for both single- and multiple-inheritance hierarchies, is to separate object creation from object initialization, as discussed in chapter 3. For example, we could rewrite the various classes as shown in listing 6.1.

The key to the solution is the class _Initializable (note the underscore, indicating a private or secret purpose). This class provides a generic constructor, which creates an empty hash-based object of whatever class is requested. Any class that inherits from _Initializable as its left-most parent, inherits this generic constructor and, therefore, doesn't need to provide its own.

The clever bit is that, having created that empty object, `_Initializable::new` then calls its _init method. Because the object is blessed into the derived class—as named by the value of `$class`—the search for the _init method starts back at the original derived class, *not* at class _Initializable.

Now, all we have to do is make sure that each class in the hierarchy provides a suitable _init method and that the _init methods of derived classes call those of their parents as well (as in `PerlGuru::_init`).

With this arrangement, if we call `PerlGuru->new(%args)`, the following sequence of events takes place:

1   Perl looks for `&PerlGuru::new`, and doesn't find it.

2   The search moves to the left-most parent class. `_Initializable::new` *is* found.

3   `_Initializable::new` creates the empty hash and blesses it into class PerlGuru.

4   `_Initializable::new` then calls the _init method of the newly blessed object.

5   That call invokes `PerlGuru::_init`.

6   `PerlGuru::_init` calls `PerlHacker::_init` on the blessed hash (see below for an explanation of the qualified method arrow syntax), which initializes the PerlHacker-ish attributes of the PerlGuru object.

7   `PerlGuru::_init` calls `PunMeister::_init` on the blessed hash, which initializes the PerlMeister-ly attributes.

8   Finally, `PerlGuru::_init` initializes its own attributes.

Note the variation of the method call syntax used to invoke `PerlHacker::_init` and `PunMeister::_init`. Normally, when a method is called using the arrow notation, Perl starts looking for the method in the class into which the object is blessed (that is, in the class whose name is returned by `ref($_[0])`. If the method name is fully qualified with a leading class name, Perl ignores the class of the object and starts the search in the namespace of the qualifier

Listing 6.1   Separating creation and initialization

```perl
package _Initializable;
use strict;

sub new
{
 my ($class, %args) = @_;
 my $self = bless {}, ref($class)||$class;
 $self->_init(%args);
 return $self;
};

package PerlHacker;
@PerlHacker::ISA = qw( _Initializable Programmer Obfuscator );

sub _init
{
 my ($self, %args) = @_;
 $self->{_name} = $args{name};
 $self->{_alias}= $args{moniker};
 $self->{_langs}= $args{languages};
}

package PunMeister;
@PunMeister::ISA = qw( _Initializable Writer Humorist OneSickPuppy );

sub _init
{
 my ($self, %args) = @_;
 $self->{_name}      = $args{name};
 $self->{_pun_gent}  = $args{pun};
}

package PerlGuru;
@PerlGuru::ISA = qw( _Initializable PerlHacker PunMeister );

sub _init
{
 my ($self, %args) = @_;
 $self->PerlHacker::_init(%args);
 $self->PunMeister::_init(%args);
 $self->{_acolytes}  = $args{followers};
 $self->{_philosophy}= $args{manifesto};
}
```

instead. This enables us, for example, to call `PerlHacker::_init` directly on the PerlGuru
object ($self->PerlHacker::_init).

It's important to understand that, even with this qualification, the search process only *starts* looking in the qualifier's namespace. For example, if `PerlHacker::_init` didn't exist, Perl would look for a suitable _init method in the ancestral classes of PerlHacker.

The success of this separation of creation and initialization requires that _Initializable be the left-most ancestor of each class or, at least, that no class inherited before _Initializable provides a new constructor.[4] It also requires that the parental _init methods invoke the _init methods of *their* parents in turn.

6.1.5 Diamonds are forfended

Even when all those conditions are met, one case that requires extra care: when the class hierarchy contains a diamond pattern (see the section on *Multiple inheritance* in chapter 1).

If a derived class inherits from an ancestor via two distinct paths, propagating _init calls up the class hierarchy will result in the ancestral _init function being called twice on the same object. At best, that's needlessly inefficient; at worst, it might cause subtle errors. For example, suppose the ancestral class's _init was responsible for incrementing a classwide object count. Any object inheriting the ancestor in a diamond pattern would be counted twice.

The solution is mercifully simple. We arrange for each object to keep track of those initializers it has visited and short circuit any second, or subsequent, visits to them. For example, if the PerlGuru class were a likely candidate for repeated initializations (that is, if we expected it to be at the top of a diamond inheritance pattern), we could protect it like this:

```
package PerlGuru;

sub _init
{
    my ($self, %args) = @_;
    return if $self->{_init}{__PACKAGE__}++;
    $self->PerlHacker::_init(%args);
    $self->PunMeister::_init(%args);
    $self->{_acolytes}= $args{followers};
    $self->{_philosophy}= $args{manifesto};
}
```

The first time `PerlGuru::_init` is called, its `$self->{_init}{PerlGuru}` attribute doesn't exist, so the if statement fails, and the initialization proceeds. However, in the process, the trailing increment operator causes the attribute to be autovivified. The resulting undef value of the attribute is then treated as a zero and incremented. Next time `PerlGuru::_init` is called, the attribute will be true, so the if will succeed, and the unwanted repeat initialization will be thwarted.

Of course, since *any* class can be inherited, it's impossible to know in advance which classes will eventually suffer from diamond-induced reinitializations. If the problem seems likely (and often it won't), the same protective line of code could be added to the start of every _init method in the hierarchy.

---

[4] Classes like _Initializable, which are used in this way and exist solely to confer some special low-level behavior on other classes, are often called *mixins*.

6.1.6 Destructors and inheritance

As you might expect, the same complications beset the automatic call of object destructors.

Since DESTROY is just a method belonging to the class, it's dispatched in the same way—by searching up the inheritance tree for the first applicable method. Once that method is found and invoked, the call ends. No other applicable method higher up the inheritance tree is subsequently called.

So, if both PerlGuru and PunMeister define a destructor, when a PerlGuru object goes out of scope, only PerlGuru::DESTROY will be automatically called. If we need the base class destructors to be called as well, we must arrange for it ourselves:

```
package PerlGuru;

sub DESTROY
{
   my ($self) = @_;

   # Avoid problems with diamond inheritance
   return if $self->{DESTROY}{__PACKAGE__}++;

   # Do whatever clean-up a PerlGuru requires
   # Then clean up the base classes…
   $self->PerlHacker::DESTROY();
   $self->PunMeister::DESTROY();
}
```

This technique works reasonably well, but has the disadvantage that we have to hard-code information about the inheritance hierarchy within the destructor call. This is unfortunate. If the inheritance relationships of a class change during development, we must now remember to update the destructor accordingly. Thus, in larger systems, this approach is a source of extra maintenance and, probably, of extra bugs as well.

There are at least two alternative solutions that reduce or eliminate the problem of invoking base class destructors. The most obvious is to replace the explicit calls to base class destructors with a more general loop:

```
package PerlGuru;

sub DESTROY
{
   my ($self) = @_;
   # Do whatever clean-up a PerlGuru requires
   # Then clean up the base classes…
   foreach my $parent ( @ISA )
   {
      next if $self->{DESTROY}{$parent}++;
      my $destructor = $parent->can("DESTROY");
      $self->$destructor() if $destructor;
   }
}
```

In this version,[5] we step through the class's inheritance list. For each direct parent of the class, we first check whether the parental destructor has already been called (that is, whether it's part of a diamond inheritance pattern). If so, we move straight on to the next parent. Otherwise, we find a reference to the correct parental destructor—using the can method (see section 6.2.2)—and call that destructor on the object if the destructor exists.

Now, if we subsequently change the inheritance hierarchy for PerlGuru, the destructor will still ensure that the destructors of all its base classes are correctly called. The same technique (and the same code) can be used in the destructors of any class in any hierarchy to ensure that all ancestral destructors are also called.

An alternative solution takes advantage of Perl's own destructor-calling mechanism. This approach is only feasible if a hierarchy does not use multiple inheritance. Since single inheritance is by far the most common type used, that's rarely a problem.

Rather than having derived class destructors explicitly call the destructor of their solitary base class, we can simply re-bless the object within its destructor. For example

```perl
package Hominidae;
sub DESTROY
{
    # Clean up Family-related information here
}

package Homo;
@ISA = ( "Hominidae" );

sub DESTROY
{
    my ($self) = @_;
    # Clean up Genus-related information here
    bless $self, $ISA[0];
}

package Neanderthalensis;
@ISA = ( "Homo" );

sub DESTROY
{
    my ($self) = @_;
    # Clean up Species-related information here
    bless $self, $ISA[0];
}

package Sapiens;
@ISA = ( "Homo" );

sub DESTROY
{
    my ($self) = @_;
```

---

[5] The destructor call loop could be written more compactly and idiomatically as

```perl
$_ && $self->$_() for (map {$_->can("DESTROY")} @ISA);
```

but those who have to understand and maintain your code will probably not appreciate it.

```
# Clean up Species-related information here
bless $self, $ISA[0];
}
```

In this class hierarchy, each class's destructor performs whatever cleanup is required and then reblesses the object being destroyed as an object of its base class (that is, $ISA[0]). Because each object in Perl has only a single scalar value indicating its class, reblessing an object means that it ceases to belong to its former class and becomes, instead, an object of the newly specified class.

When the destructor ends, the last reference to the reblessed object—the reference in the lexical variable $self—is lost. The object's newly acquired destructor—the one from the base class into which it was just blessed—is invoked, and the chain of destruction continues.

Unfortunately, this technique doesn't generalize to cases of multiple inheritance because we can only bless the object into a single class at a time. Consequently, when the current destructor ends, we can only leave the object in a state that will cause one of its ancestral destructors to be called.

6.2 TRICKS AND TRAPS

If you're building anything but the simplest inheritance hierarchies, there are some extra language features and programming techniques that will either make development a dream or a nightmare—depending on whether you know about these features or merely stumble over them in some dark corner of your code.

6.2.1 The isa() method

As the earlier sections illustrate, the effects of inheritance can be multiple and cumulative. These effects can make it a little tricky to check whether a given object—say, $hacker_ref—has inherited from a given class—say, Programmer. We can write a subroutine to perform this check for us by emulating the depth-first way that the method dispatch mechanism searches the inheritance hierarchy. For example:

```
sub inherits
{
  # Get object, name of prospective parent, and name of object's class…
  my ($caller, $target_name) = @_;
  my $class_name = ref($caller)||$caller;

  # trivial match if object is actually of requested type…
  return 1 if $class_name eq $target_name;

  # otherwise recursively check each parent of object's class
  no strict "refs";
  foreach my $parent (@{"${class_name}::ISA"})
  {
    return 1 if inherits($parent, $target_name);
  }

  # if no ancestor's match, then fail
```

```
        return;
    }

    # and later…
    if ( inherits($hacker_ref, "CyberGeek") )
    {
        # Do something CyberGeeky with $hacker_ref
    }
```

In other words, one class inherits from another either if:

- It's the same class (the trivial case), or
- One of its parents inherits from the specified class (the recursive case).

The need to determine whether an object has inherited from another is sufficiently common that Perl automatically provides a method to every object (we'll see how shortly) to do this check. The method is called isa, and it's used like this:

```
if ( $hacker_ref->isa("Programmer") )
{
    # Do something Programmerish with $hacker_ref
}
```

The isa method differs from the inherits subroutine shown above in two important respects. Firstly, it is hard-coded into the Perl executable, so it's much quicker than inherits would be. More importantly, for even greater speed isa memoizes its return values. That is, once isa has returned an answer for a particular object/class-name pair, it always returns the same answer for the same pair.

So any sneaky mucking about you might do with a class's @ISA array may not be reflected by the results isa subsequently returns. For example

```
@PerlHacker::ISA = ( "CyberGeek" );
print $hacker_ref->isa("CyberGeek");   # prints 1
@PerlHacker::ISA = ();
print $hacker_ref->isa("CyberGeek");   # also prints 1 (!)
```

The second call to isa behaves unexpectedly because isa remembers the first answer it gives for any specific object/class-name pair (e.g., $hacker_ref/CyberGeek) and regurgitates that same answer ever after, no matter what happens to the actual hierarchy involved.

6.2.2 The can() method

Sometimes we don't actually care what class an object belongs to, only whether it can perform a certain behavior; that is, whether it has a particular method. To this end, Perl automatically provides another universal method, can, which returns true only if an object or class can call the method requested:

```
if ( $hacker_ref->can("hand_optimize_assembler") )
{
    # Safe to call…
    $hacker_ref->hand_optimize_assembler($code);
}
```

The true value that the `can` method returns is actually a reference to the method that it is being asked about. In other words, if the method exists, `can` returns a reference to it.

That leads to an elegant solution if you need to call one of several alternative methods, but you're not sure which one is available through a specific object. For example, here's a generic compression subroutine that takes advantage of whichever compression algorithm a particular data object supports:

```
sub reduce
{
    my ($data_obj) = @_;
    my $reduce  = $data_obj->can("zip")
                || $data_obj->can("compress")
                || $data_obj->can("compact");
    return $data_obj->$reduce() if $reduce;
    die "data object does not provide compression method";
}
```

The subroutine first looks for a suitable compression algorithm, by calling `can` with the possible alternatives. If the data object has a method `zip`, the first call to `can` will succeed and return a reference to that method. Otherwise, the first call to `can` will fail and the second call to `can` will look for a `compress` method instead. Failing that, a third call will search for a `compact` method. Failing *that*, the entire expression will evaluate to false. Consequently, `$reduce` will contain either a reference to a suitable compression method or a false value.

If `$reduce` isn't false, the subroutine calls the appropriate compression method through the reference in `$reduce`. Note the use of the "`->$method_ref`" syntax for this purpose.

The `can` method uses the same recursive look-up algorithm as normal method dispatch. If the class into which an object is blessed doesn't have a method of the name requested, `can` checks each of the parent classes (recursively) to see if the object inherited a method from one of them. More importantly, if two or more of those classes had suitable method, `can` will return the left-most one. That is, `can` returns the one belonging to the ancestral class that appears earliest in the `@ISA` arrays of the various parent classes of the object.

For example, consider the inheritance hierarchy shown in figure 6.2, as specified by the following code:

```
package Coder;
sub write { ... }

package Documenter;
sub write { ... }
sub read { ... }

package Programmer;
@ISA = qw( Coder Documenter );

package Obfuscator;
sub write { ... }
sub read { ... }

package PerlHacker;
@ISA = qw( Programmer Obfuscator );
```

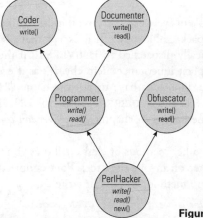

Figure 6.2   PerlHacker's inheritance hierarchy

```
sub new { … }

package main;
my $hacker = PerlHacker->new();
my $write_method = $hacker->can("write");
```

The call to `$hacker->can("write")` returns a reference to `Coder::write`, rather than `Documenter::write` or `Obfuscator::write`. This is because the class Coder is to the left of class Documentor in `@Programmer::ISA` and also to the left of class Obfuscator (because Programmer is to the left of Obfuscator in `@PerlHacker::ISA`). Figure 6.3 illustrates the inheritance paths for the `PerlHacker::write` and `PerlHacker::read` methods.

Unlike `isa`, `can` *doesn't* memoize its results. It uses the normal method caching mechanism, so run-time changes to the inheritance hierarchy *will* be reflected in the results it returns.

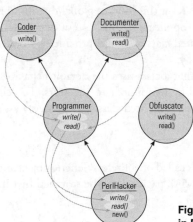

Figure 6.3   Inheritance of `read` and `write` in PerlHacker's inheritance hierarchy

6.2.3 The UNIVERSAL package

Both the `isa` and `can` methods are available in every class because they are defined in the special class UNIVERSAL. UNIVERSAL is a package like any other, except that (as indicated in section 6.1.2), method calls are automatically dispatched to UNIVERSAL if they cannot be handled by any package in an object's explicit inheritance hierarchy. It's as if every Perl class automatically inherits UNIVERSAL, except you don't have to put the name UNIVERSAL in any @ISA array. Apart from `UNIVERSAL::isa` and `UNIVERSAL::can`, the UNIVERSAL package also provides the `VERSION` method mentioned in chapter 2 (see *Version control in modules*).

More interestingly, you can add any other methods or class attributes you wish to UNIVERSAL—as long as you're careful not to step on anyone else's toes. For example, if you wanted every object of any class to provide a `debug` method, you might write

```
use Data::Dumper; # Gurusamy Sarathy's very useful CPAN module
                   # (see Chapter 14 for a full description)

sub UNIVERSAL::debug
{
   my ($package, $file, $line) = caller();
   my $subroutine = (caller(1))[3] || $package;
   print STDERR    "In $subroutine ($file:$line):\n",
                   Data::Dumper->Dump( [$_[0]] );
}
```

Now *every* object in *any* class automatically has a `debug` method:

```
my $hacker    = PerlHacker->new();
my $boyfriend = Neanderthalensis->new();
my $music     = CD::Music->new(@White_Album_data);

$hacker->debug();
$boyfriend->debug();
$music->debug();
```

There are few types of methods that warrant this kind of global distribution, mainly because few methods have the kind of universal applicability that `isa` or `can` or `debug` offer. Often, if you have a method that a set of related classes should provide, it's better to put that method in the base class of the class hierarchy.

Occasionally, we may need to ensure that a class uses the default behaviors specified by UNIVERSAL *in preference* to those specified by its immediate ancestors. To achieve this, we need to explicitly add UNIVERSAL to the list of inherited classes in the new class's @ISA array:

```
package PrefersGeneric;
@ISA = qw( UNIVERSAL Parent1 Parent2 );
```

Now, when a method, such as `debug`, is called on a PrefersGeneric object and the method is not found in PrefersGeneric, the UNIVERSAL package will be searched first instead of last.

6.2.4 The SUPER pseudo-package

The *delegation* of initializer or destructor calls to parent classes (as demonstrated in the previous sections on constructors and destructors) is a relatively common operation when using inheritance.

It's often the case that, when specifying a new method in a derived class, we would like to *reuse* the functionality provided by the same method in a base class, rather than just *replace* it. For example, to debug a class that represents quoted sections of a mail message, we might define its dump_me method to first call the dump_me method of its parent class and then perform whatever additional dumping is required by the derived class.

To do that we could write

```
package QuotedMessage;
@ISA = qw( Message );

sub dump_me
{
  my ($self) = @_;
  $self->Message::dump_me();                    # Delegate to parent…
  print STDERR "indent: $self->{_indent}\n";    # …and then do the
  print STDERR "quoter: $self->{_quote_symbol}\n";  # rest locally.
}
```

This approach is maintenance-friendly because it eliminates duplication of code between base and derived classes by reusing inherited functionality. The only drawback is that the technique requires us to hard-code the parent class's name in at least two places—in the @ISA array and (as part of) the invocation of the ancestral dump_me method. Indeed, it's possible that the name of the parent class will be hard-coded in numerous places within the class if several methods use this same delegation technique. That's maintenance *un*friendly because, if the inheritance hierarchy ever changes,[6] we'll have to hunt-and-destroy all those hard-coded names.

Perl anticipates and solves this problem by supplying a special package identifier, SUPER, which can be used instead of the name of a parent class. For example:

```
sub dump_me
{
  my ($self) = @_;
  $self->SUPER::dump_me();                      # Delegate to parent…
  print STDERR "indent: $self->{_indent}\n";    # …and then do the
  print STDERR "quoter: $self->{_quote_symbol}\n"; # rest locally.
}
```

SUPER isn't actually a generic name for the parent class of the current class. In other words, it's not a synonym for Message in the example above. Rather, it's a signal to the method-

---

[6] You might think that fundamental changes in inheritance relationships would be rare, but they can occur surprisingly often. The typical case is one where additional functionality has to be added to a system. Often the most effective means of doing so is to introduce an intermediate class between existing classes. Typically, such an intermediate class is used to abstract some part of the derived class's functionality, which is then shared by other new classes that inherit from the intermediate. For instance, we might eventually need to insert an IndentedMessage class between Message and QuotedMessage.

dispatching mechanism, telling it to start searching for a method in the parent classes of the *current* class. In other words, start looking in the parents of the class in which the current method is defined, *not* in the parent classes of the invoking object's class. Hence, SUPER is relative to the current method, not to the object through which the SUPER'd method is being invoked. This distinction is important when a derived class object uses an inherited method that calls some other method via SUPER. The example given in section 6.3.3 illustrates this important distinction.

Calling `$self->SUPER::dump_me()` still works unambiguously under multiple inheritance, even if two or more parent classes provide a `dump_me` method. Under those circumstances, the call simply invokes the left-most inherited method. That is, the call invokes the first method encountered by the recursive search of the dispatching mechanism, having ignored the current class.

Of course, there's no guarantee that the leftmost ancestral `dump_me` is what's wanted. Frequently, it isn't. Often what's desired is to invoke *all* the ancestral methods of a certain name. In that case, the usual solution is the same one we used to call multiply inherited destructors:

```
sub dump_me
{
   my ($self) = @_;
   foreach my $parent ( @ISA )
   {
      my $ancestral_dump_me = $parent->can("dump_me");
      $self->$ancestral_dump_me() if $ancestral_dump_me;
   }
   print STDERR "indent: $self->{_indent}\n";
   print STDERR "quoter: $self->{_quote_symbol}\n";
}
```

Or, more concisely

```
sub dump_me
{
   my ($self) = @_;
   $self->$_() for ( map {$_->can("dump_me")||()} @ISA );
   print STDERR "indent: $self->{_indent}\n";
   print STDERR "quoter: $self->{_quote_symbol}\n";
}
```

Either way, we iterate through the list of parental classes, and determine whether each parent can respond to a `dump_me` call. If so, we call that method directly, through the subroutine reference returned by `can`. The "...||()" in the `map` block of the second version ensures that parents that can't respond to a `dump_me` call are quietly ignored. The `map` block is evaluated in an array context so the empty array interpolates to nothing. A common mistake is to write something like `map { ($_->can("dump_me"))} @ISA` in the hope that the listifying parentheses will somehow eat the `undef` returned whenever `&can` fails, and thereby avert a nasty exception when `undef` is used as a subroutine reference. Unfortunately, that doesn't happen, since the one-element list `(undef)` is *not* the same as the empty list `()`.

6.2.5 Implementing abstract methods

Chapter 1 discussed the concept of abstract methods, which are placeholders in a parent class for methods that child classes are expected to implement. Abstract methods are also a useful means of ensuring that the abstract base classes in hierarchy are never used to directly create objects.

It's easy to define an abstract method in a Perl class. We simply define the method normally and ensure that its code throws a suitable exception. For example, each class in the Perl-Hacker hierarchy shown earlier is supposed to have a `write` method. We can ensure that every class in the hierarchy *does* have such a method by making each inherit from a suitable abstract base class with an abstract `write` method:

```perl
package Has_Write;
sub write
{
  my ($self) = @_;
  my $class = ref($self);
  croak "someone used an (abstract) Has_Write object"
    if $class eq 'Has_Write';
  croak "call to abstract method ${class}::write";
}

# and later...

package Programmer;
@ISA = qw( Coder Documenter Has_Write);

 package Obfuscator;
@ISA = qw(Has_Write);
sub write { ... }

package PerlHacker;
@ISA = qw( Obfuscator Programmer );
sub new { ... }

# etc...
```

Now, any class that inherits `write` from Has_Write without redefining it causes an exception to be thrown if that method is ever called. For example:

call to abstract method Programmer::write

Furthermore, if we ever accidentally create a Has_Write object and call its `write` method, we get a different exception:

someone used an (abstract) Has_Write object

The PerlHacker class didn't need to redefine `write`, because it inherited the redefined version from Obfuscator. But, if PerlHacker inherited Programmer before Obfuscator, then the abstract version of `write` would be left-most and would take precedence. That's also why Has_Write is specified last in each inheritance list. If any other ancestral class redefines the abstract method, the availability of that nonabstract version cancels the need for an error message.

In other words, abstract methods don't have to be redefined at *every* level of the hierarchy, just at the first nonabstract level of the left-most inheritance path.

Of course, if we intend to create many abstract methods, explicitly coding the various tests and exception generators in each abstract method would quickly become tedious. In such cases, we can instead create a utility method like this:

```
sub METHOD::ABSTRACT
{
  my ($self) = @_;
  my $object_class = ref($self);
  my ($file, $line, $method) = (caller(1))[1..3];
  my $loc = "at $file, line $line\n";
  die "call to abstract method ${method} $loc";
}
```

Because this method will be called from the actual abstract method (see below), we extract the call location and method name from one level further up the call tree than usual, via `caller(1)`.

We can then use calls to the METHOD::ABSTRACT method to declare each abstract method:

```
package Truck;

sub register       { ABSTRACT METHOD @_ }
sub tranfer_owner  { ABSTRACT METHOD @_ }
sub safety_check   { ABSTRACT METHOD @_ }
# etc.
```

And, yes, we *are* using the dreaded indirect object syntax here. Occasionally, we must let Good Sense defer to Aesthetic Sensibility.

6.2.6 Naming attributes of derived classes

One nasty little problem that can occasionally occur in complex class hierarchies is a collision of attribute names from two or more classes. Consider the two related classes shown in listing 6.2.

Objects of the base class Settable have a flag attribute called "_set", that may be set or reset by the `Settable::new` constructor and by the `Settable::set` method. Collection objects inherit this settable flag and also need to store the anonymous array of values representing a collection. The problem is that Collection uses an attribute called "_set" to store a reference to that array.

Unfortunately, since the objects that Collection creates are implemented as ordinary hashes, each object can have only a single entry with the key "_set". That means that Collection objects will attempt to use the *same entry* for both purposes. The `Settable::new` constructor first initializes the entry with the status of the settable flag. The `Collection::new` constructor immediately replaces that value with a reference to the collection's anonymous array. Any subsequent call to the inherited `Settable::set` method then wipes out that array.

Listing 6.2   When attributes collide

```perl
package Settable;

sub new
{
   my ($class, $set) = @_;
   my $self = { _set => $set };          # Was flag set?
   return bless $self, $class;
}

sub set
{
   my ($self) = @_;
   $self->{_set} = 1;                     # Set flag
}


package Collection;
@ISA = qw( Settable );

sub new
{
   my ($class, %items) = @_;
   my $self = $class->SUPER::new();
   $self->{_set} = { %items };            # Set of items in collection
   return $self;
}

sub list
{
   my ($self) = @_;
   print keys %{$self->{_set}};           # List items in collection
}
```

You might think that a problem like this is easily identified and overcome by judicious (re-)selection of names, but that's not always the case. Sometimes, for example, we may wish to inherit from a class written by someone else, perhaps one we downloaded from the CPAN. In that case, the code may be extensive or hard to understand, and it may be difficult to pinpoint every attribute that a base class uses and avoid those names in the derived class.

Remember, too, that one of the selling points of object orientation is the ability to reuse and extend existing classes without worrying about implementation details like this. This collision of attribute names makes that much more difficult.

Worse still, the potential for such collisions sets up a dependency in the other direction as well. Even if we carefully select attribute names for our derived class to avoid those already used by its base class(es), unless we control the code for those base classes, we have no guarantee that their implementation details won't change in the future. If that happens, the base class may introduce a new attribute that collides with ours.

Listing 6.3   Disaster averted

```perl
package Settable;

sub new
{
   my ($class, $set) = @_;
   my $self = { Settable_set => $set };        # Was flag set?
   return bless $self, $class;
}

sub set
{
   my ($self) = @_;
   $self->{Settable_set} = 1;                   # Set flag
}


package Collection;
@ISA = qw( Settable );

sub new
{
   my ($class, %items) = @_;
   my $self = $class->SUPER::new();
   $self->{Collection_set} = { %items };        # Set of items in collection
   return $self;
}

sub list
{
   my ($self) = @_;
   print keys %{$self->{Collection_set}};       # List items in collection
}
```

Because Perl provides no built-in answer to this problem, tradition is once again called upon to cover the gaps left by law. In other words, an unenforced but widely used cultural solution has arisen.

That solution is to prefix any attribute in a class with the name of the class, or sometimes, with a unique contraction of it. So, the "_set" attribute used by the Settable class becomes "Settable_set", while the "_set" attribute required by the Collection class becomes "Collection_set". Listing 6.3 illustrates the full set of changes required to fix the problems in listing 6.2.

The two attributes now have completely different names, at least as far as the underlying blessed hash is concerned. And, because every class name is distinct, we are immediately guaranteed that inherited attributes won't collide with any attributes we define in our new class.

Of course, that assumes that everyone plays by the rules and names their attributes in this way. Within a single project, that much discipline is usually easy to enforce, but, if you're using externally written base classes, no such guarantees exist. Nevertheless, even in that case, prefixing your own attributes with their class name will substantially reduce the chance of collisions.

Chapter 11 revisits this issue and describes a module that enables you to automatically enforce attribute name prefixing. The module can even correctly resolve collisions of unprefixed attribute named under some circumstances.

6.2.7 The empty subclass test

Setting up a base class so it can be successfully inherited is not always straightforward. We need to be careful to use the two-argument form of `bless` so that the constructor can be reused by derived classes. We need to ensure that the class name isn't inappropriately hardcoded in any method that might later be called on a derived-class object. We also want to be careful that class attributes aren't directly accessed where a derived-class object might happen across them (see the section on *Accessing class data* in chapter 3).

If the base and derived classes are both complex, it can be difficult to ensure that the inheritance has been accomplished safely and no nasty surprises lurk in an obscure method.

One relatively easy way to verify the inheritability of a base class is known as the empty subclass test. This test works by deriving a class from the base class being evaluated, but not adding any extra attributes or methods. We then use an object of the derived class as if it were a base class object and look for any behavioral disorders or other anomalies.

For example, if we wished to check that the Bit::String class (from chapter 4) can be safely inherited,[7] we might set up the following test:

```perl
use Bit::String;

# set up a gruelling workout for Bit::String objects...
sub test_bitstring
{
    my ($bitstring) = @_;
    eval { $bitstring->set(7,1); 1 }    or warn $@;
    eval { $bitstring->set(5,0); 1 }    or warn $@;
    eval { $bitstring->get(7) }         or warn $@;
    eval { !$bitstring->get(5) }        or warn $@;
    # put other suitable tests of a Bit::String in here
}

# make sure a normal Bit::String object passes the test...
test_bitstring( Bit::String->new() );

# derive an "empty" class from Bit::String...
@Bit::String::Derived::ISA = ( 'Bit::String' );

# now see if a derived object passes the same test...
test_bitstring( Bit::String::Derived->new() );
```

The `test_bitstring` subroutine should be set up to test every possible behavior of a Bit::String object, and can typically be adapted from the test code used during development

---

[7] It *can* be.

and maintenance of the Bit::String class. We then ensure the test code really is appropriate by passing it an actual Bit::String object.

Next, we (implicitly) create a class—Bit::String::Derived—deriving it from Bit::String by putting Bit::String's name in the @Bit::String::Derived::ISA array. Since the new class has no methods (or anything else) defined, every method call on a Bit::String::Derived object will be passed straight back to the appropriate method in the parental Bit::String class. In other words, a Bit::String::Derived should act exactly like a Bit::String. Only the ref function should be able to tell the difference.

Hence, if the Bit::String class was properly set up for inheritance, every test that succeeded on a Bit::String object should also succeed on a Bit::String::Derived object. And that's precisely what we test in the second call to test_bitstring.

If the test is comprehensive and both test runs produce identical results, we can be reasonably confident that other nontrivial classes derived from the Bit::String class will also work correctly—at least, as far as their Bit::String-iness is concerned.

6.2.8 Inheritance and pseudo-hashes

In chapter 4 we saw how the fields.pm module can be used to simplify the creation of classes based on pseudo-hashes, for example the Transceiver class shown in figure 4.3.

But complications arise when we wish to derive a class from one that uses pseudo-hashes. Suppose, for example, we want to create a class representing a transceiver with a finite number of simultaneous transmission channels:[8]

```
package Limited_Transceiver;
$VERSION = 1.00;
@ISA = qw ( Transceiver );

sub new
{
   # Delegate construction of object to parent class...
   my Limited_Transceiver $self = Transceiver::new(@_);

   # Add new key to pseudo-hash (if not already there) and initialize...
   $self->[0]->{_channels} = @{$self}
      unless exists $self->[0]->{_channels};
   $self->{_channels} = $_[1];
   return $self;
}

sub start_transmit
{
   my Limited_Transceiver $self = shift;
   ++$self->{transmit}
      unless $self->{receive} ||
               $self->{transmit} > $self->{_channels};
   return $self->{transmit};
}
```

---

[8] Because Transceiver::start_transmit increments the invoking object's transmission counter with no upper bound, the original Transceiver class allows any number of simultaneous transmissions.

Unfortunately, this doesn't work, even though we were careful to explicitly add the new attribute ("_channels"). The problem is that the `Transceiver::new` constructor sets up the blessed pseudo-hash with a reference to the appropriate `%FIELDS` hash—namely, `\%{"${class}::FIELDS"}`—in its first element. That means that each newly blessed Limited_Transceiver pseudo-hash starts with a reference to `%Limited_Transceiver::FIELDS`. This is a problem since the hash that knows about the "transmit" and "receive" fields is `%Transceiver::FIELDS`.

Besides, the derived constructor is just plain ugly.

Fortunately, Perl provides the small but essential amount of support needed to correctly and easily set up classes derived from a pseudo-hash-based class. The module base.pm, which is also part of the standard distribution, allows you to specify that a given class inherits from some other class also based on a pseudo-hash class. It then ensures that the correct `%FIELDS` hash is appropriately initialized.

Using base.pm, the Limited_Transceiver class would be declared as follows:

```perl
package Limited_Transceiver;
$VERSION = 2.00;
use base   qw ( Transceiver );
use fields qw ( _channels );

sub new
{
    # Delegate construction of object to parent class…
    my Limited_Transceiver $self = Transceiver::new(@_);

    # initialize…
    $self->{_channels} = $_[1];
    return $self;
}

sub start_transmit
{
  my Limited_Transceiver $self = shift;
  ++$self->{transmit}
          unless$self->{receive} ||
                $self->{transmit} > $self->{_channels};
  return $self->{transmit};
}
```

The use base directive has two effects. It pushes the string "Transceiver" onto the `@Limited_Transceiver::ISA` array, thereby ensuring that class Limited_Transceiver inherits the necessary methods from class Transceiver. It also sets up the `%Limited_Transceiver::FIELDS` hash by copying `%Transceiver::FIELDS`, thereby ensuring that Limited_Transceiver also inherits the necessary fields from Transceiver.

The use base directive can be given several base classes at once. In other words, the new class may make use of multiple inheritance. Each parent class is pushed onto the new class's `@ISA` array, and, if the current parent has a `%FIELDS` hash, its fields are added to the new class's `%FIELDS` hash. However, the base.pm module currently allows only one such base class to donate fields to the new class.

As an added feature, base.pm uses some other internal chicanery to ensure that any field whose name begins with an underscore is treated as inaccessible in derived classes, provided it is accessed through a typed lexical. In other words, if we derive another class from Limited_Transceiver:

```
package Unreliable_Transceiver;
use base   qw ( Limited_Transceiver );
use fields qw ( unreliability );

sub new
{
  my Unreliable_Transceiver $self = Limited_Transceiver::new(@_);
  $self->{unreliability} = $_[2];
  return $self;
}

sub start_transmit
{
  my Unreliable_Transceiver $self = shift;
  ++$self->{transmit}
        unless $self->{receive} ||
                $self->{transmit} > $self->{_channels} ||
                rand(100) < $self->{unreliablity};
  return $self->{transmit};
}
```

we get a compile-time error: **No such field "_channels" in variable $self of type Unreliable_Transceiver...** because the "_channels" field is treated as private to class Limited_Transceiver when accessed through the typed lexical $self.

That's nice, but it isn't true encapsulation. The handy message disappears if we forget to type the lexical and instead write

```
sub start_transmit
{
  my $self = shift;
  ++$self->{transmit}
        unless $self->{receive} ||
                $self->{transmit} > $self->{_channels} ||
                rand(100) < $self->{unreliablity};
  return $self->{transmit};
}
```

Worse still, the code works, because the "_channels" field really *is* still part of the pseudo-hash, and run-time accesses don't check accessibility. Once again, the message is that pseudo-hashes *do* provide temporary relief from object-oriented headaches, but only if used strictly as directed.[9]

---

[9] If pain persists, see Chapter 11.

6.3 EXAMPLE: INHERITING THE CD CLASS

We now have seen more than enough to effectively build a class hierarchy based on the CD::Music class. For example, we can build a new class specifically geared to storing classical music. Such a class is shown in listing 6.4.

6.3.1 Applied Laziness

This new class inherits from the hash-based version of CD::Music shown in listing 3.4, and uses several of the techniques described above to minimize the amount of code required. In fact, it's quite remarkable how little code it actually requires: no constructor or destructor of its own, no attribute accessors (or AUTOLOAD), no need to alter the inherited object counting mechanisms.

Much like the CD::Music class, CD::Music::Classical encapsulates a private class attribute, %_attr_data, that describes the new object attributes that it will offer, as well as their default values. As in the base class, this information is accessed via three class methods: _accessible, _default_for, and _standard_keys.

However, these derived versions of the methods don't just check their own class's %_attr_data attribute. Where necessary—that is, if they fail to find what they're looking for locally—they also try the corresponding method from the base class. This delegation on failure is vital because it allows all other methods inherited from CD::Music to be used directly in CD::Music::Classical.

Take the CD::Music constructor for example:

```
package CD::Music;

# ...etc...

sub new
{
  my ($caller, %arg) = @_;
  my $caller_is_obj = ref($caller);
  my $class = $caller_is_obj || $caller;
  my $self = bless {}, $class;
  foreach my $attrname ( $self->_standard_keys() )
  {
    my ($argname) = ($attrname =~ /^_(.*)/);
    if (exists $arg{$argname})
      { $self->{$attrname} = $arg{$argname} }
    elsif ($caller_is_obj)
      { $self->{$attrname} = $caller->{$attrname} }
    else
      { $self->{$attrname} = $self->_default_for($attrname) }
  }
  $self->_incr_count();
  return $self;
}
```

CD::Music::Classical can inherit and use this method without modification. The initial blessing works correctly because CD::Music::new uses the two-argument form of bless.

Listing 6.4 Deriving from the CD::Music class

```perl
use CD::Music 1.00;

package CD::Music::Classical;
@ISA = qw( CD::Music );
$VERSION = 1.00;
use strict;

{
# Encapsulated class data

   my %_attr_data =   #      DEFAULT        ACCESSIBILITY
      ( _composer    => [ '???',         'read'],
        _orchestra   => [ '???',         'read'],
        _conductor   => [ '???',         'read'],
        _soloist     => [ undef,         'read'],
      );

# Class methods, to operate on encapsulated class data

   # Is a specified object attribute accessible in a given mode
   sub _accessible
   {
      my ($self, $attr, $mode) = @_;
      return $_attr_data{$attr}[1] =~ /$mode/ if exists $_attr_data{$attr};
      return $self->SUPER::_accessible($attr,$mode);
   }

   # Classwide default value for a specified object attribute
   sub _default_for
   {
      my ($self, $attr) = @_;
      return $_attr_data{$attr}[2] if exists $_attr_data{$attr};
      return $self->SUPER::_default_for($attr);
   }

   # List of names of all specified object attributes
   sub _standard_keys
   {
      my ($self) = @_;
      ($self->SUPER::_standard_keys(), keys %_attr_data);
   }
}


1;   # Ensure that the module can be successfully use'd
```

Therefore, when it is called as CD::Music::Classical->new(@data), CD::Music::new blesses the new object, $self, into class CD::Music::Classical.

The foreach loop used to initialize the attributes of the new object also works without change. Because it calls the class method _standard_keys via $self, and because $self is of class CD::Music::Classical, the method dispatch mechanism begins searching in that class and, hence, correctly invokes CD::Music::Classical::_standard_keys. And because that method has been set up to return the keys of attributes belonging to CD::Music::Classical, *plus* those inherited from CD::Music, the initialization loop is guaranteed to set up both inherited and newly specified attributes, even though the loop itself was designed and coded before CD::Music::Classical was even conceived.

Likewise, the calls to $self->_default_for($membername) within the initialization loop invoke the derived method CD::Music::Classical::_default_for, rather than inherited method CD::Music::_default_for. In this case, if the attribute in question is specific to the derived class, the method immediately returns a value. Otherwise, it delegates the task of locating a default value to the corresponding method back in its base class.

In a similar manner, the inherited CD::Music::AUTOLOAD method:

```
sub AUTOLOAD
{
   no strict "refs";
   my ($self, $newval) = @_;
   if ($AUTOLOAD =~ /.*::get(_\w+)/ && $self->_accessible($1,'read'))
   {
      my $attr_name = $1;
      *{$AUTOLOAD} = sub { return $_[0]->{$attr_name} };
      return $self->{$attr_name}
   }
   if ($AUTOLOAD =~ /.*::set(_\w+)/ && $self->_accessible($1,'write'))
   {
      my $attr_name = $1;
      *{$AUTOLOAD} = sub { $_[0]->{$attr_name} = $_[1]; return };
      $self->{$1} = $newval;
      return
   }
   croak "No such method: $AUTOLOAD";
}
```

by virtue of its foresightful use of calls to $self->_accessible, can correctly handle requests for access to attributes of the derived class. When AUTOLOAD is invoked:

```
print $classic->get_composer();
print $classic->get_ISBN();
```

within CD::Music::AUTOLOAD, the $self object is of class CD::Music::Classical, so the method CD::Music::Classical::_assessible is called, regardless of whether the requested attribute originates in CD::Music or CD::Music::Classical. To ensure that accessibility can be correctly established for attributes of both classes, CD::Music::Classical::_assessible first checks the %_attr_data hash of CD::Music::Classical then delegates to CD::Music::_accessible if necessary.

That even a metamethod like AUTOLOAD can provide this high level of forward-compatibility with yet-to-be-declared derived classes is strong testament to the power of object orientation, and to the elegant simplicity with which Perl implements it.

The simplicity of the CD::Music::Classical class also reinforces the critical importance of good object-oriented design and appropriate programming discipline. The task of deriving from CD::Music would have been considerably harder if its constructor, its AUTOLOAD'ed accessors, and its other methods were littered with direct accesses to class attributes, or if they used a one-argument bless.

6.3.2 Class data access revisited

Up to this point, the repeated exhortation never to access class data directly, but rather always through a class method, probably just seemed like normal object-oriented paranoia (*Don't handle the attributes! Look not on the Face of the Data!*). Now that inheritance is involved, we can begin to see the value of the admonition.

Accessing the right class attribute

Every class derived from CD::Music may end up calling CD::Music::new as its own constructor. That was why we used the two-argument form of bless: to ensure that the constructor put the new object into the new (derived) class, rather than just into CD::Music.

A similar problem of ownership can occur with the object counter class attribute. In the previous section, we ignored it on the assumption that, since a CD::Music::Classical object *is-a* CD::Music object, the creation of every new CD::Music::Classical should still increment the overall count. It's likely that we *would* want the encapsulated $_count variable for CD::Music objects to increment in this way, but it's by no means certain. We might, for example, prefer the secret $_count variable associated with CD::Music::Classical to increment instead.

Fortunately, because the count is accessed through a method, rather than directly, we can easily arrange for CD::Music::Classical objects to increment and decrement the appropriate counters:

```
package CD::Music::Classical;
@ISA = qw( CD::Music );
# etc...


{
    my $_count = 0;   # counter for derived objects (only)

    sub get_count { return $_count }

    sub _incr_count
    {
        my ($self) = @_;
        ++$_count;
        $self->SUPER::_incr_count();
    }

    sub _decr_count
    {
```

```
    my ($self) = @_;
    --$_count;
    $self->SUPER::_decr_count();
}


    # Other class attributes as before
}
```

Now, when we create a new CD::Music::Classical:

```
my $classic = CD::Music::Classical->new(@data);
```

the following sequence occurs:

1 The method dispatch mechanism looks for CD::Music::Classical::new. There's no such method, so the dispatch mechanism looks for it in the parent class, finds CD::Music::new, and invokes it.

2 CD::Music::new runs. It creates the new object, blesses it into class CD::Music::Classical, initializes it, and, finally, calls $self->_incr_count().

3 The method dispatch mechanism now looks for the derived method CD::Music::Classical::_incr_count—*not* CD::Music::_incr_count—because the search always starts in the class of $self, not the class that owns the current method.

4 CD::Music::Classical::_incr_count exists, so it is executed. It increments the class attribute stored in the lexical variable $_count—that is, the my $_count declared in the same block as CD::Music::Classical::_incr_count. It then calls the inherited method CD::Music::_incr_count, via the SUPER pseudo-package.

5 CD::Music::_incr_count executes and increments the parental lexical variable $_count—that is, the my $_count declared in the same block as CD::Music::_incr_count.

Similarly, when the inherited CD::Music destructor is invoked just before the CD::Music::Classical object ceases to exist, the call to $_[0]->_decr_count() in CD::Music::DESTROY invokes CD::Music::Classical::_decr_count. This method first decrements the shared $_count attribute belonging to CD::Music::Classical, and calls CD::Music::_decr_count to adjust CD::Music's counter as well.

If we prefer, the redefined counter increment and decrement methods in CD::Music::Classical can omit the calls to $self->SUPER::_incr_count() and $self->SUPER::_decr_count(), and thereby not participate in the overall CD::Music count. The point is, having originally accessed base class count attribute via methods, we now have the flexibility to change how that attribute is accessed in derived classes.

The definition of CD::Music::Classical::get_count is also important. It ensures that if we write something like:

```
print CD::Music::Classical->get_count();
```

or:

```
print $classic->get_count();
```

the correct count—the one that counts only CD::Music::Classical objects—is returned. Without the redefinition, the method dispatch algorithm searches up the hierarchy and invokes the inherited `CD::Music::get_count`, and the count of classical CDs is inaccessible.

Of course, even with this redefinition, the overall count of CD::Music objects is still available via:

```
print CD::Music->get_count();
```

and even through individual CD::Music::Classical objects:

```
print $classic->CD::Music::get_count();
```

6.3.3 An alternative solution

Sometimes a class attribute is used solely for housekeeping inside the class or to facilitate communication between objects of the class. In such cases, the flexibility and security offered by restricting access through methods may not be needed, and the cost of a method dispatch plus a function call per access may be unacceptable. There is an alternative solution that can provide direct access to the class attribute, but still offer limited flexibility in selecting which class's attribute is accessed.

The technique[10] relies on making the class attribute accessible via each object of the class. For example, we can rework original CD::Music class like this:

```
package CD::Music;

{
   my $_count = 0;
   sub get_count{ $_count }

   sub new
   {
      my ($class) = @_;

      # blessing and initialization here

      $self->{_count} = \$_count;
      ${$self->{_count}}++;
      return $self;
   }
}

sub DESTROY
{
   my ($self) = @_;
   ${$self->{_count}}--;
}
```

In this version, each object is given an additional "`_count`" attribute, which stores a reference to the (shared) class attribute $_count. Now, any method that needs to access the class

---

[10] ...suggested by Tom Christiansen in the standard **perltoot** documentation...

attribute (such as `CD::Music::DESTROY`) can do so directly through any object of the class. Note that because `$self->{_count}` is a *reference* to the class attribute, we must explicitly dereference it: **`${$self->{_count}}`**.

The benefits of this approach become clearer when a class is derived from CD::Music. Derived classes can provide their own constructor and use it to *change* the reference stored in each derived object's `"_count"` attribute:

```perl
package CD::Music::Classical;
@ISA = qw( CD::Music );

{
    my $_count = 0;

    sub get_count { return $_count }

    sub new
    {
        my $self = $_[0]->SUPER::new(@_[1..$#_]);

        ${$self->{_count}}--;
        $self->{_count} = \$_count;
        ${$self->{_count}}++;

        return $self;
    }
}
```

Short as it is, the `CD::Music::Classical::new` constructor warrants an explanation. The first line invokes the `CD::Music::new` constructor, passing it the name of the class being created (`$_[0]`) and an array slice containing the other constructor arguments (`@_[1..$#_]`).[11] `$_[0]` might contain the class name CD::Music::Classical, or it may hold the name of an even more-derived class that has inherited `CD::Music::Classical::new`. As explained above, regardless of the class of the object through which it is invoked, the method `SUPER::new` refers to the new method inherited from a parent of the *current* class (i.e., CD::Music::Classical).

Having delegated the construction task to `CD::Music::new` and received a reference to the newly created object, the `CD::Music::Classical::new` constructor proceeds to rewire the object by replacing the reference in its `"_count"` attribute—the reference to the CD::Music counter—with a reference to the CD::Music::Classical counter. Prior to replacing the original reference, `CD::Music::Classical::new` must be careful to decrement the original CD::Music counter, in order to keep the respective counts correct.

Once a reference to the correct counter has been installed, it is immediately used to increment that counter. Of course, it would be marginally more efficient at that point simply to increment $_count directly to save a hash lookup and a dereference operation, but the version shown above more clearly illustrates the symmetry of the process. Where the cost does not

---

[11] At the cost of slightly more obscurity (but considerably less line noise) the constructor call: `$_[0]->SUPER::new(@_[1..$#_])` could also be written: `shift()->SUPER::new(@_)`

differ greatly, this style of programming is beneficial in the long run. It prompts the reader to ponder and and gain a better understanding of what's going on.[12]

The reason for messing about with references like this can be seen whenever another inherited method needs to access a class's counter attribute. For example, the inherited `CD::Music::DESTROY` method still works correctly when called on a CD::Music::Classical object. This is because `CD::Music::DESTROY` doesn't access the `$_count` class attribute directly, which would erroneously cause the destructor to always decrement the counter for CD::Music, regardless of the type of object being destroyed.

Instead, the inherited destructor accesses the counter through the reference in each object's "`_count`" attribute. For CD::Music objects, this reference is to the counter for CD::Music, whereas for CD::Music::Classical objects, the reference is to the CD::Music::Classical counter. Because the "`_count`" attribute of any object always refers to the appropriate class attribute for that type of object, the correct class attribute is always decremented, even though the destructor code never changes.

This technique is clearly faster because it avoids method calls. At first glance it also seems more limited because we are now restricted to a single accessible counter per object. A small tweak allows us to have our cake (multiple counters...) and eat it too (...accessed quickly):

```perl
package CD::Music;

{
  my $_count = 0;
  sub get_count{ $_count }

  sub new
  {
    my $class = $_[0];

    # blessing and initialization here (as before)

    $self->{_count} = [ \$_count ];
    $_count++;
    return $self;
  }
}

sub DESTROY
{
  my ($self) = @_;
  foreach my $counter ( @{$self->{_count}} )
  {
    --$$counter;
  }
}
```

---

[12] For example, in this case they are likely to ask themselves why we decrement and, then, almost immediately reincrement ${$self->{_count}}, which will, in turn, draw attention to the significance of the intervening line of code.

```
package CD::Music::Classical;
@ISA = qw( CD::Music );

{
    my $_count = 0;
    sub get_count { return $_count }

    sub new
    {
        my $self = $_[0]->SUPER::new(@_[1..$#_]);

        push @{$self->{_count}}, \$_count;
        $_count++;

        return $self;
    }
}
```

In this variation, the "_count" attribute stores an array of references to counters. The array is created and initialized in CD::Music::new. Each derived class is then free to add another reference to a counter if necessary (as does CD::Music::Classical::new). Each counter is properly adjusted when an object ceases to exist because the inherited destructor carefully walks through the object's "_count" array, decrementing each counter in turn. The count of the actual class of an object is always directly available as

```
$count = ${$cd->{_count}->[-1]};
```

It is interesting to compare the technique shown here with the use of methods to provide access to class data (as described in the previous sections). Although this technique provides better performance, it is also more complicated and subtle and, hence, likely to be harder to code and maintain. It also increases the size of each object slightly, a result which may become significant in large systems running on small machines.

More importantly, without additional layers of cleverness (see chapter 11), the presence in every object of a reference to the class attribute undoes the enforced encapsulation provided by the use of a lexical. In small systems where good manners is sufficient to ensure an unenforced interface is respected, there may not be an issue.[13] In large systems, it's an invitation to future grief.

All in all, unless maximal speed is a vital consideration, using methods to encapsulate and access class data seems the cleanest and most robust approach.

6.4 WHERE TO FIND OUT MORE

The standard perlobj and perltoot documentation both describe Perl's inheritance semantics, and the use of the UNIVERSAL package and its can and isa methods. The base.pm module comes standard with Perl.

Sean M. Burke's Class::ISA module is available from the CPAN, in the directory http://www.perl.com/CPAN/authors/id/S/SB/SBURKE/.

---

[13] Just remember that, in time, almost all useful small systems grow into essential large systems.

6.5 Summary

- The parents of a class are specified by the run-time contents of the class's @ISA array.
- In Perl, inheritance merely tells the dispatch mechanism where else to look if an object's own class doesn't provide a requested method. Attributes are not inherited.
- When searching for a suitable method, the class hierarchy is searched in a depth-first, left-to-right order.
- Only the most-derived constructor and destructor are called for each object. If inherited constructors or destructors are also required, that must be arranged manually.
- The UNIVERSAL package is the implicit ancestor of all other classes. It provides the isa and can methods, which allow inheritance relationships and class interface features to be queried at run-time.
- Invoking a method from the SUPER pseudo-package causes the method dispatch mechanism to start searching in the parents of the current method's class.
- When building or using class hierarchies, it may be necessary to prefix attribute names with their class names to avoid conflicts with inherited attributes.
- The empty subclass test is a useful way of checking the inheritability of a base class.

C H A P T E R   7

Polymorphism

Those of us who hate having injections usually appreciate when our doctor says: "Okay, I'll count to 3: …1…2…*<jab!>*…3", and the nastiness is over before it begins.

Guess what.

If you've been apprehensive about this chapter—either because you've heard polymorphism is "difficult" or because you've had trouble with it in other languages—you can relax. The nastiness is over. You've already seen everything you need to know about polymorphism in the past four chapters. This chapter merely re-presents those ideas in the accepted jargon and extends them a little.

7.1 POLYMORPHISM IN PERL

Some object-oriented languages have special syntaxes and a long list of rules, constraints, and conditions on the use of polymorphic methods. As you will have realized by now, Perl has a different attitude.

In Perl, every method of every class is potentially polymorphic as a direct consequence of the way that methods are automatically dispatched up the class hierarchy. There's no special syntax, no requirement for type-compatibility of method arguments, no need for inheritance relationships between classes. Just define your method, redefine it in any derived classes that need to act differently, and, without even knowing it, you're polymorphizing.

7.1.1 Interface polymorphism

Suppose we have an object reference—say, $datum—and we call some method—say, print_me—on it:

```
foreach my $datum ( @data )
{
    $datum->print_me();
}
```

The method dispatch mechanism determines the class of the invoking object $datum and looks in the corresponding package for a method of the appropriate name. Provided the object belongs to a class with a method named print_me, the method call succeeds and action is taken. That action depends on the class of the invoking object, even though the call syntax is always the same.

The elements in the @data array might have been blessed into completely unrelated classes:

```
my @data =(
            GIF_Image->new(file=>"camelopard.gif", format=>"interlaced"),
            XML::File->new("./lamasery.xml"),
            PGP_Coded->new("Software is *not* a munition!"),
            HTTP::Get->new("http://www.perl.org/news.html"),
            Signature->new(),
          );
```

but the same method call—$datum->print_me()—handles them all appropriately, so long as each object's class's interface provides a print_me method. Because this form of polymorphic dispatch requires only that an invoking object has the appropriate interface, it's known as *interface polymorphism*.

7.1.2 Inheritance polymorphism

Of course, the dispatch mechanism also has a fall-back strategy if the class of the invoking object *doesn't* provide a matching method. As explained earlier, it immediately searches through the object's ancestor classes for an inherited method with the correct name.

This means that, if the object belongs to a class that *inherits* a method named print_me, the method call succeeds and action is taken. Once again, that action depends on the class of the invoking object or, more accurately, on the "genealogy" of that class, even though the call syntax is still always the same. Because this form of polymorphic dispatch requires not only that an invoking object has the appropriate interface, but also that it belongs to a particular class hierarchy, it's known as *inheritance polymorphism*.

We've already seen the use of this form of polymorphism in the previous chapter. When we redefined the _accessible, _default_for, _standard_keys, and _incr_count methods of class CD::Music::Classical, we were actually making future calls to these methods polymorphic. If called through a CD::Music object, they produce the original behavior; if called through a CD::Music::Classical object, the new behavior is invoked.

It doesn't matter that the calls to these methods originate in the base class's constructor (CD::Music::new). The whole point of genuine polymorphism is that methods are dispatched according to the class to which the invoking object belongs, *not* the class that the current subroutine belongs to.[1]

7.2 EXAMPLE: POLYMORPHIC METHODS FOR THE LEXER CLASS

The use of polymorphism in deriving the CD::Music::Classical class was sneaky on a number of levels. To better see Perl's polymorphism in action, let's take a more straightforward and typical example.

Listing 5.4 showed a pretty-printer class built with the subroutine-based Lexer class presented in listing 5.3. The Lexer class was object-oriented, but the tokens it returned were not. They were simply pairs of strings representing the value and identified type of a particular input. The pretty-printer used that type information to process each token value like so:

```
while ( ($token, $_) = $lexer->extract_next($input) )
{
      /SEMICOLON/  && print ";\n", "\t" x $indent
  or /NL/         && print "\n", "\t" x $indent
  or /LCB/        && print "\n", "\t" x $indent++
                  && print "{\n", "\t" x $indent;
  or /RCB/        && print "\n", "\t" x --$indent
                  && print "}\n", "\t" x $indent
  or /HASH/       && print "\n", "\t" x $indent
                  && $lexer->resync_after($input,'NL')
  or                 print "$token ";
}
```

The presence of what amounts to a case statement in any object-oriented code is usually a sign that the object orientation has broken down, and a chance to apply polymorphism has been missed. So when we see the pretty-printer testing token types and selecting actions in response, alarm bells should be ringing.

A little further thought about the nature of tokens reveals the problem. Chapter 5 defined a token as: *a substring of the original input, with an associated label indicating what type of token it is.* A value with an associated type...sounds a lot like an object, huh?

And, of course, a token *is* just like an object. We can easily redesign the Lexer class so that, instead of returning a value string and a type string for each token, the lexer blesses the value string into the class indicated by the type string and returns the resulting object. Listing 7.1 illustrates this variation.

---

[1] This is a major difference between object-oriented Perl and statically typed languages like C++. In such languages, within a constructor method inherited from a base class, the invoking object (i.e., `this`) is treated as belonging to the base class, regardless of its actual type. In fact, calls to polymorphic methods from within a base class constructor are always dispatched to the base class version of the method (to the frequent mystification and annoyance of C++ programmers).

Listing 7.1   An object-oriented Lexer class with object-oriented tokens

```perl
package Lexer;
$VERSION = 2.00;
use strict;
use Carp;

sub new
{
  my $class = shift;
  my $code = '';
  while (my ($pattern, $token) = splice @_, 0, 2 )
  {
    $code .= '$_[0] =~ s/\A\s*?('.$pattern.')// ';
    $code .= ' and return bless \"$1", '.'"'$token';\n";
  }
  $code .= '$_[0] =~ s/\A\s*(\S)// and return \"$1"; ';
  $code .= 'return undef;';

  my $sub = eval "sub { $code }" or _croak_cleanly($@);
  bless $sub, ref($class)||$class;
}

sub _croak_cleanly
{
  $_[0] =~ m{/\\A\\s\*\((.*)\)/(.*) at .*}s;
  croak "/$1/$2";
}

sub extract_next
{
  $_[0]->($_[1]);
}

sub lookahead
{
  my ($self, $str) = @_;
  $self->($str);
}

sub extract_to
{
  my ($self) = @_;
  my @tokens = ();
  while (defined(my $token = $self->($_[1])))
  {
    push @tokens, $token;
    last if defined($_[2]) && $token->isa($_[2]);
  }
  return @tokens;
}
```

```
sub resync_after
{
   $_[0]->extract_to($_[1], $_[2]);
   return;
}

sub extract_all
{
   $_[0]->extract_to($_[1],undef);
}
```

Note how easy it is to replace value/type pairs with blessed token objects. We actually only have to change two lines from the original class, making small changes in the subroutine that implements the lexer.

The first of those small changes causes each generated rule in the lexer subroutine to return a string-based object—that is, a blessed reference to a string:

```
return bless \"$1", 'TOKEN_TYPE';      # Lexer version 2.00
```

instead of a (*value,type*) pair:

```
return ("$1", 'TOKEN_TYPE');           # Lexer version 1.00
```

The second change causes the default case to return an *unblessed* reference to an anonymous string:

```
return \"$1";
```

instead of a (*value,untyped*) pair:

```
return ("$1", '');                     # Lexer version 2.00
```

The generated lexer now returns a single reference per token. That reference is either to a string blessed into a class (indicating an expected token type), or else to an unblessed string (indicating an unknown). The classes that tokens are blessed into are specified by the token type names originally passed to Lexer::new.

At first glance, this has only made things worse. We now require an *extra* call to ref to ascertain the token type (if any). We also have to remember to dereference the reference in $token when printing it:

```
while ( $token = $lexer->extract_next($input) )
{
   $_ = ref($token);   # What kind of token is it?

      /SEMICOLON/  &&  print";\n", "\t" x $indent
   or /NL/         &&  print"\n", "\t" x $indent
   or /LCB/        &&  print"\n", "\t" x $indent++, "{\n", "\t" x $indent
   or /RCB/        &&  print"\n", "\t" x --$indent, "}\n", "\t" x $indent
   or /HASH/       &&  print"\n", "\t" x $indent
                   &&  $lexer->resync_after($input,'NL')
   or                  print "$$token ";
}
```

But the move to object-oriented tokens opens up the possibility of an entirely different solution, one both simpler and more robust.

7.3 THE SIMPLE PRETTY-PRINTER OBJECTIFIED

The whole point of polymorphism is that, if we have a series of classes that can all respond to some method call, each of those classes can do something different in response to that call. So, rather than coding up a series of type tests and associated pretty-printing actions, we can just give each token class a `pretty_print` method, and polymorphically invoke that method on each token.

Listing 7.2 shows the pretty-printer from listing 5.4, revised to make use of polymorphism. Each token type now inherits from the Pretty_Token class, which provides a default `pretty_print` method that prints the token with a single space after it. The token types that need more specialized printing behaviors, such as Semicolon, NL, LCB, and RCB, simply redefine their own versions of `pretty_print` to implement those behaviors.

Listing 7.2   A simple object-oriented pretty-printer

```
package main;
use Lexer 2.00;

my $lexer = Lexer->new ( '\d+'=> 'NUMBER',
                         '\$\w+'=> 'VARIABLE',
                         '\w+'=> 'IDENTIFIER',
                         '=|<'=> 'OPERATOR',
                         '\('=> 'LB',
                         '\)'=> 'RB',
                         '\{'=> 'LCB',
                         '\}'=> 'RCB',
                         ','=> 'COMMA',
                         ';'=> 'SEMICOLON',
                         '\n'=> 'NL',
                         '\S'=> 'UNKNOWN',
                       );

# The hierarchy of tokens...

    @NUMBER::ISA      = ( "Pretty_Token" );
    @VARIABLE::ISA    = ( "Pretty_Token" );
    @IDENTIFIER::ISA  = ( "Pretty_Token" );
    @OPERATOR::ISA    = ( "Pretty_Token" );
    @LB::ISA          = ( "Pretty_Token" );
    @RB::ISA          = ( "Pretty_Token" );
    @LCB::ISA         = ( "Pretty_Token" );
    @RCB::ISA         = ( "Pretty_Token" );
    @COMMA::ISA       = ( "Pretty_Token" );
    @SEMICOLON::ISA   = ( "Pretty_Token" );
    @NL::ISA          = ( "Pretty_Token" );
    @UNKNOWN::ISA     = ( "Pretty_Token" );
```

```
# How to print tokens...
# Each print method is called as: $token->pretty_print($level)

    sub Pretty_Token::pretty_print
        { print "${$_[0]} " }  # default behaviour

    sub SEMICOLON::pretty_print
        { print ";\n", "\t" x $_[1] }

    sub NL::pretty_print
        { print "\n", "\t" x $_[1] }

    sub LCB::pretty_print
        { print "\n", "\t" x $_[1]++;
          print "{\n", "\t" x $_[1];  }

    sub RCB::pretty_print
        { print "\n", "\t" x --$_[1];
          print "}\n", "\t" x $_[1];  }
# The pretty-printer itself...

    my $level = 0;
    my $input = join '', <>;
    foreach my $token ( $lexer->extract_all($input) )
    {
        $token->pretty_print($level);
    }
```

Having set up the necessary methods, the entire pretty-printing loop reduces to a single polymorphic method call: $token->pretty_print($level). That call causes the method dispatch mechanism to look at the type of the object referred to by $token and search up the inheritance tree for a matching pretty_print method. In this case, the dispatch mechanism either finds the method in the class itself (for tokens of type Semicolon, NL, LCB, or RCB) or in the Pretty_Token base class (for tokens of other type).

Apart from the improvement in modularity—and thus, in maintainability—this object-oriented version of the pretty-printer may even be faster than the previous version in some circumstances, especially for more realistic examples involving a large number of distinct token types—say fifty or more. That's because, if there are T distinct token types, the case statement version has to compare the type string against an average of $T/2$ token types, whereas the polymorphic version has to search at most two classes before finding the correct pretty_print method.

Of course, the individual tests *are* much cheaper than even a single method dispatch. However, while the total cost of the tests increases linearly with the number of token types used, the method dispatch process *never gets more expensive*, no matter how many token classes are added to the hierarchy.

7.4 USING INTERFACE POLYMORPHISM INSTEAD

The pretty-printer shown in figure 7.2 uses inheritance polymorphism to select the appropriate behavior in response to a given token. That is, all token types are related because every token class is derived from the Pretty_Token base class. So, every token object is guaranteed to have a `pretty_print` method—either its own or the one it inherits from Pretty_Token.

Inheritance polymorphism simplifies the main processing loop. We can call the `pretty_print` method on every token, confident that an appropriate behavior will result. But it has a down-side in that it requires an explicit specification of the inheritance relationships between the token classes and the Pretty_Token base class. If the system is large or likely to be maintained for a long time, or if the system requires other default behaviors (which could be added to the base class), that extra effort is reasonable. For a smaller or throw-away applications, it's just tedious.

Listing 7.3 shows another object-oriented pretty-printer, this one implemented using interface polymorphism instead. In this version, there's no relationship between the token classes. In fact, there is no ancestral Pretty_Token class at all. Instead of defaulting to Pretty_Token::`pretty_print`, the polymorphic call to `pretty_print` either succeeds—if the token is of a class whose interface offers a `pretty_print` method—or fails—if the token is of some other class, which doesn't.

That failure is indicated by throwing an exception (with a message such as: **can't locate object method "pretty_print" via package "Identifier"**). Rather than letting that exception kill the program, we catch it in an `eval` block, then resort to the default behavior explicitly.

There are plenty of other alternatives.[2] We can avoid the extra cost of the exception by working out beforehand whether the token will be able to handle the method call:

```
foreach my $token ( $lexer->extract_all($input) )
{
    if ( $token->can("pretty_print") )
        { $token->pretty_print($level) }
    else
        { print "$$token "; }
}
```

Or we can make sure that *every* class can handle a request to `pretty_print`, by adding the default version of that method to class UNIVERSAL:

```
sub UNIVERSAL::pretty_print { print "${$_[0]} " }

# then later...

foreach my $token ( $lexer->extract_all($input) )
{
    $token->pretty_print($level);
}
```

---

[2] ...this *is* Perl, after all.

```perl
package main;
use Lexer 2.00;

my $lexer = Lexer->new ('\d+'=> 'NUMBER',
                        '\$\w+'=> 'VARIABLE',
                        '\w+'=> 'IDENTIFIER',
                        '=|<'=> 'OPERATOR',
                        '\('=> 'LB',
                        '\)'=> 'RB',
                        '\{'=> 'LCB',
                        '\}'=> 'RCB',
                        ','=> 'COMMA',
                        ';'=> 'SEMICOLON',
                        '\n'=> 'NL',
                        '\S'=> 'UNKNOWN',
                       );

# How to print tokens...
# Each print method is called as: $token->pretty_print($level)

    sub SEMICOLON::pretty_print
         { print ";\n", "\t" x $_[1] }

    sub NL::pretty_print
         { print "\n", "\t" x $_[1] }

    sub LCB::pretty_print
         { print "\n", "\t" x $_[1]++;
           print "{\n", "\t" x $_[1];  }

    sub RCB::pretty_print
         { print "\n", "\t" x --$_[1];
           print "}\n", "\t" x $_[1];  }

# The pretty-printer itself...

  my $level = 0;
  my $input = join '', <>;
  foreach my $token ( $lexer->extract_all($input) )
  {
    eval { $token->pretty_print($level) } or print "$$token ";
  }
```

Of course, by resorting to the Mother Of All Classes, we have now effectively slipped back into inheritance polymorphism. Unfortunately, we've also given every other object in our program a pretty_print method.

As a final alternative, we can abuse the method dispatch mechanism like this:

```
foreach my $token ( $lexer->extract_all($input) )
{
   my $method_ref = $token->can("pretty_print")
                    || sub { print "${$_[0]} " };
   $token->$method_ref($level);
}
```

In this little foray into the Dark Side, we invoke the method dispatch mechanism, via the `can` method, to determine the correct polymorphic method for the object. If no suitable method is found, `can` returns `undef`, causing the right-hand side of the `||` to be selected. In that case, we use an anonymous subroutine to invent a suitable method on the spot!

Having decided how to handle the call, we invoke the appropriate method, or method substitute, through the reference in `$method_ref`. Perl doesn't care that the method invoked is sometimes just a nameless subroutine, as long as it gets the job done.

7.5 WHERE TO FIND OUT MORE

The perlobj and perltoot documentation both discuss the polymorphic effects of Perl's method dispatch semantics. The perlbot documentation also illustrates some useful tricks with inheritance.

7.6 SUMMARY

- Polymorphism is an inevitable consequence of Perl's method dispatch mechanism. Every method in every class is potentially polymorphic.
- Interface polymorphism only requires that objects provide a specific method.
- Inheritance polymorphism additionally requires that objects belong to classes in a common hierarchy.
- Polymorphic method calls are more expensive than explicit tests, but the cost of a polymorphic selection is constant, whereas the cost of explicit tests grows linearly.

CHAPTER 8

Automating class creation

After you've built a few object-oriented programs in Perl (maybe even just one), you realize that a great deal of the code required to implement any class is low-level, straightforward, repetitive, and just plain tedious to write. Fortunately, many Lazy programmers have already trodden those same wearisome paths, and the very Laziest of them have created tools to reduce the effort. This chapter looks at the two most widely used of those tools: the Class::Struct and Class::MethodMaker modules.

8.1 *THE CLASS::STRUCT MODULE*

The tedious part of constructing a class is usually the setting up of the constructor and accessor methods, especially if the constructor does nothing more than initialize the attributes of the class. If your classes have reasonably simple attributes, and you're not planning to use inheritance, Jim Miner's standard Class::Struct module[1] can save you a great deal of effort.

8.1.1 Creating classes

Class::Struct exports a single subroutine, struct, which you then use to specify a set of attributes that a particular class is to possess. Class::Struct generates and compiles some Perl code that sets up an appropriate constructor and accessors for the nominated class.

---

[1] ...which is a rewrite of Dean Roehrich's Class::Template module, which, in turn, was based on a design by Tom Christiansen.

For example, if we wanted to specify the Bug class from chapter 3 with scalar attributes *id*, *type*, and *desc*, we could set it up like so:

```
use Class::Struct;

struct Bug =>
{
   id   => '$',
   type => '$',
   desc => '$',
};
```

Class::Struct then generates code equivalent to the package shown in listing 8.1. The constructor creates an appropriate entry for each attribute in the underlying hash and blesses the hash into the Bug class.

Each accessor generated for class Bug is a method with the same name as the attribute it accesses. Each method can take a single argument, which it treats as a new value to be assigned to the attribute. If no argument is passed, the accessor returns the attribute's current value.

The `struct` subroutine can take a variety of argument types, allowing us to set up different implementations for different classes. As the code in listing 8.1 indicates, the example above sets up the Bug class so that Bug objects are implemented as hashes. The `struct` subroutine knows to base the class on hashes because the attribute set has been passed in an anonymous hash.

If, on the other hand, we pass the attribute specifications in an anonymous array:

```
struct Bug =>
[
   id   => '$',
   type => '$',
   desc => '$',
];
```

then `struct` sets the class up based on arrays instead. In other words, it generates the code shown in listing 8.2.

We can also create an array-based class by omitting the class name entirely and passing the attributes as a list (i.e., in parentheses). In that case, `struct` installs the constructor and accessors into the current package. Hence, we can rewrite the previous example as

```
package Bug;
use Class::Struct;

struct
(
   id   => '$',
   type => '$',
   desc => '$',
);
```

This form is particularly useful when we need to define other methods for a class, in addition to those created by `struct`.

Listing 8.1 Equivalent code generated by the Class::Struct module

```perl
package Bug;
use Carp;

sub new
{
  my $self = {};
  $self->{'id'} = undef;
  $self->{'type'} = undef;
  $self->{'desc'} = undef;
  bless $self;
}

sub id
{
  my ($self, $newval) = @_;
  croak 'Too many arguments to id' if @_ > 2;
  $self->{'id'} = $newval if @_ > 1;
  return $self->{'id'};
}

sub type
{
  my ($self, $newval) = @_;
  croak 'Too many arguments to type' if @_ > 2;
  $self->{'type'} = $newval if @_ > 1;
  return $self->{'type'};
}

sub desc
{
  my ($self, $newval) = @_;
  croak 'Too many arguments to desc' if @_ > 2;
  $self->{'desc'} = $newval if @_ > 1;
  return $self->{'desc'};
}
```

8.1.2 Attribute types

The new class's attribute set is passed as a series of *key=>value* pairs regardless of whether it is passed in a hash or an array. Each key specifies the name of one attribute. The corresponding value specifies the type of that attribute. The possible types are '$', '@', '%', or a class name. These types indicate whether the attribute is (respectively) a scalar, an array, a hash, or an object of the specified class.

Therefore, if we want the *desc* attribute to store a list of values and the *id* attribute to be a hash, we can write:

```perl
package Bug;
use Carp;

sub new
{
  my $self = [];
  $self->[0] = undef;
  $self->[1] = undef;
  $self->[2] = undef;
  bless $self;
}

sub id
{
  my ($self, $newval) = @_;
  croak 'Too many arguments to id' if @_ > 2;
  $self->[0] = $newval if @_ > 1;
  return $self->[0];
}

sub type
{
  my ($self, $newval) = @_;
  croak 'Too many arguments to type' if @_ > 2;
  $self->[1] = $newval if @_ > 1;
  return $self->[1];
}

sub desc
{
  my ($self, $newval) = @_;
  croak 'Too many arguments to desc' if @_ > 2;
  $self->[2] = $newval if @_ > 1;
  return $self->[2];
}
```

```perl
struct Bug =>
{
  id   => '%',          # id attribute refers to a hash
  type => '$',
  desc => '@',          # desc attribute refers to an array
};
```

Doing so changes the nature of the constructor and the accessors for the two changed attributes. The new code generated for them is shown in listing 8.3. Note that we've returned to the hash-based version of Bug objects so you should compare this version to listing 8.1. The accessors id and desc now take up to two arguments: a key or index to be looked up and a new value to be assigned. If neither is given, the accessor simply returns a reference to the hash

Listing 8.3 Bug class code with different types of attributes

```perl
package Bug;
use Carp;

sub new
{
    my $self = {};
    $self->{'id'} = {};
    $self->{'type'} = undef;
    $self->{'desc'} = [];
    bless $self;
}

sub id
{
    my ($self, $key, $newval) = @_;
    croak 'Too many arguments to id' if @_ > 3;
    $self->{'id'}->{$key} = $newval if @_ > 2;
    return $self->{'id'}->{$key} if @_ > 1;
    return $self->{'id'};
}

sub type
{
    my ($self, $newval) = @_;
    croak 'Too many arguments to type' if @_ > 2;
    $self->{'type'} = $newval if @_ > 1;
    return $self->{'type'};
}

sub desc
{
    my ($self, $index, $newval) = @_;
    croak 'Too many arguments to desc' if @_ > 3;
    $self->{'desc'}->[$index] = $newval if @_ > 2;
    return $self->{'desc'}->[$index] if @_ > 1;
    return $self->{'desc'};
}
```

or array that implements the entire attribute. If a key or index is given, the accessor returns the value of that particular entry or element of the attribute. If a new value is also given, that new value replaces the existing value for the specified entry or element.

Sometimes, it's useful to have accessors that return a reference to what they access, rather than a copy of its value. We can tell struct to generate such an accessor by prefixing the attribute's type specifier with an asterisk:

```
struct Bug =>
{
    id   => '%',
    type => '*$',        # type attribute value returned by reference
    desc => '@',
};
```

The Bug::type accessor now returns a reference to the *type* attribute, rather than a copy of its value, allowing us to write

```
$type_ref = $bug->type;
```

```
# and later…
```

```
${$type_ref} = "serious";   # same as: $bug->type("serious)
```

In a similar way, we can arrange for Bug::id and Bug::desc to return references to their individual entries or elements by specifying their types as '*%' and '*@' respectively. Of course, this approach violates the encapsulation of the Bug class by exposing the implementation of the *type* attribute, so it's almost certainly a Bad Idea.

8.1.3 Hierarchical class structures

The type specifier for an attribute can also be the name of some other class, perhaps one also built using Class::Struct. For example

```
struct BugType =>
{
    category  => '$',
    severity  => '$',
    hardware  => '$',
};
struct Bug =>
{
    id     => '%',
    type   => 'BugType',      # type attr refers to BugType object
    desc   => '@',
};
```

Now, the *type* attribute of a Bug object stores a reference to a BugType object. That nested object is automatically set up by Bug::new, which calls BugType->new() to create it. Thereafter, the Bug::type accessor returns a reference to the embedded object whenever it's called. To access the *severity* attribute within the *type* attribute, we would write

```
print "severity was: ", $bug->type->severity;
```

As with any other kind of accessor, if the Bug::type accessor is called with an argument, the existing BugType object is replaced by that argument. The accessor also checks that the argument *is* in fact a reference to a BugType object. Otherwise, an exception is thrown indicating the type mismatch. For example

```
$type = BugType->new();
$type->category("dumb user error");
$type->severity("fatal");
```

```
$type->hardware(0);

$bug->type($type);           # okay, previous object replaced

$bug->type("unknown")        # will die with "type argument is wrong class"
```

8.1.4 Initializing objects

The constructor provided to a class by struct takes no arguments and does only the most rudimentary initialization: scalar attributes remain undefined; array and hash attributes are initialized with an empty list; and class attributes have their constructor called with no arguments.[2]

In order to initialize a Bug object nontrivially, we're going to have to provide our own initialization method. For example

```
sub Bug::init
{
   my ($self, %args) = @_;
   $self->id($args{id});
   $self->desc($args{desc} || "No description");
   $self->type->category($args{category} || "unknown");
   $self->type->severity($args{severity} || "unknown");
   $self->type->hardware($args{hardware});
   return $self;
}
```

We can use that method immediately after the constructor like so:

```
my $bug = Bug->new->init(id        => "0123",
                         category  => "dumb user error",
                         severity  => "",
                         hardware  => 1,
                         desc      => "broken 'cup holder'");
```

Note that init returns a reference to the object on which it's called, so that it can be chained after the constructor in this way.

8.1.5 Inheritance and generated classes

If we look back at the constructor methods generated by struct (for example, in figure 8.1), we notice that each constructor generated by Class::Struct uses the one-argument version of bless. That's unfortunate because it means you can't derive a new class from a struct-generated class without having to reimplement the constructor in the derived class.[3]

For example, if we tried to trivially derive from the Bug class:

```
package FixedBug;
@ISA = qw( Bug );
```

---

[2] A patch that allows generated constructors to take initializer lists has been submitted, so you may find that it's possible to initialize objects directly now.

[3] A patch that fixes this problem has also been submitted, so this difficulty may soon disappear.

and then created a FixedBug object:

```
my $all_better_now = FixedBug->new();
```

the object created is actually blessed into the Bug class because the inherited `Bug::new` constructor was called, and it blessed the new object with only one argument.

To overcome this problem, we need to define a new constructor in the derived class that reblesses the new object correctly:

```
sub FixedBug::new
{
  my ($class) = @_;
  my $self = Bug->new();
  bless $self, $class;
}
```

`FixedBug::new` uses the two-argument form of `bless` to avoid propagating the same problem to any classes derived from FixedBug.

It's also important to note that Class::Struct is designed to generate classes that don't inherit from anything else. In fact, the module goes to extreme lengths to make sure you don't try to add any names to a generated class's `@ISA` array, and will throw an exception if you try. The Class::MethodMaker module described in the next section provides an alternative approach that does allow you to autogenerate classes in the middle of a hierarchy.

8.1.6 A full example—automating the CD::Music class

Listing 8.4 shows the CD::Music class, implemented using the Class::Struct module. It is interesting to compare this version with those shown in chapter 3. Although the total amount of code has been reduced, we still have to provide some components—the class attribute `$_count`, the initialization method, and the `location` accessor—by hand.

Class::Struct provides no facilities for automating the creation of class attributes, so the implementation of the shared `$_count` attribute as a lexical is the same as in previous versions of the class.

The initialization method is interesting in that it uses a symbolic reference to call the appropriate accessor (`$self->$attr(...)`) for each initialization value. In other words, it iterates through each key in the hash-like argument list and uses that key as the name of an accessor method to call, passing the corresponding initializer value (`$args{$attr}`) to that accessor. This approach is slower than a straight initialization:

```
sub init
{
  my ($self, %args) = @_;
  %{$self} = %args;
  return $self;
}
```

but has the important advantage that it catches any spurious initialization attempts. If the wrong attribute name is used, there will be no corresponding accessor. If the wrong type of initialization value is specified, the accessor will detect it.

```perl
package CD::Music;
$VERSION = 3.00;
use strict;

use Class::Struct;

{
   # Retrieve and manipulate class attribute: object count
   my $_count = 0;
   sub count { $_count }
   sub _incr_count { ++$_count }
   sub _decr_count { --$_count }
}

# define constructor and accessors
struct
(
   name      => '$', artist => '$',
   publisher => '$', ISBN   => '$',
   tracks    => '$', rating => '$',
   room      => '$', shelf  => '$',
);

# define initialization
sub init
{
   my ($self, %args) = @_;
   foreach my $attr (keys %args)
   {
      no strict "refs";
      $self->$attr( $args{$attr} );
   }
   $self->_incr_count();
   return $self;
}

# destructor adjusts object count
sub DESTROY { $_[0]->_decr_count() }

# get or set room and shelf together
sub location
{
   my ($self, $room, $shelf) = @_;
   $self->room($room) if $room;
   $self->shelf($shelf) if $shelf;
   return ($self->room, $self->shelf);
}
```

8.2 THE CLASS::METHODMAKER MODULE

Class::Struct is quite adequate for creating simple class structures. Class:Struct also has the important advantage of coming standard with the Perl distribution (so you can be sure everyone else has it too). However, if we need to generate classes with more complex and sophisticated interfaces, Class::Struct's limitations soon become apparent.

Filling that gap is Peter Seibel's CPAN module: Class::MethodMaker. It provides all of the features offered by Class::Struct—albeit, with a slightly different interface—and a great many more besides.

To use Class::MethodMaker to specify a class, we load the module and pass a list of *key* =>*value* pairs to the `use` statement. Each pair specifies a list of methods to make within the current package. In other words, the usage is conceptually similar to calling `Class::Struct::struct` with no class name and a parenthesized attribute list. The difference is that, whereas with Class::Struct each key is the name of an accessor method, and each value is a type specifier, in Class::MethodMaker, each key is a method type specifier, and each value is a method name or a list of method names.

For example to generate the basic Bug class used as an example in the previous section, we can write:

```
package Bug;

use Class::MethodMaker
   get_set => [ 'id', 'type', 'desc' ],
   new     => 'new';
```

This specifies that `Bug::id`, `Bug::type`, and `Bug::desc` are get/set accessors for scalar attributes and `Bug::new` is a constructor.

Alternatively, we can load the module with a single argument: `"-sugar"`. In that case, Class::MethodMaker sets up a special class method, `methods::make`, that allows us to define classes somewhat more poetically:[4]

```
use Class::MethodMaker '-sugar';

package Bug;

make methods
   get_set => [ 'id', 'type', 'desc' ],
   new     => 'new';
```

Class::MethodMaker offers eighteen different ways of creating methods for a class. The following subsections describe the most important of them.

---

[4] Once again we're using the dreaded indirect object syntax because it makes the resulting code look prettier, and because it's consistently described that way in Class::MethodMaker's documentation. It's still a bad idea, though.

8.2.1 Constructors

All classes created using Class::MethodMaker are based on blessed hashes. However, unlike Class::Struct, the module does not automatically create a constructor for the new class it's building. Instead, we have to explicitly request one.

The easiest way to do that is to use the `"new"` specifier as a key argument to use `Class::MethodMaker`. As shown above, the `"new"` specifier takes a string value indicating the actual name of the constructor. For example, if we want a constructor called enbug, instead of new, we specify:

```
package Bug;
use Class::MethodMaker
   new  => 'enbug';
```

Thereafter, we can create Bug objects like so:

```
$next_bug = Bug->enbug();
```

It is also possible to create two or more identical constructors at the same time, perhaps to cater to a multilingual environment:

```
package Bug;
use Class::MethodMaker
   new  => ["new", "nouveau", "neue", "tsukuru", "chu"];
```

Whatever we call it—let's stick with new for the time being—the constructor created looks like this:

```
sub Bug::new
{
   my ($class) = @_;
   my $self = {};
   bless $self, $class;
}
```

Note, in particular, that this constructor uses a two-argument blessing to create objects. Therefore, classes created using Class::MethodMaker can be inherited without redefining their constructor, unlike those built using Class::Struct.

Of course, a trivial constructor such as the one created by the `"new"` specifier is of limited use. We almost certainly need to define an init method to load some useful attribute values, as we did for Class::Struct. To support this need, Class::MethodMaker can also create constructors that *automatically* call such a method; we just specify `"new_with_init"` instead of `"new"`:

```
package Bug;
use Class::MethodMaker
    new_with_init=> 'new';
```

Now, the generated constructor looks like this:

```
sub Bug::new
{
   my ($class, @args) = @_;
   my $self = {};
   bless $self, $class;
```

```
  $self->init(@args);
  return $self;
}
```

That is, the constructor passes any extra arguments it receives to the newly created object's init method.

Of course, it would be even better if we didn't have to write init at all. Class::Method-Maker encourages this with the "new_hash_init" specifier:

```
package Bug;
use Class::MethodMaker
        new_hash_init=> 'new';
```

This version produces a constructor like this:

```
sub Bug::new
{
  my ($class, %args) = @_;
  my $self = {};
  bless $self, $class;
  foreach my $attribute (keys %args)
  {
    $self->$attribute($args{$attribute});
  }
  return $self;
}
```

This form of the constructor expects a list of *attribute=>value* pairs. Once the new object is blessed, the constructor loops through each attribute name (in $attribute) and calls the corresponding accessor method for that attribute ($self->$attribute(...)), passing the corresponding initialization value from the argument list ($args{$attribute}).

8.2.2 Scalar attributes

Scalar attributes are probably the most commonly needed components of a class. As shown above, the "get_set" key can be used to generate such attributes and the necessary accessors for them. The value for this key must be either a single string—indicating the name of one such scalar attribute—or a reference to an array of such strings—indicating one or more scalar attributes.

For each specified attribute, Class::MethodMaker creates two methods: a "get-or-set" accessor, which is exactly like the scalar accessors created by Class::Struct; and a "clear" method, which resets the value of the scalar to undef. For example, given the specification:

```
package Bug;
use Class::MethodMaker
  get_set=> [ qw( id type desc ) ];
```

or its exact equivalent

```
package Bug;
use Class::MethodMaker
  get_set=> 'id',
  get_set=> 'type',
  get_set=> 'desc';
```

Class::MethodMaker generates the methods:

```
sub Bug::id
{
  my ($self, $new) = @_;
  defined($new) and $self->{'id'} = $new;
  return $self->{'id'};
}

sub Bug::clear_id
{
  my ($self, $new) = @_;
  $self->{'id'} = undef;
}
```

as well as structurally identical methods for `Bug::type`, `Bug::clear_type`, `Bug::desc`, and `Bug::clear_desc`. Because the accessor uses `defined` to test for an argument, it can't be used to set an attribute to `undef`. Hence, the need for the `clear_...` methods.

8.2.3 Grouped scalar attributes

Sometimes, sets of attributes fall into logical groups. The `"grouped_fields"` specifier generates scalar attributes just like `"get_set"`, except that it also generates methods that return the complete list of attributes for each specified group. The value for this key must be a reference to an array of *group*=>[*attributes*] pairs. For example:

```
package Personal_Details;
use Class::MethodMaker
  grouped_fields => [
                     required => [qw(name address email)],
                     optional => [qw(phone fax age)],
                    ];
```

This specification creates "get/set" and "clear" accessors for the six scalar attributes and also generates two extra methods:

```
sub Personal_Details::required { return ('name', 'address', 'email') }
sub Personal_Details::optional { return ('phone', 'fax', 'age') }
```

We might use those methods to simplify the task of prompting for data for an object:

```
sub Personal_Details::prompt_data
{
  my ($self) = @_;
  foreach my $group ( qw(required optional) )
  {
    foreach my $attribute ( $self->$group() )
    {
      print "Enter your $attribute ($group): ";
      print "Try again: " until <> =~ /^(.*\S.*)$/ || $group !~ /required/;
      $self->$attribute($1);
    }
  }
}
```

Because we're stepping through the two attribute lists returned by `Personal_Details::required` and `Personal_Details::optional`, if we subsequently add another attribute to either group or add another group entirely, the `prompt_data` method still works correctly.

8.2.4 Flaglike attributes

Some attributes of classes act as nothing more than Boolean flags, their values indicating only whether specific conditions or properties are true for a given object. It's wasteful to devote an entire hash element to each flag, so Class::MethodMaker provides the `"boolean"` key, which allows us to create single-bit attributes.

For example, we might declare:

```
package Employee;
use Class::MethodMaker
  new     => "new",
  boolean => [ qw(is_permanent part_timer is_manager) ];
```

For each specified `"boolean"` attribute, Class::MethodMaker creates a `set_...` accessor, a `clear_...` accessor, and a combined "get/set" accessor. For example, `set_is_permanent`, `clear_is_permanent`, `is_permanent`, and so on. The "set" and "clear" accessors switch the corresponding bit-flag on or off. The "get/set" accessor sets or clears the bit-flag, depending on the truth value of its argument (if any), and returns the value of the flag.

8.2.5 Keylike attributes

Often we need to locate a particular object according to the value of one of its attributes. (For example, *find the soldier with serial number: US000001*, or *find the CD with ASIN: B000002KYR*, etc.) In other words, we want a particular attribute to act as a unique key among all objects of a given class.

We can create such an attribute using the `"key_attrib"` specifier:

```
package Soldier;
use Class::MethodMaker
  get_set   => [ qw( name rank ) ],
  key_attrib=> 'serial_num';
```

Attributes specified using `"key_attrib"` have "get/set" and "clear" accessors, just like those specified using `"get_set"`. However, for each key attribute, Class::MethodMaker also creates a class method, `find_...`, that takes a list of key values for that attribute and returns a list of references to objects whose attributes have those key values. For example

```
($monty, $patton) = Soldier->find_serial_num("GB000001", "US000001")
```

Class::MethodMaker automatically takes care of tracking any objects that have `"key_attrib"` attributes. In addition, each accessor method ensures that every object's corresponding key is unique. Whenever an object's key atrribute is changed, for example:

```
$zhukov->serial_num("CCCP000001");

# and later...

$monty->serial_num("CCCP000001");
```

the object that previously had that key value has its key attribute reset to undef. That is, after the two attribute assignments above, the "serial_num" attribute of the object referred to by $zhukov would have the value undef. No warning is issued when this happens, so it's often a good idea to check whether a key is already in use before assigning it:

```
$monty->serial_num("CCCP00001")
   unless Soldier->find_serial_num("CCCP00001");
```

This check works because, when there is no object with the specified key, find_... returns an empty list. However, that's not always the desired behavior. Sometimes it is useful if the search actually *creates* a matching object if one doesn't already exist.[5] Class::MethodMaker allows us to define key attributes whose corresponding find_... method works in just that way, by using the "key_with_create" specifier instead of using "key_attrib". For example:

```
package Encryption::Key;
use Class::MethodMaker
   new            => "new",
   boolean        => 'used',
   key_with_create => 'key';

sub unused_key
{
   my ($class, $bitstring) = @_;
   my $key = Encryption::Key->find_key($bitstring);
   return undef if $key->used;
   return $key;
}
```

The unused_key method looks for an existing Encryption::Key object with the specified *key* attribute. The find_key method either locates such an object or automatically creates a new one with the requested key by calling the method Encryption::Key->new()->key($bitstring)). The unused_key method checks if the key has been used and returns undef if it has. Otherwise, the method returns a reference to the appropriate Encryption::Key object.[6]

8.2.6 Nonscalar attributes

The "grouped_fields" specifier shown earlier sets up a logical grouping of a set of scalar attributes, which are otherwise completely separate. If we want a *physical* grouping of scalar attributes, we can use the "struct", "hash", or "list" keys instead.

The "struct" key sets up a single attribute that is an array of scalar slots. For each slot in this array, a "get/set" and a "clear" accessor is generated (exactly like all the other scalar accessors we've seen so far). In addition, a method called struct is generated, which can get or set the complete array at once.

---

[5] In the same way that "missing" entries of a hash are autovivified when they are needed.

[6] The trick, of course, is that the "used" flag of any newly created Encryption::Key object will, by default, be initialized to false. This ensures that, if the key has never been used before, unused_key will automatically create, and successfully return, a suitable Encryption::Key object.

On the other hand, sometimes we need one or more attributes, each of which is a separate array. For example, we might be implementing a scheduling object with assorted priority queues. The `"list"` specifier provides a means of creating a single attribute which acts like an array:

```
package Scheduler;
use Class::MethodMaker
  new  => "new",
  list => [qw( priority_queue normal_queue standby_queue)];
```

In a similar way, Class::MethodMaker also allows us to define attributes that are hashes, using the `"hash"` specifier.

8.2.7 Class attributes

All of the attributes described above are object attributes; their values are particular to individual objects. Class::MethodMaker also allows us to create hash attributes that are class attributes (that is, their values are shared by every object of a given class). Such shared hash attributes are specified using the `"static_hash"` specifier.

Class::MethodMaker doesn't provide a means of defining shared scalar or array attributes, but we can always use an entry in a shared hash attribute to store such a scalar or array value. For example:

```
package Bug;
use Class::MethodMaker
  static_hash => 'database';

Bug->database(queue=>[]);

# and later…

if ( Bug->database('status') eq 'locked' )
{
  warn "Can't create new bug reports. DB is locked";
  push @{Bug->database('queue')}, $request;
}
```

8.2.8 Nested objects as attributes

Like Class::Struct, Class::MethodMaker supports nested blessed objects as attributes. To set up such object attributes, we use the `"object"` specifier. Let's reimplement the same nested BugType example we used earlier. We'll use the `"-sugar"` option to avoid repeated re-use of Class::MethodMaker:

```
use Class::MethodMaker "-sugar";

package BugType;
make methods
  new_hash_init => 'new',
  get_set       => ['category', 'severity', 'hardware'];
```

```
package Bug;
make methods
   new      => 'new',
   get_set  => ['id', 'desc'],
   object   => [ BugType => 'type'];
```

The value associated with the `"object"` specifier is an anonymous array of *class-name=>definition* pairs—we only used one such pair, `BugType=>'type'`, in the above example.

The *definition* component of each of those pairs may be a single string (as above), indicating the name of the attribute object; or a list of strings, indicating the names of one or more attribute objects of the specified class; or a hash (see below).

For each attribute object specified in this way, Class::MethodMaker creates a "get/set" accessor method with the same name as the attribute (e.g., `type` in the above example). If it is called without any arguments, the accessor returns a reference to the nested object. If it is called with arguments, the accessor checks whether the first argument is a reference to another object of the appropriate type, in which case it replaces the existing nested attribute. Otherwise, the accessor assumes that the entire argument list should be passed to the constructor for the object's class to create a new object to replace the current one:

```
my $bug = Bug->new();

# Set up a new nested BugType object…
$bug->type( BugType->new(category=>"power", severity=>"meltdown") );

# or, exactly the same…
$bug->type( category=>"power", severity=>"meltdown" );

# $bug->type() returns an object reference we can use…
print $bug->type()->category();
$bug->type()->hardware(1);
```

Class::MethodMaker also provides a way to specify that the methods of a nested object should also be directly accessible through the surrounding object. For example, to print out all the information in a Bug object we currently have to write

```
print$bug->id, $bug->desc,
     $bug->type->category, $bug->type->severity, $bug->type->hardware;
```

We can, however, set up the type attribute so that calls to its accessors can be made directly on the `$bug` object itself and then automatically forwarded to the nested attribute. To do so, we use the third form of object definition where the associated specification is a hash:

```
package Bug;
make methods
   new      => 'new',
   get_set  => ['id', 'desc'],
   object   => [ BugType =>
                   {
                       slot    => 'type',
                       forward => [qw(category severity hardware)],
                   }
                ];
```

The hash has two entries: one for the key `"slot"`, which specifies the attribute object's name; and one for the key `"forward"`, which specifies an anonymous array of method names. For each method name in this array, Class::MethodMaker installs a method in the class being generated—Bug in this example. That method forwards its arguments to the same method name called on the nested attribute object. In other words, with the above definition we can now use `$bug->category()` as a synonym for `$bug->type->category()`. The full print-out of Bug data becomes:

```
print$bug->id, $bug->desc,
     $bug->category, $bug->severity, $bug->hardware;
```

The advantage of this delegation of methods to nested objects becomes obvious if the nesting is several levels deep. For example

```
print $bug->seriousness();
```

is clearly preferable to:

```
print $bug->type->severity->relative->seriousness();
```

Delegation is also useful if we later decide that a scalar attribute like `id` needs to be re-implemented as a nested object, because its semantics suddenly became more complex. For example, if we were merging two bug-tracking systems that used different ID numbering schemes, we might write something like this:

```
package BugID;
make methods
   new     => 'new',
   get_set => ['id_system_A', 'id_system_B'];

sub id { return $self->id_system_A || convert($self->id_system_B) }

package Bug;
make methods
   new     => 'new',
   get_set => 'desc',
   object  => [ BugType => 'type', # as before
                BugID   => { slot=> 'id_obj',
                             forward=> 'id',
                           }
              ];
```

Now, any existing calls to `$bug->id()` distributed throughout the code are automatically forwarded to `$bug->id_obj->id()`, ensuring that all IDs are properly converted into a standard format. Without the `"forward"` specification, any place in the code that formerly called `$bug->id()` would now throw an exception.[7]

---

[7] Similar delegation techniques can, of course, be used just as effectively in class code that has been written manually. As we have already seen, by encapsulating methods in attributes (whether coded by hand or generated by a module like Class::MethodMaker), we can insulate client code from changes in implementation details. Then, rather than locating and correcting a large number of (now-invalid) accesses to a changed attribute, we can just rewrite the affected accessor method to compensate.

8.2.9 Subroutines as attributes

Occasionally, we may want to create attributes that store subroutine references. For example, we may need to specify a particular sorting subroutine, which may be different for each object of a class. We can do this using a regular scalar attribute:

```
package List;
use Class::MethodMaker
  new_hash_init  => 'new',
  list           => 'data',
  get_set        => 'sort_order';

# and later create lists sorted in various ways…

$fwd_val = List->new(sort_order => sub { $a->val <=> $b->val });
$rev_val = List->new(sort_order => sub { $b->val <=> $a->val });
$fwd_id  = List->new(sort_order => sub { $a->id <=> $b->id  });

# and later still change the sort order for one of the lists..

$fwd_id->sort_order( sub { $a->id cmp $b->id} );
```

To actually sort such lists we can provide a sort method that accesses the subroutine reference by calling the "get/set" accessor without an argument:

```
sub List::sorted
{
  my ($self) = @_;
  return sort { $self->sort_order->() } $self->data();
}
```

Class::MethodMaker simplifies this task slightly by allowing us to define codelike attributes, using the "code" specifier:

```
package List;
use Class::MethodMaker
  new_hash_init  => 'new',
  list           => 'data',
  code           => 'sort_order';
```

The semantics of the resulting "get/set" accessor are different from those of an accessor for a normal scalar attribute. If the accessor is called with a code reference as its first argument

```
$fwd_id->sort_order( sub { $a->id cmp $b->id} );
```

it still replaces the code reference in the attribute with that argument. However, when called with any other argument list (including an empty list), the accessor actually calls the subroutine referred to by the current code reference, passing it the same argument list. Therefore, the List::sorted method can now be written like so:

```
sub List::sorted
{
  my ($self) = @_;
  return sort { $self->sort_order() } $self->data();
}
```

The `"code"` attribute effectively becomes a customized method, one that belongs uniquely to a single object rather than to its class. Unlike a regular method, when it's called, this customized pseudo-method doesn't receive a reference to the invoking object as its first argument. That doesn't matter for the `sort_order` attribute shown above, but, in other cases, it might.

To cater to those other cases, Class::MethodMaker also offers the `"method"` specifier, which acts like `"code"` except that the resulting customized method *does* receive a reference to the invoking object as its first argument. For example, we might want to create an Image class that dynamically selects its storage format depending on the size of an image. That is, smaller images are stored as bitmaps, larger images as JPEGs:

```
package Image;
use Class::MethodMaker
    new_with_init  => 'new',
    new_hash_init  => '_setup',
    get_set        => [qw(width height)],
    method         => 'store';

sub store_bitmap { … }
sub store_JPEG   { … }

sub init
{
    my ($self, %args) = @_;
    $self->_setup(%args);
    if ($self->width * $self->height > 1000)
        { $self->store(\&Image::store_JPEG) }
    else
        { $self->store(\&Image::store_bitmap) }
}

# and later…

$image->store();# store in the appropriate format
```

The `init` method sets up the customized `store` method to invoke either the `store_JPEG` or the `store_bitmap` method, depending on the overall size of the image. More importantly, when either of those methods is actually invoked—that is, when `store` is called—it is invoked as a method, with the invoking object passed as its first argument.

Note, too, that we had Class::MethodMaker create a method (`_setup`) to handle any hash-like initializers passed to `init`. This trick is handy whenever you want to use both the standard hash-like initialization offered by the `"new_hash_init"` specifier and the `init`-based initialization offered by `"new_with_init"`.

8.2.10 Abstract methods

Class::MethodMaker makes it easy to create abstract methods. The `"abstract"` specifier takes a string—or an anonymous array of strings—specifying the names of any abstract methods for the current package.

Abstract methods declared in this way don't have to be accessors. For example, we can use the Class::MethodMaker module to set up abstract methods for the Truck class (as suggested in section 6.2.5):

```
package Truck;
use Class::MethodMaker
    abstract => [qw(register tranfer_owner safety_check)];
```

Each of the named methods is set up to throw an exception immediately. For example, if class FireTruck inherited `Truck::register` without redefining it, any attempt to call `register` on a FireTruck object would produce the following exception:

Can't locate abstract method "register" in Truck called from FireTruck

8.2.11 Inheritance and generated classes

Class::MethodMaker is much more accommodating than Class::Struct when it comes to inheritance.

The constructors created by Class::MethodMaker use the two-argument form of `bless`, so it's possible to inherit from classes built using Class::MethodMaker without redefining a constructor in those derived classes.

Moreover, Class::MethodMaker doesn't care whether the package it's currently building inherits from other classes as well. It's possible to use Class::MethodMaker to extend the interface of a derived class (even when the class is derived from other classes that also use Class::MethodMaker to create some of their methods).

For example, we can easily derive the FixedBug class from Class::MethodMaker implementation of the Bug class and then use Class::MethodMaker to add extra attributes to FixedBug:

```
package Bug;
use Class::MethodMaker
    new_hash_init=> 'new',
    get_set=> [ qw( id type desc ) ];

package FixedBug;
@ISA = qw( Bug );
use Class::MethodMaker
    get_set=> [ qw( date_fixed repairer ) ];
```

8.2.12 A full example: reautomating the CD::Music class

Listing 8.5 shows the CD::Music class implemented using Class::MethodMaker.

Note that by calling `_init_args` from the `init` method, we're using the "dual constructor" trick from *Subroutines as attributes* above. We also use a shared hash attribute, *counter*, to store the classwide object counter.

Apart from the class methods and destructor method needed to control that counter, and the special `location` method, Class::MethodMaker allows us to automate the entire coding of the CD::Music class.

Compared to the Class::Struct-based version shown in figure 8.4, Class::MethodMaker's ability to define class attributes and to build dual constructors enables us to write marginally

```perl
package CD::Music;
$VERSION = 4.00;
use strict;

use Class::MethodMaker
  new_with_init  => 'new',
  new_hash_init  => '_init_args',
  static_hash    => 'counter',
  get_set        => [qw(name artist publisher ISBN
                    tracks rating room shelf )];

sub count          { $_[0]->counter('count') }
sub _incr_count  { $_[0]->counter(count=>$_[0]->counter('count')+1) }
sub _decr_count  { $_[0]->counter(count=>$_[0]->counter('count')-1) }

sub init
{
  my ($self, %args) = @_;
  $self->_init_args(%args);
  $self->_incr_count();
  return $self;
}

# destructor adjusts object count
sub DESTROY { $_[0]->_decr_count() }

# get or set room and shelf together
sub location
{
  my ($self, $room, $shelf) = @_;
  $self->room($room) if $room;
  $self->shelf($shelf) if $shelf;
  return ($self->room, $self->shelf)
}
```

less code, but apart from the noticeably simpler init method, the gain is not significant in this case. However, if we intend to inherit from CD::Music, Class::MethodMaker is the clear choice.

8.3 WHERE TO FIND OUT MORE

The Class::Struct module comes standard with Perl. The Class::MethodMaker module is available from the CPAN at: http://www.perl.com/CPAN/authors/id/PSEIBEL/. Both come with their own (brief) documentation.

The perltoot documentation also describes the Class::Struct module under the subheading *Metaclassical tools*.

8.4 SUMMARY

- The Class::Struct and Class::MethodMaker modules provide two alternatives for automatically generating classes at run time. This can make development and maintenance easier and increase the robustness of a program.
- Class::Struct can build classes based on hashes or arrays.
- It also provides a simple constructor for each class.
- Classes built with Class::Struct can neither inherit from other classes, nor (easily) be inherited from themselves.
- Class::MethodMaker always builds classes based on hashes.
- Class::MethodMaker can generate a wide range of attribute accessors, constructors, search mechanisms, and abstract methods.
- Both modules can generate accessors for attributes of scalar, array, hash, and object types. Class::MethodMaker also supports Boolean, codelike, and methodlike attributes.

C H A P T E R   9

Ties

In most languages that provide built-in data types, the behavior of those types is fixed. It's a case of "love me, love my built-in semantics!" Perl rejects this linguistic fascism by allowing us to alter the implementation and behavior of its fundamental data types: scalars, arrays, hashes, and filehandles. The key to this unusual liberty is the built-in `tie` function.

9.1 *A JACKETING TIE REQUIRED*

The `tie` function associates a specific variable or handle with an underlying data structure and a set of subroutines from a particular package. Those subroutines then mimic the behavior of that variable: assignment, retrieval of value, indexing (of arrays and hashes), iteration (of hashes), printing or reading (by filehandles). Once the variable is tied to the package containing those subroutines, they are called whenever the variable is accessed, replacing the standard interface for the particular variable. It's yet another form of polymorphism, but one applied to the intrinsic behaviors of Perl's standard data types.

If associating variables with packages and using package subroutines as an interface sounds very much like using an object and its methods, there's a good reason: it's *exactly* like using an object and its methods. Just like an object's methods, the subroutines in the package to which a variable is tied implement the interface of that variable.

The only difference is that, whereas a regular object's interface is user-defined and flexible (you can create methods with any name and argument list you like), a variable's interface is predetermined and fixed. For example, for a scalar only two methods are necessary: *fetch my value* and *store my value*. Nevertheless, Perl's `tie` mechanism is just a specialized form of object orientation.

Here's another way to think about tie-ing: according to Hollywood, the main occupations of extraterrestrial alien species appear to be:

- Finding their way inside unsuspecting humans;
- Hollowing out a little nest (usually by devouring inconvenient and unnecessary internal organs like the brain);
- Using the resulting human shell as a disguise to blend into Earth society for nefarious purposes.

Tie-ing a variable is just like that. The package that a variable is to be tied to provides a special method that eats the original variable's brain and installs a blessed object, the *implementation object*, in its place. The implementation object then provides any internal storage required by the variable, as well as methods that simulate the variable's normal behavior.

A tied variable becomes a "shell": it looks like a regular variable, it's accessed like a regular variable—but it acts like a space alien.

9.1.1 Limitations of tie-ing

There are two important limitations on tied variables and, hence, two major reasons we might choose not to use them. The first reason is performance. Tie-ing is just object-oriented programming in another guise. The subroutines that implement the behavior of a tied variable are called as methods.

That means, for example, the full polymorphic dispatch process is performed every time the value of a tied variable is retrieved or set. That imposes a substantial overhead on such operations compared to the heavily optimized performance of the hard-coded routines that implement an untied variable.

Just how big a performance hit you'll take for tie-ing a variable depends on the hardware you're using, and the sophistication of the new tied behavior. Generally, operations on a tied variable tend to be five to ten times slower. Of course, that's compensated for by the extra behaviors a tied variable may provide—which you'd have to perform separately anyway. Whether that represents an acceptable tradeoff depends on how much speed you're willing to give up in return for easier coding and increased maintainability.

The second significant limitation on tie-ing has to do with the evolving nature of Perl and the capabilities of the `tie` mechanism in particular. Until release 5.004, Perl couldn't tie filehandles at all. The interface is still incomplete as of release 5.005. For instance, there's still no way to intercept `write` operations on a tied filehandle. Similarly, earlier releases of Perl didn't fully support tie-ing of arrays.

Whether this limitation on the completeness of ties is a problem will depend entirely on what you're trying to achieve, as well as what release of Perl you're using. The problem is diminishing over time and will eventually disappear altogether, but that's of little comfort if you need a missing feature today.

9.2 TIE-ING A SCALAR

The simplest thing to tie is a scalar. To do so we simply write

```
tie $var, "Package::Name";
```

This associates a set of methods defined in the Package::Name package with the behaviors of the scalar $var. Those methods must have standard names: TIESCALAR, FETCH, STORE, and DESTROY.

The TIESCALAR method is invoked when the tie function is called on a scalar variable. It is used to create a new implementation for that scalar (i.e., to eat its brain). When the scalar is tied to a package, that package's TIESCALAR is passed the same set of arguments given to tie, except for the leading variable itself. Therefore, the above tie statement results in a call Package::Name->TIESCALAR(). If we tie the variable like this:

```
tie $var, "Package::Name", $any, $other, @args
```

the extra arguments are passed to TIESCALAR, and the call becomes Package::Name->TIESCALAR($any, $other, @args).

TIESCALAR's job is to create a new object of the appropriate class and return a reference to it. That object implements the internal state of the original variable. The blessed object itself can be any kind of object: another scalar, a hash, a closure, a typeglob, and so forth.

The FETCH method is called whenever the value of $var is requested—by printing, assigning, or incrementing it. FETCH is passed a single argument: a reference to the variable's implementation object (i.e, one created by TIESCALAR). The value that FETCH returns is used as the variable's value.

The STORE subroutine is called whenever $var's value is updated, via an assignment or increment or decrement. STORE is passed two arguments: a reference to the implementation object and the new value to be assigned. It's not expected to return a value; if it does, the value is ignored.

Like the destructor of an object, the DESTROY method is called if $var ceases to exist; that is, if its reference count reaches zero. It is called on the implementation object, not on $var itself, and may be used to tidy up any internal implementation details. Often it's not needed at all.

9.2.1 Untie-ing a scalar

There's another way in which a tied scalar's destructor may be invoked. It's possible to explicitly break the connection between a scalar and its tied implementation, using the built-in untie function:

```
untie $var;
```

After this statement is executed, the $var variable is once again a regular scalar, with the value undef. It's now completely unaffiliated with the package to which it was formerly tied.

Because that connection is severed, the variable no longer secretly houses its former implementation object. That usually means that the implementation object is no longer referred to anywhere in the program, so its destructor is called.

Generally speaking, `untie`-ing a tied variable is only important if the implementation object takes up a large amount of memory or has a nontrivial destructor that needs to be called.

9.2.2 A simple example

Let's see how those methods work together. Suppose we want a variable that automatically increments its value every time that value is examined, and that can only be assigned larger values than its current value. Such a monotonically increasing variable might be useful for allocating unique ascending ID numbers for processes, user IDS, or bar codes.

We could create a package implementing such a variable like so:

```
package Incremental;

sub TIESCALAR
{
   my ($class) = @_;
   my $implementation = 0;
   bless \$implementation, $class;
}


sub FETCH
{
   my ($implementation) = @_;
   return ++${$implementation};
}


sub STORE
{
   my ($implementation, $newval) = @_;
   croak "non-ascending assignment" unless ${$implementation} <= $newval;
   ${$implementation} = $newval;
}


sub DESTROY
{
   # Nothing to be done in this case
}
```

The constructor (`Incremental::TIESCALAR`) declares a lexical variable (`$implementation`), blesses it into the package specified by the first argument (that is, Incremental), and returns a reference to the resulting object. That object is then installed as the implementation of the scalar being tied, as shown in figure 9.1.

When the value of that tied scalar is next requested, a reference to the implementation object is passed to `Incremental::FETCH`, which dereferences it (`${$implementation}`), increments it (`++${$implementation}`), and returns the incremented value. Hence, every time the tied variable's value is queried, that value increments.

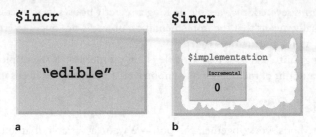

$incr

"edible"

a

$incr

$implementation

Incremental

0

b

Figure 9.1   What happens when a scalar is tied
a   Before `tie $incr, "Incremental";`
b   After `tie $incr, "Incremental";`

When a new value is assigned to the tied scalar, the STORE method is called. It first checks that the value is no less than the current value to ensure the variable remains "unidirectional." If the value is acceptable, the reference to the implementation object is deferenced, and the new value is assigned to the underlying scalar object.

The destructor is trivial (and would be omitted in real code), since there is nothing for it to do. When the tied variable's reference count becomes zero, the variable is destroyed. The only reference to implementation object is also lost, causing the implementation object itself to be destroyed. That invokes the `Incremental::DESTROY` destructor, which in this case doesn't need to do any special cleanup of the implementation object.

To actually create and use an incremental scalar, we can write the following:

```
package main;          # or wherever

tie $incr, "Incremental";# associate $incr with Incremental package

print $incr;           # calls Incremental::FETCH, prints 1
print $incr;           # calls Incremental::FETCH, prints 2
print $incr;           # calls Incremental::FETCH, prints 3

$incr = 100;           # calls Incremental::STORE

$incr += 100;          # calls Incremental::FETCH, which returns 101
                       # then Incremental::STORE, which stores 201

$incr++;               # calls Incremental::FETCH, which returns 202
                       # then Incremental::STORE, which stores 203

$next = $incr++;       # calls Incremental::FETCH, which returns 204
                       # then Incremental::FETCH, which returns 205
                       # then Incremental::STORE, which stores 206
                       # $next is assigned 204

++$incr;               # calls Incremental::FETCH, which returns 207
                       # then Incremental::STORE, which stores 208

$next = ++$incr;       # calls Incremental::FETCH, which returns 209
```

```
# then Incremental::STORE, which stores 210
# then Incremental::FETCH, which returns 211
# $next is assigned 211
```

Any access or assignment to $incr's value calls the Incremental::FETCH and Incremental::STORE methods, as expected. The add-assignment operator (+=) calls both Incremental::FETCH and Incremental::STORE—first retrieving the current value of the implementation object (after incrementing it, of course) , then adding 100, then storing the sum back into the implementation object. Operations involving -=, *=, /= or any other assignment operator do the same, although they may fail if the new value is less than the current value (e.g., $incr *= -1, $incr /= 2, $incr &= 0x0001, etc.).

The unary increment operator (++) is an interesting case. When used as a pure increment operator—that is, if the return value of the operation is ignored—it calls FETCH to get the current value, adds 1 to it, and then calls STORE to store the incremented value. On the other hand, if the return value of the preincrement *is* used—for example, assigned to $next—then the operator calls FETCH a second time to return the pre-incremented value.

Similar sequences occur for the postincrement operator. If the operation's value isn't used, there is one call to FETCH, followed by one call to STORE. If the operation's value is used, it calls FETCH (to receive the value before increment), calls FETCH again (to retrieve the value to be incremented), then calls STORE (to save the incremented value). The value returned by the first of the two FETCH calls becomes the value returned by the operation.

9.2.3 Implementing a scalar using a nonscalar

Although the previous example used a scalar as the implementation object for a tied scalar, there's no reason that any tied variable has to be implemented by an implementation object of the same type. Except for the loss of efficiency involved, we might have chosen to bless an array or a hash as the implementation object.

For example, in large applications, package variables are dangerous because of their high degree of visibility. In the section on *Lexical variables* in chapter 2, we saw how a commonly used package variable like $i can be contaminated by reuse in two or more subroutines. Any package variable is susceptible to this form of unintended coupling, and in a large program, it can be difficult to locate the source of the corruption. The Track package shown in listing 9.1 provides a simple way of finding the source of the problem.

The idea is simple. To mark a scalar package variable—say, $critical_temp—for tracking, we write:

```
Track->scalar($critical_temp);
```

This has no discernable effect on the variable[1] until we call:

```
Track->debug($critical_temp);
```

at which point the file, line, and package where the current value of $critical_temp was assigned is dumped to STDERR. The idea is to start tracking the problem variable at a point

---

[1] ...even though an alien has eaten its brain and is now living inside it.

Listing 9.1 A package for variable tracking

```perl
package Track;
$VERSION = 1.00;
use strict;

sub TIESCALAR
{
  my ($class, $val) = @_;
  bless { val => $val, src => [caller(1)] }, $class
}

sub FETCH
{
  my ($impl) = @_;
  return $impl->{val};
}

sub STORE
{
  my ($impl, $newval) = @_;
  $impl->{val} = $newval;
  $impl->{src} = [caller];
}

sub scalar
{
  tie $_[1], $_[0], $_[1];
}

sub debug
{
  my $impl = tied($_[1]);
  my ($cur_pkg, $cur_file, $cur_line) = caller;
  my ($src_pkg, $src_file, $src_line) = @{$impl->{src}};

  print STDERR "At $cur_file line $cur_line in package $cur_pkg the\n",
               "tracked variable has the value $impl->{val}, which was\n",
               "assigned at $src_file line $src_line in package $src_pkg\n";
}
```

where its value is still correct and debug it at the point where an incorrect value is first detected.

The `Track::scalar` method is the key to the whole process. It ties the variable passed as its argument—namely the variable aliased to `$_[1]`—to the Track class, passing the original value of the variant—`$_[1]` again—to the TIESCALAR constructor.

The constructor builds an anonymous hash with a `'val'` entry to store the scalar's value and a `'src'` entry to store a list of values indicating where the value was assigned. Specifically, the `'val'` entry is assigned the current value of the variable, while the `'src'` entry is assigned the package name, file name, and line number corresponding to the original call to

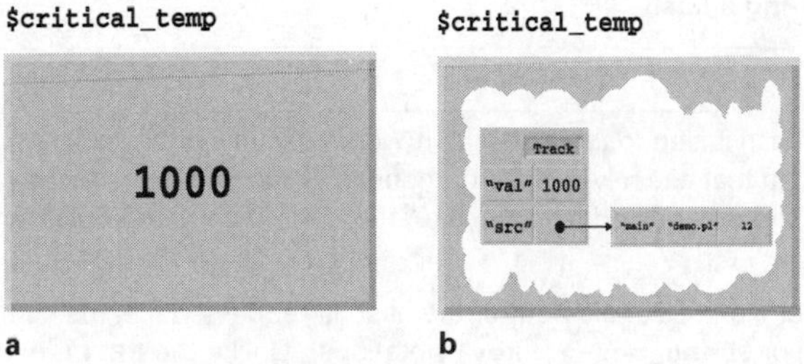

1000

a

b

Figure 9.2   Before and after tie-ing a scalar to the Track package
a   Before `Track->scalar($critical_temp);`
b   After `Track->scalar($critical_temp);`

`Track::scalar`.[2] Finally, the hash is blessed and a reference to it is returned as the new implementation object for the original scalar variable. Figure 9.2 shows a before-and-after shot of the effect.

After a variable has been tied in this way, all subsequent assignments to that variable must go through the `Track::STORE` method. That method assigns the new value to the `'val'` entry of the implementation hash, but also assigns the context information returned by `caller` to the `'src'` entry. That way, the location of the most recent assignment to a variable tied to `Track` is always stored within the implementation object.

However, because that information is hidden away inside the shell of the tied variable, the `Track::debug` method has a problem. How can it access that encapsulated data to print it out? The solution is provided by another built-in Perl function called `tied`, which takes a variable and returns a reference to its implementation object (or `undef` if the variable wasn't tied at all). Therefore, the `debug` method first calls `tied` to expose the underlying hash implementing the variable, then prints the information in that hash.

Essentially the same process is performed automatically for calls to FETCH and STORE:

```
$t = $critical_temp;    # same as: $t = tied($critical_temp)->FETCH()
$critical_temp = 100;   # same as: tied($critical_temp)->STORE(100)
```

In fact, this is how these methods receive the implementation object as their first argument.

9.3 *TIE-ING A HASH*

It's as easy to tie a hash variable to a package, as it is to tie a scalar. The only difference is that a package to which hashes are tied has to provide more methods, since a hash has a more complicated interface than a scalar. The methods needed to implement that interface are shown in table 9.1.

---

[2] Within TIESCALAR, we call `caller` with the argument 1 to make it skip back up one level of nested subroutine calls past the call to TIESCALAR itself and report on the original call to `Track::scalar`.

Table 9.1   **Methods for tie-ing a hash**

Method	Purpose
TIEHASH	called when a hash is tied to the package. It works exactly as TIESCALAR did for tied scalars, in that it receives the arguments to tie that appeared after the variable name and is expected to return a reference to a blessed implementation object.
FETCH	called whenever a particular element of the hash is requested (i.e., using the $hash{$key} or $hash_ref->{$key} notations). Unlike the FETCH method of a scalar, it is passed two arguments: a reference to the implementation object and a string containing the specified key. The value it returns is used as the value of the corresponding entry in the hash.
STORE	called whenever a value is assigned to a particular element of the hash (i.e., using the $hash{$index} = $val or $hash_ref->{$index} = $val notations). It is passed three arguments: a reference to the implementation object, a string containing the specified key, and the new value to be placed in the corresponding entry. It's not expected to return a value.
EXISTS	called whenever the exists function is applied to an entry of the tied hash (e.g., in code such as: next if exists $hash{$key}). It is passed a reference to the implementation object and a string containing the specified key. It is expected to return the appropriate true or false value.
DELETE	called whenever the delete function is applied to an entry of the tied hash (e.g., in code such as: delete $hash{$key}). It's passed a reference to the implementation object, followed by a string containing the key of the entry to delete. The value it returns is used as the result of the delete operation. If delete is used to delete two or more keys of a tied hash at the same time (e.g., delete @hash{$key1, $key2, $etc}), the DELETE method is called once for each key.
CLEAR	called whenever the entire hash is reset using the %hash = () notation. It's not expected to return a value.
FIRSTKEY	called when the "first" key of a hash is required. That is, when the built-in each function is first called on the tied hash, or at the beginning of a call to the built-in keys or values functions. FIRSTKEY is passed a reference to the implementation object and is expected to reset the tied hash's internal iterator (or rather the implementation object's simulation of that iterator). The value it returns is assumed to be the "first" key of the hash.
NEXTKEY	called every time another iterated key is required from the tied hash. That is, it is invoked every time (except the first) that the built-in each function is called or repeatedly during the execution of a call to keys or values. NEXTKEY is passed a reference to the implementation object and a string containing the most recent key iterated (i.e., the key "before" the expected next key). The value returned is assumed to be the "next" key of the hash. The subroutine should arrange to return undef after all keys have been iterated.
DESTROY	the tied hash's destructor, which is called when the tied hash ceases to exist. It is passed a reference to the implementation object. It is not expected to return a value.

9.3.1 Example: case-insensitive hashes

So let's create a hash with case-insensitive keys. That is, we'll implement a package called Insensitive::Hash that can be tied to a hash, and which implements access methods that ignore the case of the keys passed to them.

That will allow us to store a value in the entry for the key `'cat'`—for example, `$tiedhash{cat} = "meow"`—but retrieve it as `$tiedhash{CAT}`, remove it with `delete $tiedhash{Cat}`, or check on its existence via `exists $tiedhash{CaT}`, and so on. Such a facility may seem to be of dubious utility, but it might be handy in analyzing a text where we don't care whether the word *cat* appears as `'cat'` or `'Cat'`:

```
tie %count, "Insensitive::Hash";
$count{$1}++ while $text =~ m/(\S+)/g;
```

Alternatively, we might use an insensitive hash as a cache for browser search requests or as a symbol table for a programming or specification language with case-insensitive keywords. Listing 9.2 shows the implementation of the Insensitive::Hash package.

Listing 9.2 A package for case-insensitive hashes

```perl
package Insensitive::Hash;
$VERSION = 1.00;
use strict;

sub TIEHASH
{
  my ($class) = @_;
  bless {}, $class;
}

sub FETCH
{
  my ($impl, $key) = @_;
  return $impl->{lc $key}->{value};
}

sub STORE
{
  my ($impl, $key, $newval) = @_;
  $impl->{lc $key} = {key=>$key, value=>$newval};
}

sub EXISTS
{
  my ($impl, $key) = @_;
  return exists $impl->{lc $key};
}

sub DELETE
{
  my ($impl, $key) = @_;
  my $deleted_val = delete $impl->{lc $key};
```

```
        return $deleted_val->{value} if $deleted_val;
}

sub CLEAR
{
    my ($impl) = @_;
    %{$impl} = ();
}

sub FIRSTKEY
{
    my ($impl) = @_;
    keys %{$impl};
    my $first_key = each %{$impl};
    return undef unless defined $first_key;
    return $impl->{$first_key}->{key};
}

sub NEXTKEY
{
    my ($impl, $nextkey) = @_;
    my $next_key = each %{$impl};
    return undef unless defined $next_key;
    return $impl->{$next_key}->{key};
}
```

An insensitive package

The implementation object for the case-insensitive hash is another hash. The keys in that hash are lower-cased versions of the actual keys used. The value for each key is a reference to yet another hash, which stores the original (case-sensitive) key, and—finally!—the entry's actual value. When it's up and running, a hash tied to the Insensitive::Hash package has an internal structure like that shown in figure 9.3.

The interface code that Insensitive::Hash uses to accomplish all that is surprisingly simple. The code just blesses an empty anonymous hash into its class. Since, initially, no entries exist, we don't need the more complex hash of hashes structure yet.

The STORE method sets up that nested structure by converting the key to be stored to lowercase (**lc $key**), finding the corresponding entry in the implementation object (**$impl->{lc $key}**), and assigning it a reference to a new anonymous hash. That new hash stores the actual key passed and the new value for the entry ($impl->{lc $key} **= {key=>$key, value=>$newval}**).

Once such a structure is set up, the FETCH method can easily retrieve the value for a given key by first making it case insensitive (**lc $key**), using that version as a key into the implementation object (**$impl->{lc $key}**), and retrieving the 'value' entry though the resulting hash reference ($impl->{lc $key}**->{value}**).

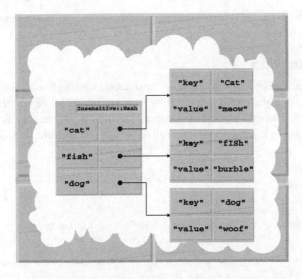

Figure 9.3 The internal structure of a tied hash

A key exists in the tied hash if its lower-case version exists in the implementation object, so the existence test in EXISTS simply lowers the case of the specified key and checks for a corresponding entry in the implementation object.

Deleting a key would normally be equally simple—merely delete the corresponding lower-case key in the implementation object—except that we also want to return the value of the deleted entry (in keeping with the normal behavior of delete). To do that, we have to take the hash reference returned by deleting the lower-cased key from the implementation object and access its 'value' entry. Of course, if the key doesn't exist in the hash, the delete returns undef, so there's no need to do anything in that case.

Clearing the entire hash is simple. We just clear the implementation object by dereferencing our reference to it (**$impl**) to get the actual hash itself (**%{**$impl**}**) and assigning an empty list to that hash.

Supporting an iterator for the hash with FIRSTKEY and NEXTKEY is the trickiest part of the package. Assuming that we want to return the actual (case-sensitive) keys under which each entry was stored, we need to return the 'key' value of the anonymous hash referred to by each entry of the implementation object.

To get the first such key, in FIRSTKEY we reset the implementation hash's own iterator by calling keys %{$impl}. We retrieve the first lower-cased key with a call to each %{$impl}. If that call returns undef, it means that there was no first key—in other words, the implementation hash is empty. So we likewise return undef to indicate that the tied hash itself is empty. If there *was* a first key, we return the value of the corresponding 'key' field ($impl->{$first_key}->{key}).

Finding the next key of a tied hash in NEXTKEY is almost exactly the same as finding the first. Once again, we call each %{$impl} to iterate through the implementation hash; once again we check for an undefined result, indicating no more keys are available; once again, we extract the 'key' field and return it. The only difference is that, unlike in FIRSTKEY, we don't reset the implementation hash's iterator before calling each on it. Therefore, we keep stepping though the implementation hash's keys each time NEXTKEY is called.

An insensitive application

We can use the Insensitive::Hash package to build an automatic indexing mechanism for text. Let's assume that each page in the text is delimited by a pair of matched tags: <PAGE>...</PAGE>. We'll use the Text::Balanced module[3] to extract and index a page at a time. Once we have the Insensitive::Hash package written, the full code of the indexing application is remarkably short:

```perl
use Insensitive::Hash;
use Text::Balanced 'extract_tagged';

# open file and load complete text
open TEXTFILE, shift(@ARGV) or die "Usage: index <textfile>\n";
local $/;
$text = <TEXTFILE>;

# create case-insensitive hash
tie %xref, "Insensitive::Hash";

# extract each page in turn…
while (my $page = extract_tagged($text,'<PAGE>'))
{
    $page_num++;
    # for each word, record that it's on the current page
    $xref{$1} = { %{$xref{$1}|{}}, $page_num => 1 }
        while $page =~ m/\G\s*(\S+)/g;
}

# for each word that was found…
foreach my $word (sort keys %xref)
{
    # extract, sort and print the list of pages where the word appeared
    print ucfirst lc $word, ": ";
    @page_list = sort {$a<=>$b} keys %{$xref{$word}};
    print join(",",@page_list), "\n";
}
```

Of course, the same application implemented using an ordinary hash is not appreciably longer than the version above. In fact, the only difference is that every place where we access any entry of the %xref hash or retrieve its keys, we need to explicitly apply lc to the key involved.

The disadvantage in that case is that we're only human and, if we miss one such point of access, an entry with a mixed-case key may immediately autovivify and cause the corresponding page number to be lost. Alternatively, the two (or more) separate entries for the same

---

[3] Available from the CPAN in the directory http://www.perl.com/CPAN/authors/id/DCONWAY/

word may result in the program printing out a series of annoyingly distinct index lists for the same word.

9.4 TIE-ING AN ARRAY

A package suitable for tie-ing an array has to be even more sophisticated than one for tie-ing a hash. Once again, we create a package with specially named methods that implement the new behavior of the tied array, but this time thirteen (!) methods are required, as shown in table 9.2.

Table 9.2   Methods for tie-ing an array

Method	Purpose
TIEARRAY	called when an array is tied to the package. Like TIESCALAR and TIEHASH, it receives the arguments to tie that appeared after the variable name, and is expected to return a reference to a blessed implementation object.
FETCH	called whenever a particular element of the array is requested (i.e., using the $array[$index] or $array_ref->[$index] notations). It's passed two arguments: a reference to the implementation object and the specified index. The value it returns is taken to be the value of the corresponding element.
STORE	called whenever a value assigned to particular element of the array is requested (i.e., $array[$index] = $val or $array_ref->[$index] = $val). It's passed three arguments: a reference to the implementation object, the index of the element to be assigned to, and the new value to be stored. It's not expected to return a value.
FETCHSIZE	called whenever the entire array is evaluated in a scalar context (e.g., in code such as: $count = @array or while ($i<@array) {...}). It's passed a reference to the implementation object and is expected to return an integer corresponding to the array's current size.
STORESIZE	called whenever the actual size of an array is *explicitly* altered (e.g., in code such as: $#array = 1000). It is passed a reference to the implementation object and the new size (i.e., 1001 for the example). It's not expected to return a value.
EXTEND	called just before the actual size of a tied array is *implicitly* altered. For example, before executing an array-to-array assignment statement such as: @tied_array = @some_other_array, Perl would call EXTEND, passing it a reference to the implementation object for @tied_array, as well as the length of @some_other_array. This constitutes a friendly warning to the implementation object that it might want to preallocate an appropriate amount of extra space to avoid the need to separately reallocate space for each of the calls to STORE that will immediately follow. The name is somewhat of a misnomer, since the size that is passed may actually be smaller than the present size of the array (if @some_other_array is shorter). Calls to EXTEND are not expected to return values.
CLEAR	called whenever the entire array is reset using the @array = () notation. It's not expected to return a value.

Table 9.2   Methods for tie-ing an array (continued)

Method	Purpose
PUSH and UNSHIFT	called whenever the built-in `push` or `unshift` functions are called on a tied array. Each is passed a reference to the implementation object, followed by the list of values to be pushed or unshifted onto the array. Neither is expected to return a value.
POP and SHIFT	called whenever the built-in `pop` or `shift` functions are called on a tied array. Each is passed a reference to the implementation object and is expected to return a scalar value that is treated as the popped or shifted value.
SPLICE	called whenever the built-in `splice` function is called on a tied array. It is passed a reference to the implementation object, followed by the offset at which the splicing is to be done and the number of elements to be spliced out. Any remaining arguments are the new values to be spliced in. It is expected to return a list of the spliced-out elements.
DESTROY	the tied array's destructor. It is called when the tied array ceases to exist and is passed a reference to the implementation object. It's not expected to return a value.

9.4.1   Example: a base/codon array

Suppose we need to access an extremely long sequence of genetic information stored in a file.[4] Given the immense size of a typical genome—well over 3 gigabytes in plaintext or just under 1 gigabyte when encoded—we will need to store the actual array of data on disk. However, for coding purposes, it is convenient if we can pretend that the data is actually stored internally in a regular Perl array. Obviously, a tied array is the ideal way to implement this masquerade.

As an added complication, sometimes we will want to treat the genetic data as an array of single characters—called *bases*—and, sometimes, as an array of three-character groups—called *codons*. For example, to simulate DNA-to-protein translation, we first need to walk an RNA polymerase enzyme down the DNA sequence base-by-base to create a messenger DNA (mDNA) strand. Then, we need to march a ribosome along the mRNA strand three bases at a time, codon-by-codon, and match up transfer DNA (tDNA) fragments to each codon to build a polypeptide.[5]

The Genome::Array package

It would be handy if we could use the same package to generate one-at-a-time and three-at-a-time genome arrays. Listing 9.3 illustrates such a package: Genome::Array. It uses a hash as the underlying implementation object for each array, and provides each of the thirteen required interface methods.

---

[4] …perhaps we're aliens assessing the bio-compatibility of the human brain.

[5] Don't let all that salacious genetics talk upset you. All we want is an array that sometimes clumps the same data one-character-per-element and sometimes three-characters-per-element.

Listing 9.3 A package for accessing genome data

```perl
package Genome::Array;
$VERSION = 1.00;
use strict;

use Carp;
use Symbol;
use Fcntl;

sub TIEARRAY
{
  my ($class, $file, $grouping) = @_;
  my $filehandle = gensym();
  sysopen $filehandle, $file, O_RDWR|O_CREAT
    or croak "Could not open genome file";
  bless
  {
    group => $grouping,
    file  => $filehandle,
  }, $class;
}

sub DESTROY
{
  my ($impl) = @_;
  close $impl->{file} or carp "Couldn't close genome file";
}

sub FETCH
{
  my ($impl, $index) = @_;
  my $element;

  # find the right offset in the file and then read in
  # and return one grouping of chars (i.e. a single element)
  sysseek($impl->{file}, $index*$impl->{group},0) &&
  sysread($impl->{file}, $element, $impl->{group});
  return $element
}

sub STORE
{
  my ($impl, $index, $newval) = @_;

  # ensure data is the right size
  croak "Bad sized data: '$newval'"
    unless length($newval) == $impl->{group};

  # ensure file is the right size
  my $oldsize = $impl->FETCHSIZE();
  my $newsize = $index+1;
```

```perl
    if ($newsize > $oldsize)
    {
      my $fill_len = $newsize - $oldsize;
      croak "Couldn't extend genome file"
       unless sysseek($impl->{file}, 0, 2)
          and syswrite($impl->{file}, "\0" x $fill_len, $fill_len);
    }


    # seek to the correct position in file and overwrite data
    croak "Couldn't write genome file"
      unless sysseek($impl->{file}, $index*$impl->{group}, 0)
         and syswrite($impl->{file}, $newval, $impl->{group});
}

sub FETCHSIZE
{
  my ($impl) = @_;
  return (-s $impl->{file})/$impl->{group};
}


sub PUSH
{
  my ($impl, $newval) = @_;
  $impl->STORE($newval, $impl->FETCHSIZE());
}


sub POP
{
  my ($impl) = @_;
  my $element;

  # seek to end of file minus one element and remember the position
  my $new_end = sysseek($impl->{file}, -$impl->{group}, 2)
    or return undef;

  # read in last element or throw exception
  croak "Couldn't pop genome file"
    unless sysread($impl->{file}, $element, $impl->{group})
       && truncate($impl->{file}, $new_end);

  return $element;
}

sub CLEAR
{
  my ($impl) = @_;
  truncate($impl->{file}, 0)
    or croak "Couldn't clear genome file";
}

sub STORESIZE
{
  my ($impl, $newsize) = @_;
```

```
        my $oldsize = $impl->FETCHSIZE();

        # either truncate the file if it's shrinking
        if ($newsize < $oldsize)
        {
          truncate($impl->{file}, $newsize * $impl->{group})
            or croak "Couldn't clear genome file";
        }
        else    # extend it since it's growing
        {
          my $fill_len = $newsize - $oldsize;
          croak "Couldn't extend genome file"
            unless sysseek($impl->{file}, 0, 2)
                and syswrite($impl->{file}, "\0" x $fill_len, $fill_len);
        }
    }

sub EXTEND    { shift()->STORESIZE(@_) }

sub UNSHIFT   { croak "No monkeying with the DNA!" }
sub SHIFT     { croak "No monkeying with the DNA!" }
sub SPLICE    { croak "No monkeying with the DNA!" }
```

The `Genome::Array::TIEARRAY` method sets up the implementation hash with a `'group'` entry that specifies the number of bases to be stored by each element (1 or 3 being the likely candidates) as well as a `'file'` entry holding a reference to an anonymous typeglob (generated using `Symbol::gensym`). The filehandle in the typeglob is connected via `sysopen` to the file where the actual data is stored. The file is opened for both reading and writing and will be created if it doesn't already exist.

The Genome::Array destructor (`DESTROY`) is nontrivial in this case, since it's useful to explicitly close the genome file as soon as it is no longer needed.

The `FETCH` method first positions the implementation object's filehandle to the appropriate point in the file, then reads the correct number of characters into the lexical scalar `$element`. The appropriate file position is the requested index multiplied by the grouping factor. That is, codon N will start at position $3N$, since each codon takes 3 characters. The correct number of characters to be read is simply the grouping factor itself—1 for bases, 3 for codons. If anything goes wrong with the seeking or reading—the likeliest problem being trying to index past the end of the file—the method returns `undef`. Otherwise the method returns the data it retrieved into `$element`.

As we might expect, the `STORE` method does essentially the opposite of `FETCH`. It checks that the new value to be stored is the right length and then verifies that the file holds that many elements. If not, it extends the file by seeking to its end and appending a suitable number of null characters. Finally, it seeks to the appropriate position in the file—again, given by the index multiplied by the grouping factor—and writes the appropriate number of characters.

Fetching the size of the entire array (via `FETCHSIZE`) is also straightforward—it's just the length of the file divided by the grouping factor.

Listing 9.4   Building proteins from DNA

```perl
package main;
use Genome::Array;

$stop_code = qr/UAA|UAG|UGA/;            # End markers for codon sequences

# Connect arrays to DNA data and mRNA data (treat each base separately)
tie @DNA, 'Genome::Array', "DNA.dat", 1;
tie @mRNA, 'Genome::Array', "mRNA.dat", 1;

POLYMERASE: foreach $base ( @DNA )       # Read DNA file one base at a time
{
   $base =~ tr/ACGU/UGCA/;               # Find complement of original base
   push @mRNA, $base;                    # Write mRNA file one base at a time
}


# Connect another array to the mRNA data (treat bases three at a time)
tie @codons, 'Genome::Array', "mRNA.dat", 3;

# Mess about with a codon (maybe add fur and whiskers?)
$codons[1023043] = 'CAT';

# interpret codons to build a protein
RIBOSOME: for (my $i=0; $i<@codons; $i++)
{
   if ($codons[$i] !~ /$stop_code/)
   {
      # add another amino acid as specified by the current codon
      $polypeptide .= find_tRNA($codons[$i]);
   }
   else
   {
      # at end of a codon sequence release and reset the amino acid chain
      express_protein($polypeptide);
      $polypeptide = "";
   }
}
```

Pushing elements is particularly easy, since it's effectively just an assignment to the (notional) element immediately after the current end of the array. Hence, it is possible to implement the PUSH method using calls to FETCHSIZE and STORE.

Popping an element is somewhat more complex, since it requires us to also truncate the file—to physically remove the last element once it's retrieved. POP first seeks to a position one grouping before the end of the file (the trailing 2 argument signifies "from the end") and records that position in $new_end. It then sysreads the appropriate grouping of characters into $element and truncates the file at the previously recorded position using the built-in truncate function. Clearing the entire array is even easier. CLEAR just truncates the file from position zero, leaving nothing.

@DNA

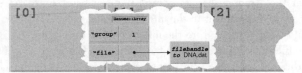

@codons

Figure 9.4   The tied @DNA and @codons arrays

When the tied array receives a STORESIZE or EXTEND request,[6] two possible courses of action exist. If the new size is smaller than the existing size, a truncate is required. Sizes are specified in terms of number of elements, so we have to multiply by the grouping factor to determine the corresponding number of chars to keep. On the other hand, if the new size is larger than the current size, we have to extend the file from the end (as in STORE) by appending the appropriate number of nulls ($newsize - $oldsize).

Incidentally, this package is a case where the hints offered by SETSIZE and EXTEND are particularly valuable. Individual append operations on a file are relatively expensive, so if we can anticipate a series of such appends and consolidate them into a single large syswrite operation, we'll have improved the tied hash's performance considerably.

The remaining access methods are all set up to throw cautionary exceptions when invoked. Shifting and unshifting involve adding text to the start of a file. Splicing requires arbitrary insertions and deletions of text somewhere within the file. On almost any common file system, adding data to the beginning or middle of a text file is expensive, since it generally requires rewriting the entire file. For gigabyte-length files, that's infeasible, so the operations are made invalid.

Applied genetics 101

Once the hard work of setting up the Genome::Array package is done, accessing and manipulating DNA data is straightforward. For example, listing 9.4 illustrates a simple program for expressing the proteins encoded in DNA.

The program first ties two genetic information files to separate arrays—@DNA and @mRNA. Figure 9.4 shows the internal structure of the @DNA array. The @mRNA array will be be identical except the filehandle would be connected to a different file. The trailing 1 argument means that the arrays are set up to treat each file as a sequence of single-character elements.

---

[6] ...since the semantics of either method are the same in this case, EXTEND has been implemented entirely in terms of STORESIZE...

The POLYMERASE: loop walks through each base in the @DNA array—that is, each single character in the DNA.dat file—and pushes its complementary base[7] onto the end of the @mRNA array—in other words, appends it to the mRNA.dat file.

Next, we tie a second array, @codons, to the mRNA.dat file (see figure 9.4 again). This array treats the data in the file as a sequence of three-base elements. Once the array is tied, these three-letter codons are directly accessible. To demonstrate this, the program changes the 1,023,044th codon to the base sequence C-A-T.[8]

Finally, we interpret and translate the codons into amino acids. The RIBOSOME: loop walks through each codon in the mRNA strand, matching tRNA fragments to each codon and assembling their associated amino acids into a polypeptide sequence. Each time the loop encounters a stop code,[9] it releases the completed polypeptide, which automatically folds itself up into a protein.

9.5 TIE-ING A FILEHANDLE

Apart from tie-ing new implementations to the three standard types of Perl variable, Perl also supports tie-ing a filehandle to a package. Such support isn't as polished as that for variables, but it does provide the basics for overriding the I/O behavior of a filehandle.

As you might expect by now, the methods that you need to define correspond to the operations that can be performed on a regular filehandle (see table 9.3).

Table 9.3 Methods for tie-ing a filehandle

Method	Purpose
TIEHANDLE	called whenever a filehandle or typeglob is tied to the package. Like the other TIE… constructors, it receives any extra arguments to tie that appeared after the filehandle itself. It's expected to return a reference to a blessed implementation object (which is usually a standard filehandle).
WRITE	called whenever the tied filehandle is written to via the low-level built-in syswrite function. It's passed a reference to the implementation object, followed by the character string to be written, the number of characters to output, and the offset within the string at which to start. In other words, it receives a reference to the implementation object plus the normal arguments of a syswrite call. The value it returns is assumed to be the number of bytes actually written.
PRINT and PRINTF	called whenever the tied filehandle is written to via the high-level built-in print and printf functions respectively. Both functions are passed a reference to the implementation object, followed by the argument list of the original call (i.e., the values to be printed, or the format and values to be printf'ed). Both methods are expected to return a true value on success and undef on failure.

[7] 'A' → 'U', 'U' → 'A', 'C' → 'G', 'G' → 'C'.

[8] …which, despite the optimistic comment, is unlikely to confer feline properties on the resulting protein.

[9] …any of the codons 'UAA', 'UAG', or 'UGA', which act like semicolons between instructions in the genetic programming language…

Table 9.3 Methods for tie-ing a filehandle (continued)

Method	Purpose
READ	called whenever the tied filehandle is read from via the low-level built-in read or sysread function. It's passed a reference to the implementation object, followed by an alias to the scalar variable to be read into, the number of characters to read, and the offset within the variable at which to place the input characters. In other words, it receives a reference to the implementation object plus the normal arguments of a sysread or read call. The value it returns is assumed to be the number of bytes actually read. Because the destination variable is passed as an alias, you need to be careful to store the input in $_[1].
GETC	called whenever the tied filehandle is used as the argument to the built-in getc function. It's passed a reference to the implementation object, and is expected to return the next character of input, or undef if there is none.
READLINE	called whenever the tied filehandle is read from using the "diamond" notation (i.e., $nextline = <TIED_HANDLE>) or the built-in readline function. It's passed a reference to the implementation object and is expected to return the next line of input, or undef if there is none.
CLOSE	called whenever the tied filehandle is closed using the built-in close function. It's passed a reference to the implementation object and is expected to return a true value if the close was completed, or undef if the close fails.
DESTROY	the destructor for the tied filehandle. It is called when the tied filehandle's implementation object is about to cease to exist and is passed a reference to that implementation object. It's not expected to return a value.

As you can see, the implementation of a replacement interface for a tied handle is incomplete. For a start, without an OPEN method, there's no way to open—or reopen—a tied handle[10] using the built-in open or sysopen functions. If that functionality is required, we typically either incorporate it into the TIEHANDLE method (and use tie instead of open):

```
tie *FILE, SomePackage, "<filename";
```

Or else, we provide our own open method and use the tied function to access it:

```
tie *FILE, SomePackage;

# and later…

tied(*FILE)->open("<filename");
```

The same problem arises with other built-in I/O functions, including eof, fileno, seek, select, sysseek, tell, truncate, and write. The only solution for those instances is to provide your own methods and call them through tied.

9.5.1 An example: filtered filehandles

Occasionally it's useful to apply a filter to an input or output stream, or, sometimes, to both. For example, we might wish to filter out nonprinting characters from an output stream sent to

---

[10] …and attempting to do so will have no effect and—worse—will generate no warnings.

a terminal, to disarm unexpected terminal control codes. Or we might want to fold all upper-case letters to low-case to render input case-insensitive. Or we might be dealing with EBCDIC data and need to convert it to Perl's native ASCII on input and then back to EBCDIC on output.

Each of these tasks *could* be performed by passing the data through a suitable subroutine after reading it in or before writing it back out. That can become messy if I/O occurs throughout a program, or we're using the full range of Perl's I/O mechanisms.

An alternative is to create a tie-able package that applies the appropriate filters to any supported I/O operation through a specific filehandle. Then, we set up the filehandle with the appropriate filters, and any kind of I/O on it automatically does the necessary filtering as well. Listing 9.5 illustrates such a package: Filtered.

Listing 9.5   A package for filtered I/O

```
package Filtered;
$VERSION = 1.00;

use strict;
use Carp;
use Symbol;

sub _no_filter { return $_[0]; }

sub TIEHANDLE
{
  my ($class, %args) = @_;
  my $handle = gensym();
  my $impl = bless { handle => gensym() }, $class;
  $impl->OPEN(%args);
  return $impl;
}

sub OPEN
{
  my ($impl, %args) = @_;
  open $impl->{handle}, $args{file}
        or croak "Could not open '$args{file}'";
  $impl->{in_filter}  = $args{in}  || \&_no_filter,
  $impl->{out_filter} = $args{out} || \&_no_filter,
}

sub SEEK
{
  my ($impl, $position, $whence) = @_;
  return sysseek($impl->{handle}, $position, $whence);
}

sub WRITE
{
  my ($impl, $buffer, $length, $offset) = @_;
```

```
  $buffer = substr($buffer, $offset||0, $length);
  $buffer = $impl->{out_filter}->($buffer);
  syswrite($impl->{handle}, $buffer, length($buffer), 0);
}

sub PRINT
{
  my ($impl, @data) = @_;
  my $filter = $impl->{out_filter};
  @data = map { $filter->($_) } @data;
  print { $impl->{handle} } @data;
}

sub PRINTF
{
  my ($impl, $format, @data) = @_;
  my $filter = $impl->{out_filter};
  print { $impl->{handle} } $filter->(sprintf $format, @data);
}

sub READ
{
  my ($impl, $data, $length, $offset) = @_;
  my $result = sysread($impl->{handle}, $data, $length);
  substr($_[1],$offset||0,$length) = $impl->{in_filter}->($data);
  return $result;
}

sub GETC
{
  my ($impl) = @_;
  $impl->{in_filter}->(getc $impl->{handle});
}

sub READLINE
{
  my ($impl) = @_;
  $impl->{in_filter}->(scalar readline(*{$impl->{handle}}));
}

 sub CLOSE
{
  my ($impl) = @_;
  close $impl->{handle};
}
```

The implementation object for a Filtered filehandle is a hash. That hash stores a reference to a typeglob, which contains the actual filehandle used for I/O, and two subroutine references, which specify the desired filtering behavior. Figure 9.5 shows the resulting internal structure.

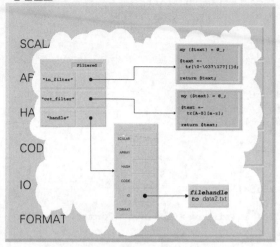

Figure 9.5 A typeglob tied to the Filtered package

The `Filtered::TIEHANDLE` method sets up the implementation object. It is passed the name of the package, followed by a set of named arguments indicating the file to be opened, and the filters to be used. `TIEHANDLE` first creates an anonymous typeglob (using `Symbol::gensym`) and places it in an anonymous hash, which is blessed as the new implementation object. To open the file, `TIEHANDLE` calls the `OPEN` method, passing it the named argument.

`OPEN` opens the filehandle stored in the implementation hash to the file specified by the `"file"` argument. If that succeeds, `OPEN` adds the references to the two filter subroutine references—the named arguments `"in"` and `"out"`—to the implementation object. If either of these subroutine references is `undef`, the default filter `no_filter` is used instead.

Keep in mind the caveat about `OPEN` mentioned in the previous section: a tied filehandle will ignore its own `OPEN` method if you pass that filehandle to the built-in `open` function. So, if FILE is a tied filehandle and we want to reopen it—say, to filter the file **data2.txt** into all lower-case—we can't write:

```
open FILE, file=>"data2.txt", in=>\&lower_case;
```

Instead we have to write:

```
tied(*FILE)->OPEN(file=>"data2.txt", in=>\&lower_case);
```

If some future version of Perl does finally enable tied filehandles to recognize and make use of an `OPEN` method, the arguments that method will require will be the same as for the built-in `read` or `sysread` functions, *not* the ones we're using here. Hence, the `OPEN` method shown in figure 9.5, and the one shown later, in figure 9.17, may not be forward-compatible.

The same restrictions are true of the `SEEK` method. It merely uses the built-in `seek` function to reposition the filehandle stored within the implementation object. But, to call it, we have to write

```
tied(*FILE)->SEEK(0,0);# Seek tied filehandle back to start of file
```

since the tie mechanism won't translate a call to the built-in seek when applied to a tied filehandle.

As indicated above, the full set of missing interface components—those that tied filehandles don't support—is extensive. Later, in section 9.7, we'll see a partial solution to this problem.

Fortunately, the remaining methods in the package *are* recognized by the tie mechanism and do work as expected. They simply interpose the appropriate filter between the program and the implementation object's filehandle. For output methods (WRITE, PRINT, PRINTF) that means applying the output filter—the subroutine whose reference is stored in $impl->{out_filter}—to the data and calling the appropriate built-in output function. In the case of PRINT, that requires us to map the filter across the array of input data.

For input methods (READ, GETC, READLINE), filtering means calling the corresponding built-in function to retrieve the data, then applying the input filter—the subroutine whose reference is stored in $impl->{in_filter}—to that data before it is returned. For the READLINE method, we had to ensure that readline was called in a scalar context so that it only reads the a single line of input.

Filtering I/O

Having set up this framework for I/O filtering, we can now easily implement the assorted filtering schemes suggested above. For example, to filter out non-printing characters from an output stream, we set up our stream like so:

```
use Filtered;

sub expurgate_unprintable
{
  my ($text) = @_;
  $text =~ tr[\0-\011\013-\037\177][]d;        # delete non-printing chars
  return $text;
}

tie *TERMINAL, Filtered, file=>">-", out=>\&expurgate_unprintable;
```

after which any output operation (i.e., a syswrite, print, or printf) through the TERMINAL filehandle removes all non-printable characters.

To fold upper-case letters to lower-case on input, we can use an anonymous subroutine and write the following:

```
use Filtered;

tie *STDIN, Filtered, file=>"-", in => sub { $_ = shift; tr/A-Z/a-z/; $_ };
```

Now, any data read from STDIN, via sysread, getc, or <>, is guaranteed to appear in lower case.

If we already have a suitable filtering subroutine, connecting it to a filehandle is just as easy. For example, to read EBCDIC data files as ASCII, then replace any occurrence of the word "mainframe" with "PC," and write the ASCII back as EBCDIC, we can make use of Chris Leach's handy Convert::EBCDIC CPAN module:

```
use Convert::EBCDIC;
use Filtered;

# open EBCDIC file…
tie *FILE, Filtered, file=>"<bigblue.dat", in=>\&ebcdic2ascii;

# process ASCII-fied data…
local $/;
$text = <FILE>;                  # read entire EBCDIC file as ASCII
$text =~ s/mainframe/PC/g;

# reopen EBCDIC file…
close FILE;
tie *FILE, Filtered, file=>">bigblue.dat", out=>\&ascii2ebcdic;
print FILE $text;                # write ASCII $text AS EBCDIC
```

9.6 INHERITING FROM A TIE-ABLE PACKAGE

Because the subroutines in a tie-able package like Insensitive::Hash or Genome::Array are really methods, we can use inheritance and polymorphism to reduce the cost of building and maintaining packages to support tied variables.

For example, suppose a package provided all the methods necessary to implement a tied hash that exactly mimicked a regular hash. We might subsequently need to implement a hash that had one nonstandard feature, for example, one that iterates its keys in alphabetical order. Our new package could inherit from the standard hash package, and we could just define new FIRSTKEY and NEXTKEY methods in the derived package to override the inherited versions and implement the extra functionality.

Such a standard hash package already exists and is distributed with every copy of Perl. It's called Tie::StdHash, and it's available as part of the Tie::Hash module that comes with the standard Perl distribution. Likewise, there are Tie::StdScalar and Tie::StdArray, which implement inheritable packages implementing tie-able versions of those other data types.

There are many other Tie::… modules in the CPAN. They cover an enormous variety of purposes, for example:

- Tie::RefHash, which allows you to use references as keys to a hash,
- Tie::DBM, which allows you to tie a hash to a DBM database file,
- Tie::Dir, which allows you to access and modify the files in a directory via a hash,
- Tie::STDERR, which allows you to tie STDERR to a file or a process,
- Tie::Cache, which implements a fixed-size least-recently-used cache.

9.6.1 Example: sorted hashes

Let's take the Tie::StdHash package and modify it to create a tied hash whose keys are always sorted.[11] Listing 9.6 shows the surprisingly small code required.

---

[11] We don't actually need to, since there are at least two CPAN modules – Tie::IxHash and Tie::LLHash – that already do more or less the same job. However, building your own is always more instructive.

Listing 9.6 A package for sorted hashes

```perl
package SortedHash;
$VERSION = 1.00;

use Tie::Hash;
@ISA = qw( Tie::StdHash );

use strict;

{
  my %key_cache = ();

  sub FIRSTKEY
  {
    my ($impl) = @_;
    delete $key_cache{$impl};
    $key_cache{$impl} = [sort keys %$impl];
    return shift @{$key_cache{$impl}};
  }

  sub NEXTKEY
  {
    my ($impl) = @_;
    return shift @{$key_cache{$impl}};
  }

  sub DESTROY
  {
    my ($impl) = @_;
    delete $key_cache{$impl};
  }
}
```

The SortedHash package inherits from Tie::StdHash by adding that package's name to its @ISA array. Now, whenever a call to FETCH or STORE or DELETE, and so forth. is received by an object implementing a SortedHash, that call is passed up the inheritance hierarchy to Tie::StdHash::FETCH, Tie::StdHash::STORE, and so on.

To give the hash the illusion of ordered storage, all we need to do is ensure that FIRSTKEY and NEXTKEY return keys in an appropriately sorted sequence. Since the inherited Tie::StdHash::FIRSTKEY and Tie::StdHash::NEXTKEY methods reproduce the normal, apparently random ordering of key iteration, we have to arrange for them to be replaced by smarter versions. That's easy to do. We just define the appropriate replacements in the derived package, where they will be seen and selected in preference to the inherited versions.

Actually arranging for the keys to be returned in the appropriate sequence is also easy, but perhaps not entirely obvious. The trick is to have FIRSTKEY build a sorted list of the hash's keys and cache that list so NEXTKEY can repeatedly pull keys from it as they are required.

The only problem is where to cache the sorted key list. We could potentially cache it back in the hash itself, under a special key (perhaps `"\0\0\0\0\0\0\0\0\0"`, or `"paynoattentiontothemanbehindthecurtain"`, or something equally improbable), but that's both ugly and likely to introduce subtle bugs. Instead, we cache the list in a private lexical hash (`%key_cache`), which is visible only to FIRSTKEY and NEXTKEY.

Each entry of `%key_cache` stores the sorted key list of one SortedHash object. The list is stored in the entry whose key is the stringified value of a reference to the implementation object. In other words, the list is stored under the key that results when the corresponding object's memory address is treated as a string. References can't generally be used as hash keys in this way—the stringification prevents them from being later reused as references—but they're okay here because all we need is a reproducible and unique key for each implementation object. A stringified reference certainly provides that.

FIRSTKEY does most of the work. It computes a sorted list of the keys in the implementation object—**sort keys %$impl**—puts that list into an anonymous array—[sort keys %$impl]—and, finally, assigns a reference to that array to the appropriate entry in the cache—**$key_cache{$impl} =** [sort keys %$impl]. Once this sorted list is set up, both FIRSTKEY and NEXTKEY iterate it by simply shifting off the first remaining element and returning it.

Finally, the SortedHash class needs a destructor to remove the cache entry for a tied hash when that hash ceases to exist. Without this destructor, the cache would preserve the cached key lists for all defunct hashes. Such lists would never be accessed again, so leaving them around would constitute a memory leak.

9.6.2 Another example: micro-tracked scalars

Of course, there's no rule that says we can only inherit from standard packages or those from the CPAN. Listing 9.7 shows a package (MicroTrack) derived from the Track package in listing 9.1. This package provides the same features as Track, except that now *every* storage operation is immediately reported.

Note how easy it was to create this new package. All we needed to do was replace the inherited STORE method with one that first reports to STDERR, then performs the necessary storage by converting itself into the inherited STORE using the `goto &subroutine` syntax.

Storing the data using `goto &{$impl->can("SUPER::STORE")}`, rather than the more obvious `$impl->SUPER::STORE($newval)`, is essential here because the ancestral storage method that will be called (i.e., Track::STORE) uses `caller` to determine where an assignment actually took place. If we had called SUPER::STORE as a regular method, then the call to `caller` inside Track::STORE would mistakenly identify MicroTrack::STORE as the source of the assignment since it would become the immediate caller.

The `goto &` syntax, however, causes MicroTrack::STORE to first locate the ancestral STORE method—`$impl->can("SUPER::STORE")`—and then be *transformed* into a call to that method—**goto &{**`$impl->can("SUPER::STORE")`**}**. As a result, the context that called MicroTrack::STORE is used as the calling context for Track::STORE. So `caller` returns the correct information in the ancestral STORE method.

Listing 9.7   A package for fine-grained variable tracking

```perl
package MicroTrack;
$VERSION = 1.00;

use Track;
@ISA = qw( Track );

use strict;

sub STORE
{
  my ($impl, $newval) = @_;
  my ($cur_pkg, $cur_file, $cur_line) = caller;
  print STDERR "At $cur_file line $cur_line in package $cur_pkg the\n",
               "tracked variable was assigned the value $newval\n";
  goto &{$impl->can("SUPER::STORE")};
}
```

9.7 *TIED VARIABLES AS OBJECTS*

A tied variable (or filehandle) can be used anywhere a regular variable (or filehandle) can be used, as long as the package to which it's tied provides methods to implement the necessary interface. One such place where a tied variable can replace a normal one, is as the implementation mechanism of a Perl class. That is, we can bless a tied variable to create an object.

9.7.1 A DNA class

For example, suppose we were designing a DNA::Sequence class. We might want to create DNA::Sequence objects storing specific genetic codes, and apply methods such as mutate, recombine, fingerprint, and so forth. to them. To build such objects, we are obviously going to bless an array (storing bases or codon sequences). Given the extended nature of such sequences, it would be handy if the array could use disk storage for the data. Clearly, the array we're going to bless as a DNA::Sequence object should be one we've already tied to the Genome::Array package.

Listing 9.8 shows an implementation of the DNA::Sequence class. The only mention of the Genome::Array package is in the DNA::Sequence::new constructor. The constructor declares a lexical array (@self), which it immediately ties to the Genome::Array package. The arguments to tie ensure that the underlying Genome::Array is connected for read/write access to the file specified by the constructor's argument and that the array data is grouped with one base per element. Finally, the constructor takes a reference to the lexical array, \@self, and uses it to bless the array into the DNA::Sequence class. DNA::Sequence objects can now be created in the usual object-oriented manner:

```perl
my $dna = DNA::Sequence->new("dna.data");
```

and the resulting object has an internal structure as shown in figure 9.6.

Listing 9.8   A class built on top of a tied array

```perl
package DNA::Sequence;
$VERSION = 1.00;
use strict;

use Genome::Array;

sub new
{
  my ($class, $datafile) = @_;
  my @self;
  tie @self, Genome::Array, "+<$datafile", 1;
  bless \@self, $class;
}

sub mutate
{
  my ($self, $changes) = @_;
  while ($changes-->0)
  {
    $self->[rand @$self] = substr("ACGT",rand(4),1);
  }
}

sub recombine
{
  my ($self, $other, $newfile) = @_;
  my $combined = DNA::Sequence->new($newfile);
  for (my $i=0; $i<@{$self} && $i<@{$other}; $i++)
  {
    $combined->[$i] = (int rand 2) ? $self->[$i] : $other->[$i];
  }
  return $combined;
}

sub fingerprint
{
  my ($self) = @_;
  my $fingerprint = 0;
  foreach my $base ( @{$self} )
  {
    $fingerprint = (($fingerprint<<1) + ord($base)) % 1e6;
  }
  return $fingerprint;
}
```

The methods of the DNA::Sequence class can completely ignore the fact that their underlying array object, @{$self}, is actually tied to an external data file. For example, the mutate method simply iterates through the number of requested mutations, arbitrarily replacing

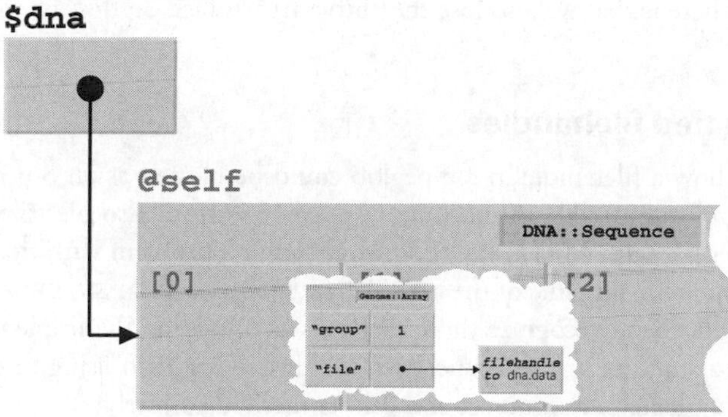

$dna

@self

DNA::Sequence

[0]   [2]

Genome::Array

"group"   1

"file"   → filehandle to dna.data

Figure 9.6   Internal structure of a DNA::Sequence object

a random element in the blessed array referred to by $self with a random base specifier. The code is identical if DNA::Sequence objects are implemented using a real Perl array, rather than one tied to the Genome::Array package.

Likewise, the recombine method crossbreeds two DNA sequences by creating a new DNA::Sequence object—referred to by $combine—and walking through the elements of two existing sequences—the invoking object and the one referred to by $other. For each element, recombine randomly selects the base value from one or the other and stores that value in the new object. Once again, the code treats each object as a simple blessed array without reference to its internal implementation as a disk file.

The obvious advantage of this "tie-then-bless" approach is that the implementation of the DNA::Sequence class becomes simple. The class's methods need only implement manipulations of the genetic data, without worrying about the complexities of shifting to and from data files.

The less obvious advantage of this approach is that, by isolating the storage considerations from the manipulation behavior, it becomes easy to migrate the code when the underlying storage mechanism changes. For example, if we were suddenly given access to a computer with 100 gigabytes of RAM, we might prefer to do all our genetic meddling in-memory to increase the speed of our algorithms. To do so, we could derive a new class from DNA::Sequence, which uses a normal array instead of a Genome::Array:

```
package DNA::Sequence::InMemory;
@ISA = qw( DNA::Sequence );

sub new
{
   my ($class, $datafile) = @_;
   open DATA, $datafile or croak "Couldn't load data";
   my @self = split //, <DATA>;
   bless \@self, $class;
}
```

The DNA::Sequence::InMemory::new constructor sets up its objects as blessed arrays with one character per element, just as DNA::Sequence::new did. All other methods inherited from DNA::Sequence then continue to work unchanged (only considerably faster). Of course, the drawback here is that we also lose the automatic storage on disk of any changes to the DNA data.

9.7.2 Object-oriented tied filehandles

In chapter 5 we saw how a filehandle in a typeglob could be blessed as an object to provide asynchronous paging of output. There's nothing to prevent us from also blessing a filehandle already tied to another package. In fact, doing so would solve a problem with tied filehandles.

That problem is the missing bits of the tied filehandle interface: OPEN, SEEK, TRUNCATE, and so on. Because Perl doesn't recognize those methods as providing the implementation for the built-in open, seek, and truncate functions, we have to resort to using tied to unpack the tied filehandle's implementation object and call its methods directly:

```
tie *FILE, Filtered, file=>">data.txt", out=>\&lower_case;

# and later…

tied(*FILE)->seek(0,0);
```

If, however, the filehandle had been blessed as an object—say of class IO::Filter—and was thereafter accessed through a reference—say, $file—we could ensure that the class provided an appropriate seek method, allowing us to write:

```
my $file = IO::Filter->new(file=>">data.txt", out=>\&lower_case);

# and later…

$file->seek(0,0);
```

Best of all, because the built-in I/O functions accept a filehandle reference instead of a filehandle, we can still use the object-oriented filehandle like a normal filehandle:

```
print $file "This WILL all be in lower case!\n";
```

Listing 9.9 shows the surprisingly compact implementation of the IO::Filter class. The IO::Filter::new constructor creates a new anonymous typeglob, using Symbol::gensym, and then ties it to the Filtered package, which takes care of opening the actual file. Finally, the constructor blesses the tied typeglob into the IO::Filter class. That produces an arrangement like the one shown in figure 9.7.

Since the resulting object is a typeglob reference, it can be used directly in I/O statements:

```
my $file = IO::Filter->new(file=>">data.txt", out=>\&lower_case);

print $file "This will be written to data.txt\n";
syswrite $file, "ditto", 5, 0;
```

And, because the typeglob $file refers to is tied to the Filtered package, those I/O operations are appropriately filtered. Better still, the typeglob reference is a blessed object, so we can also call methods on it directly:

```
$file->print("This will be filtered and then written to data.txt\n");
$file->seek(-1, 2);
$file->write("ditt-OO", 7, 0);
```

Listing 9.9 An object-oriented wrapper for the Filtered package

```perl
package IO::Filter;
$VERSION = 1.00;
use strict;

use Symbol;
use Filtered;

sub new
{
  my ($class, %args) = @_;
  my $self = gensym();
  tie *{$self}, "Filtered", %args;
  bless $self, $class;
}

sub AUTOLOAD
{
  use vars qw( $AUTOLOAD );      # Keep use strict happy
  my ($self, @args) = @_;
  $AUTOLOAD =~ s/.*:://;
  $AUTOLOAD =~ tr/a-z/A-Z/;
  tied(*{$self})->$AUTOLOAD(@args);
}
```

Of course, the IO::Filter class doesn't actually have a print, seek, or write method. Instead, it uses a single AUTOLOAD method to forward any such call directly to the implementation object of the tied filehandle. AUTOLOAD first massages the method name in $AUTOLOAD by removing any package prefix and converting what's left to upper-case (in order to match the method names of the Filtered package). It then exposes the implementation object—

$file

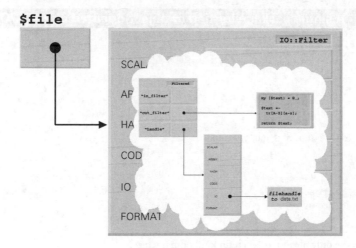

Figure 9.7 Internal structure of an IO::Filter object

`tied(*{$self}`—and calls the appropriate interface method through the symbolic reference left in `$AUTOLOAD`.

This is convenient, but relatively slow. Execution speed is not often an issue with I/O mechanisms, since the actual I/O process is usually much slower, but if it were, we could replace the `AUTOLOAD` method with an set of simple methods:

```
sub open  { tied(*{shift()})->OPEN(@_)  }
sub seek  { tied(*{shift()})->SEEK(@_)  }
sub write { tied(*{shift()})->WRITE(@_) }
sub print { tied(*{shift()})->PRINT(@_) }
sub getc  { tied(*{shift()})->GETC(@_)  }

# etc., etc.
```

Either way, the overall result is that we can now use an IO::Filter object as a normal file-handle reference, at least for those I/O functions that the tie mechanism recognizes. Or we can invoke the same filtered I/O behavior using the object-oriented interface provided by IO::Filter.

9.7.3 Blessing and tie-ing to the same package

So now we have filehandles tied to the Filtered package and, at the same time, blessed into the IO::Filter package. The next question is obvious:[12] do we actually need the two separate packages, or can we do it all with just one? The answer, of course, is that, no, we *don't* and yes, we *can*. What's not so clear, however, is whether we *should*.

Listing 9.10 shows a single class (IO::Filtered) that provides the complete implementation for both tied and object-oriented filtering filehandles. Note that it is little more that the concatenation of the methods of the packages Filtered and IO::Filter, with some slight adjustments for the change in package names. In particular, the `IO::Filtered::new` constructor now ties its filehandle to the package specified by `$class`—that is, nominally to IO::Filtered—and blesses it into the same package.

Listing 9.10 A single package for tied or object-oriented filtered I/O

```
package IO::Filtered;
$VERSION = 1.00;

use strict;
use Carp;
use Symbol;

sub _no_filter { return $_[0]; }

sub TIEHANDLE
{
  my ($class, %args) = @_;
  my $handle = gensym();
```

---

[12] Well, okay, maybe only obvious to a certain kind of masochist.

```perl
  my $impl = bless { handle => gensym() }, $class;
  $impl->OPEN(%args);
  return $impl;
}

sub OPEN
{
  my ($impl, %args) = @_;
  open $impl->{handle}, $args{file}
    or croak "Could not open '$args{file}'";
  $impl->{in_filter}  = $args{in}  || \&_no_filter,
  $impl->{out_filter} = $args{out} || \&_no_filter,
}

sub SEEK
{
  my ($impl, $position, $whence) = @_;
  return sysseek($impl->{handle}, $position, $whence);
}

sub WRITE
{
  my ($impl, $buffer, $length, $offset) = @_;
  $buffer = $impl->{out_filter}->($buffer);
  syswrite($impl->{handle}, $buffer, $length, $offset||0);
}

sub PRINT
{
  my ($impl, @data) = @_;
  my $filter = $impl->{out_filter};
  @data = map { $filter->($_) } @data;
  print { $impl->{handle} } @data;
}

sub PRINTF
{
  my ($impl, $format, @data) = @_;
  my $filter = $impl->{out_filter};
  print { $impl->{handle} } $filter->(sprintf $format, @data);
}

sub READ
{
  my ($impl, $data, $length, $offset) = @_;
  my $result = sysread($impl->{handle}, $data, $length);
  substr($_[1],$offset||0,$length) = $impl->{in_filter}->($data);
  return $result;
}

sub GETC
{
  my ($impl) = @_;
```

```
  $impl->{in_filter}->(getc $impl->{handle});
}

sub READLINE
{
  my ($impl) = @_;
  $impl->{in_filter}->(scalar readline *{$impl->{handle}});
}

 sub CLOSE
{
  my ($impl) = @_;
  close $impl->{handle};
}

sub new
{
  my ($class, %args) = @_;
  my $self = gensym();
  tie *{$self}, $class, %args;
  bless $self, $class;
}

sub AUTOLOAD
{
  use vars qw( $AUTOLOAD );      # Keep use strict happy
  my ($self, @args) = @_;
  $AUTOLOAD =~ s/.*:://;
  $AUTOLOAD =~ tr/a-z/A-Z/;
  tied(*{$self})->$AUTOLOAD(@args);
}
```

We can now choose to explicitly tie filehandles to IO::Filtered:

```
$tiedfile = \*FILE;
tie *{$tiedfile}, "IO::Filtered", file=>">passwd", out=>\&encrypt;
```

or to bless them into that package

```
$blessedfile = IO::Filtered->new(file=>">passwd", out=>\&encrypt);
```

Figure 9.8 shows the internal physical structure of an object blessed into the IO::Filtered class. Notice that it is virtually identical to the structure of an IO::Filter object (figure 9.7), the only difference being that now both the tied object and its implementation object are blessed into the same class—IO::Filtered. However, that physical similarity is misleading because the two alternatives have different internal logical structures, as figure 9.9 illustrates.

Although both the blessed and the tied versions are suitable for standard I/O operations such as

```
print $tiedfile "sEcrEtpAsswOrd";
print $blessedfile "sEcrEtpAsswOrd";
```

only the blessed version allows us to call IO::Filtered methods using the arrow notation:

$blessedfile

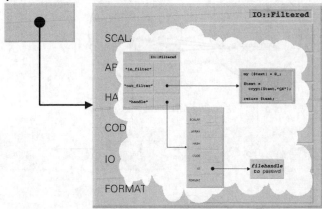

Figure 9.8 Internal structure of an IO::Filtered object

```
$blessedfile->print("sEcrEtpAsswOrd");
```

That's because a variable or filehandle that is only tied to a package is not considered to be an object belonging to that package. So, if we wrote

```
$tiedfile->print("sEcrEtpAsswOrd");
```

we would incur a fatal run-time error:

Can't call method "print" on unblessed reference

That's because the typeglob to which $tiedfile refers is not blessed into IO::Filtered; the typeglob merely tied to the package.

In other words ref($tiedfile) returns the string "GLOB", not "IO::Filtered".[13] In a similar way, a call to tied($blessedfile) returns undef, since the reference in $blessedfile isn't tied to anything (even though the thing it refers to *is*).

Those distinctions are important to bear in mind because they highlight one of the drawbacks of using a single class to both tie and bless objects. Some of the IO::Filtered package's methods, such as OPEN, READ, PRINT, expect a first argument, $impl, that is a reference to the implementation object of something *tied* to the IO::Filtered package. Others, such as open, read, print expect a first argument, $self, that is a reference to something *blessed* into IO::Filtered.[14]

Consequently, some of IO::Filtered's methods can't be directly called on an object blessed into that class. For example, if someone were accidentally to write

```
$blessedfile->PRINT("sEcrEtpAsswOrd");
```

they'd receive the fatal (and less-than-helpful) error message:

---

[13] Remember that the entire point of the tie mechanism was to *hide* the fact that a variable or filehandle is actually implemented via some package, so $tiedfile has to pretend to refer to a regular typeglob.

[14] The truly nasty bit is that both the implementation object and the regular object are blessed into IO::Filtered. However, the implementation object is a blessed typeglob, whereas the regular object is a blessed hash. It might help to stare at figure 9.8 again at this point.

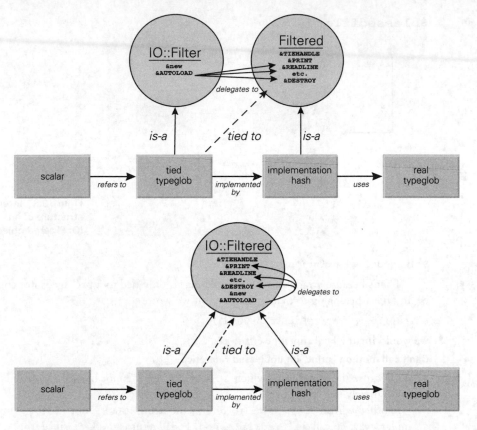

Figure 9.9 Comparative anatomy of IO::Filter and IO:Filtered objects

Not a HASH reference

All of which just emphasizes the more significant problem with tie-ing and blessing things to the same package: trying to understand the multiple relationships between the blessed and tied bits makes your head hurt.

The technique of blessing a tied filehandle is subtle enough when the components are in separate packages. When a single package has to cater to all three levels—"regular" blessing, tie-ing, and implementation blessing—the code becomes that much harder to understand and predict. All in all, it's almost certainly best to tie and bless using separate packages.

9.8 WHERE TO FIND OUT MORE

The perltie documentation describes the `tie` mechanism and the way in which Perl datatypes may be tied. *Advanced Perl Programming* also devotes a chapter to the topic.

The CPAN has a directory devoted entirely to modules that make tie-ing easier: http://www.perl.com/CPAN/modules/by_module/Tie/. The Convert::EBCDIC module is also available from the CPAN in the directory http://www.perl.com/CPAN/authors/id/CXL/.

Johan Vromans' Text::Filter module is an industrial strength version of the IO filtering packages described in this chapter. It's available from http://www.perl.com/CPAN/authors/id/JV/.

9.9 SUMMARY

- Tie-ing a variable or filehandle (using the `tie` function) replaces its internals with a user-defined implementation object.
- The implementation object must be blessed into a class that provides the methods needed to simulate the standard variable or filehandle interface.
- Once the variable or filehandle is tied, operations on it call the corresponding method on the implementation object.
- Tied variables and filehandles can also be subsequently blessed as objects. However, it's generally not a good idea to bless them into the same class to which they're tied.
- Tied variables and filehandles can be untied using the `untie` function. They revert to their normal behavior, but not their previous value. If no other references to the untied implementation object exist, it's destructor is called.

CHAPTER 10

Operator overloading

One aspect of object-oriented programming that seems to turn some people away is the constant need to call methods on objects, rather than manipulating the objects directly. It's not so much the efficiency of so many subroutine calls (although that can be a concern too); it's the sheer ugliness of the resulting code.

10.1 THE PROBLEM

Take Mark Biggar's standard Math::BigFloat module for example.[1] Math::BigFloat objects store floating point numbers as character strings and provide a range of methods for manipulating those string representations: `fneg` to negate them, `fadd` to add them, `fmul` to multiply them, and so forth.

We can use those methods to work out some calculation involving large numbers, such as the estimated difference in per-capita gross domestic product between China and the USA in 1998.[2] Given the most recent available statistics (for 1997):

---

[1] Not that there's anything inherently wrong with the `Math::BigFloat` package! On the contrary, it's well-implemented and very useful. We're just going to *use* it inappropriately in order to make a point about method-based operations in general.

[2] US $25,814.89, in case you actually needed to know.

```
%China =
(
  pop       => Math::BigFloat->new("1 221 591 778"),      # people
  gdp       => Math::BigFloat->new("3 390 000 000 000"),  # US dollars
  pop_incr  => Math::BigFloat->new("1.0093"),             # annual % change
  gdp_incr  => Math::BigFloat->new("1.097"),              # annual % change
);

%USA =
(
  pop       => Math::BigFloat->new("267 954 764"),        # people
  gdp       => Math::BigFloat->new("7 610 000 000 000"),  # US dollars
  pop_incr  => Math::BigFloat->new("1.0087"),             # annual % change
  gdp_incr  => Math::BigFloat->new("1.024"),              # annual % change
);
```

the following calculation is required:

```
$diff = Math::BigFloat->new((Math::BigFloat->new((Math::BigFloat->
        new((Math::BigFloat->new($China{gdp})->fmul($China{gdp_incr}))
        )->fdiv(Math::BigFloat->new($China{pop})->fmul($China{pop_incr}
        ))))))->fsub(Math::BigFloat->new((Math::BigFloat->new($USA{gdp}
        ->fmul($USA{gdp_incr}))))->fdiv(Math::BigFloat->new($USA{pop}->
        fmul($USA{pop_incr})))))))))->fabs());
```

Yuck. Even breaking up the computation doesn't help the readability much:

```
$cpop     = Math::BigFloat->new( $China{pop}->fmul($China{pop_incr})  );
$cgdp     = Math::BigFloat->new( $China{gdp}->fmul($China{gdp_incr})  );
$upop     = Math::BigFloat->new( $USA{pop}->fmul($USA{pop_incr})      );
$ugdp     = Math::BigFloat->new( $USA{gdp}->fmul($USA{gdp_incr})      );
$cgdp_pc  = Math::BigFloat->new( $cgdp->fdiv($cpop)                   );
$ugdp_pc  = Math::BigFloat->new( $ugdp->fdiv($upop)                   );
$sdiff    = Math::BigFloat->new( $cgdb_pc->fsub($ugdb_pc)             );
$diff     = Math::BigFloat->new( $sdiff->fabs()                      );
```

The standard method-based object-oriented interface just doesn't work here, because the numerous method calls drown the meaning of the code in a sea of arrows, parentheses, and constructors. What we'd really like to be able to write is something like:

```
$diff =
  abs( ($China{gdp} * $China{gdp_incr}) / ($China{pop} * $China{pop_incr})
     - ($USA{gdp} * $USA{gdp_incr}) / ($USA{pop} * $USA{pop_incr}) );
```

which is at least *decipherable* by normal humans.

To make that possible, we have to be able to change the meaning of operations such as $cpop * $cpop_incr, or $cgdp_pc - $ugdp_pc, or abs($sdiff) on objects of a given class. Fortunately, Perl provides a simple mechanism to do exactly that.

Changing the way Perl's built-in operators behave when applied to a user-defined type is known as *operator overloading*. Through overloading, operators can be given new semantics when applied to objects of a specific class. For example, given

```
$six = Math::BigFloat->new("6");
$seven = Math::BigFloat->new("7");
$forty_two = $six * $seven;
```

Perl might normally attempt to multiply the integer representations of the two references stored in $six and $seven; that is, the internal memory addresses of the two Math::BigFloat objects. That's unlikely to produce the desired result.

However, by overloading the multiplication operator, we can arrange for the multiplication of any two Math::BigFloat objects to produce a new Math::BigFloat object containing the correct value.[3]

10.2 PERL'S OPERATOR OVERLOADING MECHANISM

Ilya Zakharevich's overload.pm module, which comes with the standard Perl distribution, provides access to Perl's built-in mechanism for overloading operators. To overload operators for a given class, you use the module, passing the use statement a list of operator/implementation pairs:

```
package Math::BigFloat;

use overload "*"   => \&fmul,
             "+"   => "fadd",
             "neg" => sub { Math::BigInt->new($_[0]->fneg()) };
```

Each pair consists of a keyword—which specifies the operator that is to be overloaded—and a subroutine reference—which specifies a subroutine that is to be invoked when the specified operator is encountered.

The keyword must be one from the list shown in table 10.1. These are the only operators that may be overloaded. Note that simple assignment isn't one of them (more on that later). The subroutine reference may either be a reference to a named subroutine, a symbolic reference (i.e., the name of the subroutine), or a reference to an anonymous subroutine. The three alternatives may all be used in the same use overload statement.

The implementation subroutine is called any time a reference to an object of the corresponding class (in the above examples, Math::BigFloat) is an operand of the corresponding operator. If the operation was specified as a subroutine reference, it's called as a nonmethod subroutine. If it is specified as a symbolic reference (i.e., a name), it is called as a method.

In other words, if $six and $seven store Math::BigFloat objects, and multiplication, addition, and negation are overloaded as shown above, the following series of operations:

```
$six * $seven;
$six + $seven;
-$six;
```

is automatically translated to:

```
Math::BigFloat::fmul($six,$seven,"");
$six->fadd($seven,"");
(sub { Math::BigInt->new($_[0]->fneg()) })->($six,undef,"");
```

Regardless of how it is invoked, each implementation subroutine is called with three arguments:

---

[3] The Math::BigFloat module actually *does* overload the basic arithmetic operators in this way, so operations on Math::BigFloat objects do work as expected.

Table 10.1 Overloadable operations in perl

Category	Operators/Keywords	Notes
Arithmetic	"+" "-" "*" "/" "%" "**" "x" "." "neg"	"neg" implements unary negation. There is no overloading for unary identity (i.e., +$obj).
Bitwise	"<<" ">>" "&" "|" "^" "~"	"^" is bitwise exclusive OR, not exponentiation.
Assignment	"+=" "-=" "*=" "/=" "%=" "**=" "<<=" ">>=" "x=" ".=" "++" "--"	"++" and "--" are mutators and their handler is expected to actually change the value of its first argument (e.g., $_[0]->{val}++ for "++"). Handlers for other assignment operators may alter the first argument, but it is then overwritten by the return value.
Comparison	"<" "<=" ">" ">=" "==" "!=" "<=>" "lt" "le" "gt" "ge" "eq" "ne" "cmp"	All other operators may be automatically generated from the "<=>" and "cmp" operators.
Built-in functions	"atan2" "cos" "sin" "exp" "abs" "log" "sqrt"	These override the equivalent built-in function for a specific class only.
Conversions	q{""} "0+" "bool"	Automatically called when the context requires a string, number, or boolean.
Pseudo-operators	"nomethod" "fallback" "="	"=" does *not* overload the assignment operation.

1 The first operand of the operation

2 The second operand of the operation (or undef if the operation is unary, as for fneg above)

3 A flag indicating whether the operands were reversed.

The flag is needed because—as in all other object methods—the first argument must be a reference to an object of the appropriate class—in this case a reference to a Math::BigFloat. If Perl detects an operation such as:

```
6 + $seven;
```

it obviously can't translate that to:

```
6->fadd($seven,"");    # huh?
```

so it translates it to:

```
$seven->fadd(6,1);
```

and sets the third argument to a true value, to indicate that the arguments had to be reversed. Notice that in all the earlier examples, this argument was " " (i.e., false), since the first operand was always a Math::BigNum, so the arguments didn't need to be reversed.

Hence, for operations where the order of the operands matters (for example, in subtraction or division), it's common to see implementation subroutines structured like this:

```
sub subtract
{
    my ($op1, $op2, $reversed) = @_;
    ($op2,$op1) = ($op1,$op2) if $reversed;
    # then perform $op1 - $op2 as appropriate
}

use overload "-" => \&subtract;
```

Bear in mind that problems may arise if both operands of a binary operator are references to objects. If the object's classes have both overloaded the operator, it's the overloading in the *first* operand's class that is invoked. In such cases, it may be necessary to resort to multiple dispatch techniques (see chapter 13) to ensure that the appropriate subroutine is invoked regardless of the order of operands.

10.2.1 "Automagic" operators

The overload.pm module knows about the normal relationships between operations and takes advantage of them to get its job done. For example, given an implementation for a binary "-" operator, overload can automatically build a "-=" operator (since $x-=$y is normally equivalent to $x=$x-$y), a unary "neg" operator (since -$x is usually equivalent to 0-$x), and a "--" operator (since $x-- is equivalent to ($x, $x=$x-1)[0], and --$x is equivalent to $x=$x-1).

Likewise, if we provide an implementation for the three-way comparison operator ("<=>"), the overload module will figure out implementations for all other comparison operators: $x < $y (implemented as ($x<=>$y)<0), $x >= $y (implemented as ($x<=>$y)>=0), $x == $y (implemented as ($x<=>$y)==0), $x != $y (implemented as ($x<=>$y)!=0), and so forth.

These extra overloaded operators are only generated if they are not specifically defined for a package. That is

```
package Math::BigFloat;

use overload
    "-"  => sub { Math::BigFloat->new( $_[0]->fsub($_[1]) ) },
    "neg"=> sub { Math::BigFloat->new( $_[0]->fneg() ) };
```

will cause overload to autogenerate implementations for the operators "-=" and "--", but use the defined implementation for "neg", rather than generate one from "-".

Whether to provide explicit implementations for every operator or let overload mechanism build them itself is largely a choice between expediency and efficiency. Autogenerated operator implementations are rarely as efficient as those you can write yourself, but the difference in performance may not warrant the extra effort required to hand-code implementations for every variant of a single underlying operation such as subtraction.

10.2.2 Fallback operations

Occasionally, the autogeneration of certain operators may be undesirable. For example, a particular class, say DayOfTheWeek, may define a subtraction operation—to determine the interval between two days—but not a negation operation ("anti-Thursday"?) In that case, it may be important to prevent the autogeneration of the "neg" operator.

The obvious solution is to manually define a "neg" operator:

```
package DayOfTheWeek;

use overload
  "-"  => \&delta,
  "neg"=> sub { croak "Can't negate a day!" };
```

This eliminates the problem, but is tedious if many automagic operators have to be prohibited. A better solution in that case is to take advantage of the special "nomethod" and "fallback" pseudo-operators.

If we define an operator implementation for the pseudo-operator "nomethod", the corresponding subroutine is used as a last-resort implementation for operators. Consequently, a "nomethod" operator is like an AUTOLOAD subroutine for operations.

Normally, an operator implementation is looked for in the following order:

1 Check whether the required operator was explicitly overloaded. If so, call the corresponding subroutine.

2 Otherwise, check whether an implementation for the required operator can be generated automatically from some other(s). If so, create it and call it.

3 Otherwise, check whether the "nomethod" operator is defined. If so, call the corresponding subroutine.

4 Otherwise throw an exception.

This order works to maximize the chances that a useful implementation will be called for every operator, but it won't help us when our aim is to prevent "automagic" generation since the "nomethod" implemention isn't tried until after the automagic is attempted.

Fortunately, the above order can be altered by defining a value for the pseudo-operator "fallback". If "fallback" is undefined (either never specified, or else assigned the value undef), the search sequence described above is used. If "fallback" is defined and true, the sequence is the same as above, except that, instead of throwing the exception, the operation reverts to the standard Perl behavior for the operator in question. If "fallback" is defined but false, autogeneration of operators is disabled and the sequence is:

1 Check whether the required operator was explicitly overloaded.

2 Otherwise, check whether the "nomethod" operator is defined.

3 Otherwise, throw an exception.

We can therefore prevent the autogeneration of *any* unimplemented operators for the DayOfTheWeek class like this:

```
package DayOfTheWeek;

use overload
  "-"        => \&delta,
  "fallback" => 0,         # switch off autogeneration
  "nomethod" => sub { croak "Operator $_[3] makes no sense" };
```

The arguments passed to the `"nomethod"` subroutine are the same three (left operand, right operand, reversal flag) passed to an actual operator implementation subroutine, plus a fourth argument specifying the name of the operator requested. So, an operation such as

```
my $day_of_week = DayOfTheWeek->new(4);
```

```
# and later...
```

```
-$day_of_week;
```

calls the anonymous subroutine specified for `"nomethod"`, with the argument list (`$day_of_week,undef,"","neg"`) and causes a suitably informative exception to be thrown.

10.2.3 Specifying conversion operations

Another feature of the overload.pm module is the ability to redefine the way in which an object is converted in a string, numeric, or Boolean context.

To specify how an object is to be converted to a string, we overload its `"\"\""`—or "stringification"—operator.[4] The subroutine associated with this overloaded operator is called whenever an object of the corresponding class is used in a context that requires a string. For example, we can define a stringification operator for the DayOfTheWeek class:

```
package DayOfTheWeek;

my @_day_name = qw(Sun Mon Tue Wed Thu Fri Sat);
use overload
  q{""} => sub { $_day_name[$_[0]->{val}] };
```

The anonymous subroutine that implements the conversion looks up the element whose index is `$_[0]->{val}`. That's because the first argument to the subroutine is, as usual, a reference to the object in question.

The anonymous subroutine associated with `q{""}` is invoked whenever a reference to a DayOfTheWeek object is used in a context where a string is expected. The value it returns is then used as the string. For example:

```
my $day_of_week = DayOfTheWeek->new(4);
```

---

[4] The operator's name consists of two adjacent quotation marks and could more appealingly be specified as `'""'` or `q{""}`. Perversely, it rarely seems to be written any way except `"\"\""`. For clarity, we'll use `q{""}` instead.

```
# and later...

print $day_of_week, "\n";

print "($day_of_week)\n";
```

would print

Thu
(Thu)

since being passed directly to `print` or interpolated into a string are both situations in which stringification is applied. Others such contexts include:

- Being concatenated (e.g., `$day_of_week . "day"`), unless the "." operator has also been redefined,
- Being used as a hash key (e.g., `$menu{$day_of_week}`).

In a similar way, it's also possible to specify an automatic conversion performed whenever an object reference is used in a context that requires a number. For example:

```
package DayOfTheWeek;

my @_day_name = qw(Sun Mon Tue Wed Thu Fri Sat);
use overload

    q{""}=> sub { $_day_name[$_[0]->{val}] },"0+"=> sub { $_[0]->{val} };
```

The "0+" entry specifies a subroutine to be invoked when a numeric value is expected and an object reference is given. For example:

```
print "#" x $day_of_week
```

will now print:

####

because the right operand of an `x` operator is expected to be an integer. However, if DayOfTheWeek had explicitly overloaded the "x" operator, that implementation subroutine would have been called instead.

Other contexts where the "numerification" conversion is invoked include:

- Where a built-in function expects a number (e.g., `int($day_of_week)` or `substr($days,$day_of_week)`),
- Where an object is an operand of the range operator (e.g., `foreach $day (0..$day_of_week)`),
- Where an object is used as the index of an array entry (e.g., `$appointments[$day_of_week]`).

Unless the "fallback" pseudo-operator is set to a true value (see above), the operands of a nonoverloaded arithmetic operation *don't* imply a numerical context. That is, if no "+" operator is defined for class DayOfTheWeek, the expression `$day_of_week+1` doesn't convert `$day_of_week` to a number and apply normal addition. Instead, it attempts to call the missing overloaded operator "+" and fails.

The `"bool"` entry specifies a subroutine that produces a Boolean result when an object reference is used. For example:

```
package DayOfTheWeek;

my @_day_name = qw(Sun Mon Tue Wed Thu Fri Sat);
use overload
    q{""} => sub { $_day_name[$_[0]->{val}] },
    "+0"  => sub { $_[0]->{val} },
    "bool" => sub { $_[0]->{val} != 0 && $_[0]->{val} != 6 };
```

causes the specified anonymous subroutine to be called whenever a reference to a Day-OfTheWeek object appears anywhere that a true or false value is expected:

```
print "Week-end!" unless $day_of_week;
```

This correctly determines whether to print its message because the DayOfTheWeek class defines its objects to be true if the day value is between 1 and 5 (i.e., Monday to Friday).[5] The `"bool"` conversion is invoked within:

- Any control statement or statement modifier: if, unless, while, or for (e.g., while ($day_of_week) {$day_of_week->incr()}),
- The first operand of the ternary operator (e.g., print $day_of_week ? "work" : "play"),
- The block of a grep statement (e.g., grep { $_ } ($day_of_week)).

10.3 EXAMPLE: A ROMAN NUMERALS CLASS

Listing 10.1 shows a class that represents Roman numerals in the range I to MMMCMXCIX, and provides normal arithmetic on them.[6]

Listing 10.1   A Roman numerals class

```
package Number::Roman;
$VERSION = 1.00;
use strict;
use Carp;

my @unit= ( ""  , qw( I II III IV V VI VII VIII IX) );
my @ten = ( ""  , qw( X XX XXX XL L LX LXX LXXX XC) );
my @hund= ( ""  , qw( C CC CCC CD D DC DCC DCCC CM) );
my @thou= ( ""  , qw( M MM MMM) );

sub _inv { my $k = shift; map {($_[$_]=>$_*$k)} (0..$#_); }
sub _any { join "|", @_ }
my %rval= (_inv(1,@unit),_inv(10,@ten),_inv(100,@hund),_inv(1000,@thou));
```

---

[5] This is probably neither a useful nor an obvious definition of "truth" in this context and most likely indicates that the DayOfTheWeek example has now been stretched just a little too far.

[6] The ancient Romans could certainly represent and manipulate numbers larger than 3999, but they weren't restricted to ASCII.

```perl
my $rpat= join ")(", _any(@thou), _any(@hund), _any(@ten), _any(@unit);
$rpat= qr/^($rpat)$/i;
my $npat= qr/^([0-3]??)(\d??)(\d??)(\d)$/;

sub _fromRoman
{
  return unless $_[0] =~ $rpat;
  return $rval{uc $1} + $rval{uc $2} + $rval{uc $3} + $rval{uc $4};
}

sub _toRoman
{
  return unless $_[0] =~ $npat;
  return $thou[$1||0] . $hund[$2||0] . $ten[$3||0] . $unit[$4||0];
}

sub new
{
  my ($class, $num) = @_;
  $num = _fromRoman($num)||$num;
  croak qq{Unable to create Roman value for "$_[1]"}
      unless $num =~ $npat;
  bless \$num, ref($class)||$class;
}

 use overload
   '+'    => sub { my ($x,$y)=_order(@_); Number::Roman->new(int $x+$y) },
   '-'    => sub { my ($x,$y)=_order(@_); Number::Roman->new(int $x-$y) },
   '*'    => sub { my ($x,$y)=_order(@_); Number::Roman->new(int $x*$y) },
   '/'    => sub { my ($x,$y)=_order(@_); Number::Roman->new(int $x/$y) },
   '%'    => sub { my ($x,$y)=_order(@_); Number::Roman->new(int $x%$y) },
   '**'   => sub { my ($x,$y)=_order(@_); Number::Roman->new(int $x**$y) },
   '<=>'  => sub { my ($x,$y)=_order(@_); $x <=> $y },
   '++'   => "_incr",
   '--'   => "_decr",
   '""'   => sub { _toRoman(${$_[0]}) },
   '0+'   => sub { ${$_[0]} };

sub _order
{
  my ($x,$y,$reversed) = @_;
  $x = $$x if UNIVERSAL::isa($x,'Number::Roman');
  $y = $$y if UNIVERSAL::isa($y,'Number::Roman');
  return $reversed ? ($y,$x) : ($x,$y);
}

sub _incr { ${$_[0]}++ }
sub _decr { ${$_[0]}-- }

1;
```

Each Roman numeral is represented by a blessed scalar containing its numerical equivalent. Conversions between regular integers and strings representing the equivalent Roman numeral are provided by the _fromRoman and _toRoman subroutines. These make use of conversion tables (@unit, @ten, @hund, @thou, and %rval), and precompiled patterns ($rpat and $npat) that match and subdivide numbers in each format.[7]

The constructor accepts a regular number or a string containing a Roman numeral. It converts its argument to a regular number if necessary (_fromRoman($num)||$num). The constructor then tests the number against the $npat regular expression to ensure that it's in the representable range. If the resulting number is still acceptable, a reference to the lexical variable containing it ($num) is blessed into the class.

Therefore, we can write

```
my $distantia   = Number::Roman->new("LXXXVII");   # 87 stadia = 10 miles
my $tempus      = Number::Roman->new(42);          # 42 hora = 42 hours
my $gravitas    = Number::Roman->new("CLXII");     # 162 libra = 162 pounds
```

Apart from the constructor itself, the overloaded operators specified by the use overload statement form the entire public interface of the Number::Roman class. They provide the standard binary arithmetic operations, unary increment and decrement, and suitable conversions. The class relies on automagic generation to fill in the missing operations, such as all the assignment variants. There's no need to set up "nomethod" or "fallback" handling, because the constructor automatically throws an exception if any operation creates a value outside the representable range.

The binary operations all work in exactly the same way. The operands ($x and $y) are extracted from @_ by the _order subroutine, which dereferences any reference to a Number::Roman object (producing a number) and undoes any reversal of arguments. Hence, because they use _order, operators on Number::Roman can cope with mixtures of Number::Roman objects and normal numbers, in any order:

```
$velocitatis = $distantia / $tempus;

$vigoris = ($gravitas * $velocitatis**2) / 2;
```

Having converted their arguments to two numerical values in the correct order, the operators apply the appropriate numerical operation to those arguments, convert the result back to an integer, and wrap the result up in a new Number::Roman object.

There's no need to define corresponding "assignment" operators ("+=", "-=", etc.) for the arithmetic operations. The overload module will do so automagically.

The implementation of the binary "<=>" operator is slightly different from the other binary operations. The operation is required to return a value of -1, 0, or 1 and, so, cannot return a Number::Roman. The implementation subroutine still passes its arguments through _order, to dereference them and ensure that their order is correct. The resultant values are compared (using the standard <=> operator for numbers), and the result is returned immediately—

---

[7] The mechanics of the interconversion of Roman and decimal numerals are not important to this discussion and can be ignored if you wish. In fact, being able to ignore the translation details is the main reason for *having* a Number::Roman class.

without creating a Number::Roman to house it. Having defined the "<=>" operator, we need not define any other comparison. The overload module automagically creates them for us.

Unary increment and decrement are more straightforward than the binary operations. They forward the operation to the class's _incr and _decr methods. Those methods dereference their argument, and apply the corresponding numerical operator. The overloading mechanism automatically takes care of the pre- or post- semantics for a particular operation. Of course, we could just as easily implement the two operations via anonymous subroutines:[8]

```
use overload
    # etc. as before,
    '++' => sub { ${$_[0]}++ },
    '--' => sub { ${$_[0]}-- },
    # etc. as before;
```

The stringification operator (q{""}) extracts the number for a Number::Roman object and uses the _fromRoman subroutine to convert it to a character string holding the equivalent Roman numerals. Anywhere a reference to a Number::Roman object is used as a string—in particular, when it's interpolated or printed—it will be automatically converted into its Roman form. Therefore:

```
print "Velocitatis est: $velocitatis\n";
print "Vigoris est: ", ($gravitas*$velocitatis**2)/2, "\n";
```

prints out:

Velocitatis est: II
Vigoris est: CCCXXIV

The "0+" operator allows a Number::Roman reference to be used as a number, by automatically dereferencing it. For example, we can produce a graphical representation of the energy required to accelerate a two pound mass to various velocities:

```
$gravitas = Number::Roman->new(2);

for ($velocitatis=Number::Roman->new(1); $velocitatis<8; $velocitatis++)
{
    my $vigoris = ($gravitas * $velocitatis**2) / 2;
    print "$velocitatis\t", "*" x $vigoris, "\n";
}
```

to produce:

```
I    *
II   ****
III  *********
IV   ***************
V    ***********************
VI   ************************************
VII  **************************************************
VIII ****************************************************************
```

---

[8] Symbolic references were used here as an example of delegating an operation to a method. They will also help with the explanation of another feature in the next section.

10.3.1 Creating class constants

The Number::Roman package hides away almost all the difficulty in using Roman numerals, making them almost as easy to work with as Perl's built-in numeric types. The only time they're still a pain to use is at the very beginning. Creating Number::Roman objects is a nuisance because we have to code a full constructor call:

```
my $distantia  = Number::Roman->new("LXXXVII");
my $gravitas   = Number::Roman->new("CLXII");
```

whereas, with built-in numbers, we can use the appropriate constants directly, because Perl works out the type for us:

```
my $distance   = 87;    #numeric constant
my $weight     = 42;    #numeric constant
```

The same problem arises with any other type whose operators we choose to overload. For instance, all the GDP information in the example at the start of this chapter had to be wrapped up in long and code-cluttering calls to `Math::BigFloat::new`. It would be much better if we could write:

```
my $distantia = "LXXXVII";
```

or

```
$USA{gdp}      = 7610000000000;
```

and have Perl automatically convert the string or numeric constants into Number::Roman or Math::BigFloat objects. Amazingly, perl's overloading mechanism makes even this possible.

To change the way in which integers, floating-point constants, string literals, or regular expressions are interpreted in a Perl program, we can create a set of constant-interpreting handlers using the `overload::constant` subroutine. The subroutine takes a hash of arguments and expects each entry to have a key that is one of the following:

- `"integer"`, indicating the handler for decimal integers,
- `"float"`, indicating the handler for floating-point numbers,
- `"binary"`, indicating the handler for octal and hexadecimal constants,
- `"q"`, indicating the handler for string constants (i.e., in '…', "…", q{…}, and qq{…} strings, the arguments of a tr/…/…/, or the second argument of an s/…/…/),
- `"qr"`, indicating the handler for regular expressions (i.e., in the first argument of a m/…/ or an s/…/…/).

The corresponding value for each key must be a reference to a subroutine. That subroutine is responsible for providing a final value for the particular kind of constant being interpreted. The subroutine is passed three parameters:

1 A string containing the original characters in the constant,

2 The value that Perl would normally interpret the constant as,

3 A string indicating the source of the constant.

Table 10.2 shows a series of examples illustrating which handler the use of a particular constant invokes, and what arguments are passed to that handler. Note that two-part constants, such as substitutions and translations, invoke two distinct handlers in succession to handle their two components. A qw{…} string-to-list interpolator invokes a single "q" handler, which handles the entire string at once (i.e., before it is split).

Table 10.2 Invocation of constant-interpreting handlers

Constant	Handler invoked	Arguments passed (Original characters, Interpretation, Origin)		
`"double quotes"`	q	`('double quotes',`	`'double quotes',`	`'q')`
`qq{qq quotes}`	q	`('qq quotes',`	`'qq quotes',`	`'qq')`
`'single quotes'`	q	`('single quotes',`	`'single quotes',`	`'q')`
`q{q quotes}`	q	`('q quotes',`	`'q quotes',`	`'q')`
`qw{qw qwotes}`	q	`('qw qwotes',`	`'qw qwotes',`	`'q')`

`<<HERE`
`here doc`
`HERE`
	q	`("here doc\n",`	`"here doc\n",`	`'qq')`

`<<'HERE'`
`quoted here doc`
`HERE`
	q	`("quoted here doc\n",`	`"quoted here doc\n",`	`'q')`

`tr/tr_from/tr_to/`	q	`('tr_from',`	`'tr_from',`	`'tr')`
	q	`('tr_to',`	`'tr_to',`	`'tr')`
`qr{qr quotes}`	qr	`('qr quotes',`	`'qr quotes',`	`'qq')`
`s/s_pat/s_text/`	qr	`('s_pat',`	`'s_pat',`	`'qq')`
	q	`('s_text',`	`'s_text',`	`'s')`
`m/m pattern/`	qr	`('m pattern',`	`'m pattern',`	`'qq')`
`12345`	integer	`('12345',`	`12345,`	`undef)`
`12_345`	integer	`('12_345',`	`12345,`	`undef)`
`12345.0`	float	`('12345.0',`	`12345.0,`	`undef)`
`12345e1`	float	`('12345e1',`	`123450.0,`	`undef)`
`012345`	binary	`('012345',`	`5349,`	`undef)`
`0x12345`	binary	`('0x12345',`	`74565,`	`undef)`
`0xBadDeed`	binary	`('0xBadDeed',`	`19594173,`	`undef)`

The source string passed as the handler's third argument is only defined for `"q"` and `"qr"` handlers. For those handlers, it takes one of the following values:

- `'q'`, indicating that the string is from an uninterpolated context (`'…'` or `q{…}` or `qw{…}`),
- `'qq'`, indicating that the string is from an interpolated context (`"…"` or `qq{…}` or `m/…/` or the first argument of an `s/…/…/`),
- `'tr'`, indicating that the string is part of a `tr/…/…/` or `y/…/…/`,
- `'s'`, indicating that the string is the second argument of an `s/…/…/`.

Whichever handler is invoked and whatever arguments it is passed, the handler is always expected to return a scalar value, which is used in place of the usual interpretation. For example, the Math::BigFloat package can use `overload::constant` to change the way that integer and floating-point constants in a Perl program are interpreted:

```
package Math::BigFloat;
use Math::BigInt;
use overload;

my %_constant_handlers =
(
   integer => sub { return Math::BigInt->new($_[0]) },
   float   => sub { return Math::BigFloat->new($_[0]) },
);


sub import   { overload::constant %_constant_handlers }
sub unimport { overload::remove_constant %_constant_handlers }
```

This causes every literal integer or floating-point constant that appears in a Perl program—at least, those within the scope of a use `Math::BigFloat` statement—to be automatically converted to a `Math::BigInt` or `Math::BigFloat`, respectively.

We can also change the way that a program interprets strings when using the Number::Roman package:

```
package Number::Roman;

# other methods and operator overloading as before

sub _constant_handler
{
   my ($original, $std_interpretation, $source) = @_;
   return $std_interpretation unless $source =~ /q/ && $original =~ $rpat;
   return Number::Roman->new($original);
}


sub import   { overload::constant( q => \&_constant_handler ) }
sub unimport { overload::remove_constant( q => undef ) }
```

This time, the constant handler is a little more sophisticated. It first checks that the constant is coming from a single- or double-quoted string, so that translation and substitution operations do not have embedded character strings interpreted as Roman numerals:[9]

```
$medical_text =~ s/intravenous/IV/g;   # "IV", not Number::Roman->new("IV")
```

Next, the constant handler checks that the candidate string is a proper Roman numeral. If it is, then the string is replaced by the reference to a new `Roman::Number` object. Otherwise, the standard Perl interpretation of the string constant, as a constant scalar value, is returned. Quoted string constants that are valid Roman numerals are automatically converted to references to Number::Roman objects, while all other quoted strings are interpreted in the normal way. For example:

---

[9] Of course, in this particular case it wouldn't matter if such embedded strings were Romanized (except for the extra cost involved), because the `q{ " }` operator would convert them straight back to the original string. But not all classes have this kind of "exactly reversible" representation.

```
my $distantia  = "LXXXVII";
my $gravitas   = 'CLXII';
my $tempus     = "DIXIT";
```

puts references to Number::Roman objects in both `$distantia` and `$gravitas`, but a regular scalar string in `$tempus` (since although DIXIT *is* Latin,[10] it isn't a valid Roman numeral).

Note also that `overload::remove_constant` doesn't actually care about the value associated with each key it's passed, so, in this case, it's easier to pass `undef`.

10.4 *CIRCUMVENTING UNDESIRED REFERENCE SEMANTICS*

In Perl, objects are almost always accessed through references. Normally, that distinction—between the object we're using and the reference we're actually passing around—is kept clear because we have to use an arrow operator to access the object's methods or attributes. Operator overloading, however, blurs the distinction, by allowing code such as

```
$velocitatis = $distantia / $tempus;
```

in which we treat the two references in `$distantia` and `$tempus` as if they were the values of the Number::Roman objects to which they refer.

Normally, that isn't a serious problem, as our minds are well adapted to ignoring this duality, and the overloading mechanism works hard to ensure that we can do so safely. There is one situation, however, where the overloading mechanism can't automatically shield us from the "reference semantics" of objects. Consider an operation like this:

```
$v = $velocitatis;

# and later…

$v++;
```

The assignment causes both `$v` and `$velocitatis` to refer to the same object. The increment operator later causes that object's value to be incremented. Other parts of the code still using the `$velocitatis` reference will then also have the value of the referent mysteriously changed. That *may* be the desired effect, but, if so, it's obscure and inconsistent with the "value semantics" of other operations.

Operators that change the value of their operands in this way are called *mutators*, and include the increment, decrement, and operator assignment operations (`"+="`, `"*="`, etc.). The overload module provides a means of intercepting mutators and cloning the object being mutated so that the mutation only affects a copy of the object.

That interception is specified by overloading the (misleadingly named) `"="` operator:

```
package Number::Roman;

sub incr { ${$_[0]}++ }
sub copy { Number::Roman->new(${$_[0]}) }
```

---

[10] …for *"[he or she] has said"*…

```
use overload
  # etc. as before…
  '++' => "incr",
  '='  => "copy";
```

This does *not* change the behavior of assignment. Rather overloading "=" sets up a sub-routine that is called just before the implementation subroutine for any mutator is invoked. In other words, given the overloadings just specified, the code

```
$v++;
```

is effectively translated to:

```
$v = $v->copy(undef,"");
$v->incr(undef,"");
```

So, provided copy actually does make a copy of object it's called on, the previous value accessible via $velocitatis is left unchanged.

10.5 *THE USE AND ABUSE OF OPERATORS*

The operator overloading mechanism gives you a powerful mechanism with which you can alter the normal behavior of expressions and conversions involving any new class you create. The question is, *should* you?

Clearly, cases exist when overloading certain operations makes perfect sense, especially if you're creating a class to represent something with a well-defined algebra (such as large integers, complex numbers, vectors, or matrices). As illustrated by the GDP calculation at the start of this section, an appropriate set of operators can greatly improve the usability of such classes and the readability of code that uses them.

Likewise, it's often useful to overload the stringification conversion for a class. For example:

```
package CD::Music;

use overload
  q{""}  =>  sub { qq("$_[0]->{name}" by $_[0]->{artist}) };
```

That way, if someone writes:

```
my $cd = CD::Music->new(@messiah_data);

# and later…

print $cd, "\n";
```

they get something useful like:

"Messiah" by George Frideric Handel

rather than something merely accurate like:

CD::Music=HASH(0x1001c3e0)

Then there are cases where the appropriateness of specific overloadings is less certain. Consider a class implementing three-dimensional vectors, such as might be found in a graphics package:

```
$view_dir = Vector->new(x=>100,y=>0,z=>-50);
$move_dir = Vector->new(x=>20,y=>20,z=>0);

$motion_normal = $view_dir x $move_dir;
$motion_angle  = $view_dir * $move_dir;
```

Clearly for such a class "x" is an appropriate operator for the cross-product operation, but is "*" the right choice for the dot-product? It certainly conveys the multiplicative nature of the operation. It also looks somewhat like a dot (albeit a big, hairy one). But is the actual dot operator (i.e., ".") a better choice? That operator already has a strong association with concatenation in regular Perl, but a vector algebraist might well find:

```
$motion_angle = $view_dir . $move_dir;
```

more intuitive. Or perhaps not. It certainly *won't* be intuitive when the dot operator is called to concatenate two string-interpolated variables (for example, "$vector1$vector2") and, instead, produces their dot-product. And what would such mathematicians make of the "^" operator? Would they expect

```
$unit_view_dir = ^$view_dir;
```

to create a unit vector? How will they react when it produces a syntax error instead?

The problem is that, having provided some overloaded operators for a class, we have also set up an expectation in the mind of the users of that class. Because objects of the class can *sometimes* be used in the natural way, clients may expect that such objects can *always* be used that way. That will probably not be the case, so it's vital to document where the metaphor breaks down.

Another dubious use of operator overloading occurs when a certain operation is provided "for completeness," though its definition is neither justifiable nor sensible. Our earlier attempt to overload the "bool" conversion for the DayOfTheWeek class was a good example of that. Setting up such arbitrary and nonobvious operations leads to code like:

```
if ($today) { $drive->back_up() }
```

which forces everyone who comes across it to go hunting through the source code trying to work out the circumstances under which the disk actually gets archived. This is clearly a case where a normal method call is a better choice:

```
if ($today->is_business_day()) { $drive->back_up() }
```

Sometimes operator overloading is used purely to provide coding expediency, rather than to promote clarity. For example, suppose we create a database class that is entirely operator-driven:

```
use OpDBM;

my $db = OpDBM->new($dbfile);

$db += [item=>"oatmeal",   category=>"breakfast"];
$db += [item=>"marmalade", category=>"breakfast"];
$db += [item=>"potatoes",  category=>"dinner"];

my $relation = sqrt( ~$db * [category=>"breakfast"] );

print "$_->{item}\n" while ($relation++);
```

The dozen or so people on the planet who are well-versed in abstract database theory may rejoice in the decision to overload "+=" to handle insertions, "~" for database normalization, "*" to perform selections, "++" to iterate a set of records, and sqrt to implement the "Sort, Quashing Repeated Tuples" operation:

```
package OpDBM;
use overload
   '+='   => sub {$_[0]->insert_tuple( @{$_[1]} ) },
   '~'    => sub {$_[0]->normalize() },
   '*'    => sub {if ($_[2]){ $_[1]->insert_tuple( @{$_[0]} ) }
                  else { $_[0]->insert_tuple( @{$_[1]} ) } };

package OpDBM::Relation;
use overload
   '++'   => sub {$_[0]->next() },
   'sqrt' => sub {$_[0]->sort_quash_reps() };
```

To database theoreticians, the resulting code may be obvious, intuitive, and even elegant. But it's also likely to make the task of developing and maintaining such code much harder for the rest of us.

10.5.1 When to overload?

This is a "religious issue," so there's no correct answer.[11] As a general rule of thumb, overloading the algebraic operators for a class is appropriate when the same operators are used in the normal (nonprogramming) notation for whatever the class represents. Numeric and other mathematical classes are the usual candidates here.

Overloading conversion operations is also often a good idea, as it allows objects to act in standard ways programmers may expect, especially when they are stringified. Comparison operators are another reasonable candidate for overloading in most cases, provided the values represented by objects have an obvious ordering.

A few operators are sufficiently generalized in their meaning (for example, "+=" meaning "add to") that they can reasonably be overloaded in almost any suitable context. Code like

```
$db += [item=>"oatmeal", category=>"breakfast"];
```

or

```
$dictionary += "algebraist";
```

or

```
$process_group += $new_process;
```

is readily intelligible to almost any programmer.

Apart from that, it's probably best to use operator overloading sparingly, the way an expert chef uses salt. Without it, your creations may be bland and indigestible, but using it indiscriminately or too often will only raise your clients' blood pressure.

---

[11] Or perhaps: "…so there are nothing *but* correct answers, most of which are mutually exclusive."

10.6 WHERE TO FIND OUT MORE

The overload.pm module comes as part of the standard Perl distribution and has extensive documentation, including some interesting example classes.

Many other modules in the standard distribution and on the CPAN (e.g., Math::BigInt, Math::Complex, Math::Pari,[12] I18N::Collate, Data::Dumper, CGI, File::CounterFile, and Tk::Font) use operator overloading. Studying their source code can be instructive.

Chapter 13 of the *Perl Cookbook* also describes operator overloading and gives two simple example classes—one string-based and one numerical—that make use of the facility in different ways.

The CPAN provides a (non-object-oriented) Roman numeral class called Roman.pm. It's available from http://www.perl.com/CPAN/authors/id/OZAWA/.

10.7 SUMMARY

- Overloaded operators allows Perl objects to act (and interact) like built-in data types.
- Operators are overloaded by specifying a subroutine, a class method, or an anonymous subroutine that provides the necessary implementation.
- The operands are passed as arguments. Their order may have been reversed to ensure that the first argument is an object, in which case the third argument will be true.
- The overload.pm module can manufacture missing operators by combining those which *have* been specified. It's also possible to specify a catchall subroutine to handle missing operators directly.
- A module can install special conversion routines to convert objects to strings, numbers, or Boolean values and to convert literal strings, numbers, or Boolean values to objects.
- The "=" operator doesn't overload assignment. Rather, the operator specifies a duplication method to be called on an object about to have its value altered.
- Operators are best overloaded when they are syntactically compatible with the pre-existing non-programming notation for the application area.

---

[12] Math::Pari is Ilya Zakharevich's Perl interface to the extraordinarily useful PARI library for number theory and numerical computation (see ftp://megrez.ceremab.u-bordeaux.fr/pub/pari). It was to support this module that Ilya originally implemented Perl's operator overloading mechanism.

C H A P T E R   1 1

Encapsulation

Encapsulation is one of the cornerstones of object orientation, but it's the area in which Perl's support for object-oriented programming is weakest. Many would argue that enforced encapsulation is against Perl's philosophy of freedom and flexibility in programming. However, there are situations when too much freedom becomes a trap, and too much flexibility makes it hard to build solid code. Fortunately, Perl's flexibility can be turned against itself to provide a means of building objects that respect the encapsulation imposed by their classes.

11.1 *THE PERILS OF TRUST*

In practice, the lack of an built-in encapsulation mechanism rarely seems to be a problem in Perl. Most Perl programmers build classes out of standard hashes, and both they and the users of their classes get by happily with the principle of encapsulation by good manners. The lack of formal encapsulation doesn't matter because everybody plays nicely, keeps off the grass, and respects the official interface of objects. Those who don't play by the rules, who directly access a method or attribute that is supposed to be private, get what they deserve—either better performance or a nasty surprise.

The only problem is that this convivial arrangement doesn't scale very well. Leaving your front door open may be fine in a small town, but it's madness in the big city. Likewise, informal mechanisms suitable for a few hundred lines of code written by a single programmer don't work nearly as well when the code is tens of thousands of lines long and developed by a team.

Even if you could trust the entire team to maintain sufficient programming discipline to respect the notional encapsulation of attributes (a dubious proposition), accidents and mistakes happen, especially in rarely used parts of the system that only get used when demonstrating to important clients.

Moreover, deliberate decisions to circumvent the rules (usually taken in the heat of hacking, out of laziness, or for efficiency) are often inadequately documented, leading to problems much later in the development cycle. For example, consider a (notionally) private attribute of an object, which for efficiency reasons is accessed directly in an obscure part of a large system. If the implementation of the object's class changes, that attribute may cease to exist.

In a more static language, this would generate an error message when the external code next attempts to access the now nonexistent attribute. However, Perl's autovivification of hash entries may well resurrect the former attribute when it is next modified, so the now-incorrect access proceeds silently. Bugs such as this can be painfully difficult to diagnose and track down, especially if the original programmer has moved on by the time the problem is discovered.

11.2 *Encapsulation via closures*

The standard approach to enforcing encapsulation of an object's attributes is to avoid giving the user direct access to the object. At first glance, that may seem impossible; after all, you must have a reference to the object, or you can't call its methods.

The key here is the word *direct*. So long as the reference provided to the user refers to something that has been blessed into the required class, it is possible to call methods through that reference. If we somehow arrange that the blessed something cannot be used to directly access object attributes, then those attributes are safely encapsulated. The trick, of course, is to achieve that encapsulation while still allowing methods to access their own attributes directly.

Curiously, to find that kind of access control for objects, we have to travel briefly in the opposite direction and look at subroutines.

Subroutines provide an obvious form of encapsulation. If you have a subroutine—say for example, the pseudo-random number generator function rand—then the *only* way you can access the information it provides is to call it and grab the value it returns. As clients of the rand function, we have no way of directly accessing its internals. For all most of us know, it might be implemented like this:

```
{
  my @rand_val = (0.012657, 0.453662, 0.718273);
  sub rand
  {
    push @rand_val, shift @rand_val;  # "rotate" the list
    return ($_[0]||1) * $rand_val[0]; # scale and return first element
  }
}
```

The point is, there's no way to extend rand's pitifully inadequate look-up table. Outside the block in which it's defined, @rand_val is out-of-scope, and the only remaining means of accessing it is hidden inside the rand function itself.

We have seen the same technique used throughout this book, to encapsulate class attributes—for example, the $_count attribute in the CD::Music class. Outside the block in which that lexical variable is defined, the only access to it is via the closures get_count, _incr_count, etc., that were defined in the same block.

The use of a closure to provide controlled access to an otherwise inaccessible lexical works equally well when applied to the attributes of individual objects. In fact, we could actually *create* the object by blessing the access control subroutine itself.

Listing 11.1 shows another version of the simple Soldier class. Unlike the automatically generated hash-based version in chapter 8, this version of the class is implemented using closures to enforce encapsulation of its attributes.

As usual, the constructor is the most complex part of the class. It creates a lexical hash (%data) and initializes it with the appropriate entries from the argument list by assigning one hash slice (@args{@attrs}) to another (@data{@attrs}).[1]

The constructor then creates a new anonymous subroutine and stores a reference to it in $accessor. As the name implies, that subroutine will be used to access the %data hash, once the new Soldier object is fully constructed.

The anonymous accessor subroutine takes three arguments: a string indicating what kind of access is required; another string indicating which attribute is to be accessed; and the new attribute value for "set" operations. The accessor subroutine has three courses of action, depending on the arguments it is given.

If the first argument indicates a "get" request, the subroutine simply returns a copy of the requested attribute in the %data hash. The subroutine has access to %data because that hash was declared in the same lexical scope as the subroutine itself—that is, within the body of the constructor. If the first argument indicates a "set" request, the subroutine checks whether it is the "rank" attribute that is being set and, if so, assigns the new value to $data{"rank"}. Any other access request—for example, to set the "name" attribute—is impolitely rejected.

Finally, once the accessor subroutine is created, it is blessed as the new object, and a reference to it is returned from Soldier::new. At that point, the constructor ends, and the lexical variables it created would normally be destroyed. However, the %data hash escapes this fate because the anonymous subroutine still refers to it, and so Perl arranges for it to live on, incognito, until the anonymous subroutine itself is no longer accessible.

The result, illustrated in figure 11.1, is that each newly created Soldier object is a blessed subroutine, one which has the only remaining access to the lexical %data. It uses that hash as its own private storage area, getting or setting entries in %data whenever it is invoked. It's important to realize that, next time Soldier::new is invoked, a new—and entirely distinct—lexical hash, also called %data, will be created within the constructor. Then a new—and entirely distinct—anonymous subroutine will be created, blessed, and returned. That new and entirely distinct subroutine will subsequently have access to the new %data hash.

In this way, repeated calls to Soldier::new create a series of distinct hashes, each wrapped up in a personalized, anonymous, encapsulating subroutine. The subroutines are

---

[1] This method of initialization has much to recommend it: it's concise (just one assignment), declarative (valid attributes are declared in the @attrs hash), robust (only attributes specified in @attrs can ever be initialized), and easy to maintain (just add the name of any new attribute to @attrs).

Listing 11.1 The Soldier class implemented via closures

```
package Soldier;
$VERSION = 1.00;
use strict;

use Carp;

my @attrs = qw(name rank serial_num);

sub new
{
  my ($class, %args) = @_;
  my %data;
  @data{@attrs} = @args{@attrs};
  my $accessor =
    sub
    {
        my ($cmd, $attr, $newval) = @_;
        return $data{$attr}
          if $cmd eq "get";
        return $data{"rank"} = $newval
          if ($cmd eq "set" && $attr eq "rank");
        croak "Cannot $cmd attribute $attr";
    };
  bless $accessor, ref($class)||$class;
}

# These methods provide the only means of accessing object attributes
# (note that only rank can be changed)

sub get_name       { $_[0]->('get','name') }
sub get_rank       { $_[0]->('get','rank') }
sub get_serial_num { $_[0]->('get','serial_num') }

sub set_rank
{
  my ($self, $newrank) = @_;
  $self->('set','rank',$newrank);
}

1;
```

returned as objects and used to access the corresponding hash in a controlled manner. Instant encapsulation!

Oddly enough, that encapsulation is actually far stronger than is provided by most other object-oriented languages. Not even the members of its own class have direct access to a Soldier object's data. Instead, they too must request access via the encapsulating subroutine.

Hence the get_name, get_rank, and get_serial_num accessors each take the reference to a blessed subroutine through which they are invoked (i.e., $_[0]) and call that

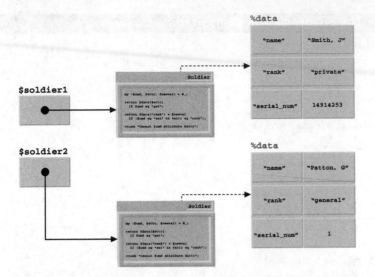

Figure 11.1 Structure of closure-based Soldier objects

subroutine, passing it an argument list requesting retrieval of the appropriate attribute value. Likewise, the `set_rank` method invokes the subroutine, asking it to update its encapsulated `$data{"rank"}` attribute with the specified new value. There is no point in providing a `set_name` or a `set_serial_num` method, since the definition of the encapsulating subroutine makes it impossible to set these attributes.

11.2.1 A variation for the paranoid

In a sense, the accessor methods of class Soldier exist only as conveniences. Instead of writing:

```
$soldier->set_rank("Colonel");
print $soldier->get_serial_num();
```

we could take advantage of the fact that we have a reference to the accessor subroutine (i.e., in `$soldier`), and call that subroutine directly:

```
$soldier->("set","rank","Colonel");
print $soldier->("get","serial_num");
```

Well, we *could* do that, but it's probably not a good idea. In fact, it would probably be better if we couldn't do it at all.

This level of paranoia may appear to have no purpose, except to "satisfy certain fastidious concerns of programming police and related puritans."[2] However, there are good reasons for

---

2 ..as suggested by Tom Christiansen in the **perltoot** man page. Of course, since the Puritans helped to found the most powerful nation in history, and the police exist to protect the personal rights and liberties of a free citizenry, it may be that Tom is actually in favor of absolute encapsulation and is praising it with faint damns.

preventing client code from accessing an object in any way except through their defined methods.

The most obvious reason is that, as maintainers of the Soldier class's code, we may later need to change the interface to the anonymous accessor subroutine or even dispense with subroutine-based objects entirely. Either of these changes will invalidate any client code that calls the accessor subroutine directly, which will result in hundreds of irate users contacting us to ask why their client code no longer works.

Furthermore, as we have already seen in chapter 5, if a class like Soldier is ever to be inherited (Soldier::Foot, Soldier::Paratrooper, Soldier::Is::A::Marine::Sir::HOO::AH, etc.), it may be vital that client code accesses Soldier attributes only via defined methods. If attributes are accessed in any other way—either directly (for example, $soldier->{"name"}), or indirectly (for example, $soldier->("get","name"))—then that client code is no longer treating the object polymorphically, and it may not work correctly when given an object of a derived class.

Fortunately, it's easy to ensure that the accessor subroutine that implements a Soldier object can only be accessed from the class's defined methods. We simply modify the Soldier constructor as follows:

```
sub new
{
    my ($class, %args) = @_;
    my %data;
    @data{@attrs} = @args{@attrs};
    my $accessor =
        sub
        {
            my ($cmd, $attr, $newval) = @_;
            croak "Invalid direct access. Use the ${cmd}_$attr method instead"
                unless caller()->isa("Soldier");
            return $data{$attr}
                if $cmd eq "get";
            return $data{"rank"} = $newval
                if ($cmd eq "set" && $attr eq "rank");
            croak "Cannot $cmd attribute $attr";
        };
    bless $accessor, ref($class)||$class;
}
```

In this version, when the anonymous accessor subroutine is called, it checks to see that it was called by a method belonging to a class that *is-a* Soldier. If not, it immediately throws an exception. This means that methods like Soldier::get_name can invoke the accessor method directly, but subroutines outside the Soldier class hierarchy cannot. We could make the access rules even stricter:

```
croak "Invalid direct access. Use the ${cmd}_$attr method instead"
    unless caller() eq "Soldier";
```

and limit access to methods of the Soldier class itself, in which case derived classes would also have to use those methods to access their own (inherited) attributes.

Ultimately, of course, nothing will stop the determined programmer from circumventing the proper interface of the Soldier class:

```
my $soldier = Soldier->new(name=>"Alexander", rank=>"General");
```

```
package Soldier;                    # Step back into the Soldier package and…
print $soldier->("get","name"); # …call the accessor directly!
```

But this technique does serve to effectively catch accidental breaches of the interface, and thereby minimize nasty surprises.

11.3 *ENCAPSULATION VIA SCALARS*

A less well-known approach to encapsulation uses scalar-based objects to implement a technique known as the *flyweight pattern*. In the flyweight pattern, objects don't carry around their own information, so that information can't be accessed directly via the object. Instead, flyweight objects merely serve as an index into a shared table of values, stored within the class itself. For example, an object may be an integer that indexes into a table of values stored as a class attribute.

Flyweight objects are most frequently used in object-oriented languages that pass objects around by value because flyweight objects remain extremely small (no matter how much data they contain). Hence, they are cheap to pass around. Because Perl objects are invariably accessed via references, this advantage is not significant.

However, the flyweight pattern still has something to offer in Perl, because it provides a simple mechanism for preventing direct access to object attributes, thereby enforcing encapsulation. As a bonus, it also provides a means of easily keeping track of every object in a class, something closure-based encapsulation doesn't provide.

11.3.1 Name, rank, and serial number

Listing 11.2 shows a flyweight implementation of the Soldier class. The entire class is contained in a pair of curly braces to ensure that any lexical variable declared within their scope is not directly accessible outside that scope. Not surprisingly, the first thing the class does is declare some lexical variables.

Listing 11.2 The Soldier class implemented via scalars

```
package Soldier;
$VERSION = 2.00;
use strict;

{
  # Table storing references to hashes containing object data
  my @_soldiers;

  # Allowable attributes and their default values
  my %_fields = (name=>'???', rank=>'???', serial_num=>-1);

  # Constructor adds object data to table and blesses a scalar
```

CHAPTER 11   ENCAPSULATION

```
    # storing the index of that data

    sub new
    {
      my ($class, %args) = @_;
      my $dataref = {%_fields};
      foreach my $field ( keys %_fields )
      {
          $dataref->{$field} = $args{$field}
             if defined $args{$field};
      }
      push @_soldiers, $dataref;
      my $object = $#_soldiers;
      bless \$object, $class;
    }

    # These methods provide the only means of accessing object attributes
    # (note that only rank can be changed)

    sub get_name         { return $_soldiers[${$_[0]}]->{name} }
    sub get_rank         { return $_soldiers[${$_[0]}]->{rank} }
    sub get_serial_num   { return $_soldiers[${$_[0]}]->{serial_num} }

    sub set_rank
    {
      my ($indexref, $newrank) = @_;
      $_soldiers[$$indexref]->{rank} = $newrank
    }

    # This class method provides an iterator over every object

    my $_cursor = -1;
    sub each
    {
      my $nextindex = ++$_cursor;
      if ($nextindex < @_soldiers)
      {
          return bless \$nextindex, ref($_[0])||$_[0];
      }
      else
      {
          $_cursor = -1;
          return undef;
      }
    }
}
```

The lexical array @_soldiers is used to store the data for each object. That data is directly accessible to the methods declared within the surrounding curly braces, but nowhere else. It is this restriction that eventually provides the desired encapsulation of object data.

The lexical hash `%_fields` performs the dual function of recording (in its keys) the names of valid attributes of a Soldier object and storing (in its values) the default values for those attributes.

The constructor begins like most others we've seen so far, by creating an anonymous hash and initializing it with the default attribute values for the class. It loops over the valid fields of the class, overwriting those default values with any corresponding argument that was passed to the constructor.

At this point, a typical constructor blesses and returns the reference in `$objref`, making the anonymous hash into the new object. Instead, `Soldier::new` pushes the hash onto the end of the encapsulated `@_soldiers` array and blesses a scalar storing the index of that newly added array element.

Thus a constructor call such as

```
my $grunt = Soldier->new(name       => "Smith, J.",
                         rank        => "private",
                         serial_num  => 149162536);
```

leaves `$grunt` with a reference to a scalar—that is, to the index of the data—rather than a reference to a hash—that is, to the data itself). Figure 11.2 illustrates the process.

Theoretically, the effect is the same. Since we have the index and know which array it refers to, we can still find the actual data. In practice, however, there's an important difference. Outside the curly braces surrounding the class, the `@_soldiers` array is inaccessible so, even though we have the index for the object's data, we can't access that data directly.

11.3.2 Controlled access

Instead, it's up to the accessor methods of the class to provide the required access. Since they are all defined within the encapsulating curly braces, they *do* have access to `@_soldiers`. So, the accessor methods can dereference the blessed index (`${$_[0]}`), index into the array to get a reference to the appropriate hash data (`$_soldiers[${$_[0]}]`), and then access the correct field of that data using the arrow notation (`$_soldiers[${$_[0]}]->{name}`).

The implementation shown in listing 11.2 doesn't provide write accessors for a Soldier's name or serial number. The lack of write access provides real data security since, without the accessors, there is no way of modifying these attributes once they are set.

Even imposing a new method on the class

```
package main;
use Soldiers;

my $general = Soldier->new( name       => "Caesar, G.J.",
                            rank        => "Prodictator",
                            serial_num  => "MMXLVIII");

# Oops, that serial number was out by one.
# Strange, there's no method to change it.
# Oh well, let's just add one ourselves...
sub Soldiers::set_serial_num { $_soldiers[${$_[0]}]->{serial_num} = $_[1] }
```

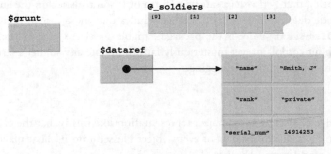

a After `my $dataref = {%_fields};` and `foreach my $field...`

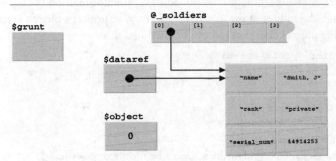

b After `push @_soldiers, $dataref;` and `my $object = $#_soldiers`

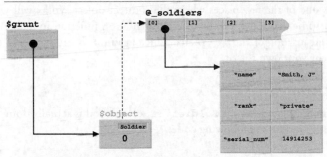

c After `bless \$object, $class;` and constructor returns

Figure 11.2 Construction of a Soldier object

```
# ...and use it...
```

```
$general->set_serial_num("MMXLIX");
```

will not circumvent encapsulation. Although the new method *is* in the class's namespace (and hence, callable through its objects), it *isn't* in the lexical scope of the original encapsulating curly braces, so it doesn't have access to the lexical @_soldiers array.

It's worth noting that Perl visits a satisfying form of Instant Justice on the author of this code. Since the code doesn't use strict, Perl concludes that the @_soldiers array being modified in Soldier::set_rank is the package variable @main::_soldiers. Thus, the code executes without complaint, yet mysteriously fails to update any soldier's serial number, leading to happy hours of fruitless debugging.

11.3.3 Roll call

The other advantage of a scalar-based object representation like this is that the class itself has direct and continuing access to the data of every object blessed into it. That makes it easy to provide class methods to iterate that data.

The Soldier class demonstrates this by providing an iterator method (Soldier::each), which steps through the indices of the @_soldiers array, returning a blessed version of each index (i.e., a Soldier object). The method can be used like this:

```
while (my $soldier = Soldier->each)
{
    printf "name: %s\nrank: %s\n s/n: %d\n\n",
        $soldier->get_name(),
        $soldier->get_rank(),
        $soldier->get_serial_num();
}
```

By the way, as elegant as it might look, don't be tempted to write

```
while (my $soldier = each Soldier) {...}
```

hoping that this is one of the few places where the indirect object syntax will work. It isn't. Instead, Perl will assume you wanted to use the built-in each function to iterate the package hash %Soldier, and just forgot the "%" prefix. Once again, use strict will prevent Perl from helping you cut your own throat.

11.3.4 A question of identity

It's instructive to contemplate what the Soldier::each method is actually doing, every time it returns an object. Consider the following code:

```
use Soldier;

my $soldier_ref1 = Soldier->new(name=>"Temuchin", rank=>"Khan");
my $soldier_ref2 = Soldier->each;
```

Assuming that this is the entire program, then the objects referred to by $soldier_ref1 and $soldier_ref2 should be the same. And, in almost every important sense, they *are*. They have the same name, rank, and serial number, and any changes made via $soldier_ref1->set_rank() will be reflected in subsequent calls to $soldier_ref2->get_rank(). However, the two references themselves do not compare equal, because the two blessed scalar objects to which they refer are distinct (though they have the same value).

Each time it needs to return a given index of @_soldiers, Soldier::each creates an entirely new blessed scalar object containing that index. Because that object has the same value as the original object for the given data, it is logically equivalent to the original, and only distinguishable by its distinct address. Such objects are sometimes called *proxies*, since they act in place of the original object.

11.3.5 A variation for the truly paranoid

Although it's useful that two physically distinct objects can be logically identical, there's a down-side: that duality also means that any Soldier object can be converted to any other Soldier object, *even if there is no preexisting reference to that other object in the current scope.*

For example, consider the following code

```
use Soldier;
OUTER:
{
    INNER:
    {
        my $commander = Soldier->new(name=>"Smythe, Sir X.A.StJ.",
                                     rank=>"Field Marshall");
    }
    my $private1 = Soldier->new( name=>"Smith, J.",
                                 rank=>"Private");

    $$private = 0;                   # Guess the right index
    bless $private, Soldier;         # and become…
    print $private->get_rank();      # …Field Marshall!
}
```

Even though the outer scope has lost access to the $commander object before the $private object is even created, $private can still steal $commander's identity by changing (and reblessing) the index stored in its object.

If this kind of referential "bed-swapping" is unacceptable, or if it is important that all references to the same Soldier object always compare equal, then a slightly more sophisticated approach, such as that shown in listing 11.3, is required.

Listing 11.3 A more secure version of Soldier class, implemented via scalars

```
package Soldier;
$VERSION = 3.00;
use strict;

{
    # Hash table storing references to hashes containing object data
    my %_soldiers;

    # Allowable attributes and their default values
    my %_fields = (name=>'???', rank=>'???', serial_num=>-1);

    # Constructor adds object data to hash table and blesses a scalar
    # storing the key of that data

    sub new
    {
```

```
                  my ($class, %args) = @_;

                  # Build the data for the object…
                  my $dataref = {%_fields};
                  foreach my $field ( keys %_fields )
                  {
                     $dataref->{$field} = $args{$field}
                        if defined $args{$field};
                  }

                  # Build a unique unguessable key…
                  $dataref->{_key} = rand
                     until $dataref->{_key} && !exists $_soldiers{$dataref->{_key}};

                  # Insert the data into the table and return the key…
                  $_soldiers{$dataref->{_key}} = $dataref;
                  bless \$dataref->{_key}, $class;
               }
               # These methods provide the only means of accessing object attributes
               # (note that only rank can be changed)

               sub get_name{ return $_soldiers{${$_[0]}}->{name} }
               sub get_rank{ return $_soldiers{${$_[0]}}->{rank} }
               sub get_serial_num{ return $_soldiers{${$_[0]}}->{serial_num} }

               sub set_rank
               {
                  my ($keyref, $newrank) = @_;
                  $_soldiers{$$keyref}->{rank} = $newrank
               }
               # This class method provides an iterator over every object

               sub each
               {
                  my $nextkey = each %_soldiers;
                  return \$_soldiers{$nextkey}->{_key} if defined $nextkey;
                  return undef;
               }
            }
```

Version 2.00 of the Soldier class makes it much harder to locate the data for a particular object by guessing its location in the internal @_soldiers array. Instead of the array, with its orderly and predictable sequence of indices, this version uses a hash table (%_soldiers), and chooses hash keys that are much harder to guess.

The keys are generated by a call to the built-in rand function, which produces floating point numbers in the range zero to one. When these numbers are stringified to produce hash keys, they are typically rendered to 15 decimal digits, all of which are independently random (assuming double precision on a 32-bit architecture). Hence, the odds of guessing a particular key are one in a quadrillion.

The code itself does not even trust these odds and uses a `while` loop to guarantee that a given key is never reused for separately constructed objects.

Each key is stored as an entry in the hash of data belonging to its object. The tricky bit is that this scalar entry is then blessed to *become* the object itself. Trying to visualize and understand the relationships between keys, data, and objects in this version will almost certainly give you a headache, mainly because—in a complete reversal of normal object-oriented physics—objects are now stored *inside* their own data! Figure 11.3 illustrates how the constructor call:

```
my $grunt = Soldier->new(name       => "Smith, J.",
                         rank       => "private",
                         serial_num => 149162536);
```

would be handled. You may find it helpful to compare the sequence illustrated, with the corresponding sequence in figure 11.2.

The benefit of this fascinating arrangement is that it's now *very* unlikely that any piece of code will be able to guess the key of an otherwise inaccessible Soldier object (and thereby assume its identity).

Moreover, since the original objects are actually stored as one of their own attributes, it's possible for `Soldiers::each` to return a reference to the original objects, rather than having to manufacture a proxy. This guarantees that the object references returned by `Soldier::new` and `Soldier::each` always compare equal for a given object.

In fact, `Soldiers::each` is considerably simplified in this version, since all it needs to do is to use the built-in each function to iterate through the entries of `%_soldiers` hash and extract a reference to the original object from each entry.

11.4 ENCAPSULATION VIA TIES

Other object-oriented languages support varying degrees of encapsulation. For example, C++ and Java programmers can declare object and class data members as public, protected, or private, to restrict access to them to certain well-defined scopes. Likewise, attributes of Eiffel classes can be declared with an export list that specifies the classes that can access them.

The closest Perl comes to an explicit encapsulation feature is the behavior of the fields.pm and base.pm modules (as described in chapters 4 and 6). Pseudo-hash fields whose name starts with an underscore are not imported by a call to use base, and thus, to some extent, they mimic private attributes. Unfortunately, all this really means is that derived class objects don't have a `%FIELDS` entry for underscored fields inherited from a base class. Such fields can still be accessed anywhere.

So far we have seen two clever techniques for encapsulating the attributes of a class: within a closure and via a scalar implementing the flyweight pattern. Both techniques effectively provided a bottleneck that controls access to object attributes. These techniques work well, but they are all-or-nothing propositions. Every attribute is encapsulated, even from methods of the same class. Moreover, both techniques are moderately complicated to understand and code, particularly by beginners—who are most likely to need the safety net of explicit encapsulation.

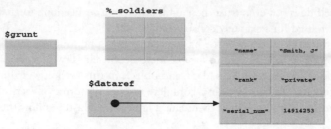

a After **my $dataref = {%_fields};** and **foreach my $field...**

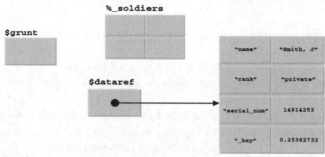

b After **$dataref->{_key} = rand while...**

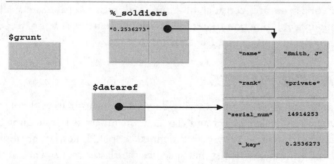

c After **$_soldiers{$dataref->{_key}} = $dataref;**

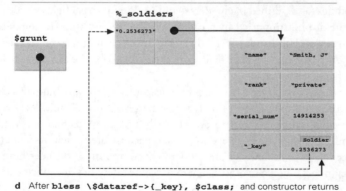

d After **bless \$dataref->{_key}, $class;** and constructor returns

Figure 11.3   Construction of a paranoid Soldier object

What we really need is a mechanism that builds objects using a simple hash-like data type and yet is able to specify different levels of accessibility to individual attributes stored in that hash.

11.4.1 A limited-access hash

The Tie::SecureHash module, which is available from the CPAN, provides a flexible means of restricting access to individual attributes of a hash. The module mimics a normal hash, via the standard `tie` mechanism described in chapter 9, but allows keys to be fully qualified as if they were independent package variables. Using these qualifiers, the module restricts attribute accessibility to specific namespaces.

A Tie::SecureHash object—let's call it a securehash—is created in one of two ways: either by tie-ing an existing hash to the Tie::SecureHash module:

```
my %securehash;
tie %securehash, Tie::SecureHash;
```

or by calling the constructor `Tie::SecureHash::new`:

```
my $securehash_ref = Tie::SecureHash->new();
```

The value returned by `Tie::SecureHash::new` is a reference to an anonymous securehash, which has also been blessed into the Tie::SecureHash class. (See chapter 9 for an explanation of how a single package can be used both to tie and bless an object.)

Generally speaking, the resulting securehash acts like a regular Perl hash. You can:

- Access individual entries using normal hash access syntaxes: `$securehash{$key}` or `$securehash_ref->{$key}`;
- Confirm the existence of specific entries: `exists $securehash_ref->{$key}`,
- Obtain a list of the keys and values that it currently contains: `keys %securehash`, `values %{$securehash_ref}`;
- Iterate through the entire hash: `each %securehash`.

The Tie::SecureHash module also provides object methods corresponding to most of these features—such as `$securehash_ref->values()`, `$securehash_ref->each()`, `$securehash_ref->exists($key)`, and so forth—which may be invoked on securehashes that were created with `Tie::SecureHash::new`.

The following subsections look at each aspect of using a securehash, concentrating on how it differs from a regular hash.

11.4.2 Constructing a securehash

Although you can create a securehash by explicitly tie-ing an existing hash to the Tie::Secure-Hash package, it's an ungainly way of producing one.[3] Since securehashes are designed to be used as the basis of regular Perl classes, the `Tie::SecureHash::new` method provides a convenient way of obtaining a reference to a "pre-blessed" securehash.

---

[3] It also makes optimization using the "fast" option difficult (see section 11.4.8).

`Tie::SecureHash::new` takes a single optional argument that specifies the class you want the new securehash blessed into. So, instead of writing a constructor like this:

```
sub new
{
    my ($class, %args) = @_;
    my %hash;
    tie %hash, Tie::SecureHash;
    my $self = bless \%hash, $class;

    # initialization here

    return $self;
}
```

you can just write

```
sub new
{
    my ($class, %args) = @_;
    my $self = Tie::SecureHash->new($class);

    # initialization here

    return $self;
}
```

If `Tie::SecureHash::new` is called without the optional argument, it blesses the securehash into class Tie::SecureHash itself.

11.4.3 Declaring securehash entries

Securehashes differ from regular Perl hashes in several respects. Perhaps the most important difference is that securehash entries are not autovivifying. In fact, specific entries cannot be accessed at all until they have been declared to exist.

A securehash entry is declared by referring to it through a *qualified key*. A qualified key is a string consisting of one or more characters except ' : ', preceded by a standard Perl package qualifier. For example, the following are all qualified keys, suitable for specifying entries in a securehash:

```
'MyClass::key'          # key: 'key',          qualifier: 'MyClass::'
'MyClass::a key'        # key: 'a key',        qualifier: 'MyClass::'
'CD::Music::_tracks'    # key: '_tracks',      qualifier: 'CD::Music::'
'Railroad::_tracks'     # key: '_tracks',      qualifier: 'Railroad::'
'PerlGuru::__password'  # key: '__password',   qualifier: 'PerlGuru::'
'main::mainkey'         # key: 'mainkey',      qualifier: 'main::'
'::mainkey'             # key: 'mainkey',      qualifier: 'main::' (implicitly)
```

Each qualifier indicates the package that owns the key. Hence, the first two keys above are owned by class MyClass and the last two by the main package. Qualified keys with the same key but different qualifiers—for example, `'Railroad::_tracks'` and `'CD::Music::_tracks'`—are treated as being distinct, even if they label two entries in the same securehash.

Hence, the qualifiers are just like the classname prefixes used in chapter 6[4] to prevent derived class attributes from clobbering those of the same name inherited from the base class. Indeed, as we'll see shortly, qualifiers serve exactly the same purpose in securehashes.

To create an entry in a securehash, it must first be referred to by its fully qualified name. This would typically happen in a class's constructor:

```
package File;

sub new
{
  my ($class) = @_;
  my $self = Tie::SecureHash->new($class);

  $self->{"File::name"}     = $_[1];
  $self->{"File::_type"}    = $_[2];
  $self->{"File::__handle"} = $_[3];

  return $self;
}
```

The class whose name is used as a qualifier to declare an entry is thereafter considered to be the owner of that entry. Owner classes have special access privileges to their attributes, as described in the next section. Because of that special relationship, an entry can only be declared within the namespace of its owner's package. In other words, the qualifier for any entry declaration must be the name of the current package, as in the example above.

Once the entries have been declared, they can subsequently be accessed (subject to the constraints explained in the next section) either by their fully qualified key or their actual key, so long as it's unambiguous. For example:

```
sub File::dump
{
  my ($self) = @_;

  print "Dumping file $self->{name}\n";        # Just use key
  print "(of type $self->{File::_type}):\n";   # Use qualified key

  while (my $nextline = readline(*{$self->{__handle}}))     # Just use key
  {
    print " > $nextline";
  }
}
```

11.4.4 Accessing securehash entries

The use of underscores in some of the key names shown above is not an accident. Securehashes are aware of the usual Perl conventions about leading underscores. More importantly, they *enforce* those conventions.

---

[4] ...in the subsection *Naming attributes of derived classes*...

If the unqualified key of a securehash begins with a single underscore, access to the entry for that key is restricted to its owner class and any classes derived from the owner. If the unqualified key of a securehash begins with two or more underscores, access to the entry for that key is restricted to its owner class alone. Entries with unqualified keys that don't begin with an underscore are accessible everywhere. In other words, in C++/Java parlance:

- No leading underscore indicates a public attribute.
- One leading underscore signifies a protected attribute.
- Two or more leading underscores mark an attribute as private.

For example, in the `File::new` constructor shown above, the attribute with the key `"name"` is universally accessible, the attribute with the key `"_type"` is accessible within class File or any class derived from it, and the attribute with the key `"__handle"` is only accessible within class File itself.

This arrangement is similar to the usual Perl conventions regarding the labeling of attributes although the distinction between protected and private is rarely made in Perl classes. The difference here is that Tie::SecureHash polices the intended accessibilities at run time. Whenever a piece of code attempts to access a securehash entry, the securehash checks whether the key indicates that the entry is legally accessible to that code. If it isn't, the securehash throws an exception. For example:

```
package ASCII_File;
@ISA = qw( File );
use strict;

use IO::File;
sub open
{
   my ($self) = @_;
   $self->{__handle} = IO::File->new($self->{name});
}
```

throws an exception stating: **Private key 'File::__handle' of tied SecureHash is inaccessible from package ASCII_File.** The leading underscores of the key `'__handle'` indicate that it's a private attribute, and the qualifier indicates that it's private to the package File.

Similarly, an access attempt such as:

```
package main;

my $file = File->new();
print $file->{_type};
```

dies with the message: **Protected key 'File::_type' of tied SecureHash is inaccessible from package main**, since the leading underscore indicates that the `"_type"` entry is accessible only within the hierarchy derived from the class in which the entry was created (i.e., File), and therefore not accessible from the main package.[5]

---

[5] ...unless, of course, `@main::ISA = ('File')`. But that's unlikely.

For additional security, private attributes have a further access restriction. They can only be accessed within the source file in which they were originally declared. That catches most accidental abuses of encapsulation[6] such as:

```
use File;                    # Import class File (i.e., from some other file)

package File;                # Reopen the class...

sub reset_handle            # ...and rummage around inside
{
  my ($self, $newval) = @_;
  $self->{__handle} = $newval;
}
```

The leading underscores of the attribute name clearly indicate it is intended to be private and should therefore be left alone. If class File had been implemented using a regular Perl hash, messing about with such an attribute would merely constitute a dangerous breach of Perl etiquette. However, because $self is a securehash, it is, instead, a fatal error.

11.4.5 Iterating a securehash

The issue of entry accessibility extends to iterations. The built-in functions each, keys, and values, when applied to a securehash, respect the accessibility constraints of its entries.

This means that the each iterator only returns those entries accessible at the point where the iteration occurs. In other words, if $file contains a reference to a File object, then the number of entries printed out by a loop such as:

```
while ( ($key, $value) = each %{$file} )
{
  print "$key => $value\n"
}
```

depends on where the loop is executed. The four possibilities are:

- The loop executes in package File in the source file in which File::new was originally declared. In this case, all three entries—that is, those with the keys "name", "_type", and "__handle"—are accessible, and so all three are returned by each.
- The loop executes within the logical bounds of package File, but in the physical bounds of some other source file. In this case, two entries (for "name", and "_type") are returned. The "__handle" entry is be skipped because it's only accessible in the file in which it was originally declared.
- The loop executes a package derived from File. Once again, two entries ("name" and "_type") are returned. This time the "__handle" entry is skipped because it's only accessible from the class in which it was originally declared.
- The loop executes in a package not derived from File. Only the public entry ("name") is returned. The "__handle" entry is skipped because it is only accessible from the class in

---

[6] Though determined encapsulation abusers can always resort to the #line directive and effectively wish themselves into any source file they choose.

which it was originally declared. The "_type" entry would be skipped because it is accessible only from the hierarchy of the class in which it was originally declared.

Thus, for a securehash, each (and likewise keys and values) only iterates through the currently accessible entries, and silently skips the rest. It's also worth noting that each and keys both return fully qualified keys, which can be used to access the iterated entry unambiguously (see the next section).

11.4.6 Ambiguous keys in a securehash

The ability to access securehash entries by unqualified keys is an important convenience. It can also be a useful programming technique when using inheritance, since, as we'll see in a moment, it allows us to create polymorphic attributes. But it also creates problems under some circumstances.

The convenience aspect is obvious. Requiring that securehash keys always be fully qualified would go against the cardinal virtue of Laziness. Who would bother to use a securehash if they always had to write $self->{CD::Music::__rating}, instead of $self->{__rating}? In most cases, the securehash contains only a single matching unqualified key, so it is redundant to require it to be qualified.

However, the use of inheritance can bring complications. It should be possible to derive one class from another without worrying about conflicts with inherited attributes. But, as we saw in chapter 6, when using a standard hash as the basis of an object, it's all too easy to set up name collisions between a class's attributes and those of an ancestral class.

Let's recreate the collection class with the settable flag from chapter 6, using securehashes instead:

```perl
package Settable;
use Tie::SecureHash;

sub new
{
    my ($class, $set) = @_;
    my $self = Tie::SecureHash->new($class);
    $self->{Settable::_set} = $set;              # Is the Settable object set?
    return $self;
}

sub set
{
    my ($self) = @_;
    $self->{_set} = 1;                           # Access Settable_set
}

package Collection;
@ISA = qw( Settable );

sub new
{
    my ($class, %items) = @_;
```

```
          my $self = $class->SUPER::new();
          $self->{Collection::_set} = { %items };      # Set of items in collection
          return $self;
      }


      sub list
      {
          my ($self) = @_;
          print keys %{$self->{_set}};                 # Collection::_set or
                                                        # Settable_set?

      }
```

We would probably expect that Collection::list would be smart enough to work out that accesses to the key "_set" in the Collection class should refer to "Collection::_set", rather than "Settable::_set". And, indeed, Tie::SecureHash resolves such ambiguous cases in exactly that way. The key whose owner is the least distance away up the inheritance hierarchy is the one selected. Hence, unlike those stored in a normal hash, object attributes stored in a securehash can behave polymorphically. Just like methods, attributes declared in derived classes can supersede those of the same name that were inherited from a base class, instead of colliding with them.

The concept of an attribute being the least distance away up the hierarchy means "…with respect to the class that *owns the current method*," not "…with respect to the *actual class* of the object." Otherwise, there would be problems if a Collection object called the inherited Settable::set method. In that case, there are still two "_set" keys in the securehash, but we want the appropriate one for the Settable portion of the Collection object. If the securehash looked at the type of the object (Collection), rather than the location of the method (in Settable), it would guess wrongly.

That's not to say that a securehash can always correctly interpret an unqualified key. Take the following example:

```
package Chemical;

sub new
{
    my ($class, $chem_name) = @_;
    my $self = Tie::SecureHash->new($class);
    $self->{Chemical::name} = $chem_name;
    return $self;
}

package Medicine;
@ISA = qw( Chemical );

sub new
{
    my ($class, $product_name, $chemical_name) = @_;
    my $self = Chemical->new($class, $chemical_name);
    $self->{Medicine::name} = $product_name;
    return $self;
}
```

Within any methods of the Chemical class, the unqualified public key `"name"` is always resolved to `"Chemical::name"`. Likewise, within Medicine's methods, the same key is unambiguously resolved to `"Medicine::name"`. But suppose we attempt to use the unqualified key from the main package? That is:

```
package main;
my $nostrum = Medicine->new("Didroxyfen", "dihydrogen oxide");
print $nostrum->{name};
```

Since we're not attempting to access either `"name"` entry from the namespace of its owner, there's no way to decide which entry was intended. Tie::SecureHash sidesteps the issue by immediately throwing an exception that explains the difficulty.

Of course, there's no problem if we remember to fully qualify any access to a public attribute of a securehash outside its class hierarchy. An even better solution is not to use public attributes in the first place!

Unfortunately, even if we virtuously avoid declaring public keys, ambiguity can still arise within a class hierarchy. The problem lies, as usual, with multiple inheritance. If a class inherits protected attributes with the same unqualified key from two ancestral classes, any subsequent unqualified attempt to access one of those attributes is inherently ambiguous. Listing 11.4 shows a particularly nasty case.

The reference to `$self->{_handle}` in `IO::okay` is inherently ambiguous. There are two matching keys—`"Reader::_handle"` and `"Writer::_handle"`—in the securehash referred to by `$self`, and each of their owners is equally close to the IO class in the inheritance tree, since both are owned by an immediate parent of the current class.

In this case, Tie::SecureHash has two options:

- Implement a resolution process similar to the dispatch process for methods (that is, resolve the unqualified key to the one owned by the left-most depth-first ancestor);
- Simply flag an ambiguity.

Since the situation really is ambiguous, securehashes choose the second alternative and throw an exception listing the accessible qualified keys that made the unqualified key ambiguous. Once again, the problem disappears if we say exactly what we mean and use a fully qualified key instead:

```
sub okay
{
  my ($self) = @_;
  return !$self->{Writer::_handle}->error();
}
```

It's important to note that Tie::SecureHash only ever considers accessible keys when determining whether an unqualified key is ambiguous.[7] That means, for example, that even though entries for both keys `"Reader::_handle"` and `"Writer::_handle"` may be present in the securehash object, the `Reader::next` method can unambiguously resolve an

---

[7] In contrast, for example, to C++, where an unqualified member access under multiple inheritance will be flagged as ambiguous even if only one of the possible targets is actually accessible at that point.

Listing 11.4 Key ambiguity within a derived class

```
package Reader;

sub init
{
    my ($self, $source) = @_;
    $self->{Reader::_handle}= new IO::File("<$source");
    $self->{Reader::__lastread}= undef;
}

sub next
{
    my ($self) = @_;
    $self->{__lastread} = $self->{_handle}->readline(); # "Reader::_handle"
}

package Writer;

sub init
{
    my ($self, $destination) = @_;
    $self->{Writer::_handle} = new IO::File(">$destination");
}

package IO;
@ISA = qw( Reader Writer );

sub new
{
    my ($class, $source, $destination) = @_;
    my $self = Tie::SecureHandle->new($class);
    $self->Reader::init($source);
    $self->Writer::init($destination);
    $self->{IO::__mode} = "read";
    return $self;
}

sub okay
{
    my ($self) = @_;
    return !$self->{_handle}->error();                    # Which "_handle"???
}
```

unqualified access to $self->{_handle} since only the "Reader::_handle" entry is accessible from package Reader.

11.4.7 Debugging a securehash

Because two or more keys in a secure hash can have the same unqualified name, and because the accessibility rules for keys are moderately complex, the behavior of securehashes blessed into complex inheritance hierarchies can be difficult to debug in some cases. Moreover, since securehashes strictly enforce encapsulation in a most un-Perl-like manner, they can reveal unsuspected problems in a class design. Hence, it's important to be able to debug securehashes effectively.

The Tie::SecureHash module provides a method (debug) that may be called to dump the contents of a securehash to STDERR. The method can be called on any securehash—regardless of the class into which it's been blessed—with an explicit method call. For example, if we were debugging the IO::okay method discussed in the previous section, we might modify it:

```
sub okay
{
    my ($self) = @_;
    $self->Tie::SecureHash::debug();
    return !$self->{_handle}->error();
}
```

Alternatively, the class using a Tie::SecureHash can inherit from it as well, to make Tie::SecureHash::debug directly available through its objects:

```
package IO;
@ISA = qw( Reader Writer Tie::SecureHash );

sub okay
{
    my ($self) = @_;
    $self->debug();
    return !$self->{Writer::_handle}->error();
}
```

Either way, when IO::okay is called, the debug method will print:

In subroutine 'IO::okay' called from package 'IO':

> **Writer::**
>   **(?) '_handle' => 'IO::File=GLOB(0x10028ba0)'**
>   **>>> Ambiguous unless fully qualified. Could be:**
>   **>>>   Reader::_handle**
>   **>>>   Writer::_handle**
>
> **IO::**
>   **(+) '__mode' => 'read'**
>
> **Reader::**
>   **(?) '_handle' => undef**
>   **>>> Ambiguous unless fully qualified. Could be:**
>   **>>>   Reader::_handle**
>   **>>>   Writer::_handle**
>
>   **(–) '__lastread' => undef**
>   **>>> Private entry of Reader::**
>   **>>> is inaccessible from IO.**

In other words, Tie::SecureHash::debug reports the current location details[8] and the key and value of each entry of the securehash, categorized by owner. More importantly, it reports the accessibility of each entry at the point where it was called. Entries preceded by a "(+)" are accessible, entries preceded by a "(–)" are not, and entries preceded by a "(?)" are accessible but ambiguous unless the key is fully qualified.

11.4.8 "Fast" securehashes

Securehashes provide an easy means of controlling the accessibility of object attributes on a per-attribute basis. Unfortunately, that ease and flexibility comes at a cost.

As explained in chapter 9, accessing the entries of tied hashes is often five to ten times slower than for untied hashes. Add to that the cost of the tests that a securehash has to perform before it can grant access to an entry, and the cost blows out to between ten and twenty times as much as for an untied hash. That makes the use of securehashes impractical in most production code.

With this problem in mind, the Tie::SecureHash module provides a way to have your cake (properly encapsulated attributes…) and eat it too (…accessed at untied hash speeds). The trick lies in observing that the actual enforcement of access restrictions is only required when a piece of code attempts to violate those restrictions. In other words, if no one ever breaks the law, you don't need any actual police to enforce it.

The solution is to develop the application using Tie::SecureHash to enforce proper encapsulation, then optimize the final code by converting every securehash to a regular hash (which provides no enforcement). As long as the development code has been fully tested, the enforcement code provided by the securehashes is no longer required.

To convert from securehashes to regular hashes, it's not necessary to change any of the code that *accesses* a securehash, only the code that *creates* it. That's because a securehash's interface mimics that of a regular hash,[9] so code that accesses one will access the other just as well. It's a form of polymorphism: keeping the interface the same means the client code doesn't have to worry about the implementation at all.

Of course, in the typical large application in which you might want to use securehashes, hunting for every situation where a securehash is created and replacing that securehash with a regular hash can be time-consuming and error-prone. If we have to locate every call to Tie::SecureHash::new and every use of tie %somehash, Tie::SecureHash, we're likely to miss at least one.

To reduce that burden, the Tie::Securehash module provides a special "fast" mode, in which a call to Tie::SecureHash::new returns a reference to an ordinary hash, rather than to a securehash. Hence, in fast mode, we don't have to replace any call to Tie::Secure-Hash::new, since it correctly adjusts its behavior automatically. Of course, that doesn't solve the problem of any raw tie %somehash, Tie::SecureHash, but that's just another reason to use Tie::SecureHash::new instead.

---

[8] Access violations often occur because methods are not actually called from the expected package (or file), or they're not defined in the class in which they're assumed to be.

[9] Well, almost. See section 11.4.9 for the single exception.

Fast mode is activated by importing the entire module with an extra argument:

```
use Tie::SecureHash "fast";
```

Converting to fast mode: an example

Developing securehash-based classes that can later be converted to fast mode requires three phases of coding. First, we create the code using securehashes:

```
package Color;
use Tie::SecureHash;

sub new
{
    my $self = Tie::SecureHash->new($_[0]);
    $self->{red}            = $_[1];
    $self->{Colour::green}  = $_[2];
    $self->{Component::blue} = $_[3];
    $self->{Color::__bright} = 0.299*$_[1] + 0.587*$_[2] + 0.114*$_[3];
    return $self;
}


package main;

my $color = Color->new(128,255,255);
print $color->{Color::__bright};
```

Then, we debug the code to eliminate the error messages that the securehashes will have produced in response to access violations:

```
package Color;
use Tie::SecureHash;

sub new
{
    my $self = Tie::SecureHash->new($_[0]);
    $self->{Color::red}      = $_[1];   # Add missing owner name
    $self->{Color::green}    = $_[2];   # Correct wrongly spelt owner name
    $self->{Color::blue}     = $_[3];   # Replace wrong owner name
    $self->{Color::__bright} = 0.299*$_[1] + 0.587*$_[2] + 0.114*$_[3];
    return $self;
}


# add accessor for private attribute
sub brightness { return $_[0]->{Color::__bright} }

package main;

my $color = Color->new(128,255,255);
print $color->brightness;   # use accessor instead of private attribute
```

Finally, we optimize the entire code, converting every securehash to a regular hash by activating fast mode:

```
package Color;
use Tie::SecureHash "fast"; # switch to "fast" mode

sub new
{
    my $self = Tie::SecureHash->new($_[0]);
    $self->{Color::red}      = $_[1];
    $self->{Color::green}    = $_[2];
    $self->{Color::blue}     = $_[3];
    $self->{Color::__bright} = 0.299*$_[1] + 0.587*$_[2] + 0.114*$_[3];
    return $self;
}

sub brightness { return $_[0]->{Color::__bright} }

package main;

my $color = Color->new(128,255,255);
print $color->brightness;
```

Apart from that one extra argument to use Tie::Securehash, the debugged source code doesn't change in any way. But Tie::SecureHash::new now returns a reference to a regular hash and, although the code works exactly as before, access to attributes has been greatly accelerated.

11.4.9 "Strict" securehashes

This develop-with-restrictions-then-run-without-them approach works well provided we accept two limitations: always use Tie::SecureHash::new to create securehashes, and never use unqualified keys to access them.

The need to use Tie::SecureHash::new was explained above. If the Color::new constructor had been implemented like this

```
sub new
{
    my %securehash;
    tie %securehash, Tie::SecureHash;
    my $self = bless \%securehash, $_[0];
    $self->{Color::red}      = $_[1];
    $self->{Color::green}    = $_[2];
    $self->{Color::blue}     = $_[3];
    $self->{Color::__bright} = 0.299*$_[1] + 0.587*$_[2] + 0.114*$_[3];
    return $self;
}
```

then, even with fast mode activated, the constructor still ties the object to the Tie::SecureHash class. The resulting code works, but slowly. So, the source code has to be manually changed when moving to fast mode—by replacing the tie statement. In other words, Tie::Secure-

`Hash::new` knows about fast mode and can adjust for it, but the built-in `tie` function doesn't and can't.[10]

The second restriction is a more significant problem. One of the useful features of a securehash is that, once an entry has been declared with its full qualifier, you can thereafter refer to it without the qualifier and expect the securehash to get it right in all unambiguous cases. However, if we're replacing the securehash with a regular hash, that "do what I mean" intelligence disappears. Since a regular hash doesn't recognize an unqualified key as being the same as a fully qualified key, this can lead to subtle bugs when the securehashes are removed. For example, if we code `Color::brightness` like so:

```
sub brightness { return $_[0]->{__bright} }
```

it works perfectly as long as Color objects are implemented as securehashes, but silently breaks as soon as the securehashes are replaced by regular hashes in fast mode.

That's because, although the constructor stores the brightness value under the key `"Color::__bright"`, the `brightness` method looks it up under the key `"__bright"`. Since a regular hash considers these two keys to be completely unrelated, it won't redirect the access request to the `"Color::__bright"` entry. Instead, it autovivifies an entry for the key `"__bright"` and returns that new entry's `undef` value, which would probably then be automatically converted to zero. Oops!

These two restrictions are not particularly onerous, but they can be difficult to apply consistently in a large application.[11] To make conversion to fast mode easier, Tie::SecureHash offers another mode called "strict." Like fast mode, this mode can be invoked by importing the module with the appropriate argument:

```
use Tie::SecureHash "strict";
```

In strict mode, securehashes control access in their normal way, except that they also produce warnings whenever a hash is explicitly tied to Tie::SecureHash and whenever an unqualified key is used to access a securehash. Thus, code that uses securehashes and runs without warnings in strict mode is guaranteed to behave identically in fast mode.

11.4.10 The formal access rules

The access rules for a securehash are designed to provide secure encapsulation with minimal inconvenience and maximal intuitiveness—so that keys need only be qualified when they are created and where they would be ambiguous. However, to produce this appearance of transparency, the formal access rules are quite complicated. The following subsections list them explicitly. Unless you're planning to use the module immediately, you may like to skip this bit for now.

---

[10] Actually, the way Tie::SecureHash is set up, any attempt to tie a securehash while in fast mode causes a warning to be generated. That doesn't make converting such code back to regular hashes any easier, but at least it tells you where the problems are.

[11] ...or to retrofit to an existing one when the decision to use fast mode is made only after the code is complete.

All entries

- No entry for an unqualified key is autovivifying. Each entry must be declared before it is used. Qualified keys *do* autovivify their entry, so an entry may be declared as part of its initial use.
- The key of each entry must be explicitly qualified (in the form `"<owner>::<key>"`) when an entry is declared.
- An entry is owned by the package whose name was used as the explicit qualifier in its declaration.
- Entries must be declared by code that's within the namespace of their owner's package and file.
- An unqualified key is always interpreted as referring to the key owned by the current package, if such a key exists, no matter how many other accessible matching keys the hash may also contain.
- Otherwise, accesses through an unqualified key throw an exception if the number of *accessible* matching keys in the securehash is not 1 (either ...**key does not exist**... if the number is zero, or ...**key is ambiguous**... if it is greater than 1).
- A fully qualified key is never ambiguous, though it may be nonexistent, or inaccessible from a particular namespace.

Public entries

- Public accessibility of entries is indicated by their unqualified key beginning with a character other than an underscore.
- Public entries may be subsequently accessed from any package in any source file.
- A public entry's key is ambiguous if it isn't explicitly qualified, *and* no matching key is owned by the current package, *and* two or more matching unqualified keys are owned by any other packages.

Protected entries

- Protected accessibility of entries is indicated by their unqualified key beginning with a single underscore.
- Protected entries may subsequently be accessed from any package (P) in any source file, provided that at the point of access, P is, or inherits from, the owner package (*Owner*). That is, a protected entry is accessible in any package P, where `P->isa("Owner")` is true.
- Protected keys declared to be owned by a given package will hide entries with the same unqualified key inherited from parent classes of that package. Any inherited entry hidden in this way is inaccessible from the namespace of the derived class, unless accessed via a qualified key.
- A protected key is ambiguous if it's not explicitly qualified, *and* no matching key is owned by the current package, *and* two or more accessible matching keys are owned by two or more other packages, *and* those other packages are inherited by the current package through two distinct entries in its inheritance hierarchy.

Private entries

- Private accessibility of entries is indicated by their unqualified key beginning with two or more underscores.
- Private entries can be accessed only from within the namespace of their owner package, and only from the source file in which they were originally declared.
- Unqualified private keys are never ambiguous. Because private entries are only ever accessible from a single class, there can be at most only one accessible matching private key.

11.5 WHERE TO FIND OUT MORE

Tom Christiansen's perltoot tutorial has an excellent description of the use of closures to enforce encapsulation. Closures themselves are discussed in the perlref, perlsub, and perlfaq7 documentation and in chapter 4 of *Advanced Perl Programming*.

The flyweight pattern is discussed at great length in *Design Patterns* (although in the context of C++, not Perl).

The Tie::SecureHash is available from the CPAN in the directory http://www.perl.com/CPAN/authors/id/DCONWAY/.

11.6 SUMMARY

- Techniques for enforcing encapsulation of Perl objects rely on hiding the interface of the datatype that is implementing each object, typically by taking advantage of the limited scope of lexical variables.
- One approach is to use a closure as an object. The closure itself provides restricted access to out-of-scope lexicals, which in turn store attribute values.
- Alternatively, a scalar object can be used to hold an index into a lexical table that stores the actual objects. This approach is known as the *flyweight pattern*.
- The Tie::SecureHash module simulates a regular hash, but provides three levels of enforced encapsulation on individual entries.
- Hashes tied to Tie::SecureHash are slower than regular hashes, so the module is best used in development and then removed (using the fast option) in production code.

CHAPTER 12

Genericity

The ability to specify generic code structures, independent of the details of class type, is an important component of most object-oriented languages. Anyone who has ever had to rewrite the List class to cater for different types of elements (List_of_CDs, List_of_Soldiers, List_of_Lexers, List_of_List_of_Dates, etc.) knows that generic types and subroutines are a powerful means of reducing code duplication and simplifying maintenance. In fact, some would contend that genericity is more important than hierarchical abstraction in this respect.

Surprisingly, Perl offers no explicit built-in mechanism for creating generic classes or generic subroutines.[1] There are no templates, no metaclasses, no parametric types, no class generators. The reason is simple: they aren't needed.

12.1 WHY PERL DOESN'T NEED SPECIAL GENERIC MECHANISMS

Explicit mechanisms for specifying generic structures are usually found in languages with static typing, where the type of each object is determined—and fixed—during compilation. Such languages need a way of separating the generic *form* of a data structure from the type-specific implementation of that data structure, for a given set of classes (usually called its *type parameters*).

---

[1] ...except, perhaps, the AUTOLOAD mechanism, which can be viewed as a run-time generic method that reproduces the functionality and, to some extent, the internal structure of the specific methods it replaces.

In other words, such languages need a way of indicating a placeholder for a type, so that it's possible to specify something general like:

"Let L be a list of objects of type *<whatever>*. To insert a new element E (also of type *<whatever>*), for each object O already in the L, use a subroutine S to compare O and E. The first time the comparison is false, insert E before O in the list, and set the current element pointer to the newly inserted element."

Then the compiler can fill in the placeholders with actual types, usually with the assistance of additional syntax to bind specified types to the placeholder *<whatever>*.

Perl's type system is completely different from this. Perl objects don't have statically associated class types; objects can be reblessed at any time. Perl variables don't have static types either;[2] they can store objects blessed into any class (or into no class at all). So, in Perl, we can get away with specifying a generic list insertion as follows:

"Let L be a list of objects (of any type, as usual). To insert a new element E (of any type), for each object O already in the L, use a subroutine S to compare O and E. The first time the comparison is false, insert E before O in the list, and set the current element pointer to the newly inserted element."

Or, in actual Perl code:

```
sub List::insert
{
   my ($L, $E, $S) = @_;
   my $index;
   for ($index=0; $index < @{$L->{elements}}; $index++)
   {
      my $O = $L->{elements}->[$index];
      last unless $S->($O, $E);
   }
   splice @{$L->{elements}}, $index, 0, $E;
   $L->{current} = $index;
}
```

The dynamic typing of Perl variables means that there is no need for placeholders, since any scalar variable will happily hold a reference to an object of any class, and arguments of any type(s) may be passed to any subroutine.

Of course, there's a price to pay. The earlier statically typed version has access to more information, namely, the type of object the list is supposed to store. With this information, it can pick up errors at compile time such as attempting to insert an object E of the wrong type, or using the wrong comparison subroutine. In the Perl version, these problems would not surface until the code is actually executed—and perhaps not even then.

Another reason why Perl has no need for explicit genericity is Perl's excellent range of built-in datatypes. As the above code example illustrates, Perl's powerful arrays, hashes, references to data, and subroutines, and so forth, are already generically capable of storing—or referring to—any Perl data-type. Thus, when implementing the insertion subroutine for our

---

[2] Not even with typed lexicals, where the associated class name is merely a hint to the compiler as to their intended use.

generic list class, we can just use a regular Perl array as the basis of the class, confident that it will be able to cope with whatever kind of objects we choose to store.

12.2 USING SPECIFIC MECHANISMS ANYWAY

Yet another reason why Perl doesn't need explicit genericity is that it provides other powerful mechanisms that can achieve the same effects. Closures, for example, are a general means of binding specific data (and hence data-types) into a generic subroutine. The `eval` function provides an even more powerful code-generation mechanism, allowing us to build an entire class, using interpolated variables as placeholders. This section explains both of these techniques.

12.2.1 Closures as generic methods

One problem with the generic `List::insert` code shown above is that the user has to pass a reference to some comparison subroutine, which is accessed via `$S`, each time they wish to do an insertion. That's tedious and unnecessary.

A better solution is to provide a method that *generates* variants of the `List::insert` method with the appropriate comparison subroutine hard-wired in. For example, we can write:

```
sub List::generate_insert
{
  my ($class, $S) = @_;
  return sub
  {
    my ($L, $E) = @_;
    my $index;
    for ($index=0; $index < @{$L->{elements}}; $index++)
    {
        my $O = $L->{elements}[$index];
        last unless $S->($O, $E);
    }
    splice @{$L->{elements}}, $index, 0, $E;
  }
}
```

`List::generate_insert` takes a single argument, which is a reference to a subroutine. It creates and returns a new anonymous subroutine functionally identical to `List::insert`, except that it no longer requires a third (`$S`) argument. Instead, the lexical variable `$S`, which was created in the first line of `List::generate_insert`, is used. `$S` is still in scope when the anonymous subroutine is created, so it's okay to use it within that subroutine. And because the subroutine uses it, `$S` survives the end of the call to `List::generate_insert`. The technique is almost identical to the way we created a private `$_count` variable for the CD::Music class.

Of course, to make it usable, we still have to associate the newly created anonymous subroutine with the `insert` method of a specific class. If, for example, we want `List_of_Employee::insert` to use the anonymous subroutine we can simply assign the result of the call to `List::generate_insert` to the appropriate typeglob:

```
*List_of_Employee::insert = List->generate_insert(\&List_of_Employee::_compare);
```

We pass `List::generate_insert` a reference to the subroutine `List_of_Employee::_compare`, so that the new class's `insert` method uses its own `_compare`. This approach gives us some flexibility in deciding which comparison subroutine is used by which `insert`. For instance, we might want to ensure the same sorting order for both general employees and management level staff:

```
*List_of_Manager::insert = List->generate_insert(\&List_of_Employee::_compare);
```

On the other hand, this might be a coding error (and a difficult one to detect, at that). If each specific list class's `insert` must *always* use the same class's `_compare`, we can rewrite the `List::generate_insert` method to produce a safer generator method:

```
sub List::generate_insert_for
{
  my ($class, $newclass) = @_;
  no strict "refs";
  my $S = \&{"${newclass}::_compare"};
  *{"${newclass}::insert"}  = sub
  {
    my ($L, $E) = @_;
    my $index;
    for ($index=0; $index < @{$L->{elements}}; $index++)
    {
      my $O = $L->{elements}[$index];
      last unless $S->($O, $E);
    }
    splice @{$L->{elements}}, $index, 0, $E;
  }
}
```

Instead of a reference to the comparison function, this version takes the name of the new class as its argument. It uses that class name to build the name of the appropriate comparison subroutine—`"${newclass}::_compare"`. That name is used as a symbolic reference to the subroutine itself (`&{"${newclass}::_compare"}`), which is converted to a normal reference via a leading backslash (`\&{"${newclass}::_compare"}`). The anonymous subroutine is then constructed exactly as before, but now it is automatically assigned it to the correct typeglob, which is also accessed via a symbolic reference (`*{"${newclass}::insert"}`).

So, now, to create a suitable `List_of_Manager::insert` method, we write:

```
List->generate_insert_for("List_of_Employee");
```

This same approach can easily be extended to generate the other necessary methods for a list class:

```
List->generate_first_for("List_of_Employee");
List->generate_next_for("List_of_Employee");
List->generate_insert_for("List_of_Employee");
List->generate_delete_for("List_of_Employee");
```

or, better still, aggregated into a single subroutine:

```
sub List::generate_methods_for
{
  my ($class, $newclass) = @_;
  List->generate_first_for($newclass);
  List->generate_next_for($newclass);
  List->generate_insert_for($newclass);
  List->generate_delete_for($newclass);
}
```

Even better, that subroutine could be called `List::import` instead of `List::generate_methods_for`. Remember that `import` is automatically called whenever a module is used, so we can put the generic method generators of class List into a List.pm module and create list classes whenever they are needed like so:

```
use List "List_of_Employee";
use List "List_of_Tasks";
use List "ClientList";
# etc., etc.
```

Of course, we would then need to declare the `_compare` subroutines in BEGIN blocks to make sure each is available when each new list type is used into existence during compilation:

```
BEGIN
{
  sub List_of_Employee::_compare
  {
    return $_[0]->{ID} < $_[1]->{ID}
  }
}

use List "List_of_Employee";
```

Otherwise, there is no way to create the necessary reference to it within `List::generate_insert_for`.

Alternatively, we can go back to passing the comparison subroutine explicitly (as a second argument to `List::generate_insert_for`):

```
sub List::generate_insert_for
{
  my ($class, $newclass, $S) = @_;
  no strict "refs";
  *{"${newclass}::insert"}  = sub
  {
    my ($L, $E) = @_;
    my $index;
    for ($index=0; $index < @{$L->{elements}}; $index++)
    {
     my $O = $L->{elements}[$index];
     last unless $S->($O, $E);
    }
    splice @{$L->{elements}}, $index, 0, $E;
  }
}
```

We would then modify `List::import` accordingly:

```
sub List::import
{
    my ($class, $newclass, $comparison_sub) = @_;
    List->generate_first_for($newclass);
    List->generate_next_for($newclass);
    List->generate_insert_for($newclass,$comparison_sub);
    List->generate_delete_for($newclass);
}
```

and create entire classes in a single line:

```
use List "List_Employee", sub {$_[0]->{ID} < $_[1]->{ID}};
use List "Manager::List", sub {$_[0]->{revenue} > $_[1]->{revenue}};

# and later...

my $minions = List_Employee->new();
my $masters = Manager::List->new();
```

Listing 12.1 shows the complete generic List class, as it would be specified in the List.pm module.

Listing 12.1   The List module

```
package List;
$VERSION = 1.00;
use strict;
no strict "refs";

sub List::import
{
    my ($class, $newclass, $comparison_sub) = @_;
    List->generate_new_for($newclass);
    List->generate_first_for($newclass);
    List->generate_next_for($newclass);
    List->generate_insert_for($newclass,$comparison_sub);
    List->generate_delete_for($newclass);
}

sub List::generate_new_for
{
    my ($class, $newclass) = @_;
    *{"${newclass}::new"} = sub
    {
        my ($class, @data) = @_;
        bless {
                current => 0,
                data    => [@data],
            }, ref($class)||$class;
    }
}

sub List::generate_first_for
{
```

```
    my ($class, $newclass) = @_;
    *{"${newclass}::first"} = sub
    {
      my ($self) = @_;
      return \$self->{data}[$self->{current}]
            if ($self->{current}=0) < @{$self->{data}};
    }
  }


sub List::generate_next_for
{
    my ($class, $newclass) = @_;
    *{"${newclass}::next"} = sub
    {
      my ($self) = @_;
      return \$self->{data}[$self->{current}]
            if (++$self->{current}) < @{$self->{data}};
    }
}


sub List::generate_insert_for
{
    my ($class, $newclass, $compare) = @_;
    *{"${newclass}::insert"} = sub
    {
      my ($self, $newelem) = @_;
      my $index;
      for ($index=0; $index < @{$self->{data}}; $index++)
      {
            my $nextelem = $self->{data}[$index];
            last unless $compare->($nextelem, $newelem);
      }
      splice @{$self->{data}}, $index, 0, $newelem;
      $self->{current} = $index;
    }
}


sub List::generate_delete_for
{
    my ($class, $newclass) = @_;
    *{"${newclass}::delete"} = sub
    {
      my ($self) = @_;
      splice @{$self->{data}}, $self->{current}, 1;
    }
}

1;   # to ensure the "use" succeeds
```

The same approach can be adapted to any generic class that requires specific subroutine references, class name strings, or other class-specific data to be interpolated into some placeholder within the generic code. The values to be interpolated are passed as arguments to use and distributed to the appropriate generator subroutines by the generic class's import method.

12.2.2 Eval-ing generic classes

There are two main drawbacks to the approach described in the previous section. First, invoking the comparison subroutine through a reference (i.e., $s) is relatively slow, which is unfortunate in a fundamental data structure like a list. Secondly, the use of different generate_... methods, each with an embedded anonymous subroutine representing a single generic method, fragments the generic class and makes it more difficult to understand and maintain.

Both problems can be overcome at once by changing the way the individual subroutines are generated. Instead of creating an anonymous subroutine and assigning it into a typeglob, we can use an eval to convert a block of text (containing the specification of the generic class) into actual Perl code. Listing 12.2 shows the generic List class from listing 12.1 modified in this way.

Listing 12.2 The List module using eval

```
package List;
$VERSION = 2.00;
use strict;

sub _replace
{
   my ($substitute, $text) = @_;
   $text =~ s/\Q$_/$substitute->{$_}/g foreach (keys %$substitute);
   return $text;
}

my $code;
sub import
{
   my ($class, $newclass, $compare) = @_;
   unless (defined $code) { local $/; $code = <DATA> }
   eval _replace {'<<CLASS>>'=>$newclass, '<<COMPARE>>'=>$compare} => $code;
}
1;    # to ensure the "use" succeeds
__DATA__
package <<CLASS>>;

sub new
{
   my ($class, @data) = @_;
   bless { current => 0, data => [@data] }, ref($class)||$class;
}

sub compare { <<COMPARE>> }

sub first
{
```

```
    my ($self) = @_;
    return \($self->{data}[$self->{current}])
      if ($self->{current}=0) < @{$self->{data}};
}

sub next
{
    my ($self) = @_;
    return \($self->{data}[$self->{current}])
      if (++$self->{current}) < @{$self->{data}};
}

sub insert
{
    my ($self, $newelem) = @_;
    my $index;
    for ($index=0; $index < @{$self->{data}}; $index++)
    {
        my $nextelem = $self->{data}[$index];
        last unless compare($nextelem, $newelem);
    }
    splice @{$self->{data}}, $index, 0, $newelem;
    $self->{current} = $index;
}

sub delete
{
    my ($self) = @_;
    splice @{$self->{data}}, $self->{current}, 1;
}
```

The _replace subroutine takes a reference to an anonymous hash as its first argument and a string as its second. The hash specifies a series of substitutions to perform on the string. Each key of the hash is a literal pattern; each value is the corresponding replacement text.

The List::import subroutine effectively performs the same job as the previous version, but in a different way. It first extracts the name of the new class and the code for that class's _compare subroutine from the argument list.

Then, if necessary, it reads in the template for the List class, as specified after the token __DATA__, and stores it in the package lexical variable $code. This read is only performed the very first time a use List is issued in a program, after which the text is cached in $code.

To generate the specific code needed we could also have used a here document, or an interpolation module such as Interpolation or Text::Template,[3] or even the standard sprintf function. However, reading from <DATA> allows us to cleanly distinguish between the actual code implementing the List.pm module (everything before __DATA__) and the code template it uses (everything after __DATA__).

---

[3] Both by Mark-Jason Dominus, and available from the CPAN.

The template code is passed through _replace to put the new class's name and the comparison code into the appropriate placeholders. Once these slots have been filled in, the (now-specific) code is evaled into the current program.

The remainder of the file consists of the code template for the generic list class. The entire class is laid out—with the placeholders <<CLASS>> and <<COMPARE>> for the generic bits—making the structure, function, and level of genericity of the class much clearer.

This version of the List class is used in much the same one-line manner as the previous one. The only difference is that the comparison code is now specified as a string (in single quotes to avoid the embarrassment of premature interpolation):

```
use List "List_Employee", '$_[0]->{ID} < $_[1]->{ID}';
use List "Manager::List", '$_[0]->{revenue} > $_[1]->{revenue}';

# and later...

my $minions = List_Employee->new();
my $masters = Manager::List->new();
```

Once again, the technique can be easily adapted to generate generic classes for any purpose and with any number of place-holders.

12.3 *IMPLICIT GENERICS VIA POLYMORPHISM*

Despite the occasional need for the techniques shown above, Perl's normal blend of dynamic typing, interface polymorphism, and string-based class names (as arguments to bless) is so powerful that it's almost always enough to do the job without such tricks.

Let's look at a complete example of a generic tree container class and see how it can be used to implement treelike structures as diverse as binary search trees and numerical heaps.

12.3.1 The generic Tree class

The class, as shown in listing 12.3, is very simple. Its constructor takes the name of another class, which specifies the type of node to be stored. It stores this name and creates an empty root node of the corresponding type. Because Tree::new takes an argument used to specify another type, it is immediately generic, since we can now create trees to store different kinds of nodes using the same method:

```
my $bst_str  = Tree->new("BinarySearch::StringKey");
my $bst_num  = Tree->new("BinarySearch::NumericKey");
my $heap_num = Tree->new("Heap");
```

The _check_root method ensures that there *is* a root node in every tree, which is vital since all other methods of the class rely on being able to invoke methods on the root node. If it finds that the root node no longer exists, _check_root recreates it, using the class name stored in the "_node_type" attribute.

The "_node_type" attribute is the heart of the genericity of class Tree. It acts as a placeholder for a (specific) type name, which is then used by the (generic) Tree::_check_root method to create nodes of different types. The tree class as a whole is generic because, even though every Tree object uses a set of public methods defined by the one source code, the

Listing 12.3 A generic tree class

```perl
package Tree;
$VERSION = 1.00;
use strict;

sub new
{
  my ($class, $node_type) = @_;
  bless  {
            _node_type => $node_type,
            _root      => $node_type->new()
         }, ref($class)||$class;
}

sub _check_root
{
  my ($self) = @_;
  $self->{_root} = $self->{_node_type}->new()
    unless $self->{_root};
}

sub find
{
  my ($self, $key) = @_;
  $self->_check_root();
  return $self->{_root}->find($key);
}

sub insert
{
  my ($self, $key, $value) = @_;
  $self->_check_root();
  return $self->{_root}->insert($key,$value);
}

sub pop
{
  my ($self) = @_;
  $self->_check_root();
  return $self->{_root}->pop();
}

1;
```

semantics of those methods differ, according to the actual type of root node in the tree. That root node type in turn depends on the value of the "_node_type" placeholder that an individual Tree stores.

This difference in semantics occurs because the public methods of Tree all delegate their respective tasks directly to the root node. For example, the `Tree::find` method calls the utility method `_check_root` to ensure that the tree has a root object (creating one for it, if necessary) and then invokes the `find` method of that root object, passing it the target information to be located. Likewise, `Tree::insert` calls the root node's `insert` method, and `Tree::pop` calls the root's `pop`.

Indeed, the three methods are effectively identical in structure: *get self, get arguments, get root node, call corresponding method of root with arguments*. This suggests that we can increase our use of genericity by replacing `Tree::find`, `Tree::insert`, and `Tree::pop` with a single `Tree::AUTOLOAD` method:

```
use vars '$AUTOLOAD'   # keep 'use strict' happy
sub Tree::AUTOLOAD
{
  my ($self, @args) = @_;
  $AUTOLOAD =~ s/^.*:://;
  $self->_check_root();
  my $method = $self->{root}->can($AUTOLOAD);
  croak "Tree($self->{_node_type} can't $AUTOLOAD"
    unless $method;
  $self->{_root}->$method(@args);
}
```

This method is invoked whenever some method is called on a Tree object—for example, `$bst_str->find("enlightenment")`. When invoked, the `$AUTOLOAD` variable contains the fully qualified name of the method being requested: `"Tree::find"`. `Tree::AUTOLOAD` first truncates this to the actual method name (`"find"`) by stripping everything up to the last `"::"`. It then ensures that the root node exists and tests whether that node will be able to respond to the specified method. If not, it throws an exception. Otherwise it calls the method directly, using the subroutine reference returned by `can`.

Using an AUTOLOAD like this is almost certainly a good idea, as it allows the tree to adopt *any* behavior that a specific node class might provide, rather than being restricted to only finding, inserting, and popping. For example, a specific node class—say UnbalancedTree—might provide an `UnbalancedTree::rebalance` method to manually rebalance a tree. If `Tree::AUTOLOAD` were defined, we could easily rebalance a suitable tree:

```
my $checkbook_records = Tree->new("UnbalancedTree");

# and later...

$checkbook_records->rebalance();
```

If we had used a heap instead (or any other node type that doesn't support rebalancing)

```
my $checkbook_records = Tree->new("Heap");

# and later...

$checkbook_records->rebalance();
```

an exception would have been thrown: **Tree(Heap) can't rebalance**.

12.3.2 A specific node class

Although the Tree class doesn't care what individual node classes look like—that's the point of genericity—it's instructive to look at several such classes to see how they go about honoring their commitments to the Tree class. The classes also demonstrate some interesting object-oriented programming techniques in their own right.

Listing 12.4 illustrates a node class, BinarySearch::StringKey, that turns the generic Tree class into a binary search tree with keys that are strings. The constructor builds an object by blessing a hash with four attributes, which will store the key and value of the node, as well as references to its left and right child nodes.

Listing 12.4 A node class implementing a binary search tree with string key

```
package BinarySearch::StringKey;
$VERSION = 1.00;
use strict;

sub _compare
{
    return "left"          if $_[1] lt $_[2];
    return "right"         if $_[1] gt $_[2];
    return "";
}

sub new
{
    my $class = ref($_[0])||$_[0];
    bless{
            key     => undef,
            value   => undef,
            left    => undef,
            right   => undef,
        }, $class;
}
sub find
{
    my ($self, $key) = @_;
    my $compare = $self->_compare($key,$self->{key});

    return $self->{value} unless $compare;
    return eval { $self->{$compare}->find($key) };
}
sub insert
{
    my ($self, $key, $value) = @_;
    if (!defined($self->{key}))
    {
        $self->{key} = $key;
        return $self->{value} = $value;
    }
```

```
    my $compare = $self->_compare($key,$self->{key});
    return $self->{value} = $value unless $compare;

    $self->{$compare} = $self->new() unless $self->{$compare};
    return $self->{$compare}->insert($key,$value);
}

sub pop
{
    my ($self) = @_;
    return () unless defined $self->{key};
    return $self->{left}->pop($self) if defined $self->{left};
    $_[0] = $self->{right};
    return ($self->{key}, $self->{value});
}

1;
```

BinarySearch::StringKey next defines a method (_compare) that can be used to determine the relative positions of two given keys. If the first key is lexicographically before the second key, the first key must appear to the left of the second in the tree. If it is greater, the first key must be to the right. Otherwise the keys are identical, a case the _compare method indicates by returning the empty string.

The `find` method implements the standard binary search algorithm for trees. It consults the compare method to determine where the key in question is likely to be found. If compare returns an empty string, the key *has* been found in the current node, so find returns the current value. Otherwise, the value returned by compare indicates the name of child node in which the key may be found, either `"left"` or `"right"`. In that case find invokes itself recursively on the node referenced by the attribute of the same name—$self->{"left"} or $self->{"right"}.

The `eval` block is used to catch and disarm the explosion that occurs if the current node doesn't have an appropriate left or right child. This would normally cause an error indicating an illegal attempt to call a method through an undefined reference—that is, the undefined value of the attribute $self->{$compare}. The eval catches the exception and transmutes it into a simple undef, which is the ideal value to return when indicating a failure to find the requested key. Exceptiophobes may replace the eval block:

```
return eval { $self->{$compare}->find($key) };
```

with a boring (but probably more maintainable)

```
return $self->{$compare} ? $self->{$compare}->find($key) : undef;
```

The insertion routine for class BinarySearch::StringKey also implements a standard algorithm. The simplest case is where the current node is empty (that is, where there is no defined key), in which case `insert` just fills it up with the new key and value and returns. The next best case is where the current node already has the required key, as indicated by _compare returning an empty string. In this case, we need only assign the new value indicated and we're done.

The remaining case is where `compare` indicates that the new node should be inserted to the left or right of the current one. If there is no appropriate left or right child, `insert` creates one by cloning itself.[4] Having ensured that the appropriate child exists, `insert` recursively hands that child the task of inserting the specified data.

Popping is an operation usually defined on stacks, rather than trees. Hence, Binary-Search::StringKey is at liberty to define this operation any way it likes.[5] In this case, `pop` is defined to delete the node with the lexicographically smallest key and return that node's key and value as a two-element list. How this is achieved bears a detailed explanation.

As with insertion, three distinct cases must be handled. The first case is where `pop` is invoked on a node that does not have a defined key. This can happen only if the node is the root of an empty tree. (Remember that `Tree::_check_root` ensures that every tree always has a root node, creating an empty one if need be.) In that case, nothing is left to pop, so an empty list can be returned to indicate failure.

The next case is where the current node has a left child. The `insert` method ensures that any left child has a key lexicographically before its parent's key so, in this second case, the value to be popped must reside somewhere in the left subtree. Therefore, the task of popping the next value can be delegated to the left child of the current node—that is, `return $self-> {left}->pop($self) if defined $self->{left}`.

The final case is the awkward one. If it has no left child, the current node must have the "least" key. In that case, the current node must be destroyed and have its values returned. To get rid of the node itself, we need to ensure that there are no references to it anywhere in the tree. In other words, we have to remove the reference to it that's in its parent's `"left"` attribute. This might seem difficult to achieve, given that nodes don't have pointers to their parent nodes, but we can accomplish the task easily by assigning `undef` to `$_[0]`—though why this is so may not be immediately obvious.

Recall that the elements of the `@_` array are special in that they are *aliases* for the original arguments to a subroutine or method, rather than copies of those arguments. That means that any assignment to an element of `@_` changes the value of the corresponding argument in the subroutine or method that called the current one. In a method, that means the assignment `$_ [0] = undef` assigns an undefined value to the object reference through which the method was invoked.

In the case of the `pop` method, that object was either `$t->{_root}`—where `$t` refers to the containing Tree object—or else `$p->{left}`—where `$p` refers to the current node's parent.

In either case, assigning an `undef` causes the parent, or the containing tree, to lose the only external reference to the current node, apart from the one still contained in the lexical `$self`. That means that, at the end of the current method call, when the lexical `$self` goes

---

[4] The constructor carefully blesses nodes into the class specified by `ref($class)||$class` so that `new` acts as a copier as well as a constructor. This ability is required of all node classes to be used by Tree.

[5] Of course, this is also true for all its other methods. Teleologically speaking, it's the way in which methods are defined that gives a particular node class its semantics, not vice versa.

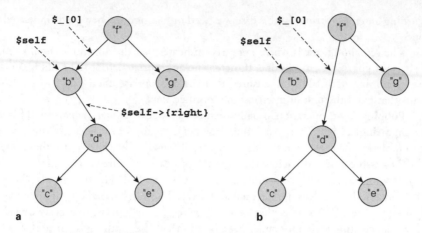

Figure 12.1   Deleting a left-most note without losing its right subtree
a   Before $_[0] = self->(right);
b   After $_[0] = self->(right);

out of scope, there will be no existing references to the current node, and so it will be garbage collected.[6]

The only problem is that, if the current node has a right subtree, that subtree will also be lost. That's clearly unacceptable. The solution, as illustrated in figure 12.1, is to replace the current node with its own right subtree ($_[0] = $self->{right}). If the subtree is non-existent, this is equivalent to assigning undef, as described above. If the subtree does exist, this ensures that its nodes are preserved and that the ordering of the tree is maintained.

Having now successfully condemned the current node, pop can finally extract its key and value and return them in a list as required.

12.3.3   Building related node classes

Having gone to all that trouble, it would be gratifying if we could extract additional functionality from the BinarySearch::StringKey class. If nothing else, it might soothe the headache we developed trying to understand how BinarySearch::StringKey::pop works.

Taking a second look at the class, it becomes clear that many of the decisions that each method makes are determined by the values returned by the method Binary-Search::StringKey::_compare. Whether find should search left or right for a node and where insert should put new data both depend directly on what _compare says about the relationship between a specified key and the key of the current node. Indirectly, this decision determines the ordering of the entire tree of nodes and, therefore, the behavior of pop as well.

The _compare method is designed to correctly handle keys that are strings. This could lead to problems if the keys are numbers, since the ordering of strings of digits ("1", "11",

---

[6]   If the current node was the root node of the surrounding tree, the assignment to $_[0] causes the root node to cease to exist. That's why the Tree class provides the _check_root method: to reinstate it if necessary.

"12", "2", "21", "22", etc.) is not the same as for actual numbers (1, 2, 11, 12, 21, 22, etc.) Thus if we wanted to use numerical keys in a Tree, we need to create a new node class: BinarySearch::NumericKey.

But, as far as Perl is concerned, the only relevant difference between numbers and strings lies in the behavior of their comparison operators. So we ought to be able to construct the BinarySearch::NumericKey class simply by borrowing, or inheriting, all that complex yet useful behavior from BinarySearch::StringKey and replacing the inappropriate _compare method:

```perl
package BinarySearch::NumericKey;
@ISA = qw( BinarySearch::StringKey );
$VERSION = 1.00;
use strict;


sub _compare
{
   return "left"  if $_[1] < $_[2];
   return "right" if $_[1] > $_[2];
   return "";
}
```

Now, when a BinarySearch::NumericKey object is asked to locate a particular key—that is, when it has find invoked on it—BinarySearch::StringKey::find is called and, in turn, calls $self->_compare($key,$self->{key}). Because $self actually refers to a BinarySearch::NumericKey object, BinarySearch::NumericKey::_compare is invoked and performs a numeric comparison. This ensures that the insertion occurs in such a way that the expected order of the numeric keys is preserved.

In a similar way, we can create a BinarySearch::DescendingStringKey class, which reverses the ordering of nodes:

```perl
package BinarySearch::DescendingStringKey;
@ISA = qw( BinarySearch::StringKey );
$VERSION = 1.00;
use strict;

my %reverse = ( "left"=>"right", "right"=>"left", ""=>"" );

sub _compare
{
   my ($self, @keys) = @_;
   return $reverse{ $self->SUPER::_compare(@keys) };
}
```

12.3.4 Cleaning up the act: an abstract base class

If we intend to create additional BinarySearch::... subclasses in this way, it soon becomes clear that BinarySearch::StringKey has no claim to special status, and does not deserve to be the ancestor of all the others.

Instead, we might chose to restructure the entire hierarchy so that BinarySearch::StringKey, BinarySearch::NumericKey, BinarySearch::DescendingStringKey, and so forth, all inherit from some common ancestor—say, BinarySearch—which defines all their shared methods—in fact, everything except _compare. Each derived class, *including* Binary-

Search::StringKey, would then inherit from BinarySearch and redefine the appropriate _compare method.

BinarySearch probably doesn't need its own _compare method, since there's no obvious default behavior for comparisons. If we simply omit `BinarySearch::_compare`, any class that inherits BinarySearch but fails to redefine compare is prone to an exception: **Can't locate object method "compare" via package "BinarySearch"**. The fact that the base class doesn't provide enough functionality to stand on its own can be looked on as a feature.[7]

As explained in chapter 1, such classes are known as *abstract base classes* and are typically used to provide some common functionality to a collection of derived classes, but with the intention that objects of the base class itself are never actually used. Some languages even prevent objects from being created if their class includes uninstantiated polymorphic methods, such as the missing `BinarySearch::_compare`. Perl, of course, views this as the worse kind of fascism and contents itself with simply killing your program when you do something as stupid as that.

If you prefer an epitaph more indicative of the problem, you might choose to provide an abstract version of `BinarySearch::_compare` (as described in chapter 6), which could correctly identify the problem. It might even distinguish between attempts to use a BinarySearch object directly and failures to redefine _compare in a derived class:

```
package BinarySearch;

use Carp;

# all the useful methods (as previously in BinarySearch::StringKey)

sub _compare
{
  my $callers_class = ref($_[0]);
  if ($callers_class eq "BinarySearch")
  {
    croak "BinarySearch is an abstract base class.
          Attempt to call non-existent method BinarySearch::_compare"
  }
  else
  {
    croak "Class $callers_class inherited the abstract base class
          BinarySearch but failed to redefine the _compare method.
          Attempt to call non-existent method ${callers_class}::_compare";
  }
}
```

12.3.5 An unrelated node class

Listing 12.5 shows a node class completely unrelated to binary search trees. A heap is a tree-like data structure in which the organizing rule is that every node must be greater in value than any node in its subtree. Figure 12.2 illustrates the difference between a heap and a binary search tree storing the same data.

---

[7] As can *any* bug, provided it's suitably documented!

Listing 12.5   A node class implementing a numeric heap

```perl
package Heap;
$VERSION = 1.00;
use strict;

sub _ordered_child
{
  my ($self, $which) = @_;
  my $left= $self->{left} && $self->{left}->{weight}|| 0;
  my $right= $self->{right} && $self->{right}->{weight}|| 0;
  my @order= ($left < $right) ? ("left","right") : ("right","left");
  return $order[$which];
}


sub new
{
  my ($class, $value, $left, $right) = @_;
  bless {
          value   => $value,
          left    => $left,
          right   => $right,
          weight  => ( defined($value) ? 1 : 0 ) +
                     ( defined($left)  ? $left->{weight} : 0 ) +
                     ( defined($right) ? $right->{weight} : 0 ),
        }, ref($class)||$class;
}
sub find
{
  my ($self, $value) = @_;

  return 1 if $value == $self->{value};
  return eval { $self->{left}->find($value) }
      || eval { $self->{right}->find($value) };
}


sub insert
{
  my ($self, $newvalue) = @_;

  return if defined $self->{value} && $self->{value} == $newvalue;
  $self->{weight}++;
  return $self->{value} = $newvalue
    if (!defined $self->{value});
  if ($self->{value} > $newvalue)
  {
    my $child = $self->_ordered_child(0);
    $self->{$child} = $self->new() unless $self->{$child};
    $self->{$child}->insert($newvalue);
  }
  else
  {
```

```
        $_[0] = $self->new($newvalue, $self, $self->{right});
        $self->{right} = undef;
    }
}


sub pop
{
    my ($self) = @_;
    my $popval = $self->{value};
    if (!$self->{left} && !$self->{right})
        { $_[0] = undef; }
    elsif ($self->{left} && !$self->{right})
        { $self->{value} = $self->{left}->pop() }
    elsif (!$self->{left} && $self->{right})
        { $self->{value} = $self->{right}->pop() }
    elsif ($self->{left}->{value} >= $self->{right}->{value})
        { $self->{value} = $self->{left}->pop() }
    else
        { $self->{value} = $self->{right}->pop() }
    return $popval;
}


1;
```

The Heap class provides all the public methods (new, find, insert, pop) required of a node for the Tree class. However, instead of a _compare method, those public methods need a way to determine the heavier subtree of a given node—in other words, the subtree which contains the most nodes. This is important because, when adding a new node, we may chose

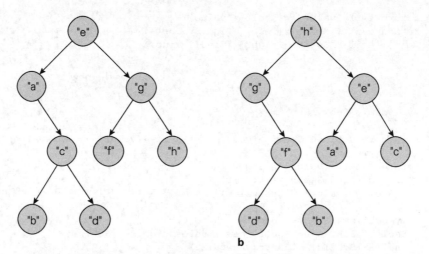

b

Figure 12.2   A binary search tree and a heap storing the same set of data
a   Data stored in a binary search tree
b   Data stored in a "top-heavy" heap

to add it to either the left or right of a given node. We would prefer to add it to the subtree that currently has the fewest nodes in order to keep the heap as well-balanced as possible.

Hence, the _ordered_child method compares the weight attribute of each child (making allowances for nonexistent children, whose weight is zero) and returns the attribute name of the appropriate child (i.e., "left" or "right"). _ordered_child takes a single numerical argument (0 or 1), which indicates whether the "lighter" or the "heavier" child is required.

The Heap constructor takes a node value and references to two subtrees and constructs a new node, automatically determining its weight. That weight is the combined weights of the two subtrees—either of which may be zero—plus 1 if the new node is not itself empty. As in the BinarySearch::... classes, the constructor is careful to bless into ref($class)||$class, so it can be invoked either as a class method or through a specific object.

Finding a specific value in a heap is less efficient than finding a key in a binary search tree. Because the ordering of a heap is "vertical," rather than "left-to-right," Heap::find may have to search both left and right subtrees if the required value isn't found in the current node. Once again we've wrapped each recursive call in a soothing eval block to avoid having to cope explicitly with nonexistent subtrees.

Insertion into a heap is more complicated than insertion into a binary search tree.[8] There are three distinct cases that must be handled, although they have the common feature that each causes the weight of the current node to increment (since the value will be inserted either at the current node or in a subtree).

In the first case, the current node is empty. It is also the simplest, because all that is required is to set the nodes "value" attribute to the new value, and return.

In the second case, the current node's value is greater than the new value. This implies that the new value must be inserted somewhere further down the heap, so insert selects the lighter subtree, $self->_ordered_child(0), creates that child if necessary, and then recursively inserts the new value into that child.

In the final case, the current node stores a value no greater than the new value. In that case, insert has to insert the new value at the position of the current node. To do this, it creates a new node in place of the current node—by assigning it to $_[0], just as Binary-Search::StringKey::insert did. This new node is created containing the new value and has subtrees holding the current node and its left subtree—as the new node's left child—and the current node's right child—as the new node's right child. Figure 12.3 illustrates this complex transformation.

Popping a heap is conceptually straightforward: just remove the root node and promote the larger of its two children. Again, there are three cases. If the node has no children, there is nothing to promote, so the current node can be deleted—once again, by assigning undef to $_[0]. If the node has only one child, that child's value can be promoted by recursively popping it and assigning the returned value to the current node. If both children exist, the child whose value is larger is the one recursively popped (or the left one, if their values are the same).

---

[8] This is mainly because insertion into a binary search tree can only occur at leaf nodes (i.e., those which have no children), whereas, in a heap, a value bigger than any leaf node may need to be inserted somewhere in the middle. Allowing for duplicate values in the heap also complicates matters slightly.

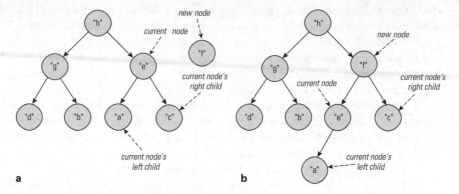

Figure 12.3   Inserting into the middle of a heap
a   Node "f" to be inserted where node "e" is
b   Node "f" inserted by splitting the children of node "e"

The recursive call to pop in the second and third cases ensures that the top-heavy structure of the entire heap is preserved and the heap kept as small as possible. Once the correct child has been promoted, the original value of the current node, which was preserved in $popval, is returned.

12.3.6   Putting it all together

Having examined a few types of node class, we can observe the way in which the type of node given to a Tree changes its semantics by considering the following example:

```
use Tree;
use BinarySearch::StringKey;
use BinarySearch::NumericKey;
use Heap;

my $bst_str   = Tree->new("BinarySearch::StringKey");
my $bst_num   = Tree->new("BinarySearch::NumericKey");
my $heap_num  = Tree->new("Heap");

@value[8..12] = qw( eight nine ten eleven twelve );

foreach $n (8..12)
{
   $bst_str->insert($n, $value[$n]);
   $bst_num->insert($n, $value[$n]);
   $heap_num->insert($n);
}
print "$key=>$value\n" while ($key, $value) = $bst_str->pop();
print "$key=>$value\n" while ($key, $value) = $bst_num->pop();
print "$value\n"       while defined($value = $heap_num->pop());
```

The code constructs three Tree objects—$bst_str, $bst_num, and $heap—passing them distinct node types. It then initializes an array of values, and uses a foreach loop to insert identical elements from that array into each tree. Note the different insertion syntax for the tree storing Heap nodes, which store only a single value rather than a key/value pair.

The last three lines step through each tree's content, popping nodes and printing them. Observe again that the syntax of popping differs slightly for $heap, because Heap::pop returns a single scalar value, rather than a pair in a list.[9]

It's also important to note that the *semantics* for insertion to $bst_str and $bst_num also differ, due to the distinct node types they were given. Both BinarySearch::StringKey and BinarySearch::NumericKey insert into a tree node by using their _compare method to determine whether the key belongs in the current node or in one of its children. The insertion methods themselves are syntactically identical (since BinarySearch::NumericKey inherits from BinarySearch::StringKey).

However, because class BinarySearch::NumericKey redefines its version of the _compare method, the semantics of the shared insertion method are subtly different when called on objects of each class. Specifically, BinarySearch::NumericKey::insert uses the standard numeric ordering when comparing two node keys, while BinarySearch::StringKey::insert uses the standard string ordering. Hence, the loop that pops $bst_str prints:

```
10=>ten
11=>eleven
12=>twelve
8=>eight
9=>nine
```

whereas the loop popping $bst_num prints:

```
8=>eight
9=>nine
10=>ten
11=>eleven
12=>twelve
```

12.3.7 A philosophical note

The design and implementation of the Tree class and its node classes represent perhaps the purest form of object-oriented programming we've yet seen.

The Tree class performs almost all of its duties simply by sending messages (method invocations plus arguments) to other objects. Those other objects, the nodes, have no central control or organizer. They achieve their task of implementing the full behavior of the Tree by exchanging messages that cause them to collaboratively create, preserve, and ultimately destroy a structure that they impose upon themselves.

Thus, they implement an *emergent system*: one with no centralized control, and in which the interesting behavior is never explicitly coded, but just emerges from the much simpler interactions of its individual components. The node objects within a Tree are therefore less like a traditional data structure and more like a flock of birds in flight, an ensemble of dancers

---

[9] The fact that Tree::insert and Tree::pop can adapt without any code changes to these different node types is an indication of the power of Perl's built-in genericity.

improvising, or a group of musicians jamming. Each individual reacts in simple ways to local and immediate cues, but collectively the group produces complex and choreographed behavior.

12.4 WHERE TO FIND OUT MORE

The Interpolation and Text::Template modules, which can be used to simplify the generation of `evaled` generic classes, are available from the CPAN in the directory http://www.perl.com/CPAN/authors/id/MJD/.

12.5 SUMMARY

- Perl's dynamic typing of variables and interface polymorphism handle most situations where generic techniques would be required in other languages.
- In the few cases where generic programming is needed in Perl, it can easily be implemented using closures with lexical variables acting as placeholders within a subroutine.
- Alternatively, it is sometimes easier to use the built-in `eval` function to generate new code at run time, filling in placeholders in the generic text with relevant code fragments.

C H A P T E R   1 3

Multiple dispatch

Sometimes the standard polymorphic dispatch mechanism isn't sophisticated enough to cope with the complexities of finding the right method to handle a given situation. For example, in a graphical user interface (GUI), objects representing events may be passed to objects representing windows. What happens next depends not only on the type of window and, also, on the type of event.

It's not enough to polymorphically invoke a `receive_event` method on the window object, since that won't distinguish between the possible kinds of event. Nor can we polymorphically invoke a `send_to_window` method on the event object, since that won't distinguish between the possible kinds of window. What we really want is to polymorphically select a suitable method for the appropriate *combination* of window and event. This chapter looks at how to accomplish that.

13.1 WHAT IS MULTIPLE DISPATCH?

In object-oriented Perl, the subroutine to be called in response to a method invocation is selected polymorphically. That means the subroutine invoked is the one defined in the class that the invoking object belongs to. So, a call to `$objref->method(@args)` invokes *CLASSNAME*::method, where *CLASSNAME* is the class name returned by ref(`$objref`).

If the class in question doesn't have a suitable method, the dispatch procedure searches upwards through the superclasses of the original class, looking for an appropriate subroutine. If that search fails, the dispatch procedure attempts to invoke an AUTOLOAD subroutine somewhere in the inheritance hierarchy.

The important point is that the subroutine the method dispatcher eventually selects is determined by the class of the original invoking object—that is, according to the class of the first argument.

For most applications, the ability to select behavior based on the type of a single argument is sufficient. In terms of their expressive power, such *single dispatch* mechanisms provide the same functionality as a case statement. The class of the method's first argument is the selector value, and the polymorphic methods that can be invoked correspond to the cases that could be selected. Alternatively, you can think of a polymorphic method as a one-dimensional look-up table, where the first argument's type is the key, and the method to be invoked is the corresponding value.[1]

However, some applications—such as the GUI event handler mentioned above—need to select the most applicable polymorphic method on the basis of more than one argument. Therefore, they require a more complex dispatching behavior, something equivalent to nested `if` statements or multidimensional tables. The object-oriented equivalent of those constructs is called *multiple dispatch*.

Multiple dispatch works by considering the classes of *all* of a method's arguments, and searching for a subroutine with a corresponding set of typed parameters. Typical situations where multiple dispatch is needed include:

- Processing events in a GUI or a real-time system, where the correct response to an event depends not just on the object that receives it, but also on the type of event and the current mode of the interface (i.e., whether or not it's active, what types of events are enabled, etc.)
- Performing image-processing operations between different types of images, such as a blend between two images that may be in different formats. Using multiple dispatch, the common case where the two images are in the same format can be handled by one optimized subroutine. Cases where conversions are required can be delegated to a more general, but probably less efficient, method.
- Handling binary operations on different numeric types: *integer, rational, arbitrary-precision*, etc. Often the return type of such an operation depends on the types of both operands: *integer + integer* gives *integer; integer + rational* gives *rational; arbitrary-precision + rational* gives *arbitrary-precision*, and so forth. Multiple dispatch allows a separate method to be supplied for each combination of operands, then enables the program to automatically find the right one each time.

---

[1] In fact, many languages (including Perl) use such look-up tables to implement or optimize calls to polymorphic methods.

- Implementing simulations in which a diversity of objects interact. For example, in a physical simulation, the way two colliding objects interact depends on the nature of both (e.g., hard/hard, hard/brittle, soft/hard, brittle/sticky, etc.) Using multiple dispatch, handlers for each type of object-object interaction can be coded separately. The correct handler is selected automatically on the basis of the types of objects involved.

Generally speaking, multiple dispatch is needed whenever two or more objects belonging to different class hierarchies are going to interact, and we need to do different things depending on the combination of the actual types of those objects.

Multiple dispatch isn't the same thing as overloaded functions in C++ or Java. In those languages, you can define two or more methods with the same name but different parameter lists, and the compiler works out which one to call, based on the nominal types of the arguments you specify. In other words, the compiler analyzes the argument type information, selects the corresponding target method, and hard-codes a call to it. That means that if you call the overloaded method with a set of arguments belonging to derived classes, you still invoke the method that handles the original base-class arguments.

With multiple dispatch, on the other hand, the method called is always chosen polymorphically by examining the actual run-time types of each of the objects you passed as arguments, not the compile-time types of the pointers or references through which those arguments were passed. Hence, if you pass derived objects as arguments, you get the method that handles derived objects.

13.2 MULTIPLE DISPATCH VIA SINGLE DISPATCH AND CASES

Let's consider a typical object-oriented implementation of a GUI. There would probably be classes for different types of windows:

```
package Window;
package ModalWindow;        @ISA = qw( Window );
package MovableWindow;      @ISA = qw( Window );
package ResizableWindow;    @ISA = qw( MovableWindow );
```

and events:

```
package Event;
package ReshapeEvent;        @ISA = qw( Event );
package AcceptEvent;         @ISA = qw( Event );
package MoveEvent;           @ISA = qw( ReshapeEvent );
package ResizeEvent;         @ISA = qw( ReshapeEvent );
package MoveAndResizeEvent;  @ISA = qw( MoveEvent ResizeEvent );
```

and modes that the entire interface may be in:

```
package Mode;
package OnMode;     @ISA = qw( Mode );
package ModalMode;  @ISA = qw( Mode );
package OffMode;    @ISA = qw( Mode );
```

Figure 13.1 illustrates the structure of these three hierarchies.

But what happens when we want a Window to handle a specific Event in a certain Mode? That happens repeatedly in the GUI's event loop:

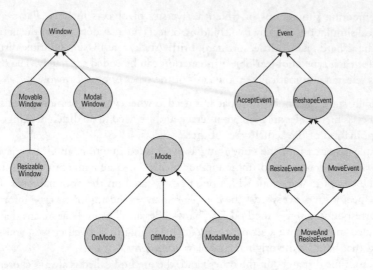

Figure 13.1 The Window, Event, and Mode class hierarchies

```
while ($next_event = shift @event_queue)
{
   $focus_window->receive_event($next_event, $current_mode);
}
```

Each class in the Window hierarchy needs a polymorphic method (receive_event) that expects two arguments—an Event and a Mode—and determines how to handle the resulting combination. Listing 13.1 shows an implementation of the Window hierarchy with suitable methods.

Listing 13.1 Window subclasses with polymorphic `receive_event` methods

```
package Window;

my $_id = 1;
sub new { bless { _id => $_id++ }, $_[0] }

sub receive_event
{
   my ($self, $event, $mode) = @_;
   if ($event->isa(Event) && $mode->isa(OffMode))
      { print "No window operations available in OffMode\n" }
   else
      { print  "Window $self->{_id} can't handle a ",ref($event),
               " event in ", ref($mode), " mode\n" }
}

package ModalWindow; @ISA = qw( Window );
```

```
sub receive_event
{
  my ($self, $event, $mode) = @_;
  if ($event->isa(AcceptEvent))
  {
    if ($mode->isa(OffMode))
            { print "Modal window $self->{_id} can't accept in OffMode!\n"
}
    else
            { print "Modal window $self->{_id} accepts!\n" }
  }
  elsif ($event->isa(ReshapeEvent))
    { print "Modal windows can't handle reshape events\n" }
  else
    { $self->SUPER::receive_event($event,$mode) }
}

package MovableWindow; @ISA = qw( Window );

sub receive_event
{
  my ($self, $event, $mode) = @_;
  if ($event->isa(MoveEvent) && $mode->isa(OnMode))
    { print "Moving window $self->{_id}!\n" }
  else
    { $self->SUPER::receive_event($event,$mode) }
}

package ResizableWindow; @ISA = qw( MovableWindow );

sub receive_event
{
  my ($self, $event, $mode) = @_;
  if ($event->isa(MoveAndResizeEvent) && $mode->isa(OnMode))
    { print "Moving and resizing window $self->{_id}!\n" }
  elsif ($event->isa(ResizeEvent) && $mode->isa(OnMode))
    { print "Resizing window $self->{_id}!\n" }
  else
    { $self->SUPER::receive_event($event,$mode) }
}
```

Each receive_event method has what amounts to a nested case statement inside it, so this technique is sometimes known as "tests-in-methods." The if statements are needed to work out which combination of argument types has actually been received and, thus, what action to take. Also note that the last alternative in each method is always the same: give up and pass the arguments to the parent class in the hope that an ancestral class will be able to handle them.

The cases directly tested don't explicitly cover all possible combinations of argument types. To do so would require a total of 96 alternatives (4 window classes × 6 event types × 4 modes). Instead, the handlers rely on inheritance relationships. For example, there is no specific test to detect a ResizableWindow object receiving a MoveEvent in OffMode. If that actually ever happens, the following sequence ensues:

1 `ResizableWindow::receive_event` is called, and tests for the cases it handles. None match, so it executes the `else` block, invoking its parent class's `receive_event` method on the same set of arguments.

2 In response, `MovableWindow::receive_event` is called, and tests for the cases that it handles. Once again, none match, so its `else` block is selected and invokes the grandparental `receive_event` method on the same arguments.

3 That means that `Window::receive_event` is called, and it, too, tests its cases. The first case discovers that the MoveEvent argument can be treated as an Event—since the MoveEvent class inherits from Event. Then it discovers that the modes also match exactly. Hence it executes the code of the first case.

The result is that the arguments (ResizableWindow, MoveEvent, OffMode) have collectively been treated as if their types were (Window, Event, OffMode). Since there was no case to explicitly handle the actual combination given, `receive_event` has located a case that will handle it more generally—by *abstracting* the first two arguments.

This type of best fit behavior is extremely useful because it means we can code the cases we want to handle specially and provide one or more catchall cases (that is, handlers that take base-class parameter types) to deal with any other combination of arguments.

Normally, a polymorphic method like `receive_event` selects the subroutine to call on the basis of the type of its first argument alone and, if necessary, works its way up that argument's inheritance tree to find a suitable method. Here, in contrast, it's as if the `receive_event` were able to select the appropriate action on the basis of the combined types of all three arguments, working its way up all three inheritance hierarchies at once to find a suitable response.

That's polymorphism with a vengeance.

13.3 MULTIPLE DISPATCH VIA A TABLE

Of course, vengeance always comes at a price. In this instance, instead of the already high cost of doing a single polymorphic dispatch on the `receive_event` method, the dispatch mechanism now has to do that dispatch, test the various cases, and then, perhaps, redispatch `receive_event` to a parent class and repeat the tests there as well.

It would be far better if the call to `receive_event` went directly to a single method, which determined the classes of the arguments involved, looked up the appropriate handler in some table, and invoked that handler directly. No multiple tests, no redispatch; just one subroutine call, one table look up, and the handler is invoked. Listing 13.2 illustrates the implementation of just such a method.

Listing 13.2   Window base class with a table-based receive event method

```
package Window;

my $_id = 1;
sub new { bless { _id => $_id++ }, $_[0] }

my %table;

sub init
{
   my ($param1,$param2,$param3,$handler) = @_;
   foreach my $p1 ( @$param1 ) {
      foreach my $p2 ( @$param2) {
         foreach my $p3 ( @$param3) {
            $table{$p1}{$p2}{$p3} = $handler;
         }
      }
   }
}
my $windows = [qw(Window ModalWindow MovableWindow ResizableWindow )];
my $events  = [qw(Event ReshapeEvent AcceptEvent
                  MoveEvent ResizeEvent MoveAndResizeEvent )];
my $modes   = [qw(Mode OnMode OffMode ModalMode )];

init $windows, $events, $modes                               #case 0
   => sub { print   "Window $_[0]->{_id} can't handle a ",
                     ref($_[1]), " event in ", ref($_[2]), " mode\n" };

init $windows, $events, [qw(OffMode)]                        #case 1
   => sub { print "No window operations available in OffMode\n" };

init [qw(ModalWindow)],                                      #case 2
     [qw(ReshapeEvent ResizeEvent MoveEvent MoveAndResizeEvent)],
     $modes
   => sub { print "Modal windows can't handle reshape events\n" };

init [qw(ModalWindow)], [qw(AcceptEvent)], $modes            #case 3
   => sub { print "Modal window $_[0]->{_id} accepts!\n" };

init [qw(ModalWindow)], [qw(AcceptEvent)], [qw(OffMode)]     #case 4
   => sub { print "Modal window $_[0]->{_id} can't accept in OffMode!\n" };

init [qw(MovableWindow ResizableWindow)],                   #case 5
     [qw(MoveEvent MoveAndResizeEvent)],
     [qw(OnMode)]
   => sub { print "Moving window $_[0]->{_id}!\n" };

init [qw(ResizableWindow)], [qw(ResizeEvent)], [qw(OnMode)]  #case 6
   => sub { print "Resizing window $_[0]->{_id}!\n" };

init [qw(ResizableWindow)], [qw(MoveAndResizeEvent)], [qw(OnMode)]#case 7
```

```
       => sub { print "Moving and resizing window $_[0]->{_id}!\n" };

sub receive_event
{
  my ($type1, $type2, $type3) = (ref($_[0]),ref($_[1]),ref($_[2]));
  my $handler = $table{$type1}{$type2}{$type3};
  die "No suitable handler found" unless $handler;
  $handler->(@_);
}
```

This version of the Window hierarchy uses a three-dimensional *dispatch table*, stored in the lexical hash %table. Each dimension of the dispatch table represents the range of possible parameter types of one of the three arguments passed to the receive_event method: the first dimension representing the Window argument; the second, representing the Event argument; the third, the Mode argument.

The table must have entries for each possible combination of Window, Event, and Mode subclasses. To make this less tedious—remember, there are 96 distinct combinations—the init subroutine is provided. This subroutine takes three references to arrays and a reference to an anonymous subroutine. The three arrays specify the respective sets of parameter types for which the anonymous subroutine should be used as a handler.

For example, the call

```
init [qw(ModalWindow)],
     [qw(ReshapeEvent ResizeEvent MoveEvent MoveAndResizeEvent)],
     [qw(Mode OnMode ModalMode OffMode)]
        => sub { print "Modal windows can't handle reshape events\n" };
```

means:

Locate every dispatch table entry corresponding to a call where the first argument is a ModalWindow; and the second argument is either a ReshapeEvent or ResizeEvent or MoveEvent or MoveAndResizeEvent; and the third argument is any mode (Mode or OnMode or OffMode or ModalMode). To each such entry, assign a reference to the specified anonymous subroutine.

The nested foreach loops in init iterate through the class names in each array, installing a reference to the handler subroutine ($handler) in the corresponding entries in the dispatch table. In other words, each array specifies a set of parameter classes, whose objects may appear as the corresponding argument. The same specified handler is called for any combination of parameters chosen from those classes.

Typically, there is no special handler for most combinations of parameter types, so most of the dispatch table entries correspond to cases that use the most generic possible behavior. Therefore, the first step in setting up the dispatch table is to initialize the entire table to point to a general handler (#case 0). That is

```
init $windows, $events, $modes
    => sub
        { print "Window $_[0]->{_id} can't handle a ",
          ref($_[1]), " event in ", ref($_[2]), " mode\n" };
```

The three lexical variables—$windows, $events, and $modes—are set up with complete lists of each hierarchy's subclasses, specifically to make this general initialization easier.

Once the universal catchall case has been set up, particular table entries can be overwritten to redirect them to more-specialized handlers. First (#case 1), every combination of arguments that includes an OffMode parameter is reinitialized to refer to the handler specific to OffMode. Then (#case 2), every combination with a ModalWindow, a ReshapeEvent (or any derived class) and a Mode (or any derived class) is given a special handler. Next (#case 3), a handler is installed for the (ModalWindow, AcceptEvent, *any-kind-of-mode*) combination and then (#case 4) one for the more specific (ModalWindow,AcceptEvent,OffMode) combination. The initialization process continues until all handlers are correctly set up.

Once the table is complete, implementing the actual receive_event method is straightforward. The method simply determines the class of the three arguments, by applying ref to each of them, and looks up the corresponding entry in %table to retrieve the appropriate handler. If the entry isn't defined, an exception is thrown. Otherwise, the handler is called, and passed the original argument list.

As promised, a single receive_event method handles every call on any type of Window object. To make sure that happens, the method is defined in the base class—that is, in Window—and the derived classes simply inherit it unchanged.

Because this change to the internals of the multiple dispatch mechanism is safely encapsulated within the receive_event method, the GUI's event loop:

```
while ($next_event = shift @event_queue)
{
    $focus_window->receive_event($next_event, $current_mode);
}
```

doesn't have to change at all when a dispatch table is used instead of "tests-in-methods."

13.3.1 Determining the table initialization order

Obviously, the whole technique only works if the dispatch table is correctly initialized, which in turn requires that we install the handlers in the correct order. That order is determined by the relationships within and between the set of classes that each argument accepts.

For example, consider the two initializations

```
#initialization A
init[qw(Window)], [qw(Event)], [qw(Mode OnMode OffMode ModalMode)]
  => sub { print "universal handler" };

#initialization B
init [qw(Window)], [qw(Event ResizeEvent)], [qw(OffMode)]
  => sub { print "specific OffMode handler" };
```

If these initializations occur in the opposite order, the entry for the combination (Modal-Window, AcceptEvent, OffMode) is initially set to the OffMode handler, only to be immediately—and incorrectly— overwritten with the more general "universal" handler.

This same problem may occur wherever there is an overlap in the set of cases covered by two handlers. Some kind of rule is obviously needed to determine the order in which a given set of table initializations should occur.

To determine the correct order for any two initializations, we need to work out which of the handlers is the more general—that is, which one covers the widest range of cases. Typically, either one handler will cover a superset of the other handler's cases (in which case, it's obviously the more general of the two and should be initialized first), or each handler will cover a nonoverlapping set of cases (in which case, the initialization order doesn't matter), or else there will be some noninclusive overlap in the cases covered (which is a damn nuisance).

Ignoring the problem of overlapping coverage for the moment (we'll deal with it in the next section), it's relatively straightforward to determine which of the two handlers should be initialized first. To do so, we have to find the least-derived class name in each parameter set of each handler. That is, for each argument of each handler, we have to determine the one class within its parameter set that is an ancestor for all other classes in the same set. For example, within a set such as `[qw(ReshapeEvent Event ResizeEvent)]`, the least-derived class is Event since it's the ancestor of the other two.

Once we've determined the two lists of least-derived parameter types, we use them to compare the two handlers in question argument-by-argument. The goal is to find an argument position for which the least-derived parameter in one handler is an ancestral class of the least-derived parameter in the other handler.

For example, looking at initializations A and B above, we can see that, for A, the least-derived parameter classes of the three arguments are (Window, Event, Mode). That's because the first two parameter sets have only one candidate each (Window and Event, respectively), so those classes are automatically the least-derived for those parameters. For the third parameter set there are four candidates, but Mode is the base class of the other three, so it's clearly the least-derived. By similar logic, the least-derived parameter classes in initialization B are (Window, Event, OffMode).

Having now determined the least-derived parameter class in each argument position of both handlers, we can compare them, one argument position at a time. For their first arguments, the least-derived class of each handler is Window, so they're equal at that point. Likewise, the least-derived class for both handlers' second arguments is Event, so they're still equal. Only when we compare the final arguments is there a difference: Mode vs OffMode. Since Mode is an ancestor of OffMode, initialization A wins. Winning implies that initialization A sets up the more general of the two handlers—since at least one of its parameters is more general than B's—and, hence, should be performed first.

13.3.2 Ordering problems

Working out the correct order for two—or more—initializations is not always so straightforward, even when each parameter set has only a single element. Consider the following case:

```
# initialization C
init [qw(Window)], [qw(AcceptEvent)], [qw(OffMode)],
   => sub { print "Window $_[0]->{_id} can't accept in OffMode!\n" };

# initialization D
init [qw(ModalWindow)], [qw(Event)], [qw(Mode)]
   => sub { print "Modal window $_[0]->{_id} can't handle event!\n" };
```

Comparing the parameter sets for the first argument position suggests that initialization C should be done first since Window is an ancestor of ModalWindow. However, the opposite conclusion is reached when you compare the second parameters: Event is the base class of AcceptEvent, so initialization D should come first. The final parameter types also suggest that initialization D should be done first since OffMode is derived from Mode.

Cases such as this one are, in fact, inherently ambiguous. Suppose, for example, that the actual set of arguments passed to `receive_event` were (ModalWindow, AcceptEvent, OffMode). Clearly, the handler for (Window, Event, OffMode) can handle these arguments: it will just polymorphically treat the ModalWindow argument as a Window. Equally clearly, the (ModalWindow, AcceptEvent, Mode) handler can handle the call, by treating the AcceptEvent argument polymorphically as an Event and the OffMode argument polymorphically as a Mode.

There are several ways to resolve this ambiguity. We might decide that the initialization with the greatest number of more general arguments should come first, in which case initialization D wins with two ancestral parameter types to C's one.

Or we might still follow the algorithm described in the previous section, and effectively give priority to the left-most parameter where a difference occurs. In that case, initialization C wins because the difference in the first parameters favors it. This approach is the multiple dispatch equivalent of Perl's "left-most ancestor wins" single dispatch policy.

Or we might choose to complain that the two handlers really do make the (ModalWindow, AcceptEvent, OffMode) combination ambiguous and demand that a third handler be provided specifically for that case.

Generally speaking, it doesn't matter which resolution policy we choose to apply, as long as it's well documented and used consistently. The few languages with built-in support for multimethods generally opt for giving left-most arguments priority, but that's mainly because it's an easy rule for language designers to implement and programmers to remember; it doesn't necessarily lead to more predictable or appropriate dispatching behavior.

13.4 COMPARING THE TWO APPROACHES

Having now looked at two different approaches to implementing multiple dispatch—tests-in-methods and dispatch tables—the obvious question is: *which is better?*

Multiple dispatch via tables is clearly superior in terms of execution speed. For the implementations shown above, a single call to a handler is dispatched through a dispatch table approximately twice as fast as through a method with embedded tests. That translates to an average improvement of around 20 percent in real applications, where the cost of actually executing the handler typically dominates the cost of invoking it.

Many implementers also find dispatch tables easier to maintain, since the calls to `init` explicitly document the expected behavior for every combination of argument classes. On the other hand, experienced object-oriented programmers may find the use of methods with nested tests more illuminating because the polymorphism of the initial single dispatch and the subsequent calls to `isa` allows them to reason abstractly about the overall behavior of the handlers.

Despite its poorer run-time performance, the tests-in-methods approach has another indisputable advantage over a fixed dispatch table: it's able to handle requests involving arguments of classes not explicitly named in the handlers.

For example, suppose we derive a new type of window from ResizableWindow—let's call it CollapsableWindow—and a new mode from OnMode—say, ActiveMode. If the GUI event hander is called on a set of arguments with classes (CollapsableWindow, ResizeEvent, ActiveMode), then the tests-in-methods version of the handler initially calls the inherited method ResizableWindow::receive_event:

```
sub ResizableWindow::receive_event
{
  my ($self, $event, $mode) = @_;
  if ($event->isa(MoveAndResizeEvent) && $mode->isa(OnMode))
    { print "Moving and resizing window $self->{_id}!\n" }
  elsif ($event->isa(ResizeEvent) && $mode->isa(OnMode))
    { print "Resizing window $self->{_id}!\n" }
  else
    { $self->SUPER::receive_event($event,$mode) }
}
```

because that's the one that CollapsableWindow inherits.

That method tries each of its tests and discovers that the second test succeeds, because the ResizeEvent object *is-a* ResizeEvent (obviously), and the ActiveMode object *is-a* OnMode (because it inherits directly from that class). Hence, even though there's no specific code to handle the many new argument combinations created by adding two new classes, the existing handlers can still use inheritance relationships to treat all three arguments polymorphically.

In contrast, if you use the dispatch table approach, the receive_event method inherited from class Window:

```
sub Window::receive_event
{
  my ($type1, $type2, $type3) = (ref($_[0]),ref($_[1]),ref($_[2]));
  my $handler = $table{$type1}{$type2}{$type3};
  die "No suitable handler found" unless $handler;
  $handler->(@_);
}
```

is called. It attempts to look up the entry for the new combination in %table, but fails to find one, since no entries for either CollapsableWindow or ActiveMode are ever initialized. Instead of handling the request in some reasonable way, this version of receive_event throws an exception.

Therefore, to add the new classes into the table-dispatched application, we have to ensure that we've also covered all possible combinations of those classes with appropriate extra initializations. For example, to cover the (CollapsableWindow, ResizeEvent, ActiveMode) combination, we can extend the initialization

```
init[qw(ResizableWindow)],
    [qw(ResizeEvent)],
    [qw(OnMode)]
        => sub { print "Resizing window $_[0]->{_id}!\n" };
```

to:

```
init[qw  (ResizableWindow CollapsableWindow)],
    [qw  (ResizeEvent)],
    [qw  (OnMode ActiveMode)]
        => sub { print "Resizing window $_[0]->{_id}!\n" };
```

13.5 DYNAMIC DISPATCH TABLES

Of course, it's not particularly difficult to redesign the dispatch table mechanism so that it can automatically treat unfamiliar argument types polymorphically. To do so, we need to supply a means of extending the dispatch table whenever we encounter an unknown combination of types. That means, on failing to find a suitable entry in the dispatch table, receive_event has to search upwards through the various argument hierarchies until it finds a combination of ancestral parameter classes that does have an entry in the table. Figure 13.2 illustrates that search for a subset of the full table.

Each node represents a particular combination of argument types. If the node is dark, there is a handler for the combination. Light nodes represent combinations for which no handler has yet been installed. The search performed in such cases is represented by the dashed arrows. The search is constrained to move only in the same direction as the inheritance arrows,[2] even if it must bypass a handler node physically closer than the one it eventually reaches.

Listing 13.3 illustrates the surprisingly extensive additions required to provide this new behavior. The central concern of those additions is what happens when the table doesn't specify a handler for a particular set of arguments. And what happens is that receive_event compiles a list of the ancestral classes of each argument, then searches through the full set of combinations of those ancestors, in three nested foreach loops, looking for a combination with an entry in the table. If such an entry is found, it's guaranteed to handle the actual argument types.[3]

The ancestors subroutine is used to compute the set of ancestral classes for each argument. Starting with a list consisting of the class itself, it iteratively splices the parents of each class into the list (using the symbolic reference @{"$ancestors[$i]::ISA"}). Each parent list is spliced in just after the class itself. This eventually produces a depth-first, left-to-right listing of the ancestors of the original class.

Having determined the ancestry of each argument, receive_event iterates through three nested foreach loops, stepping through every combination of possible argument types until it finds a suitable handler. The order of the nested loops (i.e., foreach (@ancestors1)... foreach (@ancestors2)... foreach (@ancestors3)) is important here because that sequence gives priority to the left-most argument. In other words, combinations featuring the most-derived classes of the left-most arguments are tried first. This is an extension of the left-most ancestor wins ambiguity resolution policy.

---

[2] ...because the *is-a* relationship, by which argument objects are generalized, is unidirectional, it only applies when going up a hierarchy...

[3] One of the consequences of an inheritance relationship is that each object conceptually *is-a* instance of every one of its ancestral types, and can be treated as such whenever necessary.

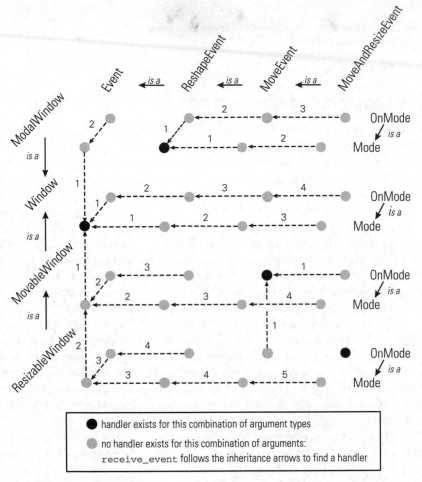

Figure 13.2 Multiple dispatch with a dynamic table

Most importantly, once a handler is found for a previously unknown set of argument types, that handler is assigned to the corresponding entry of the dispatch table. That way, the next time the same set of argument types is used, the search won't have to be repeated.

Because `receive_event` can now cope with missing table entries, the initialization process can be made much simpler. It's no longer necessary to ensure that every possible combination of argument classes has a handler, since a suitable polymorphic substitute for any missing combination will be automatically located when the table is forced to extend. As long as we remember to initialize the critical default case, (Window,Event,Mode), every actual combination of arguments will find its way back to that handler unless a more specific handler is encountered first.

```perl
package Window;

my $_id = 1;
sub new { bless { _id => $_id++ }, $_[0] }

my %table;

sub init
{
   my ($param1,$param2,$param3,$handler) = @_;
   $table{$param1}{$param2}{$param3} = $handler;
}

init "Window", "Event", "Mode"
   => sub { print"Window $_[0]->{_id} can't handle a ",
           ref($_[1]), " event in ", ref($_[2]), " mode\n" };

init "Window", "Event", "OffMode"
   => sub { print "No window operations available in OffMode\n" };

init "ModalWindow", "ReshapeEvent", "Mode"
   => sub { print "Modal windows can't handle reshape events\n" };

init "ModalWindow", "AcceptEvent", "Mode"
   => sub { print "Modal window $_[0]->{_id} accepts!\n" };

init "ModalWindow", "AcceptEvent", "OffMode"
   => sub { print "Modal window $_[0]->{_id} can't accept in OffMode!\n" };

init "MovableWindow", "MoveEvent", "OnMode"
   => sub { print "Moving window $_[0]->{_id}!\n" };

init "ResizableWindow", "ResizeEvent", "OnMode"
   => sub { print "Resizing window $_[0]->{_id}!\n" };

init "ResizableWindow", "MoveAndResizeEvent", "OnMode"
   => sub { print "Moving and resizing window $_[0]->{_id}!\n" };

sub ancestors
{
   no strict "refs";
   my @ancestors = @_;
   for (my $i=0; $i<@ancestors; $i++)
      { splice @ancestors, $i+1, 0, @{"$ancestors[$i]::ISA"} }
   return @ancestors;
}

sub receive_event
{
```

```
my ($type1, $type2, $type3) = (ref($_[0]),ref($_[1]),ref($_[2]));
my $handler = $table{$type1}{$type2}{$type3};
if (!$handler)
{
   my @ancestors1 = ancestors($type1);
   my @ancestors2 = ancestors($type2);
   my @ancestors3 = ancestors($type3);

   SEARCH:foreach my $anc1 ( @ancestors1 )
     {
        foreach my $anc2 ( @ancestors2 )
        {
           foreach my $anc3 ( @ancestors3 )
           {
              $handler = $table{$anc1}{$anc2}{$anc3};
              next unless $handler;
              $table{$type1}{$type2}{$type3} = $handler;
              last SEARCH;
           }
        }
     }
}

die "No handler defined for ($type1,$type2,$type3)"
   unless $handler;
$handler->(@_);
}
```

Hence, the init subroutine can be greatly simplified, so that it merely initializes the entry for the three least-derived classes handled by a particular handler. Those single class names can now be passed as strings rather than in anonymous arrays.

13.5.1 No free lunch...

Extending the dispatch table mechanism in this way comes at a cost. For a start, it greatly complicates receive_event, which is unfortunate if we plan to use a number of different multiply-dispatched methods and need to implement a distinct dispatch table mechanism for each.

The greater complexity of the mechanism also reduces the dispatch table's raw performance by around 60 percent for each call in which the table has to be extended. Amortized over many calls, this reduces the real-world performance by around 15 to 20 percent—once all combinations have been handled at least once and the table is fully extended.

The simplified initialization process compensates somewhat for this loss of performance. Unlike the tests-in-methods approach, which distributes the possible handlers amongst numerous methods throughout the first argument's class hierarchy, the dynamic, table-driven dispatch collects the alternatives together and specifies them in a generic way that makes the dispatch process much easier to predict. Better still, because each initialization sets up only a single table entry, it doesn't matter what order they're applied in.

13.6 SOME LINGERING DIFFICULTIES

The hand-crafted approaches to multiple dispatch shown above are fine for small applications where it's relatively easy to work out the necessary tests (in the tests-in-methods approach) or to construct suitable dispatching mechanisms (for a dispatch table).

But the number of possible cases, and potential handlers, grows with the product of the size of the class hierarchies involved, and that way lies madness. For example, adding a single new type of window to the GUI adds twenty-four extra cases (1 new window type × 6 existing events × 4 existing modes). By adding a single class, we just made the already complex task of setting up handlers about 25 percent more difficult.

Moreover, most of us simply aren't able to directly perceive the consequences of simultaneous changes in multiple interacting hierarchies.[4] Imagine adding that extra window subclass, and a few extra events specific to it, and then throwing in another possible mode. Do any of the existing handlers become ambiguous? If so, the dispatch of existing cases may also be affected. How many additional handlers will be required? If you're using tests-in-methods, will the order of testing have to change? And what happens if that new window subclass inherits from two existing classes, for example, combining MovableWindow and ModalWindow to create a MovableModalWindow?

In such cases, it can be particularly hard to ensure that all possible combinations of arguments are covered, and that method calls are dispatched in a consistent and predictable manner. Even if you do manage to encode the correct set of choices, testing and maintenance can become a nightmare. And, on top of everything else, you still have to rebuild a separate dispatch table, look-up method, and extension mechanism for each new multiply dispatched method you add.

Life would be much easier if we could define a set of identically-named methods with distinct parameter lists. Then the program would automagically find the right one. Such a set of multiply dispatched methods is known as a *multimethod*, and each alternative method in the set is known as a *variant*.

Alas, Perl has no mechanism for specifying parameter types or overloading subroutine names. And certainly there's no mechanism for automatically selecting between (hypothetically) overloaded subroutines on the basis of the inheritance relationships of those (unspecifiable) parameter types.

And that's where the Class::Multimethods module comes in.

13.7 THE CLASS::MULTIMETHODS MODULE

The Class::Multimethods module generalizes and automates the dynamic dispatch table technique described earlier. It exports a subroutine called `multimethod` that takes the place of the dynamic dispatch table's `init` subroutine and can be used to specify multimethods of the type described above.

---

[4] Consider, for example, the many unforeseen consequences to England's monarchy when the `Windsor` hierarchy started interacting with the `Spenser` and `Ferguson` family trees.

The `multimethod` subroutine takes the name of the desired multimethod, followed by a parameter list (of class names), and a subroutine reference. Unlike the `init` subroutine used by the dynamic dispatch tables, each variant defined using `multimethod` can be given any number of parameters. The call to `multimethod` generates an implementation of a single variant of the requested multimethod within the current class. By using several calls to `multimethod`, we can set up a collection of variants, thereby creating a usable multimethod.

Listing 13.4 shows the Window class reimplemented using Class::Multimethods. The new class is effectively an automated version of the dynamic dispatch table shown in listing 13.3. Once again, the GUI's event loop:

```
while ($next_event = shift @event_queue)
{
    $focus_window->receive_event($next_event, $current_mode);
}
```

correctly dispatches each event to the appropriate variant of the `receive_event` multimethod for the given combination of arguments derived from classes Window, Event, and Mode. More importantly, if no variant of the multimethod matches exactly, the call is dispatched to the closest compatible alternative.

13.7.1 Identifying the nearest multimethod

The usefulness of any multiple dispatch technique depends on how intelligently the dispatch mechanism performs its *dispatch resolution*—that is, how well the dispatch mechanism decides which variant of a multimethod is nearest to the arguments provided.

In the dynamic dispatch table shown previously, that decision was based on a depth-first, left-to-right analysis of the inheritance hierarchies of the arguments, giving the left-most argument's hierarchy precedence. That's an easy algorithm to understand, and one that corresponds well to Perl's built-in notions of left-most, depth-first search for singly dispatched methods. But it doesn't always select the most appropriate method.

For example, given a multimethod call with a combination of arguments such as (ResizableWindow, MoveAndResizeEvent, OffMode), a depth-first algorithm might dispatch them to the variant for (ResizableWindow, Event, Mode).[5] That's unfortunate, since the variant for (MovableWindow, MoveAndResizeEvent, OffMode) would clearly be a better choice.

In trying to quantify what makes (MovableWindow, MoveAndResizeEvent, OffMode) a better choice, the obvious answer is that—on average—its parameter types are nearer to the actual arguments in their respective inheritance hierarchies. That means that their behaviors are more specific to the actual arguments. It's better to treat a ResizableWindow a little more generically—say, as a MovableWindow—if it means we don't have to treat the MoveAndResizeEvent and OffMode objects as completely abstract Event and Mode objects.

In other words, in selecting a most appropriate variant, we'd prefer to go as short a distance up each argument's inheritance hierarchy as possible. That calls for a breadth-first rather than a depth-first approach.

---

[5] …because it walked all the way up the inheritance trees of the right-most arguments first, reached the ancestral Window and Mode classes, and happened to find a match.

```
package Window;

my $_id = 1;
sub new { bless { _id => $_id++ }, $_[0] }

use Class::Multimethods;

multimethod receive_event
   => ("Window", "Event", "Mode")
      => sub { print"Window $_[0]->{_id} can't handle a ",
              ref($_[1]), " event in ", ref($_[2]), " mode\n" };

multimethod receive_event
   => ("Window", "Event", "OffMode")
      => sub { print "No window operations available in OffMode\n" };

multimethod receive_event
   => ("ModalWindow", "ReshapeEvent", "Mode")
      => sub { print "Modal windows can't handle reshape events\n" };

multimethod receive_event
   => ("ModalWindow", "AcceptEvent", "Mode")
      => sub { print "Modal window $_[0]->{_id} accepts!\n" };

multimethod receive_event
   => ("ModalWindow", "AcceptEvent", "OffMode")
      => sub { print "Window $_[0]->{_id} can't accept in OffMode!\n" };

multimethod receive_event
   => ("MovableWindow", "MoveEvent", "OnMode")
      => sub { print "Moving window $_[0]->{_id}!\n" };

multimethod receive_event
   => ("ResizableWindow", "ResizeEvent", "OnMode")
      => sub { print "Resizing window $_[0]->{_id}!\n" };

multimethod receive_event
   => ("ResizableWindow", "MoveAndResizeEvent", "OnMode")
      => sub { print "Moving and resizing window $_[0]->{_id}!\n" };
```

13.7.2 Finding the nearest multimethod

And a breadth-first dispatch resolution algorithm is exactly what Class::Multimethods uses. When asked to select a variant to handle a particular multimethod call, it follows these five steps:

1   If the types of the arguments given, as determined by `ref`, exactly match the parameter types of any variant of the multimethod, that variant is called immediately, and the dispatch process is complete.

2   Otherwise, Class::Multimethods compiles a list of *viable targets*. A viable target is a variant of the multimethod with the correct number of parameters, where each parameter type is a base class of the respective argument's actual type in the actual call. That means that if the actual arguments passed to the multimethod are of types X, Y, and Z, a viable target will have parameter types A, B, and C, where X->isa(A), Y->isa(B), and Z->isa(C).

3   If there's only one viable target, it's called immediately, and the dispatch process is complete. If there are no viable targets, the dispatch fails, and an exception is thrown.[6]

4   Otherwise, Class::Multimethod examines each viable target and computes its *inheritance distance* to the actual set of arguments. The inheritance distance from a single argument to the corresponding parameter is the number of inheritance steps between their respective classes (working *up* the tree from argument to parameter). If there is no inheritance path between them, the distance is infinite. The inheritance distance for a set of arguments is just the sum of their individual inheritance distances.

   Hence, if a specific argument is of the same class as the corresponding parameter, the inheritance distance to that parameter is zero. If the argument is of a class that is an immediate child of the parameter type, the inheritance distance is 1. If the argument is of a class that is a "grandchild" of the parameter type, the inheritance distance is 2. For example, the numbered links in figure 13.2 show the inheritance distances for various argument sets passed to the `receive_event` multimethod.

5   Class::Multimethod chooses the viable target with the smallest inheritance distance as the *actual target*. If more than one viable target has the same smallest distance, the call is ambiguous. In that case, the dispatch process fails, and an exception is thrown.[6] If there is only a single actual target, Class::Multimethod records its identity in a special cache. That way, the distance computations don't have to be repeated next time the same set of argument types is used.[7] The actual target is then called, and the dispatch process is complete.

That's a fairly complex definition of nearest. To gain a better appreciation of how the Class::Multimethods dispatch process works, let's consider the example where arguments of types (ResizableWindow,MoveEvent,OffMode) are passed to the `receive_event` multimethod. Here's how Class::Multimethods handles the call:

1. Exact match?

The available variants of the `receive_event` multimethod are:

---

[6]   ...but see the subsection on *Handling resolution failure*, section 13.7.4, below.

[7]   As with the dynamic dispatch table, the caching of this information is vital because it ensures that the average cost of calling multimethods approaches the cost of a single table look-up per call and, so, is comparable to the cost of using tests-in-methods or fixed dispatch tables.

```
multimethod receive_event => (Window, Event, OffMode)
multimethod receive_event => (Window, Event, Mode)
multimethod receive_event => (ModalWindow, ReshapeEvent, Mode)
multimethod receive_event => (ModalWindow, AcceptEvent, OffMode)
multimethod receive_event => (ModalWindow, AcceptEvent, Mode)
multimethod receive_event => (MovableWindow, MoveEvent, OnMode)
multimethod receive_event => (ResizableWindow, ResizeEvent, OnMode)
multimethod receive_event => (ResizableWindow, MoveAndResizeEvent, OnMode)
```

None of these has a parameter list (ResizableWindow, MoveEvent, OffMode), so no exact match can be invoked directly.

2. Viable targets?

Class::Multimethods compiles the list of viable targets, namely:

```
multimethod receive_event => (Window, Event, OffMode)
multimethod receive_event => (Window, Event, Mode)
```

The (Window, Event, OffMode) variant is viable because its first parameter type, Window, is a grandparent of the actual type of the first argument, ResizableWindow; the second parameter type, Event, is a parent of MoveEvent; and the last argument, OffMode, matches the type of the corresponding argument exactly.

The (Window, Event, Mode) is also viable. Once again, Window is a grandparent of ResizableWindow, and Event is a parent of MoveEvent. The last parameter type, Mode, is also compatible since it's the parent class of the last argument type (OffMode).

None of the other six variants is viable. For example, the (ModalWindow, ReshapeEvent, Mode) variant is rejected because ModalWindow isn't a superclass of ResizableWindow even though ReshapeEvent and Mode *are* superclasses of MoveEvent and OffMode respectively.

Likewise, the other five candidates fail to be viable due to various incompatibilities in one or more of their parameter types:

```
multimethod receive_event=> (ModalWindow,    AcceptEvent,        OffMode)
                       #    no               no                  no

multimethod receive_event=> (ModalWindow,    AcceptEvent,        Mode)
                       #    no               no                  yes

multimethod receive_event=> (MovableWindow,  MoveEvent,          OnMode)
                       #    yes              yes                 no

multimethod receive_event=> (ResizableWindow, ResizeEvent,       OnMode)
                       #    yes              yes                 no

multimethod receive_event=> (ResizableWindow, MoveAndResizeEvent, OnMode)
                       #    yes              no                  no
```

3. One or fewer viable targets?

Step 2 leaves two viable targets, so neither can be called immediately. However, there's still the possibility that the call *can* be dispatched to one of them.

4. Computation of inheritance distances

For the first viable target:

```
multimethod receive_event => (Window, Event, OffMode)
```

the inheritance distance of the first parameter is two inheritance steps (ResizableWindow *is-a* MovableWindow *is-a* Window). For the second parameter, the distance from MoveEvent to Event is one inheritance step (MoveEvent *is-a* Event). For the third parameter, the distance from OffMode to OffMode is, of course, zero. Hence, the total distance from the actual argument set to the first viable target is 3.

For the second viable target:

```
multimethod receive_event => (Window, Event, Mode)
```

the distance from class ResizableWindow to Window is once again 2, and the distance from MoveEvent to Event is still 1. The distance from OffMode to Mode is also 1, since OffMode directly inherits from Mode. Hence, the distance to the second viable target is 4.

5. Selection of least distant target

Because the first viable candidate has a smaller inheritance distance than the second, it is selected as the actual target. Class::Multimethod records the fact in its dispatch cache, noting that any future calls to `receive_event` with the argument types (ResizableWindow, MoveEvent, OffMode) should be sent straight to the variant with parameters (Window, Event, OffMode). Finally, the actual target is invoked and passed the original argument list.

13.7.3 Implications of breadth-first multimethod dispatch

It's important to note the differences between the dispatch processes for a multimethod and a regular Perl polymorphic method, since the more complex multimethod dispatch procedure can lead to unexpected results, especially if the multimethod has only a single argument.

The minimal inheritance distance criterion for selecting a multimethod variant is equivalent to a breadth-first parallel search of the inheritance hierarchies of all the multimethod's arguments. In fact, that's how the multiple dispatch mechanism is actually implemented in Class::Multimethods, since it's more efficient to search for and evaluate viable targets incrementally than blithely calculate the distance to every multimethod at once.

In contrast, regular methods are dispatched via a sequential depth-first search of the hierarchy of the first argument only. That makes for faster dispatching, but it does mean that the first parent of a class is more strongly inherited than the rest,[8] and, hence, tends to determine which inherited method is called.

Differences for multiple arguments from multiple hierarchies

To see the consequences of these two approaches, let's consider the A_..., B_..., and C_... hierarchies shown in figure 13.3 and implemented in listing 13.5. In each class, the method

---

[8] Left-most ancestor wins again. One way to think about it is to pretend that the left-most parent has the dominant genes.

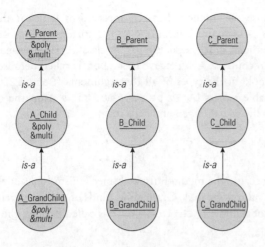

Figure 13.3 Class hierarchies illustrating the differences between dispatch of methods and multimethods

`poly` and the multimethod `multi` are identical in structure. They differ only in how calls to them are dispatched. That difference between method dispatch and multimethod dispatch becomes clear when the following code is executed:

```
package main;

my ($aref1, $aref2) = (A_Parent->new(), A_Grandchild->new());
my ($bref1, $bref2) = (B_Parent->new(), B_Grandchild->new());
my ($cref1, $cref2) = (C_Parent->new(), C_Grandchild->new());

# case 1
$aref1->poly($bref2,$cref2);
$aref1->multi($bref2,$cref2);

# case 2
$aref2->poly($bref1,$cref1);
$aref2->multi($bref1,$cref1);

# case 3
$aref2->poly($bref2,$cref2);
$aref2->multi($bref2,$cref2);
```

In case 1, the following lines are printed:

dispatched to A_Parent::poly
dispatched to A_Parent::multi

`A_Parent::poly` is called because the method dispatch mechanism looks at the type of the first argument (`$aref1`), starts searching for a matching subroutine in the corresponding package (A_Parent), immediately finds a suitable match, and calls it. In contrast, `A_Parent::multi` is called because the multimethod dispatch mechanism looks at the types of all the arguments (`$aref1`, `$bref2`, `$cref2`), compiles a list of viable targets (`A_Parent::multi` is the only one), selects the one viable target as the actual target, and calls it.

Case 2 prints the following:

dispatched to A_Child::poly
dispatched to A_Parent::multi

A_Child::poly is called because the method dispatch mechanism looks at the type of $aref2, and starts searching for a matching subroutine in the corresponding package (A_Grandchild). It fails to find one there, so it checks the parent class (A_Child) where it finds and calls a suitable subroutine. In contrast, A_Parent::multi is called because the multimethod dispatch mechanism looks at the types of all the arguments ($aref2, $bref1, $cref1), compiles a list of viable targets (A_Parent::multi is again the only one), selects that single viable target as the actual target, and calls it.

Case 3 prints:

dispatched to A_Child::poly
dispatched to A_Child::multi

A_Child::poly is called because the method dispatch mechanism looks at the type of $aref2, fails to find a matching subroutine in A_Grandchild, finds one in the parent class A_Child, and calls that matching subroutine. A_Child::multi is called because the multimethod dispatch mechanism:

1 looks at the types of all the arguments ($aref2, $bref2, $cref2);

2 compiles a list of viable targets (both A_Parent::multi and A_Child::multi are now viable);

3 computes their relative inheritance distances from the actual argument types (6 for A_Parent::multi and 3 for A_Child::multi);

4 selects A_Child::multi as the single "closest" actual target;

5 calls it.

In this third case, the outcomes are similar: a method of class A_Child is selected in preference to a method of class A_Parent. However, the reasons for each selection are different. A_Child::poly is selected because the first argument is closer to class A_Child than to class A_Parent. A_Child::multi is chosen because the complete set of arguments is *collectively* closer to the combination (A_Child,B_Child,C_Child) than to (A_Parent,B_Parent,C_Parent).

Differences for single arguments from the same hierarchy

It is not so surprising that multimethods handle the dispatch of calls with more than one argument in a special manner. After all, that's why they were invented. What *is* surprising is that such differences in dispatch behavior are not confined to cases involving multiple arguments from different inheritance hierarchies. They can also occur when dispatching methods with a single argument belonging to a single hierarchy.

Consider the D_... hierarchy shown in figure 13.4 and implemented in listing 13.6. The following two calls:

```
my $dref = D_Grandchild->new();

$dref->poly();
$dref->multi();
```

```perl
# The "A" class hierarchy
package A_Parent;
use Class::Multimethods;

multimethod multi => (A_Parent, B_Parent, C_Parent)
  => sub { print "dispatched to A_Parent::multi\n" };

sub poly { print "dispatched to A_Parent::poly\n" }


package A_Child;
@A_Child::ISA = (A_Parent);
use Class::Multimethods;

multimethod multi => (A_Child, B_Child, C_Child)
  => sub { print "dispatched to A_Child::multi\n" };

sub poly { print "dispatched to A_Child::poly\n" }


package A_Grandchild;
@A_Grandchild::ISA = (A_Child);


# The "B" class hierarchy
package B_Parent;

package B_Child;
@B_Child::ISA = (B_Parent);

package B_Grandchild;
@B_Grandchild::ISA = (B_Child);


# The "C" class hierarchy
package C_Parent;

package C_Child;
@C_Child::ISA = (C_Parent);

package C_Grandchild;
@C_Grandchild::ISA = (C_Child);
```

dispatch on the same single argument, $dref, consider a similar set of possible target methods—those inherited from D_Parent, D_OtherParent, and D_OtherChild—but end up in different places:

dispatched to D_Parent::poly
dispatched to D_OtherChild::multi

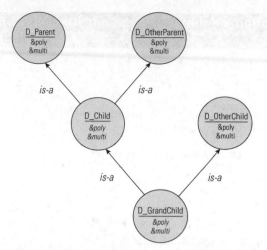

Figure 13.4 Another class hierarchy illustrating the difference between dispatch of methods and multimethods

The call to the `poly` method looks at the class of `$dref`, finds no matching subroutine in D_Grandchild, and recursively tries the left-most parent class (D_Child). Failing to find a match there, it again tries the left-most parent (D_Parent), finally finding a suitable method, which it immediately calls.

In contrast, the call to the `multi` multimethod first assembles a list of viable targets. This list consists of `D_Parent::multi`, `D_OtherParent::multi`, and `D_OtherChild::multi`. Computing the inheritance distances from D_Grandchild (the class of the argument `$dref`) to each viable target yields 2, 2, and 1 respectively, so `D_OtherChild::multi` becomes the final target and is called.

In other words, even with a single argument to consider, the regular Perl polymorphic method chooses the first suitable method that a class inherits, while a Class::Multimethods multimethod chooses the closest suitable inherited method.

13.7.4 Handling resolution failure

It's relatively easy to create a set of multimethod variants so that particular combinations of argument types cannot be correctly dispatched. For example, consider the following variants of a multimethod called `put_peg`:

```
multimethod put_peg => (RoundPeg,Hole)
   => sub { print "a round peg in any old hole\n"; };

multimethod put_peg => (Peg,SquareHole)
   => sub { print "any old peg in a square hole\n"; };

multimethod put_peg => (Peg,Hole)
   => sub { print "any old peg in any old hole\n"; };
```

If `put_peg` is called like this:

```
put_peg( RoundPeg->new(), SquareHole->new() );
```

```
# The "D" class hierarchy
package D_Parent;
use Class::Multimethods;

    multimethod multi => (D_Parent)
       => sub { print "dispatched to D_Parent::multi\n" };

    sub poly { print "dispatched to D_Parent::poly\n" }


package D_OtherParent;
use Class::Multimethods;

    multimethod multi => (D_OtherParent)
       => sub { print "dispatched to D_OtherParent::multi\n" };

    sub poly { print "dispatched to D_OtherParent::poly\n" }


package D_Child;
@D_Child::ISA = (D_Parent, D_OtherParent);


package D_OtherChild;
use Class::Multimethods;

    multimethod multi => (D_OtherChild)
       => sub { print "dispatched to D_OtherChild::multi\n" };

    sub poly { print "dispatched to D_OtherChild::poly\n" }


package D_Grandchild;
@D_Grandchild::ISA = (D_Child, D_OtherChild);
```

Class::Multimethods can't dispatch the call, because it cannot decide between the (RoundPeg, Hole) and (Peg, SquareHole) variants, each of which is the same inheritance distance—one derivation—from the actual arguments.

The default behavior of Class::Multimethods in such a situation is to throw an exception:

Cannot resolve call to multimethod put_peg(RoundPeg,SquareHole).
The multimethods:
   put_peg(RoundPeg,Hole)
   put_peg(Peg,SquareHole)
are equally viable.

Sometimes, however, the more specialized variants of a multimethod like put_peg are only optimizations. A more general case, such as the (Peg,Hole) variant, would suffice as a default where such an ambiguity exists. If that's the case, it's possible to tell Class::Multimethods to resolve the ambiguity by calling that generic variant. To do so, we use the resolve_ambiguous subroutine, which is automatically exported by Class::Multimethods:

```
resolve_ambiguous put_peg => (Peg,Hole);
```

That is, we specify the name of the multimethod being disambiguated and the signature of the variant to be used in ambiguous cases. Of course, the specified variant must actually exist at the time of the call. If it doesn't, Class::Multimethod gives up and throws the usual equally viable exception anyway.

Alternatively, if no variant is suitable as a default, you can register a reference to a subroutine to be called instead:

```
resolve_ambiguous put_peg => \&disambiguator;
```

Now, whenever put_peg can't dispatch a call because it's ambiguous, disambiguator is called instead, with the same argument list as put_peg was given. Of course, resolve_ambiguous doesn't care which subroutine it's given a reference to, so we can just as easily also use an anonymous subroutine:

```
resolve_ambiguous put_peg
    => sub { print "can't put a ", ref($_[0]), " into a ", ref($_[1]), "\n" };
```

Multiple dispatch can also fail if *no* suitable variants are available to handle a particular call. For example:

```
put_peg( JPEG->new(), Loophole->new() );
```

would normally produce the exception

No viable candidate for call to multimethod put_peg(JPeg,Loophole)

because classes JPEG and Loophole aren't in the Peg and Hole hierarchies, and so there's no inheritance path back to a more general variant.

To catch such cases, you can use the resolve_no_match subroutine, also exported from Class::Multimethods. resolve_no_match registers a multimethod variant—or subroutine reference—to be used whenever the dispatch mechanism can't find a suitable variant for a given multimethod call. For example:

```
resolve_no_match put_peg => sub
{
    my ($p_type, $h_type) = @_;

    $_[0]->show($_[1])  if $p_type =~ /[JM]PEG/;
    call_plumber()      if $p_type eq 'ClothesPeg' && $h_type eq 'DrainHole';
    $_[1]->crush($_[0]) if $h_type eq 'BlackHole';

    # etc.
};
```

As with resolve_ambiguous, the variant or subroutine that resolve_no_match registers is called with the same set of arguments that was passed to the original multimethod call.

13.7.5 Defining multimethods outside their classes

Class::Multimethod is laid back about how you use it. Having implemented its own sophisticated dispatch procedure, it can cheerfully ignore the constraints imposed by the normal Perl method dispatch mechanism.[9] For example, it doesn't matter which packages the individual variants of a multimethod are defined in. Every variant of a multimethod is visible to the underlying multimethod dispatcher, no matter where it was created. Notice, for instance, that the receive_event variants in listing 13.4 are all defined in class Window, even though most of them don't take a Window object as their first argument.

There's no need to declare the multimethod in every other class in the Window hierarchy because the normal Perl method inheritance mechanism ensures that it's automatically visible in all derived classes. However, the dispatch mechanism will be more efficient if the multimethod *is* declared separately in every subclass, since Perl won't have to search up the inheritance tree to find the multimethod declaration and perform its own multimethod dispatch procedure as well.

To declare, but not define, a multimethod within the assorted Window subclasses, we can call multimethod with just the name of the multimethod (that is, without specifying its parameter types or a reference to its associated subroutine). For example:

```
package ModalWindow;
use Class::Multimethods;
multimethod 'receive_event';

package MovableWindow;
use Class::Multimethods;
multimethod 'receive_event';

# etc.
```

It's a little tedious to have to import Class::Multimethods into every class and declare the multimethod as well, so the module also provides a shortcut. If the use Class::Multi-Methods statement is specified with the name of one or more multimethods, it automatically declares each of them in the current package. For example:

```
package ModalWindow;
use Class::Multimethods 'receive_event';

package ModalWindow;
use Class::Multimethods 'receive_event';

# etc.
```

Whether it's better to define multimethod variants in separate classes or collect them in a single class is largely a matter of personal preference. You might take the view that, as methods of individual classes, they belong with those classes. Alternatively, it could be argued that a multimethod is really a behavior *of the class hierarchy as a whole*, and so it makes sense to collect all the variants in one place somewhere near the code implementing the hierarchy (say, at the end of all the related classes). Yet another school of thought observes that a multimethod implements a behavior that emerges from the interactions of the hierarchies containing *all* its arguments, so there's no reason to put its variants near any particular hierarchy.

---

[9] It is a tribute to the brilliance of Perl's design that it's possible for a user-defined module to circumvent so fundamental a mechanism as method dispatch.

Ultimately, like so many things in life, it doesn't really matter what you choose to do, only that you do it consistently. However, experience indicates that multimethods with more than three or four variants are usually easier to comprehend and to maintain if all their variants are kept together.

13.7.6 Multimethods as regular subroutines

Although we've gone to the trouble of setting them up as object methods, Class::Multimethod doesn't care whether multimethods are called as methods or as regular subroutines.

In fact, because they use their own dispatch mechanism, multimethod calls are the one exception to the rule about *always* calling a method using the arrow syntax. When `receive_event` is implemented using Class::Multimethods, the GUI event loop shown previously can just as easily be coded as:

```
package main;
use Class::Multimethods 'receive_event';

while ($next_event = shift @event_queue)
{
    receive_event($focus_window, $next_event, $current_mode);
}
```

and the correct method would still be called in each case.[10] The call would even be marginally faster, since it doesn't need to work its way through Perl's normal method dispatch process first.

Of course, dispensing with the method call syntax also implies that multimethods can be used as regular subroutines in non-object-oriented contexts. In other words, Class::Multimethods also provides general subroutine overloading. For example:

```
package main;
use IO;
use Class::Multimethods;

multimethod test => (IO::File) => sub
{
    $_[0]->print("This should go in a file\n");
};

multimethod test => (IO::Pipe) => sub
{
    $_[0]->print("This should go down a pipe\n");
};

multimethod test => (IO::Socket) => sub
{
    $_[0]->print("This should go out a socket\n");
};

# and later...

test($some_io_handle);    # calls whichever variant is appropriate
```

---

[10] Note, however, that it *was* necessary to declare the multimethod within the main namespace, since there's now no invoking object to help Perl locate `receive_event`.

13.7.7 Nonclass types as parameters

Yet another thing Class::Multimethods doesn't care about is whether the parameter types for each multimethod variant are the names of real classes or just the identifiers returned when raw Perl data types are passed to the built-in `ref` function. That means we could also define multimethod variants like this:

```
multimethod stringify => (ARRAY) => sub
{
  my @arg = @{$_[0]};
  return "[" . join(", ",@arg) . "]";
};

multimethod stringify => (HASH) => sub
{
  my %arg = %{$_[0]};
  return "{" . join(", ", map("$_=>$arg{$_}",keys %arg)) . "}";
};

multimethod stringify => (CODE) => sub
{
  return "sub {???}";
};

# and later…

print stringify( [1,2,3] ), "\n";
print stringify( {a=>1,b=>2,c=>3} ), "\n";
print stringify( $array_or_hash_ref ), "\n";
```

Provided we remember that the parameter types ARRAY, HASH, and CODE really mean reference to array, reference to hash, and reference to subroutine, the names of built-in types—those returned by `ref`—are perfectly acceptable as multimethod parameters.

That's a nice bonus, but there's a problem. Because `ref` returns an empty string when given any literal string or numeric value, the following code

```
print stringify( 2001 ), "\n";
print stringify( "a multiple dispatch oddity" ), "\n";
```

produces a nasty surprise

No viable candidate for call to multimethod stringify at line 1

The problem is that the dispatch resolution process first calls `ref(2001)` to get the class name for the first argument. That call returns `undef` since 2001 isn't a reference at all. The `undef` is subsequently converted to an empty string when used as a class name, and since there's no `stringify` variant with an empty string as its parameter type, there are no viable targets for the multimethod call. Hence, the exception.

To overcome this limitation, Class::Multimethods allows two special pseudo-typenames within the parameter lists of multimethod variants. The first pseudo-type, `'$'`, is the class to which Class::Multimethods *pretends* all scalar values belong. Thus, we could make the two recalcitrant stringifications of scalars work correctly by defining:

```
multimethod stringify => ('$') => sub
{
    return qq{"$_[0]"};
};
```

With that definition in place, the two calls:

```
print stringify( 2001 ), "\n";
print stringify( "a multiple dispatch oddity" ), "\n";
```

would produce:

"2001"
"a multiple dispatch oddity"

That solves the problem, but not as elegantly as we might like. It would be better if numeric values were left unquoted. To this end, Class::Multimethods offers a second pseudo-type, '#', which represents the class it pretends numeric scalar values belong to. If we now also define:

```
multimethod stringify => ('#') => sub
{
    return $_[0];
};
```

then the two calls to stringify now produce:

2001
"a multiple dispatch oddity"

the first having been dispatched to the '#' variant, rather than to the '$' version.

From an object-oriented point of view, it's interesting to note that Class::Multimethod treats the pseudo-type '#' as a subclass of the pseudo-type '$' (that is, a numeric scalar is a special case of a scalar). That's why, before the '#' variant of stringify was defined, the call to stringify(2001) still managed to call the '$' variant.

13.7.8 Last resort parameters

Sometimes it's useful to define multimethod variants that ignore one or more parameters when determining the actual target of a dispatch. For example, our stringify multimethod caters only to scalars and to references to arrays, hashes, and subroutines. It throws an exception if it encounters anything else (such as a reference to a scalar, a precompiled pattern, a typeglob, or another reference).

Of course, in this particular example, we *can* code individual variants for each of these argument types, though it is tedious. However, if we also need to support the stringification of references to blessed objects of various classes, the problem quickly becomes unmanageable, since there is a potentially endless supply of cases to be covered.

To overcome this problem in the Laziest possible way, Class::Multimethods supports one extra pseudo-type, '*', which matches a value or reference of any type.

Hence, we can code our catchall case as:

```
multimethod stringify => ('*') => sub
{
    return "<<".ref($_[0]).">>";
};
```

Now, any attempt to stringify something for which there is no more specific variant

```
print stringify(\1), "\n";
print stringify(qr/^=head[12]/), "\n";
print stringify(CD::Music->new()), "\n";
```

is handled by the '*' variant and results in stringifications like this:

<<SCALAR>>
<<Regexp>>
<<CD::Music>>

The presence of the '*' specifier does complicate the dispatch resolution process slightly. It matches any argument, but is designed to be used only as a last resort—when all more specific alternatives have failed. In order to allow those other variants to take precedence, the Class::Multimethods dispatch mechanism doesn't include variants with a '*' parameter in its list of viable targets at all, unless there is no viable target without a '*' parameter. All of which means that '*' parameters really *are* a last resort. For example, given the two variants:

```
multimethod receive_event => (Window, Event, Mode)
   => sub { print "W-E-M\n" };

multimethod receive_event => (ResizableWindow, MoveAndResizeEvent, '*')
   => sub{ print "W-M-*\n" };
```

a call to `receive_event` with argument types (ResizableWindow, MoveAndResizeEvent, OnMode) selects the variant with parameters (Window, Event, Mode), even though two of the three parameters of the '*'-ed variant are much closer to the actual argument types.

13.7.9 Recursive multiple dispatch

As defined above, the `stringify` multimethod still fails rather badly on nested data structures. For example:

```
print stringify( { a=>[1,2,3], b=>{b1=>4,b2=>5}, c=>sub{3} } );
```

will print out something like:

{a=>ARRAY(0x1001c23e), b=>HASH(0x10023ae6), c=>CODE(0x10027698)}

That's because, when the hash reference is passed to the HASH variant of `stringify`, each key and value is simply interpolated directly into the returned string rather than being individually stringified.

Fortunately, a small tweak to the ARRAY and HASH variants solves the problem:

```
multimethod stringify => (ARRAY) => sub
{
  my @arg = map { stringify($_) } @{$_[0]};
  return "[" . join(", ",@arg) . "]";
};

multimethod stringify => (HASH) => sub
{
  my %arg = map { stringify($_) } %{$_[0]};
  return "{" . join(", ", map("$_=>$arg{$_}",keys %arg)) . "}";
};
```

The difference here is that each element in the array or hash is recursively stringified, within the map block, *before* the container itself is processed. Because stringify is a multimethod, these recursive calls automatically select the correct variant for each element, so nested references and values are correctly processed.

Now the call:

```
print stringify( { a=>[1,2,3], b=>{b1=>4,b2=>5}, c=>sub{3} } );
```

prints:

{"a"=>[1, 2, 3], "b"=>{"b1"=>4, "b2"=>5}, "c"=>sub{???}}

13.7.10 Debugging a multimethod

As some of the preceding examples indicate, it isn't difficult to set up a multimethod with enough variants to make its behavior impossible to casually predict, especially when its arguments are drawn from complicated hierarchies.

To help prevent multimethods becoming obfuscated in this manner, Class::Multimethods provides a (nonexported) subroutine called analyse. This subroutine takes the name of a multimethod and generates a report (to STDERR) listing the behavior of that multimethod under all possible argument combinations. Because it's not exported, Class::Multimethods::analyse must be called by its fully qualified name. For example

```
use Class::Multimethods;

multimethod test => (IO::File)
  => sub { $_[0]->print("This should go in a file\n") };

multimethod test => (IO::Pipe)
  => sub { $_[0]->("This should go down a pipe\n") };

multimethod test => (IO::Socket)
  => sub { $_[0]->("This should go out a socket\n") };
```

Class::Multimethods::analyse("test");

The combinations of argument types to be analyzed are determined by examining the parameter lists of each variant of the multimethod and compiling a list of classes in the same inheritance hierarchy as any of those parameter classes. The analyse subroutine iterates through every possible combination of argument types and reports which variant, if any, would have been called for that set of arguments. Combinations that result in ambiguities or failure to dispatch are reported separately.

Even more usefully for argument sets where a single variant would be sucessfully dispatched, analyse also reports any other viable candidates—in other words, other variants that can handle the call, but which are further away from the argument list. This can be especially useful in determining why a particular variant was not called as expected.

The analyse subroutine can also take extra parameters to narrow the analysis to specific argument combinations. Each combination to be explicitly analyzed is specified as an anonymous array. For example, if we are puzzled over apparent discrepancies in the way the receive_event multimethod dispatched the specific argument combinations (ModalWindow, AcceptEvent, Mode) and (ModalWindow, Event, OnMode), we can analyze them in isolation by writing

```
Class::Multimethods::analyse( "receive_event",
                              [ModalWindow,AcceptEvent,Mode],
                              [ModalWindow,Event,OnMode],
                            );
```

13.8 COMPARING THE THREE APPROACHES

We've now seen three approaches to implementing multimethods in Perl: building polymorphic tests into ordinary methods, hand-crafting dispatch tables, and using the Class::Multimethods module.

Compared to the first two approaches, Class::Multimethods is much easier to use. It supplies the dispatch mechanism automatically, so the only code to be written is the actual behavior of the variants. That probably also makes code that uses the module more robust, since Class::Multimethods' dispatch mechanism has already been carefully debugged.

The breadth-first dispatch implemented by Class::Multimethods differs from the left-most ancestor wins strategy of the tests-in-methods approach and the dynamic dispatch table.[11] The breadth-first strategy is more predictable—that is, likelier to invoke the expected variant—in many cases, and, in those cases where it isn't any better than the other two, it's no worse either.

At present, however, the module offers no alternative to breadth-first search, so if you need to dispatch using some other strategy—for example, if one argument really *is* more important than the others—you'll still need to build your own mechanism.

Another important issue is that of run-time performance. Individual calls to multimethods built with the Class::Multimethods module are dispatched approximately one-third as fast as calls through an equivalent hand-crafted static dispatch table, and about half as fast as calls through a comparable tests-in-methods hierarchy.

That loss of performance may be significant if a multimethod is used frequently—for collision detection in a simulation, for example, or event handling in a GUI. Often, however, the difference in speed can be ignored because the multimethods being dispatched are themselves so expensive that variations in dispatch performance are relatively unimportant.

13.9 WHERE TO FIND OUT MORE

The Class::Multimethods module is available from the CPAN, in the directory http://www.perl.com/CPAN/authors/id/DCONWAY/.

13.10 SUMMARY

- Multiple dispatch is a polymorphic method-call technique that selects the subroutine to invoke according to the combined types of all arguments to a call, rather than just on the type of the first argument.

---

[11] Although, of course, we *could* rewrite the ancestors subroutine of the dynamic dispatch table version to use a breadth-first approach.

- Multiple dispatch can be simulated in Perl by nesting `if` statements in a singly dispatched method. The statements use the `isa` method to determine the actual types of the other arguments and respond accordingly.
- A faster alternative is to set up a multidimensional table of references to subroutines (handlers) for all possible combinations of argument types. Methods are dispatched by looking up the table entry for the argument types given and then calling the corresponding subroutine.
- To cope with arguments of derived types, such dispatch tables must be able to extend themselves at run time. Extending a table involves searching up the arguments' respective inheritance hierarchies to find a handler (in the current table) for a combination of ancestral parameter types.
- The Class::Multimethods module automates and greatly simplifies the task of setting up dynamic dispatch tables to implement multimethods.

C H A P T E R   1 4

Persistent objects

One of the most useful features of inanimate objects in the Real World is that when you leave them somewhere, they're often still there when you come back.[1] Unfortunately, software objects aren't nearly so obliging. Consequently, you have to keep recreating them every time you run their program.

Persistent programming is an attempt to overcome that problem, by arranging for data objects to retain their existence, identity, and contents between executions of the program that created them. Perl provides many means of grafting persistence onto object-oriented code. This chapter examines a few of them.

14.1 *THE INGREDIENTS*

To enable data to persist between executions of a program, the program—or the programming language—needs to provide four basic services. It must:

- Associate a unique identifier with the persistent data (*identity*);
- Create an accurate external representation of the data, suitable for storage between executions (*encoding* or *serialization*);
- Store and retrieve that external representation of the data between executions (*storage*);
- Reliably ensure that the internal and external representations of the data are synchronized at certain times (*coordination*).

---

[1] Unless, of course, you live with a two-year-old or some other small inquisitive domestic creature.

In a typical coarse-grained persistent program, these services are used as follows. When the program is executed, the persistence mechanism reinstates any external representation of persistent data. This involves locating the storage for the data, extracting the external representation, decoding it to an internal representation—sometimes described as thawing it—determining its identity, and assigning it to the appropriate variable. At the end of the program, the persistence mechanism saves the contents of each internal persistent variable. This involves extracting the data from the variable, converting it to an external representation—known as encoding or "freezing"—and then storing it. In other words, the persistence mechanism is responsible for converting between internal and external representations, and does so at either end of the program's execution.

Coarse-grained persistence is susceptible to data loss if the program terminates unexpectedly and is unable to save its persistent data to permanent storage. In cases where data integrity is critical, or system reliability is poor, an application may need to implement fine-grained persistence, in which the representations of the internal and external data are synchronized every time the data changes. That is, any change to the internal data causes the persistence mechanism to immediately save that data to external storage. This scheme is far less susceptible to data corruption,[2] but is also considerably more expensive since *every* change to the value of *any* persistent variable now requires a write to disk.

14.1.1 Identity

All data in a program, whether persistent or transient, needs an unambiguous identity, so that it can be located when needed. In many programming languages—including Perl—the identity of a datum is imposed by the variable that stores it. From one perspective, variables provide a kind of persistence of data *within* a program: they preserve values for use in other parts of the program at other points in the execution.

Localized and lexical variables impart a temporary identity on data, whereas global (package) variables impose a permanent identity—at least within the lifetime of the program itself. If we confine our discussion to unlocalized package variables, we can reasonably pretend that the identity of a piece of data is synonymous with the name of the variable containing it.

Applying that view to the problem of persistence, we require the value that a package variable was storing at the end of one execution of a program to be restored to that variable at the beginning of the next execution. Or, looking at it the other way, we require that a specific datum (whose identity is specified by virtue of being stored in a particular package variable) must be given the same identity—that is, be stored in the same variable—next time the program is run.

Establishing and maintaining identity is usually a major obstacle when implementing persistence in a nonpersistent programming language. Most such languages only allow the internal memory address of a given variable—a pointer or reference—to be accessed by the program itself and provide no run-time mechanism for determining a variable's name, scope, or type. This makes it difficult to generate unique and consistent identities for data since there is no

---

[2] …but not immune to it. For example, the program might receive a fatal signal in the middle of saving some persistent data.

guarantee that a given memory address will be repeatedly allocated to the same variable in each separate execution of a program.

Yet again, Perl is pleasantly different. Perl programs have full run-time access to their own symbol tables, and allow variables to be accessed via strings containing their names. Provided we confine our ambitions to package variables, we can easily arrange for each persistent datum to be given a unique and reproducible identity.

Even if the Perl symbol table isn't directly accessible, the availability of hashes still permits a form of persistent identity to be established for particular data. Since each value in a hash is identified with a unique key, if we store data in a single hash whose contents are restored each time the program runs, then each value in the hash will be persistent and uniquely identifiable.

14.1.2 Encoding/serialization

Once a datum can be identified in a reproducible manner, the next step towards making it persist is to find some way to represent it accurately outside the program. This is necessary because the formats used to store data within a program typically involve information, such as internal pointers or references to memory addresses, that is specific to a particular execution of the program.

If this execution-specific data were to be stored away in its raw state, then, when the program is next invoked and that persistent data is restored, it is extremely unlikely that the different memory addresses would all conveniently line-up with their previous data. It's far more likely that the various parts of the data would be stored in entirely different memory addresses, so the restored pointers and references now refer to completely unrelated data.

Hence, the values of any pointers or references within a data structure need to be converted into a consistent set of abstract addresses that are correctly related to each other, but entirely unrelated to the actual locations where the data was previously stored. This process is called "unswizzling." Next time the program is executed, these abstract addresses can be coherently mapped, or swizzled, back into the new address space to restore the internal relationships of the parts of the data.

Encoding is also required because persistent data has to hibernate somewhere on disk between program executions. Most modern file-systems use files that store only sequences of bytes. Therefore, in order to store a datum, it must be converted to a single sequence of characters (or bits). This process is called serialization, or flattening, or marshalling.

Once again, Perl makes the task, if not painless, at least possible. Because the type of any value can be ascertained (via a call to ref), it is possible to develop Perl code that can analyze the type and contents of a variable, determine its structure, and convert that structure to an execution-independent sequence of characters.

There are three freely available modules on the CPAN that automate the task of serializing and later reconstructing arbitrary data structures: Storable, FreezeThaw, and Data::Dumper. The following subsections look briefly at each of these and illustrate their approaches to serialization using the following test data:

```
$str = "string";
$num = 668;
$ref = \$str;
@arr = (1,2,\$str);
%hsh = (a=>1,z=>\$arr[1]);
```

Note that the last three variables contain references to other variables (or parts thereof). If an encoding module is to be usable, it must preserve these relationships when encoding and decoding.

The Storable module

Rafaël Manfredi's Storable module provides two subroutines: `Storable::freeze` and `Storable::thaw`, that encode and decode a single arbitrary data structure to a binary format. The `freeze` subroutine takes a single reference to a scalar, array, or hash and converts the contents of the variable to a character string. So, to encode two or more values simultaneously, they must be boxed in an array.

For example, we can serialize the complete set of test data above as follows:

```
use Storable qw(freeze thaw);

# encode data and relationships...
  $encoding = freeze [\$str, \$num, \$ref, \@arr, \%hsh];
```

which would produce the following string in `$encoding`:

```
"\002\0044321\004\004\004\002\000\000\000\005\004\n\006stringXX\004\006\000
\000\002\234XX\004\004\000\000\000\000\002XX\004\002\000\000\000\003\010\20
1X\010\202X\004\000\000\000\000\002XXX\004\003\000\000\000\002\010\201X\000
\000\000\001a\004\000\000\000\000\nX\000\000\000\001zXXX"
```

This string is actually considerably more compact than it appears. (It occupies only 92 bytes.) It looks longer here because it consists largely of non-printable characters, which have been rendered above as `"\nnn"` escapes.

When decoded:

```
# decode data...
  $anon_array = thaw $encoding;
```

that string recreates exactly the anonymous array—now referred to by `$anon_array`—that was originally passed to `freeze`, including the relationships between the variables. However, that re-creation represents an exact *copy* of the originals and their interrelationships, rather than a reconstruction of the originals themselves. In order to restore the original package variables and their relationships, we need to add:

```
# decode data...
  $anon_array = thaw $encoding;

# ...and reinstate in variables...
  ( *str, *num, *ref, *arr, *hsh ) = @$anon_array;
```

This assigns each recreated reference in the array referred to by `$anon_array` back to the original package variable, via an assignment to the appropriate typeglob.

Storable also provides subroutines for storing to, and retrieving from, a named disk file:

```
store $data_ref, "save_file";

# and later…

$data_ref = retrieve "save_file";
```

The module also has subroutines for storing data through an open filehandle, storing data in a machine independent order and deep-copying data (that is, when copying a reference, copy the entire data object referred to, not just the reference).

The FreezeThaw module

Ilya Zakharevich's FreezeThaw module also offers `freeze` and `thaw` methods, but has a slightly different interface. `FreezeThaw::freeze` takes a list of scalar arguments—normally references—and freezes them together, preserving any referential relationships between them. `FreezeThaw::thaw` takes the encoded string and converts it back to an array of references.

To encode and decode our test data using FreezeThaw, we would write

```
use FreezeThaw qw(freeze thaw);

# encode data and relationships…
  $encoding = freeze (\$str, \$num, \$ref, \@arr, \%hsh);

# decode data…
  @array = thaw $encoding;

# …and reinstate in variables…
  ( *str, *num, *ref, *arr, *hsh ) = @array;
```

FreezeThaw uses a different encoding scheme to Storable and manages to be even more frugal with space. The code above puts the following string

```
"FrT;!0|\_\$6|string@1|@5|<0|\$3|668\<0|@3|$1|1$1|2<0|%4|$1|a$1|z$1|1\$1|2"
```

into encoding and requires only 73 bytes to encode the five interrelated pieces of data.

FreezeThaw is also more sophisticated than Storable when it comes to encoding and decoding blessed data (see section 14.2).

The Data::Dumper module

Gurusamy Sarathy's Data::Dumper module is different in its approach to encoding: it uses the Perl language itself as its encoding scheme. That is, the `Data::Dumper::Dump` subroutine—Data::Dumper's equivalent of `freeze`—takes an anonymous array of variables, and a second array listing their names, and converts them into a character string containing a series of beautifully-formatted Perl statements.

For example, when given the five variables of our test set

```
# encode data and relationships…
  $encoding = Data::Dumper->Dump( [    $str, $num, $ref, \@arr, \%hsh],
                                  [qw(  str   num   ref   *arr   *hsh )] );
```

`Dump` returns the following string to be assigned to `$encoding`:

```
q{
    $str = 'string';
    $num = 668;
    $ref = \$str;
    @arr =(
            1,
            2,
            $ref
        );
    %hsh =(
            'a' => 1,
            'z' => \$arr[1]
        );
}
```

Although it's an uninterpolated character string, the return value contains text that is bona fide Perl source code. If executed, that source code will fully reconstruct the original contents and interrelationships of the original variables.

Because its encoded representation is simple Perl, Data::Dumper doesn't need a special subroutine to decode it. Instead, you just apply `eval` to the string:

```
# decode data and reinstate in variables...
  eval $encoding;
```

You don't even have to muck about assigning the decoded contents to an array of type-globs; the evaluated string automatically assigns the correct data to the correct variables.

Of course, the downside is that the standard Data::Dumper encoding scheme isn't optimally compact. Encoding the five test variables required 151 bytes, over half of which are white space characters. Fortunately Data::Dumper provides an option that dispenses with the lovely layout, thereby reducing the same encoding to an remarkably compact 74 bytes:

```
q{$str='string';$num=668;$ref=\$str;@arr=(1,2,$ref);%hsh=(a=>1,z=>\$arr[1])
;}
```

Data::Dumper also provides several formatting options for the code strings it produces. You can independently control padding, layout, indentation, and even "`eval`-ability." This helps the module to moonlight as a useful debugging tool—producing comprehensible representations of misbehaving data structures—and also makes it useful in some code-generation contexts.

Like FreezeThaw, Data::Dumper also has special tricks when encoding blessed objects (see below), though it isn't quite as flexible as FreezeThaw in that regard.

14.1.3 Storage

Once the data has been suitably serialized, we have to store it somewhere on disk. To do this, we can write it into a standard disk file, or we can use one of the simple database modules from the CPAN (NDBM_File, GDBM_File, ODBM_File, DB_File) or a full relational database such as Oracle (via the DBI and DBD::Oracle modules), Ingres (DBI plus DBD::Ingres), Sybase (DBI plus DBD::Sybase), and so on.

Flat files

If we use one of the serialization modules described above to encode all the persistent data in a program at once, we produce a single, possibly very long, character string. The easiest way to store this string might well be to just write it out to a file on disk.

This approach can be particularly effective if we use Data::Dumper as our encoding mechanism since, in that case, the encoding is really just a short Perl script that recreates the data when executed. If that script were written to a disk file

```
open STORAGE, ">persistent.dat"
    and print STORAGE $encoding
    and close STORAGE
or die "can't save persistent data";
```

then the complete code to reinstate it would simply be

```
do "persistent.dat";
```

It's hard to make persistence much simpler than that!

Simple databases

Sometimes however, we want fast and reliable access to the encodings of individual objects stored on disk (we'll see examples of this shortly). In such cases, a proper database system is a better choice.

If the data for each object is still serialized as a single string, then we can use one of the simple database systems supported by the tie mechanism. In this approach to storage, we create a tied hash that's attached to the desired database, then assign the encoded representation of the object to the entry for a specific key of that hash. That key might, for example, be the full name of the variable storing the persistent data.

To tie a simple database—let's call it persistent.db—to a hash—say %pers_db—we use the tie function as follows:

```
use DB_File;
use Fcntl;

tie %pers_db, "DB_File", "persistent.db", O_CREAT|O_RDWR, 0640, $DB_HASH;
```

In this case we are tie-ing the hash %pers_db to a database in the Berkley DB format. The arguments to tie are:

- %pers_db: the hash to which the database is to be tied.
- "DB_File": the name of the Perl module that implements the necessary methods to tie a hash to that particular kind of database.
- "persistent.db": the name of the database file to which the hash is to be tied.
- O_CREAT|O_RDWR: a set of bit-flags (as used by the sysopen function), indicating the kind of access to be provided. O_CREAT specifies that the database file is to be created if it doesn't already exist. O_RDWR specifies that the database should be opened for both reading and writing. The constants themselves come from the Fcntl module.
- 0640: an octal value specifying the maximal access permission to be given to the new database file, if it needs to be created. This number is filtered through the user's umask to

determine the actual access permissions for the file. 0640 means that maximal permissions allowed for the file are read/write access for the user, read-only access for the user's group, and no access for other users. A more permissive value of 0666, which permits read/write access for everyone, subject to the user's umask, is also a common choice.

• $DB_HASH: a variable exported by the DB_File module. It contains a predefined reference that tells the database how to act—in this case, as a hash of key/value pairs.

The set-up code would be similar for any of the other simple databases: ndbm, odbm, gdbm, sdbm, and so on, except for the last argument, which is unique to Berkeley DB. The documentation accompanying their respective Perl modules (NDBM_File, ODBM_File, GDBM_File, SDBM_File, etc.) describes the specifics of tie-ing each type of database.

Once the database is open, storing serialized objects in it is as easy as assigning a string to a hash entry. In fact, that's exactly what you do. For example, having tied %pers_db to persistent.db, we can encode the values of the test variables and save them in the database as follows:

```
use FreezeThaw "freeze";

$pers_db{"str"} = freeze(\$str);
$pers_db{"num"} = freeze(\$num);
$pers_db{"ref"} = freeze(\$ref);
$pers_db{"arr"} = freeze(\@arr);
$pers_db{"hsh"} = freeze(\%hsh);
```

Extracting the data back to its original package variables is similarly straightforward. We retrieve the relevant entry of the %per_db hash, decode it, and assign the resulting reference back to the appropriate typeglob:

```
use FreezeThaw "thaw";

(*str) = thaw( $pers_db{"str"} );
(*num) = thaw( $pers_db{"num"} );
(*ref) = thaw( $pers_db{"ref"} );
(*arr) = thaw( $pers_db{"arr"} );
(*hsh) = thaw( $pers_db{"hsh"} );
```

In other words, once the database is tied to a hash, each record is accessible as an entry of that hash.

Relational databases

Occasionally, it may be preferable to use a full relational database like Oracle or Sybase to store persistent data. For example, we may want to perform complex queries or generate reports on the persistent data in other applications, or we may be working on a machine that only has this kind of database installed.

The easiest way to use such databases is through the interface provide by Tim Bunce's DBI module. The DBI module defines a set of classes that provides a standard interface to many SQL-based relational databases (and numerous others besides). The details specific to each particular database are then encoded in a separate module (DBD::Oracle, DBD::Sybase, DBD::Informix, etc.) that is passed to DBI when setting up access to a particular database.

Again, let's assume the data is encoded as a single string.[3] We'll use Tim's own DBD::Oracle driver module to connect to an Oracle database, called persistence.orc:

```
use DBI;
use DBD::Oracle;

my $db = DBI->connect("dbi:Oracle:persistence.orc", $user, $password)
    or die "Couldn't not connect to persistence database";

# etc.
```

The `DBI::connect` method is a constructor for a database interface object and returns a reference to the new object, which is then stored in `$db`. In DBI parlance, however, that reference is called a database handle, so that's what we'll call it here.

The first argument to `connect` specifies the driver module and database file to be used. (The format is `"dbi:driver_module:database_source_name"`.) The remaining arguments are the username and password required for access to most databases.

Once the database connection is established, serialized objects can be stored and retrieved by creating appropriate SQL statements and sending them to the database via methods called on the database handle. For example, to encode and store the contents of the test variables, we can write:

```
# Create a table to store the data (if necessary)...
  my $create_table =
    "CREATE TABLE persistent_data
      ( var_name CHAR(128) PRIMARY KEY,
        encoding CHAR(2000) )";

  $db->do($create_table);
# Create a statement for inserting data into the table...
  my $insert_data = 'INSERT INTO persistent_data VALUES ( ?, ? )';
  my $insert_stat = $db->prepare($insert_data);


# Encode and store the data...
  use FreezeThaw "freeze";

  $insert_stat->execute( "str", freeze(\$str) );
  $insert_stat->execute( "num", freeze(\$num) );
  $insert_stat->execute( "ref", freeze(\$ref) );
  $insert_stat->execute( "arr", freeze(\@arr) );
  $insert_stat->execute( "hsh", freeze(\%hsh) );

  $db->commit();
```

We first set up a table called "persistent_data" with two fields: "var_name" and "encoding". The `do` method takes a string argument containing an SQL command—in this case a "CREATE TABLE..." command—and executes it. Of course, normally, it is only necessary to

---

[3] Of course, with a relational database we *could* set individual fields to represent the attributes of a hash, but then we'd have to worry about conversions, and we'd *still* have to encode any nested data structures.

set up the table the first time the database is used, unless we're also planning to delete it again when the data is reloaded (see below).

Next, we set up another SQL statement—"INSERT INTO..."—that inserts a new row of data into the "persistent_data" table. The values for the row's two fields are "?" placeholders, which we will need to fill in each time we wish to insert some data.

The "INSERT" statement is set up as a separate object by passing the SQL string to the prepare method. The object returned[4] (known as a "statement handle") can then be used to perform insertions on the original database by calling its execute method. Of course, each time the statement handle is executed, the "?" placeholders in the original SQL statement must be filled in. This is achieved by passing those values as arguments when execute is called.

After the insertions are made, we also need to tell the database to make the changes permanent by calling commit on the original database handle.

Extracting the data is more complicated. To retrieve the data for a variable whose name is stored in $var_name, we need to extract the corresponding encoding field from the table using a qualified "SELECT..." statement:

```
$select_statement =
   "SELECT encoding FROM persistence_data WHERE var_name = '$varname'";
```

But, as we need to extract *all* the encodings from the table to reinstate the complete set of persistent variables, it's more efficient to use a single unqualified "SELECT..." statement:

```
$select_statement =
   "SELECT var_name, encoding FROM persistence_data";
```

and then process the matching records one at a time (see below).

Because the unqualified "SELECT..." is going to return a number of rows of data, the DBI module requires us to create another statement handle to provide access to that information. This statement object can be applied to the database—once again, by calling its execute method—and subsequently queried to retrieve individual rows—using its fetchrow_array method.

Therefore, complete restoration of the four variables looks like this:

```
# Create a statement handle to collect all the returned data...
   my $extract_data =
      "SELECT var_name, encoding FROM persistence_data";

   my $statement = $db->prepare($extract_data);

# Extract the data from the database into the statement handle...
   $statement->execute();

# Extract each row of data from the statement handle,
# decoding it, and reinstating the corresponding variable...
```

---

[4] Note that each time it's called, the prepare method creates and initializes a new statement handle object. Thus prepare is a constructor, but one always called as an object method, rather than as a class method.

```
    while ( ($var_name, $encoding) = $statement->fetchrow_array() )
    {
        (*{$var_name}) = thaw( $encoding );
    }
```

```
# Set the statement handle free...
$statement->finish();
```

```
# Remove the table (if necessary)...
    $db->do("DROP TABLE persistent_data");
    $db->commit();
```

It's sometimes necessary to delete the table every time the persistent data is reinstated within a program, so that other applications will not try to access the data while it's in play. Alternatively, depending on the type of database we're using, it may be possible to lock the table so other application only have read access (or no access at all) while the program executes.

The DBI module and the SQL language together provide a sophisticated means of achieving the same end of storing data externally. For more details, you should consult the documentation that comes with DBI.pm and the DBD::... driver module for your particular database.

14.1.4 Coordination

Useful as they are, none of the modules described above is a complete package for implementing persistence. Though together they can provide a means by which data can be converted to an externally-stored representation, none provides a control mechanism that ensures data actually *is* converted or stored at the appropriate time.

The coordination mechanism has to ensure that persistent data is uniquely identified in a process-independent manner; that it is encoded and decoded in a manner that preserves values and their interrelationships; and that the encoded data is stored reliably and retrieved as needed.

Ideally, a coordination mechanism should accomplish these tasks with little or no prompting from the programmer—in other words, it should be *automatic*. The mechanism should also place as few constraints as possible on the nature and organization of the data so that persistence can be added into an existing system with little if any modification to code— that is, the persistence mechanism should be *orthogonal*. Ideally, we would like something as simple as a (hypothetical) persistent specifier, so that a variable can be made persistent merely by writing

```
persistent $obj;
```

thereafter, all the messiness of coordinating the identification, encoding, storage, retrieval, decoding, and re-creation of that object's data is handled automagically.

Coordinating those tasks for coarse-grained persistence is relatively simple in Perl and can be fully automated and completely orthogonal. We can even implement a persistent subroutine with almost exactly the semantics described above.

Coarse-grained persistence requires only that data be brought in from disk at the start of a program and written back at the end. Most programming languages provide a means of performing a task like this at either end of a program's execution. Perl and awk offer explicit

BEGIN, INIT, and END blocks, while C++ and Java normally rely on the constructors and destructors of global objects. Even in C and Pascal, you can at least hard-code statements at the beginning and end of the main program.

Coordinating fine-grained persistence is more challenging. A general solution tends to be more invasive—that is, less orthogonal—because fine-grained persistence requires the program to detect any case in which any part of any persistent datum changes. This *can* be achieved in Perl, but does require some explicit coding, since there is no way to automatically detect and intercept changes to the elements of an arbitrary array or a hash, not even using a tied variable.

14.2 OBJECT-ORIENTED PERSISTENCE

An added complication arises when making blessed objects persistent. A blessed object is a collection of data with an associated class. Hence, to correctly encode such an object, it's essential to record both the data and the class into which the object was blessed.

14.2.1 Encoding objects

Fortunately that's not particularly difficult in Perl, since ref can be used to ascertain the name of any object's class. Decoding the data for a persistent object and reblessing that object into the correct class is also relatively easy. So long as we can access the class name as a string, we can bless an object into that class with the two-argument form of bless. All three packages described in section 14.1.2 automatically detect blessed data and encode and decode it correctly.

For example, when Data::Dumper is asked to encode a blessed object:

```
package Act;

sub new
{
   my ($class, %data) = @_;
   bless { %data }, $class;
}

package main;
use Data::Dumper;

$data = { age=>34, shoe_size=>9 };
$obj  = Act->new(age=>34, shoe_size=>9);

print Data::Dumper->Dump([$data,$obj],[qw(data obj)]);
```

it recognizes the blessing of the data referred to by the second variable and produces the following reconstruction string:

```
q{
   $data={
          'shoe_size' => 9,
          'age' => 34,
        };
```

```
$obj=bless({
        'shoe_size' => 9,
        'age' => 34,
        }, 'Act' );
}
```

14.2.2 Object-oriented encoding

Better still, the Data::Dumper module provides two run-time configuration variables: $Data::Dumper::Freezer and $Data::Dumper::Toaster. Each may be assigned a string specifying the name of a method to be invoked as part of the encoding or decoding process. For example:

```
use Data::Dumper;
$Data::Dumper::Freezer = "tidy_up";
$Data::Dumper::Toaster = "rebuild";
```

Whenever $Data::Dumper::Freezer is set to a string containing the name of a method, Data::Dumper::Dump calls that method on any blessed object immediately before it is encoded. Hence, if $Data::Dumper::Freezer is set as above, a call like

```
# encode data and relationships...
  $encoding = Data::Dumper->Dump([$obj],["obj"]);
```

causes $obj->tidy_up() to be called before $obj is encoded. This may be useful to allow $obj to delete any unnecessary internal housekeeping data structures or, perhaps, eliminate some cached information relevant to the current process only.

If $Data::Dumper::Toaster is set to a nonempty string, Data::Dumper::Dump includes a call to the method of that name as part of the encoded string. In other words, that method is called when eval is used to reanimate the encoded object. For example, if $Data::Dumper::Toaster is also set as above, the call to Data::Dumper::Dump produces a string like this:

```
q{
    $obj= bless( {
                  'shoe_size' => 9,
                  'age' => 34,
                }, 'Act' )->rebuild();
}
```

which, when eval-ed, invokes the rebuild method on the newly blessed Act object.

The FreezeThaw module is even cleverer. When asked to encode a blessed object, it calls that object's own Freeze method and returns whatever that method returns. That is:

```
$encoding = FreezeThaw::freeze($obj);
($obj) = FreezeThaw::thaw($encoding);
```

is really equivalent to:

```
$encoding = $obj->Freeze($_options);
($obj) = Act->Thaw($encoding,$_options);
```

where `$_options` is a reference to an object containing configuration options. FreezeThaw passes this object to the method to allow it to conform to the overall configuration for the package. See the module's documentation for the gory details.

Giving each object control over its own encoding provides a great deal of flexibility. For example, if the object is keeping an access count, it may choose not to encode that information since it may no longer be relevant the next time the program is invoked. But what if the object's class doesn't define a suitable `Freeze` or `Thaw` method?

Here is where FreezeThaw is at its most clever. When the package is first imported, it installs two additional subroutines: `UNIVERSAL::Freeze` and `UNIVERSAL::Thaw`. This ensures that *every* class now has a suitable `Freeze` or `Thaw` method, if not its own, then the one it inherits from class UNIVERSAL. `UNIVERSAL::Freeze` and `UNIVERSAL::Thaw` implement the default freeze-everything semantics applied to non-blessed data. Thus, a class may choose to specify its own encoding behavior or do nothing and inherit the default.

We can even use this feature to allow an object to record how often it has been frozen:

```
package CountFreezings;

sub Freeze
{
   my ($self, $_options) = @_;
   $self->{_freezings}++;
   $self->UNIVERSAL::Freeze($_options);
}
```

Now, when we freeze an object of any class that inherits from CountFreezings, Count-Freezings::Freeze receives the freeze request. It increments the freeze count in the object (`$self->{_freezings}++`) and allows the default freezing behavior (`$self->UNIVER-SAL::Freeze($_options)`) to take over.

14.3 COARSE-GRAINED PERSISTENCE

Implementing coarse-grained persistence for objects of a particular class is easy. We merely have to ensure that, when the program starts, the data for such objects is retrieved from disk and, when the program ends, the data is written back to disk. We'll first consider how to hard-code this for a specially designed class. Then we'll see how the technique can be generalized to provide automatic and orthogonal persistence for any class and, indeed, for unblessed data as well.

14.3.1 Class-specific persistence

An object consists of a collection of attributes accessed through a set of methods. For an object to be persistent, its attributes must be retrieved and stored at either end of a program. Those attributes are usually implemented as a hash, where each attribute is a single entry within the hash, and is accessed via a key that is the attribute's name. Thus, to make an object persistent, we must create a persistent hash.

A persistent hash is a reasonable description of a database. In fact, in Perl, a tied hash is the usual interface to a database. So, if we can arrange for an object to store itself in a database

Listing 14.1   A non-persistent contacts class

```perl
package Contact;
$VERSION = 1.00;
use strict;

sub new
{
  my ($class, %init) = @_;
  bless {
          name    => $init{name},
          phone   => $init{phone},
          fax     => $init{fax},
          email   => $init{email},
        }, $class;
}

sub get_name  { $_[0]->{name} }
sub get_phone { $_[0]->{phone} }
sub set_phone { $_[0]->{phone} = $_[1] }
sub get_fax   { $_[0]->{fax} }
sub set_fax   { $_[0]->{fax} = $_[1] }
sub get_email { $_[0]->{email} }
sub set_email { $_[0]->{email} = $_[1] }

sub print
{
  my ($self) = @_;
  print $self->get_name(), ":\n";
  print "\tPhone:", $self->get_phone(), "\n";
  print "\tFax:", $self->get_fax(), "\n";
  print "\tEmail:", $self->get_email(), "\n";
}

1;
```

at the end of a program and retrieve itself from that database next time the program executes, we will have made the object persist.

Unless the object's attributes are improbably large, which particular database we use is almost irrelevant. As long as the database can store keys and associated strings of an appropriate length, we are able to encode each attribute of an object—using one of the encoding modules described above—and use the attribute's name as a key under which to store it in the database.

To illustrate the technique, we'll implement a class of persistent objects suitable for recording basic contacts information. Listing 14.1 lists the basic, nonpersistent, Contact class. The constructor creates a blessed hash and initializes it with any suitable arguments given. The accessor functions provide read access to all attributes and write access to all but the name attribute. The `print` method prints out an object's data

Listing 14.2 shows the Contact::Persistent class, which is derived from class Contact. It provides its objects with coarse-grained persistence by storing them in a Berkeley DB database

Listing 14.2 A persistent contacts class

```
use Contact;

package Contact::Persistent;
$VERSION = 2.00;
@ISA = qw( Contact );
use strict;

use DB_File;
use Fcntl;

my %persistent = ();
sub persistent
{
  no strict;
  my ($class, $varname, $filename) = @_;
  $varname =~ s/^\$((\w|::)+)$/$1/
    or croak "Invalid persistent variable name: $varname";
  $varname = (caller)[0]."::$varname" unless $varname =~ /::/;
  $persistent{$varname} = $filename;
  if (tie local %db, 'DB_File', $filename, O_RDWR, 0640)
  {
    ${$varname} = bless { %db }, $class;
    untie %db;
  }
  return ${$varname};
}

END
{
  no strict;
  while (my ($varname, $filename) = each %persistent)
  {
    tie local %db, 'DB_File', $filename, O_CREAT|O_RDWR, 0640
      or croak "Unable to open persistent database $filename ($!)";
    %db = %${$varname};
    untie %db;
  }
}

1;
```

(though any other Unix database could be substituted simply by replacing "DB_File" with the appropriate alternative: "NDBM_File", "GDBM_File", "SDBM_File", etc.).

The derived class first loads the DB_File module—to provide access to the databases—and the Fcntl module—to access the file control constants needed to open them. Next, it defines a lexical hash, %persistent, which will be used to record the identities of any persistent objects.

That recording is done in the `Contact::Persistent::persistent` method, which takes two arguments: the name of a scalar package variable (`$varname`), and the name of the database file in which it's to be stored (`$filename`). For example:

```
package main;

Contact::Persistent->persistent( '$me'           => 'mydata' );
Contact::Persistent->persistent( '$Spouse::unit' => 'herdata' );
Contact::Persistent->persistent( '$employer'     => 'theirdata' );
```

When invoked, the `persistent` method first extracts the variable's name, by chopping off the leading `"$"` and prepending a suitable package name—the name of the calling package—if the variable was specified without one. For example, after "extraction," the three variable names specified above become

```
"main::me"
"Spouse::unit"
"main::employer"
```

Invalid scalar variable names such as:

```
Contact::Persistent->persistent( '%us'           => 'ourdata' );
Contact::Persistent->persistent( '@them'          => 'theirdata' );
Contact::Persistent->persistent( '$Those::%&^@%' => 'theirdata.too' );
```

are also caught and vilified.

The extracted variable name is used as a key to store the corresponding file name in the `%persistent` cache. That information will be needed again at the end of the program in order to save the persistent objects back to disk.

Next, `persistent` attempts to tie a local hash to the named database file. If it can, it proceeds to copy the data stored in the database to an anonymous hash, which is then blessed. A reference to the reconstructed object is assigned to the named variable—which is why it had to be a scalar—using `$varname` as a symbolic reference—which is why we need `no strict`.

This reconstruction step is skipped if the database doesn't exist. That occurs the first time that the program is run because the object's data has not yet been saved. In that case, the named global variable is not initialized at all, which makes it easy to initialize it within the program:

```
Contact::Persistent->persistent( '$me'=> 'mydata' );
$me = Contact::Persistent->new(name=>"Damian") unless defined $me;
```

Or, since `Persistent` returns the reference stored in the named variable, it's also possible to write

```
Contact::Persistent->persistent( '$me'=> 'mydata' )
   or $me = Contact::Persistent->new(name=>"Damian");
```

Within `persistent` the newly created object is blessed into the class named by the first argument, *not* straight into Contact::Persistent. This means that objects of classes derived from Contact::Persistent can also be made persistent:

```
@Contact::Persistent::Personal::ISA  = ( "Contact::Persistent" );
@Contact::Persistent::CIA::ISA       = ( "Contact::Persistent" );

Contact::Persistent::Personal->persistent( '$therapist' => 'shrinkdata' );
Contact::Persistent::CIA->persistent(      '$agent_x'   => 'covertdata' );
```

Because `persistent` blesses reconstructed objects into the class through which it is invoked, `$therapist` receives a Contact::Persistent::Personal object rather than a Contact::Persistent object.

Finally, the local database is untied to close it and `persistent` returns the value, if any, of the named package variable.

The overall effect of a call to `Contact::persistent` is to recreate the previous contents of a Contact::Persistent object and to mark the package variable that stores it as housing persistent data. That marking is used at the end of the program by the END block that follows the definition of `persistent`.

The END block iterates through each variable-name/file-name pair stored in `%persistent`. For each pair, it opens the corresponding database file or issues a warning if something goes wrong. Then, the END block copies and stores the contents of the object referred to by the variable and closes the database. Thus, every package variable registered via a call to `persistent` is automatically saved to its own database file at the end of the program. In this respect, the END block within a class is being used like a destructor for class attributes.

This scheme can only make package variables persistent, since the Contact::Persistent module will not have symbol table access to lexical variables from other scopes and, hence, can't load or store them.

14.3.2 Some improvements

For a simple class like Contact, the technique described above is adequate and moderately robust. For more complicated cases, however, it has six glaring deficiencies:

- It will lose data if the program terminates without invoking the END block—that is, if it receives a fatal signal;
- It can handle only scalar attributes and will fail if any attribute stores a reference to an array or to a hash;
- It relies on the user to correctly specify the actual class of each object when calling `persistent`;
- It uses a separate database for each object, which is cumbersome and wasteful;
- It confines persistence to a single class hierarchy;
- It fails to preserve any interrelationships between persistent variables because each variable is encoded separately, so the encoder doesn't recognize the relationships.

We'll fix the first four of those problems in this section, and the last two in the next.

The first problem, data loss, is easily dealt with. We need to ensure that any fatal signal causes the process to exit normally—with the usual clean-up—rather than terminating the process immediately. To do that, we can modify `persistent` so that it also installs a signal handler to catch this case:

```
sub persistent
{
    $SIG{'INT'} = sub { exit(0) };
    no strict;
    my ($class, $varname, $filename) = @_;
```

```
# etc. as before
}
```

Now, unless some other part of the program changes the signal handler, when an interrupt signal is received, the program calls `exit`, which performs the END block and ensures that the data is saved. The handler is set up in `persistent` so that it is only installed if at least one persistent variable is specified. However, catching interrupt signals still doesn't guarantee data integrity. The signal may have been received, and the handler invoked, in the middle of modification to an object; that is, while one of its methods was executing. This is likely to leave the object in an invalid state and corrupt the data saved for it. Alternatively, the program might receive a kill signal, which can't be caught.

The second problem—inability to handle nested data structures within an object—is also easy to overcome. We merely ensure that the END handler serializes each attribute before storing it and that `persistent` properly decodes it again when reconstructing the object. We can use any of the three encoding modules described above. Listing 14.3 shows the necessary modifications to `persistent` and the END block, implemented with Storable. The only change to either is a loop that steps through each attribute, decoding or encoding it as appropriate. However, now the attributes of a Contact::Persistent object can store anything:

```
Contact::Persistent->persistent( '$me' => 'mydata' );

# and later…

$me->set_phone( ["555-6787", "1800-AUTHOR"] );
```

because those additional loops convert each attribute value to a string representation that the database can store.

We can overcome the third and fourth problems—relying on the programmer to get the class right, and storing objects in separate databases—by taking the encoding process one step further and encoding each entire object as a single string.

If each object is encoded in this way, then decoding it automatically reblesses it into the correct class. Better still, we can store the representations of all persistent objects in a single database, since each object is now a single string and can be indexed by its variable name. Listing 14.4 shows the changes to the original Contact::Persistent class (from listing 14.2) that are required to implement this scheme. Note that, for this version, we've swapped to Data::Dumper for the encoding, just to show that the choice of serializer is irrelevant to the various techniques.

The most significant change to the class is that its interface has been altered.[5] Specifically, the persistence mechanism is now accessed differently. For a start, the addition of an `import` method means that the Contact module is now going to do something whenever it's used. It's now going to expect an extra argument to `use`, which specifies the single persistence database that all the Contact::Persistent objects will be stored in. It then opens the database and ties it to the lexical hash `%db` (or dies trying).

---

[5] Interface changes are always the most significant because they directly affect every person who is using the previous version of your class and who will now need to change their code.

Listing 14.3   A persistent contacts class with encoded attributes

```perl
use Contact;

package Contact::Persistent;
$VERSION = 2.10;
@ISA = qw( Contact );
use strict;

use Storable qw( freeze thaw );

my %persistent = ();

sub persistent
{
    $SIG{'INT'} = sub { $SIG{'INT'} = 'IGNORE'; exit(0) };
    no strict;
    my ($class, $varname, $filename) = @_;
    $varname =~ s/^\$((\w|::)+)$/$1/
        or croak "Invalid persistent variable name: $varname";
    $varname = (caller)[0]."::$varname" unless $varname =~ /::/;
    $persistent{$varname} = $filename;
    if (tie local %db, 'DB_File', $filename, O_RDWR, 0640)
    {
        ${$varname} = bless { %db }, $class;
        foreach my $key (keys %${$varname})
        {
            ${$varname}->{$key} = ${thaw( ${$varname}->{$key} )}
        }
        untie %db;
    }
    return ${$varname};
}

END
{
    no strict;
    while (my ($varname, $filename) = each %persistent)
    {
        tie local %db, 'DB_File', $filename, O_CREAT|O_RDWR, 0640
            or croak "Unable to open persistent database $filename ($!)";
        foreach my $key (keys %${$varname})
        {
            ${$varname}->{$key} = freeze( \${$varname}->{$key} )
        }
        %db = %${$varname};
        untie %db;
    }
}
```

Listing 14.4   A persistent contacts class in a single database

```
use Contact;

package Contact::Persistent;
$VERSION = 2.20;
@ISA = qw( Contact );
use strict;

use Carp;
use DB_File;
use Fcntl;
use Data::Dumper;

my %db;

sub import
{
  my ($class, $filename) = @_;
  croak "Usage: use $class '<database>'" unless $filename;
  tie %db, 'DB_File', $filename, O_CREAT|O_RDWR, 0640
    or croak "Unable to open persistent database $filename ($!)";
}

 sub persistent
{
  $SIG{'INT'} = sub { $SIG{'INT'} = 'IGNORE'; exit(0) };
  no strict;
  my ($class, $varname) = @_;
  $varname =~ s/^\$((\w|::)+)$/$1/
    or croak "Invalid persistent variable name: $varname";
  $varname = (caller)[0]."::$varname" unless $varname =~ /::/;
  if (exists $db{$varname})
    { eval $db{$varname} }
  else
    { $db{$varname} = "" }
  return ${$varname};
}

END
{
  no strict;
  foreach my $varname (keys %db)
  {
    $db{$varname} = Data::Dumper->Dump([${$varname}],[$varname]);
  }
  untie %db;
}


1;
```

The persistent method also changes. It no longer needs a second argument specifying the object's storage file, since all objects are stored in the file attached to %db. Instead, it checks whether %db has a meaningful entry for the variable in question and, if so, evals it into existence (recall that eval is Data::Dumper's equivalent to thaw). If the entry for the variable was empty, or nonexistent, persistent sets the entry to an empty string. This ensures that the variable's name is recorded (as a key in %db) so that the END block subsequently knows to save it.

The END block does that saving by iterating through each key of the %db hash. For each key, it uses Data::Dumper to encode the corresponding variable, ${$varname}, then stores it back in the database by assigning it to $db{$varname}. Having updated the database, the END block then closes it by untie-ing %db.

The result is that we can specify persistent contacts like so:

```
package main;

use Contact::Persistent "contacts.db";

# and later...

Contact::Persistent->persistent( '$me' )
    or $me = Contact::Persistent->new(%my_data);

Contact::Persistent::Personal->persistent( '$therapist' );
    or $therapist = Contact::Persistent::Personal->new(%shrink_data);

Contact::Persistent::CIA->persistent( '$agent_x' );
    or $agent_x = Contact::Persistent::CIA->new(%classified_data);
```

and have them all saved in a single database file (i.e., contacts.db).

14.3.3 Coarse-grained persistence for any data

To achieve the last two goals—persistence for objects of any class and preserving interrelationships between persistent objects—we have to isolate the persistence mechanism from class Contact::Persistence and push the serialization scheme back yet another level. In other words, we have to encode all the persistent variables together into a single string. Listing 14.5 illustrates a module, Persistence, that does this.

The Persistence module uses the standard Exporter module to export a single subroutine called persistent. This subroutine takes the place of the Contact::Persistent::persistent method.

The module declares two package variables: a hash (%pers_var), that's used to collect the persistent variables; and a scalar ($storage_file), that records the name of the text file in which their encoded representations will be stored. The Persistence module can use a regular disk file for persistent storage because all the persistent variables will eventually be encoded together into a single string. Since the string can be written to a flat file, we can avoid the complexities and overheads of a full database.

Listing 14.5   A class-independent persistence module

```perl
package Persistence;
$VERSION = 1.00;

require Exporter;
@ISA = qw(Exporter);
@EXPORT = qw( persistent );
use strict;
use Carp;
use Data::Dumper;
$Data::Dumper::Purity = 1;

use vars qw( %pers_var $storage_file );

sub import
{
  my ($class, $file) = @_;
  if (defined $file)
  {
    croak "Storage file specified twice" if defined($storage_file);
    $storage_file = $file;
    do $storage_file;
    $SIG{'INT'} = sub { $SIG{'INT'} = 'IGNORE'; exit(0) };
  }
  $class->export_to_level(1,@_[2..$#_]);
}

sub persistent
{
  no strict 'refs';
  my ($varname) = @_;
  my ($package) = caller;
  my ($type,$symname) = ($varname =~ /^(.)((\w|::)+)$/);
  my $success;
  $symname = "${package}::$symname" unless $symname =~ /::/;
  $varname = "$type$symname";
  if ($type eq '$')
    { ${$symname} = ${$success = $pers_var{$varname}}
      if defined $pers_var{$varname}; }
  elsif ($type =~ /[%@]/)
    { *{$symname} = $success = $pers_var{$varname}
      if defined $pers_var{$varname}; }
  else
    { croak "Can't make $varname persistent" }
  $pers_var{$varname} = undef;
  return $success;
}

END
{
  no strict;
```

```
foreach my $varname (keys %pers_var)
{
   my ($type,$symname) = ($varname =~ /(.)(.*)/);
   if ($type eq '$')   { $pers_var{$varname} = \${$symname} }
   elsif ($type eq '@'){ $pers_var{$varname} = \@{$symname} }
   elsif ($type eq '%'){ $pers_var{$varname} = \%{$symname} }
}

open STORAGE, ">$storage_file"
   and print STORAGE Data::Dumper->Dump([\%pers_var],["*pers_var"])
   and close STORAGE
or die qq{Couldn't save persistent data: $!};
}

1;
```

The import method is defined to catch any call to use Persistence. If the use statement also specifies a file name—use Persistence "persistent.dat"—then the name of the file is stored in $storage_file for later use by the END block. Note that croak-ing if the $storage_file variable is already set ensures that use Persistence can be called only once with a file name, though it may be called any number of times without a file, so as to import the persistent method into various namespaces.

The contents of the storage file are evaluated, using the do $storage_file statement. Once again, we're using Data::Dumper, so eval-ing the contents of the storage file is a tidy and efficient way of reconstructing the persistent data.

The import method next sets up a signal handler to commute any trappable interrupt signal to an exit, thereby ensuring the END block will be invoked. Finally, it calls Exporter::export_to_level, passing any arguments specified after the file name. Calling export_to_level causes the subroutines specified in the @EXPORT array to be exported in the usual manner. We have to do it ourselves because we overrode the normal Exporter::import method (by defining Persistence::import).

The single exported subroutine—Persistence::persistent—replaces Contact::Persistent::persistent from the previous examples. It serves exactly the same purpose, namely, to mark specific variables as housing persistent data, and restore their stored values. However, this version of persistent is a little more general in applicability. It can be passed the name of any package scalar, array, or hash, thereby allowing nonscalars to also be made persistent.

If the variable isn't of one of those types, persistent complains and dies. Otherwise, persistent restores its value, either by direct assignment if it's a scalar or, else, by assigning the corresponding array or hash reference to the appropriate typeglob for the package variable, which is accessed through a symbolic reference: *{$symname}.

You might well ask how %pers_var happened to *have* an appropriate entry containing a reference to the persistent data. The answer is that the END block is going to assign references to each persistent variable to the corresponding entries of %pers_var, then encode %pers_var, and all those variables, into a single string. Thus, the file that import evaluates with its `do $storage_file` command will contain a script for reconstructing `%pers_var` and, with it, the values of all the persistent variables.[6]

Finally, `persistent` assigns an undefined value to the `%pers_vars` entry for the specified variable. This has two important effects: it records the variable's name—as a key—so that the END block knows to save the variable, and it ensures that any future call to `persistent` that specifies the same variable has no effect, since the `"if defined $pers_var{$var-name}"` guarding the typeglob assignment will then fail.

The END block carries out the same functions as the END block in the Contact::Persistent module: it saves the values of the various variables that `persistent` recorded as being persistent. As promised earlier, it uses Data::Dumper (with its purity set to 1 so that complex relationships between the variables being saved are correctly preserved).

The END block iterates through the name of each persistent variable, as specified by the keys of `%pers_var`, and assigns a reference to each variable into the `%pers_var` entry with the corresponding key. The references are generated by taking a symbolic reference to the variable (**`$symname`**), dereferencing it with the appropriate type dereferencer (**`${$symname}`**, **`@{$symname}`**, or **`%{$symname}`**), and taking a reference to the resulting variable (**`\${$sym-name}`**, **`\@{$symname}`**, or **`\%{$symname}`**).

Having aggregated the necessary references into a single variable, the END block opens a file handle, encodes that single variable, and writes its representation to the specified storage file. Because all the persistent variables are encoded simultaneously, Data::Dumper—or either of the other two serialization modules, if we chose to use them instead—is able to detect and preserve their interrelationships in the encoded representation.

Now, we don't need to create a specific Contact::Persistent class. We can use the (non-persistent) Contact class and mark *some* of its objects as persistent:

```
use Contact;
use Persistence "contacts.db";

# and later...

persistent '$me'
    or $me = Contact->new(%my_data);

persistent '$therapist'
    or $therapist = Contact::Personal->new(%shrink_data);

persistent '$agent_x'
    or $agent_x = Contact::CIA->new(%classified_data);
```

Because the Persistence module is now totally decoupled from the Contact class, we can easily make objects of other classes persistent as well:

```
use CD::Music;
use Bit::String;
```

---

[6] It's kind of a *Back to the Future* arrangement. The program can rely on `do $storage_file` to reconstitute the persistent values in `%pers_var` because, *in a previous existence,* the program's END block already put those persistent values into `%pers_var` and then saved that hash to the storage file.

```
persistent '$bach'
    or $bach = CD::Music->new(@eine_kleine_Bach_data);

persistent '$isprime'
    or $isprime = Bit::String->new(primes(1..1000000);
```

or even confer immortality on common unblessed values:

```
persistent '$name'
    or $name = "Damian";

persistent '%corrections'
    or %corrections ={
                        "recieved"         => "received",
                        "wierdness"        => "weirdness",
                        "undocumented bug" => "retro-feature",
                     };
```

14.3.4 Assessing the technique

The mechanism implemented by the Persistence module meets the needs of many applications requiring persistent data. The persistence conferred on package variables is automatic: once a variable is marked persistent, its value is automatically saved and restored every time the program is run without the need for any further user intervention. The persistence is also orthogonal: it can be applied to any class or built-in data type that the Data::Dumper serialization module can encode.

Orthogonality also works in the other direction. The internal serialization mechanism that Persistence uses can be changed to Storable or FreezeThaw without affecting the syntax or behavior of any program using the Persistence module. Likewise, the storage mechanism can be changed from a flat file to a database, without any impact on client code.

In fact, the Persistence module could easily be made generic, so that a serialization module and a storage mechanism would each be specified when the Persistence module is imported.

14.4 *FINE-GRAINED PERSISTENCE*

The fundamentals of fine-grained persistence—identity, encoding, storage, and coordination—are almost exactly the same as in the coarse-grained persistence techniques described so far. The difference is that the external representation of each persistent object has to be updated every time the object's data changes.

In general such updates are difficult to achieve without some assistance from the objects themselves, since there are no built-in mechanisms in Perl to detect assignments to nested arrays or hashes. (Although it *is* possible to detect assignments to unnested data structures by tie-ing them.)

This section illustrates several approaches to fine-grained persistence. All of them require cooperation on the part of the objects being made to persist; none are as automatic or orthogonal as the final coarse-grained technique described above.

14.4.1 Disk files as objects

The simplest way to ensure that an object's internal and external representations are always synchronized is to make those representations one and the same. In other words, use the external representation as the internal representation.

Listing 14.6 shows a Bit::String::FinelyPersistent class, derived from the Bit::String class shown in chapter 4. Bit::String::FinelyPersistent objects act just like Bit::String objects, except they also provide fine-grained persistence.

Listing 14.6   A persistent Bit::String subclass

```
use Bit::String;

package Bit::String::FinelyPersistent;
@ISA = qw( Bit::String );
$VERSION = 1.00;
use strict;

use Carp;
use Symbol;
use Fcntl;

sub new
{
    my ($class, $file, $size) = splice(@_,0,3);
    my $filehandle = gensym;
    sysopen($filehandle, $file, O_RDWR|O_CREAT)
        || croak "Can't open persistence file: $file";
    my $init_string = join('',map({$_?'1':'0'} @_)).'0'x($size-@_);
    syswrite($filehandle, $init_string, $size)
        || croak "Can't initialize persistence file: $file"
            unless -s $filehandle;
    bless $filehandle, $class;
}

sub get
{
    my ($self,$bitnum) = @_;
    return undef if $bitnum >= $self->bitcount();
    my $bit;
    sysseek($self, $bitnum, 0)
        && sysread($self, $bit, 1)
        || croak "Couldn't read bit $bitnum";
    return $bit;
}

sub set
{
    my ($self,$bitnum,$newval) = @_;
    return undef if $bitnum >= $self->bitcount();
    sysseek($self, $bitnum, 0)
        && syswrite($self, ($newval?"1":"0"), 1)
```

```
          || croak "Couldn't write bit $bitnum";
}

sub complement
{
  my ($self) = @_;
  my $bits;
  sysseek($self, 0, 0)
   && sysread($self, $bits, $self->bitcount())
    || croak "Couldn't read bits to create complement";
  return Bit::String->new(split(//,$bits))->complement();
}

sub bitcount
{
  my ($self) = @_;
  return -s $self;
}

1;
```

Bit-strings are ideal candidates for implementing fine-grained persistence. They have an extremely simple internal structure which makes them easy to represent externally and simple access methods, which are easily modified to ensure synchronization of internal and external representations.

More importantly, though, there are good reasons for *wanting* to make bit-strings persistent. One common use of a bit-string is to house a collection of flags, such as a set of program options, a file creation permissions mask, or a lookup table indicating which elements of some other array have a certain property such as "primality" or "validity" or "readiness." Such data often needs to be preserved between executions of a program, either because the user expects the information to be "sticky" or because the data was expensive to compute.

The Bit::String::FinelyPersistent class works by blessing a filehandle, or rather the type-glob containing it. That filehandle is attached to a disk file. The disk file provides storage for the actual bit-string. Thus, bits are never stored internally. Accesses to individual bits of the bit-string are actually reads on the disk file, while changes to bits are writes. The technique is essentially the same as the one used to implement the Genome::Array class in chapter 9, though the Bit::String::FinelyPersistent class has a much simpler interface.

To make it all work, the module redefines the constructor, get, and set accessors, and the complement and bitcount methods defined in Bit::String. In fact, only the print method is actually inherited unscathed. Thus, the use of inheritance here is more symbolic—of the common purpose of the two classes—than functional.

Nevertheless, the Bit::String::FinelyPersistent class illustrates a major advantage of inheritance. Although it provides exactly the same features and interface as its parent class, internally the two classes have almost nothing in common. Whereas the Bit::String class implements each of its objects as a pack'ed character string, Bit::String::FinelyPersistent objects are actually blessed filehandles, connected to a disk file storing the bits as individual "1" or "0" characters.

The advantage is that clients of the class don't have to worry, or even know, about those internal differences, and can easily add or remove persistence to bit-strings with minimal changes to the code that uses them.

The constructor takes two arguments, specifying the name of the disk file to be used and the size of the bit-string to be created (and, hence, the size of the storage file itself). Any additional arguments are treated as true/false initialization values just as in the Bit::String class.

The constructor first creates an anonymous typeglob using the `Symbol::gensym` subroutine and stores a reference to it in `$filehandle`—since it's the filehandle within the typeglob that we're actually interested in. The typeglob will eventually be blessed as the new Bit::String::FinelyPersistent object. The constructor then opens the specified file for both read and write access (`O_RDWR`), creating it if necessary (`O_CREAT`).

Next, the constructor checks the length of the newly opened file (`-s $filehandle`) to see if it already existed. If it was just created, the file's size will be zero, so `-s $filehandle` will return false. In that case, the constructor writes the initialization values to the file, by first mapping them to a list of 1's and 0's (**map({$_?'1':'0'} @_)**), concatenating the list (**join('',map({$_?'1':'0'} @_)**), then appending enough additional zeroes (`join(map({$_?'1':'0'} @_).`**'0'x($size-@_)**) to pad the resulting string to the requested size.

Finally, the typeglob containing the filehandle is blessed into the class and returned as the new Bit::String::Persistent object.

The accessor methods, `get` and `set`, use that filehandle—their invoking object—to access the file character that corresponds to the bit they are requested to access. Both accessors first check whether the requested bit (`$bitnum`) is in the range stored in the file. If it is not, they immediately return `undef` to indicate an out-of-range error. Otherwise, they seek to the specified character in the file. Recall that each character represents a single bit, so seeking to the position `$bitnum` takes the filehandle to the correct point in the file. Having reached the appropriate point in the file, the `get` accessor simply reads a single character, thereby retrieving the requested bit. The `set` accessor, on the other hand, writes a single character—either "1" or "0", depending on the truth-status of the value it is given—thereby storing the requested bit.

The constructor and accessors all use `syswrite`, `sysread`, and `sysseek`, rather than the more commonly used `print`, `read`, and `seek`. Apart from their greater efficiency, these sys... functions bypass the normal buffering of Perl I/O, which ensures that the file is updated immediately and minimizes the chance that an ill-timed signal will cause data to be lost.

The `complement` method cheats a little.[7] It extracts all the bits from the file by seeking to the start and reading `$self->bitcount()` characters. It splits the resulting string into an array of individual bits (**split //,$bits**)) and builds a new (nonpersistent) Bit::String object containing those bits (**Bit::String->new**(split(//,$bits)**)). Then, it returns the complement of that Bit::String object (`Bit::String->new(split(//,$bits))->`**complement()**).

---

[7] Or if you prefer: "...reuses existing superclass functionality in a polymophic manner, in the best traditions of object orientation."

Lastly, the implementation of the `bitcount` method is extremely simple. Since Bit::String::FinelyPersistent bit-strings are stored as one file character per bit, `bitcount` just returns the length of the file to which its filehandle is attached: `-s $self`.

14.4.2 Memory-mapped files as objects

If your operating system supports memory mapping—via the `mmap` system call—the Bit::String::FinelyPersistent class can be made even simpler, and far more efficient. Memory mapping is a technique through which the memory required by a scalar variable is provided not from the program's internal address space, but, instead, a disk file.

In other words, memory mapping is an automation of the file reading and writing technique shown in the previous section. It's also an optimization of the previous technique, since memory-mapped access to a file is typically two to five times faster that standard reads and writes, depending on your system's architecture.

Perl supports memory mapping on systems that provide it—via Malcolm Beattie's Mmap module. Listing 14.7 uses that module to reimplement Bit::String::FinelyPersistent using memory mapping. Compared to the version in listing 14.6, its constructor is marginally more complex, but its other methods are much simpler.

Listing 14.7   A persistent memory-mapped Bit::String subclass

```
use Bit::String;

package Bit::String::FinelyPersistent;
@ISA = qw( Bit::String );
$VERSION = 2.00;
use strict;

use Carp;
use Mmap;

sub new
{
   my ($class, $file, $size) = splice(@_,0,3);
   my $filehandle = gensym;
   sysopen($filehandle, $file, O_RDWR|O_CREAT)
      || croak "Can't open persistence file: $file";
   my $init_string = join('',map({$_?'1':'0'} @_)).'0'x($size-@_);
   syswrite($filehandle, $init_string, $size)
      || croak "Can't initialize persistence file: $file"
         unless -s $filehandle;
   my $str;
   mmap($str, $size, PROT_READ|PROT_WRITE, MAP_SHARED, $filehandle)
      || croak "Can't map object to file: $file";
   bless \$str, ref($class)||$class;
}

sub get
{
   my ($self,$bitnum) = @_;
```

```
    return undef if $bitnum >= $self->bitcount();
    return substr($$self, $bitnum, 1);
}

sub set
{
    my ($self,$bitnum,$newval) = @_;
    return undef if $bitnum >= $self->bitcount();
    substr($$self, $bitnum, 1) = $newval?"1":"0";
}

sub complement
{
    my ($self) = @_;
    return Bit::String->new(split(//,$$self))->complement();
}

sub bitcount
{
    my ($self) = @_;
    return length($$self);
}

1;
```

The constructor is essentially the same as before, except it no longer blesses the anonymous typeglob that stores the filehandle. Instead, it memory maps the filehandle onto the variable $str, using the mmap subroutine supplied by the Mmap module. The arguments to mmap are:

- $str: the scalar variable to which the file is to be memory mapped, in this case, a lexical variable,
- $size: the number of bytes of the file that are to be mapped to the object, in this case, all of them,
- PROT_READ|PROT_WRITE: a set of access flags, in this case, both read and write access are permitted. The constants are exported by the Mmap module,
- MAP_SHARED: a flag indicating how paging of the mapped file should be handled. See the mmap(2) documentation on your local system for intimate details on this—or else just ignore it, like the rest of us do,
- $filehandle: a reference to the typeglob containing the filehandle for the file to be mapped, in this case, a handle for the file we just opened and initialized.

The effect of the call to mmap is to make the scalar variable $str use the file as its memory for any string it might hold. Any assignment to that string—or into it, via substr—is written straight to the file. The data returned by any read access is read directly from it. Having set up $str this way, the constructor blesses it into the class and returns a reference to it.

The accessor methods, get and set, can now be greatly simplified. Because the blessed string ($$self) uses the same memory as the file, we can access the file character at position

`$bitnum` by accessing the single character at that position in `$$self`—that is, `sub-str($$self,$bitnum,1)`. The `get` method returns the result of this expression, while `set` assigns to it. The Mmap module takes care of the (notional) reading, writing, and seeking required to synchronize `$$self`'s internal representation with the memory mapped disk file.

The `complement` method is also greatly simplified. To access the complete set of bits for the bit-string, we can use the value of the entire memory-mapped string—that is, `$$self`—directly. As before, this is split, fed to `Bit::String::new`, and the resulting object complemented. Similarly, the `bitcount` method simply returns the length of the complete memory-mapped string.

14.4.3 Tied databases as objects

Yet another approach to implementing fine-grained persistence is to attach the internal representation of an object to an external file by `tie`-ing a hash to a database. The technique is similar to the coarse-grained persistence mechanism illustrated by listing 14.2. The only difference is that, now, instead of only `tie`-ing a hash at either end of an object's existence, in `persistent` and the END block, we keep the tied hash around and use *it* as the object.

The move from accessing database records only at the program boundaries to accessing them throughout the program simplifies the structure of the persistent class considerably. Listing 14.8 shows the class Contact::FinelyPersistent. Note how much cleaner it is than the equivalent coarse-grained Contact::Persistent subclass in listing 14.2.

Once again, we have a triumph for inheritance: Contact::FinelyPersistent has only to redefine its constructor before reusing all of the accessor methods (`get_name`, `set_phone`, `print`, etc.) that it inherits from Contact. This is because the new constructor takes the hash that will become the new Contact::FinelyPersistent object and ties it directly to an external file. Thereafter, any modifications to the object's values will be automatically propagated back to the file.

There is no need for a `persistent` method because, as the class name suggests, every Contact::FinelyPersistent object is automatically persistent and doesn't need to be explicitly marked as such. There is no need for an END block either because every operation on a Contact::FinelyPersistent object automatically saves the object back to its persistence file. So, at the end of the program every object will already be synchronized with its external representation.

The Contact::FinelyPersistent class uses Gurusamy Sarathy's MLDBM module to access each object's database, rather than DB_File, or SDBM_File, etc. "MLDBM" stands for "Multi-Level Database Module." The module allows nested hashes and arrays to be stored in a simple key/value database.[8]

It manages this impressive feat by interposing an encoding/decoding layer—normally Data::Dumper, but you can specify FreezeThaw or Storable instead—between the tied hash and an underlying database module—SDBM_File by default, but that too is configurable. Each tied MLDBM hash is implemented internally by a real hash with two entries:

---

[8] The MLDBM module itself makes excellent use of many object-oriented techniques described in earlier chapters: interface polymorphism, inheritance, delegation, attribute accessors, aggregation, tie-ing, generic methods, and abstract methods. The source code is definitely worth studying.

Listing 14.8   A Contact subclass with fine-grained persistence

```perl
use Contact;

package Contact::FinelyPersistent;
$VERSION = 1.00;
@ISA = qw ( Contact );
use strict;

use MLDBM;
use Fcntl;
use Carp;

sub new
{
  my ($class, $file, %init) = @_;
  my $already_exists = -s "$file.pag";
  my %hash;
  tie %hash, 'MLDBM', $file, O_RDWR|O_CREAT, 0640
    or croak "Unable to connect to persistence file: $file ($!)";
  unless ($already_exists)
  {
    %hash = (
              name  => $init{name},
              phone => $init{phone},
              fax   => $init{fax},
              email => $init{email},
            );
  }
  bless \%hash, ref($class)||$class;
}

1;
```

- "SR", which stores a reference to a special serialization object. It is the serialize and deserialize methods of this object that are called to encode or decode data whenever MLDBM::STORE or MLDBM::FETCH are invoked.
- "DB", which stores a reference to *another* tied hash, which is tied to the standard SDBM_File database access module.

Figure 14.1 illustrates the arrangement.

Contact::FinelyPersistent uses DB_File as MLDBM's underlying database and Freeze-Thaw as its encoding module, specifying them as extra parameters when MLDBM is imported.[9] The constructor creates a lexical hash (%hash) and uses MLDBM to tie it to the database specified by the $file argument. If the database did not previously exist—that is if the size of its .pag file was zero before the tie—it is initialized by assigning the relevant entries from %init to %hash. These initialization values can be scalars, array references, or hash references since

---

[9] These modules were chosen instead of the defaults because they have much better performance .

```
%hash
```

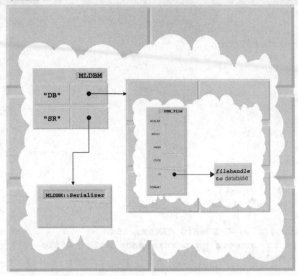

Figure 14.1   The structure of an MLDBM-tied hash

MLDBM automatically serializes them when they are assigned and will decode them again when they are next accessed.

Having connected the new Contact::FinelyPersistent object to its database and initialized it, all that remains is to bless the hash into the class and return a reference to it. Thereafter, the object looks and acts just like a blessed hash, except that each modification to it is immediately and automatically encoded (by FreezeThaw) and stored (by DB_File) in the specified database. That's why the other methods inherited from Contact work just as well for Contact::FinelyPersistent objects. For example, the `Contact::set_phone` method

```
sub set_phone { $_[0]->{phone} = $_[1] }
```

assigns to the phone entry of the tied hash, which causes MLDBM to encode the new value and pass it to DB_File, which stores it directly into the object's database. Then, when the `Contact::get_phone` method

```
sub get_phone { $_[0]->{phone} }
```

is next called, it requests the value of the phone entry from the tied hash, which causes DB_File to retrieve the corresponding value from the database and pass it to MLDBM, which decodes it.

This is all very convenient for a simple case like the Contact class, but, in general, the methods of classes based on MLDBM databases must be carefully designed if they are to access subentries of a tied hash. For example, if the phone entry for a Contact::FinelyPersistent object is a reference to an array of strings

```
$me->set_phone( ["555-6787", "1800-AUTHOR"] );
```

and we wish to add a method (`set_phone_i`), to replace a given phone number in that array, we have to write it like this:

```
sub Contact::FinelyPersistent::set_phone_i
{
   my ($self, $i, $newval) = @_;  # get args
   my $temp = $self->{phone};     # create temporary phone data
   $temp->[$i] = $newval;         # update temporary phone data
   $self->{phone} = $temp;        # update original phone data
}
```

rather than the more obvious:

```
sub Contact::FinelyPersistent::set_phone_i
{
   my ($self, $i, $newval) = @_;     # get args
   $self->{phone}->[$i] = $newval;   # try to update original data directly
}
```

The problem is that Perl's tied hashes don't support modifications to nested subentries. The expression $self->{phone} returns a copy of the data in that entry (that is, a copy of the phone list), so assigning $newval directly to $self->{phone}->[$i] (in the second version) puts the new value into the $i-th element of the copy, not into the original. In contrast, the first version (with $temp) works correctly because it explicitly captures the copy returned by $self->{phone}, assigns into it, and writes the complete updated copy back to the original entry in the database.

14.4.4 Fine-grained persistence for any class

Just as we generalized the coarse-grained Contact::Persistent class to create the Persistence module, we can abstract any of the mechanisms used to implement Contact::FinelyPersistent to create a FinePersistence module.

Listing 14.9 shows such a module. Unfortunately, although the fine-grained persistence it confers *is* orthogonal and can be applied to objects of any suitable class, it's *not* completely automatic because it requires a small amount of cooperation by the inheriting class, as described below.

Listing 14.9 A module for conferring fine-grained persistence on any class

```
package FinePersistence;
$VERSION = 1.00;

require Exporter;
@ISA = qw(Exporter);
@EXPORT = qw(persistent changes);
use strict;
use Carp;

use vars qw( %pers_var $storage_file);

sub import
{
   my ($class, $file) = @_;
   if (defined $file)
```

```perl
    {
        croak "Storage file specified twice" if defined($storage_file);
        $storage_file = $file;
        do $storage_file;
        $SIG{'INT'} = sub { $SIG{'INT'} = 'IGNORE'; exit(0) };
    }
    $class->export_to_level(1,@_[2..$#_]);
}

sub persistent
{
    no strict;
    my ($varname) = @_;
    my ($package) = caller;
    my $success = 0;
    my ($type,$symname) = ($varname =~ /^(.)((\w|::)+)$/);
    $symname = "${package}::$symname" unless $symname =~ /::/;
    $varname = "$type$symname";
    if ($type eq '$')
        { *{$symname} = $success = $pers_var{$varname}
            if defined $pers_var{$varname} }
    else
        { croak "Can't make $varname finely persistent" }
    $pers_var{$varname} = undef;
    return $success;
}

sub changes { $_[0] = FinePersistence::Updater->new() }

package FinePersistence::Updater;
use Data::Dumper;
$Data::Dumper::Purity = 1;

sub new { bless {}, ref($_[0])||$_[0] }

sub DESTROY
{
    foreach my $varname (keys %FinePersistence::pers_var)
    {
        no strict;
        my $symname = substr($varname,1);
        $FinePersistence::pers_var{$varname} = \${$symname};
    }

    open STORAGE, ">$FinePersistence::storage_file"
        and print STORAGE Data::Dumper->Dump([\%FinePersistence::pers_var],
                                             ["*pers_var"])
        and close STORAGE
    or die qq{Couldn't save persistent data: $!};
}

1;
```

The initial sections of the FinePersistence module are identical to the (coarse-grained) Persistence module. Once again, the lexical %pers_var is used to collect all persistent variables, and the import method restores them when the module is first use-d. The persistent subroutine marks objects as persisting and reinstates their stored values from %per_var. The subroutine's implementation is *almost* the same as in figure 14.5, except that this version is restricted to operating on scalars. This change is necessary because FinePersistence only works for blessed objects, and scalars are the only type of variable that can directly store an object reference.[10]

Not surprisingly then, marking package variables as holding persistent objects is done just as it was with the Persistence module:

```
package main;

use FinePersistence "persistence_file";

# create Contact subclass called Contact::FinelyPersistent
# (see below)

persistent '$me'
   or $me = Contact::FinelyPersistent->new(@mydata);

persistent '$Spouse::unit'
   or $me = Contact::FinelyPersistent->new(@herdata);

persistent '$Secret::agent_x'
   or $me = Contact::FinelyPersistent->new(@we_could_tell_you,
                                           @but_then_we'd_have_to_kill_you);
```

The differences between the Persistence module and FinePersistence have to do with the way each goes about storing the persistent data it controls. The Persistence module uses a single END block to collect, encode, and store the values of persistent variables. FinePersistence uses objects of a special *helper class*, FinePersistence::Updater, to control these tasks.

The FinePersistence::changes subroutine is exported to assist in the creation of these *helper objects*. It takes a single scalar argument, to which it assigns a reference to a new FinePersistence::Updater object. Because $_[0] aliases the corresponding argument passed to changes, assigning the reference directly to $_[0] actually assigns it to the original argument variable. The reason for this slightly unusual approach—assigning to an argument rather than just returning the reference directly—is aesthetic and will become apparent in a moment.

The constructor of the FinePersistence::Updater class blesses an empty hash and returns a reference to it. It could equally well bless an empty array or scalar because we don't care about the contents of FinePersistence::Updater objects, only their lifetimes.

In fact, the FinePersistence::Updater class really exists only to provide its objects with a destructor. That destructor acts just like the END block of the Persistence module, collecting references to persistent variables (in %pers_var), encoding them together (with Data::Dump-

---

[10] Of course, an array element and a hash entry can also store a reference, but individually they are both really scalars. The version of FinePersistence shown in figure 14.9 doesn't allow such embedded scalars to be made persistent, though it wouldn't be difficult to add that capacity.

er), and storing them in the specified file, overwriting it each time. Consequently, every time a FinePersistence::Updater object ceases to exist, the complete set of persistent variables is collected, encoded, and stored.

The postmortem behavior of these helper objects is the key to the fine-grained persistence that FinePersistence confers on classes that use it. For example, Listing 14.10 shows how to add fine-grained persistence to the Contact and Bit::String classes.

Creating persistent versions of these classes is easy. We simply create a new subclass and redefine any method that changes the value of an object. Methods that *don't* change the object can be inherited as-is, since the persistence mechanism can safely ignore them. The redefined methods are all structurally identical, consisting of a call to `changes`, followed by an invocation of the inherited method.

The call to `changes` creates a helper object (a FinePersistence::Updater) and assigns a reference to it to the lexical variable `$value`.[11] When `$value` ceases to exist at the end of the method, the helper object's destructor is called, which causes all persistent variables to be resaved. This ensures that the external representations of all persistent objects are updated *after* any of their value-changing methods is invoked.

At first glance, this appears wasteful, since the FinePersistence::Updater destructor resaves all persistent objects every time any of them changes. It certainly is more expensive than updating only the individual object that changes, but global updating is also essential in the general case. That's because the only way that the serialization module can preserve the interrelationships within a group of objects is to encode the entire group at the same time. Since we have no way of knowing how the objects that FinePersistence controls interrelate, we have to play it safe and re-encode everything each time anything changes.

After all, the change might easily involve assigning a reference to one persistent object in an attribute to another, perhaps as part of a persistent binary search tree. If that assignment replaced a previously-stored reference to another persistent object, the relationships between three objects have altered, and all three must be reserialized to preserve that change.

14.4.5 Easier persistence through genericity

Because the structure of every redefined method is identical in any derived class that uses the FinePersistence module, we have a good opportunity to apply some genericity. For example, FinePersistence might provide an additional exported function, perhaps `save_after`, like this:

```
package FinePersistence;
@EXPORT = qw(persistent changes save_after);

# etc. as before...

my $generic_method =
q{
   package %s;
```

---

[11] This usage explains why `changes` assigns to its first argument—because that allows us to poetically declare that a method: `changes my $value`.

```perl
use Contact;

package Contact::FinelyPersistent;
$VERSION = 2.00;
@ISA = qw( Contact );
use strict;

use FinePersistence;

sub set_phone
{
  changes my $value;
  my ($self, @args) = @_;
  $self->SUPER::set_phone(@args);
}


sub set_fax
{
  changes my $value;
  my ($self, @args) = @_;
  $self->SUPER::set_fax(@args);
}


sub set_email
{
  changes my $value;
  my ($self, @args) = @_;
  $self->SUPER::set_email(@args);
}



use Bit::String;

package Bit::String::FinelyPersistent;
$VERSION = 2.00;
@ISA = qw( Bit::String );
use strict;

use FinePersistence;

sub set
{
  changes my $value;
  my ($self, @args) = @_;
  $self->SUPER::set(@args);
}
```

```
    sub %s
    {
        changes my $value;
        my ($self, @args) = @_;
        $self->SUPER::%s(@args);
    }
};

sub save_after
{
    my ($owner) = caller;
    foreach my $method_name ( @_ )
    {
        croak "No such method was inherited: $method_name"
            unless $owner->can($method_name);
        eval sprintf($generic_method, $owner, $method_name, $method_name);
    }
}
```

The `save_after` function determines the name of the package ($owner) from which it was called and steps through its arguments, checking that each is a valid method name for the $owner class, via a call to the standard `can` method. It then interpolates each valid method name into a generic subroutine template, stored in $generic_method, using `sprintf`. Finally, `save_after` evaluates this interpolated string to define each new method.

The result is that `save_after` takes a list of inherited method names and, for each, builds the standard redefined method required by FinePersistence. The creation of the persistent versions of Contact and Bit::String is now trivial:

```
package Contact::FinelyPersistent;
$VERSION = 3.00;
@ISA = qw( Contact );
use FinePersistence;
save_after qw( set_phone set_fax set_email );

package Bit::String::FinelyPersistent;
$VERSION = 3.00;
@ISA = qw( Bit::String );
use FinePersistence;
save_after qw( set );
```

Of course, given that these two simplified class definitions are now also structurally identical, we can repeat the trick at the next level up and define an exported `define_persistent` subroutine:

```
package FinePersistence;
@EXPORT = qw(persistent changes save_after define_persistent);

# etc. as before...

my $generic_subclass =
q{
    package %s::FinelyPersistent;
    @%s::FinelyPersistent::ISA = qw( %s );
```

```
    use FinePersistence;
    save_after qw( %s );
};

sub define_persistent
{
  my $owner = shift;
  my $save_afters =  join(" ",@_);
  eval sprintf($generic_subclass, $owner, $owner, $owner, $save_afters);
}
```

Then we can reduce the two class definitions to:

```
use FinePersistence;

define_persistent 'Contact' => qw( set_phone set_fax set_email );
define_persistent 'Bit::String'=> qw( set );
```

14.4.6 Assessing the technique

Fine-grained persistence for specific classes can be most easily provided by attaching each persistent object to a separate file, either by a filehandle, memory mapping, or tie-ing a hash to a database. The accessors of the persistent class have to be specifically coded to ensure that data is correctly "written through" to the file whenever it changes. Nested data structures within such special-purpose objects also present difficulties because of the limitations of Perl's `tie` mechanism.

Generalizing fine-grained persistence to any class is also possible, but, again, it requires special coding for some accessors. Therefore, fine-grained persistence cannot be applied directly to a preexisting class, but requires the definition of a special derived class with suitably redefined accessors. Fortunately, every such derived class is structurally similar, which allows us to use generic techniques to minimize the effort required.

As with coarse-grained persistence techniques, the identity of an object is either imposed by the name of its individual storage file—as passed to its constructor—or the name of the package variable that stores it—as passed to `persistent`.

On balance, unless your application specifically needs the extra robustness of fine-grained persistence, you're almost certainly better off just using the non-intrusive generalized coarse-grained persistence technique described earlier.

14.5 WHERE TO FIND OUT MORE

Several simple database access modules (DB_File, GDBM_File, NDBM_File, and SDBM_File) come with the standard Perl distribution. The serialization modules Data::Dumper, FreezeThaw, and Storable are all available from the CPAN, as are the relational database access modules (DBI, DBD::Oracle, DBD::Sybase, etc.) There's also a home page for the DBI module: http://www.symbolstone.org/technology/perl/DBI/.

The CPAN has several database solutions to persistent objects. For example, Paul Sharpe's excellent DbFramework classes (found in the directory http://www.perl.com/CPAN/authors/id/PSHARPE/) includes a DbFramework::Persistent module. More recently, Jean-Louis

Leroy's Tangram module, available from http://www.perl.com/CPAN/authors/id/J/JL/JLLE-ROY/, provides a declarative approach to specifying persistent classes.

The *Perl Cookbook* has recipes for serialization, database access, and simple persistence. *Advanced Perl Programming* also discusses these issues, and explores another approach to object-oriented persistence.

14.6 SUMMARY

- Persistent systems enable the contents of variables to be automatically preserved between executions of a program. Such systems require components to identify, encode, store, retrieve, decode, and reinstate data. They also require mechanisms to coordinate these activities.
- In Perl, the easiest way to identify a package variable is by its fully qualified name. Alternatively, the keys of a special hash can be used to provide unique identifiers for their corresponding values.
- The CPAN provides several modules to automate the encoding and decoding of arbitrary hierarchical data structures. The main constraint is that objects with nested cross-references must be encoded simultaneously, to allow the modules to detect and preserve referential interrelationships.
- Once encoded, persistent data may be stored in flat files or databases.
- Coarse-grained persistence only restores and saves the state of persistent variables at the start and end of a program's execution. This form of persistence can be fully automated, but may result in data loss if the program terminates unexpectedly.
- Fine-grained persistence restores the state of persistent variables at the start of a program, and saves their state every time it changes. Compared to coarse-grained techniques, this approach is less susceptible to data loss, but cannot be as easily automated.

APPENDIX A

Quick reference guide

This appendix summarizes the important concepts and syntax of object-oriented Perl.

Table A.1   Classes and objects (Chapters 3 to 5)

Concept	Syntax
A class is a package.	```package Class::Name;``` ```use strict;```

An object method is a subroutine in the class package that expects an object reference as its first argument.	```sub method_name```
	```{```
	``` my ($self, @other_args) = @_;```
	``` # whatever```
	```}```

A class method is a subroutine in the class package that expects a class name as its first argument.	```sub class_method_name```
	```{```
	``` my ($class, @other_args) = @_;```
	``` # whatever```
	```}```

A constructor is a subroutine in a package (i.e., a method in the class). It uses the bless function to mark a datatype (usually a hash) as an object.	```sub new```
	```{```
	``` my ($class, @args) = @_;```
	``` my $self = bless {}, ref($class) || $class;```
	``` # initialize object here```
	``` return $self;```
	```}```

Objects can also be based on anonymous arrays	```my $self = bless [], $class;```

Table A.1 Classes and objects (Chapters 3 to 5) (continued)

Concept	Syntax
| or scalars (usually lexicals) | ```perl
my $implementation;
$self = bless \$implementation, $class;
``` |
| or typeglobs | ```perl
use Symbol;
my $self = bless gensym(), $class;
``` |
| or precompiled regular expressions | ```perl
my ($class, $pattern) = @_;
my $self = bless qr/$pattern/, $class;
``` |
| or subroutines. | ```perl
my $implementation = sub {
  #whatever
};
my $self = bless $implementation, $class;
``` |
| Object attributes are usually accessed via a method called an accessor. Typically, a single accessor is used to both get and set each attribute. | ```perl
sub attribute_name
{
  my ($self, $newval) = @_;
  $self->{attribute_name} = $newval if @_ > 1;
  return $self->{attribute_name};
}
``` |
| Class attributes are usually implemented by a lexical within the class package. Accessors are declared in the same namespace. The accessors are visible outside the declaration block; the lexical itself is not. | ```perl
{
  my $_class_attribute_name = $init;
  sub class_attribute_name
  {
    my ($class, $newval) = @_;
    $_class_attribute_name = $newval if @_ > 1;
    return $_class_attribute_name;
  }
}
``` |
| A destructor is a method with the special name DESTROY. It is called automatically when an object's reference count reaches zero. | ```perl
sub DESTROY
{
  my ($self) = @_;
  # any object clean-up here
}
``` |
| An object is normally created by calling a class's constructor. | ```perl
my $obj_ref = Class::Name->new(@init_args);
``` |
| All methods are called using the "arrow" notation. | ```perl
$obj_ref->method_name($arg1, $arg2, $etc);

my $val = $obj_ref->attribute_name(); # get
$obj_ref->attribute_name($new_value); # set
``` |
```

Table A.2 Inheritance and polymorphism (Chapters 6 and 7)

Concept	Syntax
A derived class is a package whose @ISA array lists its parent classes.	```package DerivedClass::Name;``` ```@ISA = qw(Parent1 Parent2 Etc);```

Derived classes may not need their own constructor if the one they inherit is sufficient (it must use the two-argument form of bless). Otherwise, they may define a constructor that delegates object creation to their ancestor (using the SUPER pseudo-class).	```sub DerivedClass::Name::new```
	 ```{```
	 ``` my ($class, @args) = @_;```
	 ``` my $self = $class->SUPER::new(@args);```
	 ``` # initialize derived bits of object here```
	 ``` return $self;```
	 ```}```

Every method in Perl is polymorphic and may be overridden in any derived class.	```package Even::More::DerivedClass::Name;```
	 ```@ISA = qw(DerivedClass::Name);```
	
	 ```sub inherited_method_name```
	 ```{```
	 ``` # whatever```
	 ```}```

When a method is called on a derived-class object, if it's not found in the derived class, the ancestral classes are searched depth-first, left-to-right; then the UNIVERSAL class; then the search repeats, looking for an AUTOLOAD subroutine instead.	```sub AUTOLOAD```
	 ```{```
	 ``` my ($self, @args) = @_;```
	 ``` my ($methodname) = $AUTOLOAD=~/.*::(\w+)$/;```
	 ``` # build or simulate missing method```
	 ```}```

Table A.3 Automated class creation (Chapter 8)

Concept	Syntax

The standard Class::Struct module creates a constructor and attribute accessors for the named hash-based class. Attributes can be scalars, arrays, hashes, or other objects.	```use Class::Struct;```
	
	 ```struct Class::Name =>```
	 ```{```
	 ``` attr1 => '$', # scalar attribute```
	 ``` attr2 => '@', # array attribute```
	 ``` attr3 => '%', # hash attribute```
	 ``` attr4 => 'Type', # object attribute```
	 ```};```

The module can also implement named array-based classes.	```struct Class::Name =>```
	 ```[```
	 ``` attr1 => '$', # scalar attribute```
	 ``` attr2 => '@', # array attribute```
	 ``` attr3 => '%', # hash attribute```
	 ``` attr4 => 'Type', # object attribute```
	 ```];```

Table A.3   Automated class creation (Chapter 8) (continued)

Concept	Syntax

Alternatively, it can provide accessors to the current class.
If attribute types are specified with a leading *, they are returned by reference instead of by value. (This feature is independent of the array or hash basis of the class.)
	```package Class::Name;```
	```use Class::Struct;```
	
	```struct```
	```(```
	``` attr1 => '*$', # scalar reference attribute```
	``` attr2 => '*@', # array reference attribute```
	``` attr3 => '*%', # hash reference attribute```
	```);```

The Class::MethodMaker module always installs methods into the current class.
Constructors can be specified that take no arguments, or named arguments, or may be made to call a user-defined init method.
	```package Class::Name;```
	
	```use Class::MethodMaker```
	``` new => 'create_empty',```
	``` new_hash_init => 'create_with_args',```
	``` new_with_init => 'create_and_call_init';```

Attributes can be scalars, grouped scalars, flags, keys, lists, or hashes.
Attributes can be specified singly (using a string) or several at a time (using a reference to an array of strings).
	```use Class::MethodMaker```
	``` get_set => 'name',```
	``` grouped_fields => [name => [qw(first last)]],```
	``` boolean => [qw(flag1 flag2 flag3)],```
	``` key_attrib => 'id_number',```
	``` struct => [qw(name rank serial_num)],```
	``` list => [qw(names dates)],```
	``` hash => 'found';```

Attributes can also be nested objects.	```use Class::MethodMaker``` ``` object => [OtherType => 'obj_attr'];```

Classes can delegate methods to the methods of their object attributes.	```use Class::MethodMaker```
	``` object => [OtherType => { slot => 'obj_attr',```
	``` forward => 'method'}```
	```];```

Hash-like class attributes can also be declared.	```use Class::MethodMaker``` ``` static_hash => 'shared_data';```

Attributes that are subroutines or special per-object methods can be created.	```use Class::MethodMaker```
	``` code => 'iterator_function',```
	``` method => 'print_me';```

Passing a subroutine reference to the accessor replaces the attribute.	```$obj->iterator_function(sub {each %somehash});``` ```$obj->print_me(\&some_method);```
Passing any other arguments (or none) calls the subroutine.	```while ($obj->iterator_function())``` ``` { $obj->print_me() }```
Methods declared "abstract" throw exceptions if they're ever invoked.	```use Class::MethodMaker``` ``` abstract => 'redefine_me_later_or_else';```

Table A.4   Ties (Chapter 9)

Concept	Syntax
| The `tie` function takes a variable or a typeglob, plus package name and arranges for that package to provide the interface for the variable or filehandle. | ```perl
tie $scalar, "Package_Name", @other_args;
tie @array,  "Package_Name", @other_args;
tie %hash,   "Package_Name", @other_args;
tie *glob,   "Package_Name", @other_args;
``` |
| When `tie` is called, it passes the package name and any extra arguments to the package's appropriate TIE... method (TIESCALAR, TIEARRAY, TIEHASH, or TIEHANDLE). | ```perl
package Package_Name;

sub TIESCALAR
{
  my ($class, @otherargs) = @_;
  bless { value => undef }, $class;
}
``` |
| That method must return an object, blessed into a class, that provides the necessary interface methods for the type of variable tied. | ```perl
sub Package_Name::FETCH
{
  my ($implementation) = @_;
  return $implementation->{value};
}


sub Package_Name::STORE
{
  my ($implementation, $newval) = @_;
  $implementation->{value} = $newval;
}
``` |

Table A.5   Operator overloading (Chapter 10)

Concept	Syntax
| A class may overload operators on its objects using the standard overload.pm module. When the module is imported, a list of operator names is specified, each with an associated method name or a subroutine reference indicating how it is implemented. | ```perl
package DayOfTheWeek;

use overload
  "+"   => "add_days",    # call as method
  "-"   => \&delta_days,  # call as subroutine
  "neg" => sub { die "can't negate Days" };
``` |
| When an operation involving objects of the class is performed, the corresponding method or subroutine is called. | ```perl
print $day + 7; # print $day->add_days(7,"");
print 31-$day; # print delta_days($day,31,1);
print -$day; # throws "can't negate Days"
``` |
| The method or subroutine called receives three arguments: the object, the other argument (which may also be an object), and a flag indicating whether the order of arguments was reversed (to ensure an object was the first argument). | ```perl
sub delta_days
{
  my ($x, $y, $reversed) = @_;
  ($x,$y) = ($y,$x) if $reversed;
  # do subtraction here
}
``` |

Table A.5   Operator overloading (Chapter 10) (continued)

Concept	Syntax
| The "=" operator specifies a cloning subroutine (*not* an assignment mechanism), which is called just before any mutator operation is applied to an object. | ```perl
use overload
    "++" => "increment",
    "="  => "copy";

$obj++;   # ( $obj=$obj->copy() )->increment();
``` |
| The q{""}, "0+" and "bool" keys are used to specify conversions when an object is evaluated in a string, numeric, or Boolean context. | ```perl
use overload
    q{""}   => "stringify",
    "0+"    => "numerate",
    "bool"  => "booleanize";

if ($obj) # if ($obj->booleanize())
{
    $str .= $obj;   # $str .= $obj->stringify();
    $num += $obj;   # $num += $obj->numerate();
}
``` |

Table A.6   Encapsulation (Chapter 11)

Concept	Syntax
| Attributes can be encapsulated using closure-based objects... | ```perl
package Class::Name;

sub new
{ my ($class) = @_;
  my %data = { r_attr=>undef, rw_attr=>undef };
  my $closure = sub
    { my ($attr, $val) = @_;
      die "$attr is read-only"
          if @_>1 && $attr ne 'rw_attr';
      $data{$attr} = $newval if @_>1;
      return $data{$attr};
    };
  bless $closure, $class;
}

sub r_attr  { shift()->('r_attr',@_) }
sub rw_attr { shift()->('rw_attr',@_) }
``` |
```

Table A.6 Encapsulation (Chapter 11) (continued)

Concept	Syntax
| ...or scalar-based objects (the flyweight pattern)... | ```perl
package Class::Name;
my @data = ();

sub new
{ my ($class) = @_;
  push @data, {r_attr=>undef, rw_attr=>undef};
  my $scalar = $#data;
  bless \$scalar, $class;
}

sub r_attr
{ my ($self) = @_;
  die "r_attr is read-only" if @_>1;
  return $data[$$self]->{r_attr};
}

sub rw_attr
{ my ($self, $val) = @_;
  $data[$$self]->{rw_attr} = $val if @_>1;
  return $data[$$self]->{rw_attr};
}
``` |
| ...or by tie-ing them with the Tie:: SecureHash module. | ```perl
package Class::Name;
use Tie::SecureHash;

sub new
{ my ($class) = @_;
  my $self = Tie::SecureHash->new($class);
  $self->{Class::Name::_r_attr} = undef;
  $self->{Class::Name::_rw_attr} = undef;
  return $self;
}

sub r_attr
{ my ($self) = @_;
  die "r_attr is read-only" if @_>1;
  return $self->{_r_attr};
}

sub rw_attr
{ my ($self, $val) = @_;
  $self->{_rw_attr} = $val if @_>1;
  return $self->{_rw_attr};
}
``` |

Table A.7   Genericity (Chapter 12)

Concept	Syntax
Genericity in Perl is usually achieved via closures…	(see below)

```
package SortedList;

sub import
{
 my ($class,$COMPARE_SUB) = @_;
 my ($CALLER) = caller();
 no strict "refs";

 *{$CALLER."::new"} = sub
 { my ($class, @data) = @_;
   bless { curr=>0, data=>[@data] }, $class;
 };

 *{$CALLER."::insert"} = sub
 { my ($self, $newval) = @_;
   my $arr = $self->{data};
   @$arr = sort $COMPARE_SUB (@$arr,$newval);
 };

 *{$CALLER."::delete"} = sub
 { my ($self) = @_;
   splice @{$self->{data}}, $self->{curr}, 1;
 };

 *{$CALLER."::first"} = sub
 { my ($self) = @_;
   return $self->{data}->[$self->{curr}=0];
 };

 *{$CALLER."::next"} = sub
 { my ($self) = @_;
   return $self->{data}->[++$self->{curr}];
 };

 return 1;
}
```

Table A.7 Genericity (Chapter 12) (continued)

Concept	Syntax
...or else by eval-ing a string template	(see code below)

```
package SortedList;

sub import
{
 my ($class,$COMPARE_TEXT) = @_;
 my ($CALLER) = caller();

 eval <<EOCLASS;
   package $CALLER;
   sub insert
   { my ($self, $newval) = @_;
     my $arr = $self->{data};
     @$arr = sort {$COMPARE_TEXT}
             @$arr,$newval;
   };

   sub new    {...} # implementation as above
   sub delete {...} # implementation as above
   sub first  {...} # implementation as above
   sub next   {...} # implementation as above

EOCLASS

 return 1;
}
```

A P P E N D I X   B

What you might know instead

Many people come to Perl on the rebound from some other language: hurt, confused, disillusioned, looking for comfort. Many of us who learn object-oriented Perl are already painfully familiar with object orientation in some other form. This appendix briefly summarizes the similarities and differences between Perl and four of the better-known object-oriented languages: Smalltalk, C++, Java, and Eiffel.

If you're familiar with one or more of those languages, the following sections may help you get a better grasp on Perl's unique approach to object orientation, by comparison and contrast. If you've never used any of these languages, the following sections can give you a general idea of several other approaches to the same issues.

Each of these comparisons assumes that you're well versed in the other language and at least noddingly acquainted with object-oriented Perl (for example, that you've read the first half of this book).

In other words, this appendix is designed to help someone moving from another language to Perl, rather than someone interested in jumping from Perl to that other language. Specifically, each section couches its description of object-oriented Perl constructs in the terminology of the language with which Perl is being compared.

B.1   PERL AND SMALLTALK

Although Simula 67 was the first programming language to offer all the major components of object-oriented programming, Smalltalk is generally considered to be the first significant object-oriented programming language. Developed in the early 1970s by Alan Kay and his team at Xerox PARC, Smalltalk had evolved into a widely used and relatively stable language by the early 80s. This section assumes you're familiar with the most widely used variant of Smalltalk: Smalltalk-80.

B.1.1 Objects

Perl's general notion of an object—that is, something that has a unique identity, a capacity to store data, and an ability to respond to requests—is surprisingly similar to that of Smalltalk. However, unlike Smalltalk, Perl doesn't require that every datum in a program, including primitive numbers and characters, must be an object. Object-oriented and non-object-oriented Perl can be freely intermixed in a way quite foreign to Smalltalk.

In Smalltalk, every object is accessed through a variable storing a reference to it. Perl objects are (almost always) stored and accessed in the same way. Like Smalltalk variables, the Perl scalars used to store object references are dynamically typed and can be made to refer to any kind of object. Like Smalltalk objects, Perl objects are automatically garbage-collected.

Regardless of their actual class, all Smalltalk objects are record-like collections of attributes, called "instance variables," each of which is uniquely named. Perl is more flexible, allowing an object to be a based on a record-like hash, or an array, or a scalar, or just about any other Perl datatype. Smalltalk also provides a built-in mechanism for declaring class attributes (class instance variables). Perl doesn't provide such a mechanism, but the same effect can be achieved by taking advantage of the scoping rules of lexical variables (chapter 3).

In both Smalltalk and Perl, objects are created by invoking a method, usually called new in both languages.

B.1.2 Classes

In Smalltalk, each object is an instance of a class. Classes are defined in a template provided by the programming environment, or specified by a subclass message sent to an existing class object. In Perl, each class is also a template, but one completely defined by the methods specified in a given package. Perl has no standard concept like a Smalltalk class object, though the capabilities can certainly be simulated (chapter 8).

Like Smalltalk classes, Perl packages have a name and a list of method definitions. Unlike Smalltalk, Perl classes do not directly specify the attributes (instance variables) that are accessible to objects of the class.[1] Instead, it is the responsibility of the Perl class's constructor—its new method—to set up any necessary attributes.

B.1.3 Methods

Smalltalk methods are defined as unary subroutines, binary operators, or keyword selectors in which the method name is implicitly the concatenation of the selector arguments. Perl methods are always just regular named subroutines, which may take any number of arguments

---

[1] …unless the Perl programmer uses a module such as fields.pm (chapter 4), or Class::Struct or Class:: MethodMaker (chapter 8).

(chapter 3). However, Perl methods may also be camouflaged as unary and binary operators using the overload.pm module (chapter 10).

Perl has no built-in dispatch mechanism like a Smalltalk keyword message to a selector, but can provide named arguments to a method call, by treating its argument list as if it were a hash initialization (chapter 3). Unlike Smalltalk methods, Perl methods don't automatically enforce a fixed-length parameter list, even though non-object-oriented Perl subroutines can do so.

Methods are invoked in Smalltalk by sending a message to an object. Such messages consist of the name of the variable referring to the object, followed by the name of the message, which may be implied as the set of selector arguments. Perl methods are invoked in a similar manner (chapter 3) by specifying the name of the variable containing an object reference, followed by the name of the method, and, then, a list of any arguments to the method. In Perl, an arrow is placed between the object reference and the method name.

In Smalltalk, the name of a method being invoked may be parameterized using a selector literal, which allows the name of the method to be specified as a string passed to an object's perform method. Perl provides a simpler mechanism: the method name in any method invocation may be replaced by a scalar variable that contains a reference to the desired method (chapter 3).

While both Smalltalk and Perl methods can return values, the values that Perl returns are not limited to object references, but can be any Perl datatype. Both languages ensure that all methods always return some value: in Smalltalk, if no return value is specified, then the method returns a reference to the invoking object; in Perl, the default return value is the value of last evaluated statement. In this respect, a Perl method is more like a Smalltalk block constructor.

Perl has no built-in mechanism for cascading messages to a particular object, although method invocations can be chained together if each method happens to return a reference to the original object.

Within each method, Smalltalk provides a reference to the object that received the invoking message, through the special identifier self. In Perl, a reference to the invoking object is always passed as the first argument and typically immediately assigned to a scalar variable called $self.

Both languages allow methods to be defined as class methods, rather than object methods. Class methods in Smalltalk are essentially just object methods of the class object—they can even refer to self to access the class object. Class methods in Perl are essentially just object methods which are called by naming the class, rather than invoking through an object (chapter 3).

B.1.4 Encapsulation

Smalltalk objects are strongly encapsulated, so it's not possible to directly access their attributes except within the methods of the class. Instead, the program manipulates those attributes by sending messages to an object, which then performs the necessary computations using its own encapsulated data.

Perl, by contrast, has no enforced encapsulation of object attributes, which are all accessible by any other part of the program (chapter 3). It's possible to set up mechanisms in Perl to provide strong encapsulation (chapter 11), but this must be done manually.

Instead of strong encapsulation, Perl relies on encapsulation by good manners, in that it's customary to politely avoid accessing object attributes directly except within a class's methods.

B.1.5 Inheritance

Unlike Smalltalk classes, which always have a single superclass, each Perl package may inherit from more than one class or from no explicit superclass at all (chapter 6).

In Smalltalk, the inheritance relationships are fixed when classes are defined.[2] In Perl, inheritance relationships are determined dynamically by the contents of the @ISA array belonging to each class. Such relationships are dynamic because run-time changes to the contents of a class's @ISA array actually change its inheritance.

Both Perl and Smalltalk have a primordial class that is the ultimate ancestor of all others. In Smalltalk, it's the Object class; in Perl, it's called UNIVERSAL.

Both languages grant full access to attributes inherited from ancestral classes but in different ways. Smalltalk automatically imports inherited instance variables and reencapsulates them in each subclass. Perl, because it provides no enforced encapsulation, has no need to.

B.1.6 Polymorphism

As in Smalltalk, Perl methods are inherently interface polymorphic (chapter 7). Any method may be invoked on any object that provides a suitable interface. Perl provides no standard mechanism, like the Smalltalk protocol, for controlling such interfaces, although it may be simulated easily enough (chapters 6 and 8).

In both languages, any method inherited from a superclass may be overridden in the subclass. Both languages also provide a mechanism—the super identifier in Smalltalk, the SUPER:: pseudo-package in Perl—for delegating control back to an otherwise overridden method.

Smalltalk's Object protocol provides the class message, with which the actual class of an object can be determined, and the isMemberOf: and isKindOf: messages, with which an object's membership in a specific class hierarchy can be interrogated. Perl provides similar mechanisms: the ref function to determine object classification,[3] and the UNIVERSAL::isa method to determine hierarchy membership (chapter 6).

Smalltalk also provides the respondsTo: message, which can be used to determine if an object conforms to part of a specified protocol (that is, whether it can accept a specific message). In Perl, the UNIVERSAL::can method fulfils the same role.

---

[2] In fact, they're determined by the class to which the subclass message is sent.

[3] ref($object) is actually the equivalent of object class name in Smalltalk, since Perl classes aren't objects and, hence, are always accessed symbolically by their package name.

B.1.7 Control structures and exception handling

Smalltalk is a pure object-oriented language in that even its selection and iteration control structures are implemented as messages passed to objects, in particular to the objects named `true` and `false`. Perl provides explicit imperative control structures: `if`, `unless`, `while`, `until`, and `for` statements.

In Smalltalk, exceptions—like almost everything else—are represented by objects, and exception handlers are implemented by `on:do:` selectors inherited from specific classes. Object-oriented Perl, in contrast, uses the same exception handling techniques as regular Perl (`die` to throw exceptions, `eval` to catch them). More significantly, unlike Smalltalk exceptions, Perl exceptions are always non-resumable.

B.1.8 Comparative syntax

Table B.1 shows the translation of fundamental Smalltalk programming constructs to their Perl equivalents.

Table B.1   Selected comparative syntax for Smalltalk and object-oriented Perl

Construct	Smalltalk	Perl
Comment	`"Comments in double quotes"`	`# comment from '#' to eol`
Undefined literal	`nil`	`undef`
Assignment	`variable := value`	`$variable = value;`
Temporary variable	`| variable |`	`my $variable;`
Conditional execution	`condition ifTrue: [actions]` `ifFalse: [actions]`	`if (condition) { actions }` `else            { actions }`
Iterative execution	`[condition]` `whileTrue: [actions]`	`while (condition)` `{ actions }`
Counted repetition	`1 to: 10 do: [:i| actions ]`	`foreach my $i (1..10) {actions}`
Class definition	`Object subclass: #className`	`package className;`
Class derivation	`superclassObject` `subclass: #subclassName`	`package subclassName;` `@ISA = qw( superclassName );`
Attribute specification	`Object subclass: #className` `instance_variables: 'a b'`	`bless {a=>value, b=>value},` `className;`
Class attribute specification	`Object subclass: #className` `classVariableNames: 'c'`	`package className;` `{ my $c` `sub c` `{ $c = $_[1] if @_>1; $c }` `}`
Object instantiation	`variable := className new`	`$variable = className->new();`
Method definition	`methodName` `actions` `^ returnedValue`	`sub methodName` `{ actions;` `return returnValue; }`
Access to message target	`self`	`my ($self) = @_;`
Access to superclass method	`super methodName`	`$self->SUPER::methodName()`

Table B.1 Selected comparative syntax for Smalltalk and object-oriented Perl (continued)

Construct	Smalltalk	Perl
Method invocation (message dispatch)	`object methodName`	`$object->methodName()`
Class method invocation	`classObject methodName`	`className->methodName()`
"Named" method arguments (selectors)	`object arg1: value arg2: value`	`$object->method( arg1=>value, arg2=>value);`
Parametric method invocation	`object #methodName`	`$method = "methodName"; $object->$method();`
Class type identification	`object class name`	`ref($object)`
Class hierarchy membership	`object isKindOf: superclassObj`	`$object->isa("superclassName")`
Exception handlers	`[actions] on: exceptionClassObject do: [exception:	handle]`	`unless (eval { actions; 1 }) { handle }`
Raising an exception	`exceptionClassObject signal`	`die "exceptionText";`

B.1.9 Where to find out more

The most widely used references for Smalltalk are probably Budd's *A Little Smalltalk* and Goldberg and Rubin's *Smalltalk-80: The language*. A more recent text that provides an integrated introduction to Smalltalk and object-oriented programming in general is Liu's *Smalltalk, Objects, and Design*.

The Smalltalk Industry Council (STIC) is an advocacy group promoting the use of Smalltalk. Their website is at http://www.stic.org/. The University of Illinois hosts an archive site for Smalltalk components, documentation, tutorials, and FAQs (roughly analogous in content to Perl's CPAN) at http://st-www.cs.uiuc.edu/. There is also an active Smalltalk-related newsgroup: comp.lang.smalltalk.

B.2 PERL AND C++

For better or worse, to much of the programming world, C++ *is* object-oriented programming. Devised by Bjarne Stroustrup at the Bell Research Laboratories in the early 80s as an object-oriented successor to the C programming language, C++ has undergone perhaps the most public and collaborative evolution of any programming language, culminating in the recent ANSI C++ standard.

Like Perl, C++ is a hybrid language with object-oriented features layered over an original imperative language. Syntactically and semantically, its non-object-oriented components are almost completely backwards compatible with the C programming language, while its object-oriented features draw most heavily on Simula.

B.2.1 Objects

C++ objects are structured regions of memory that store one or more typed data members. In other words, every object is a record of various fields. In Perl, too, objects may be recordlike structures (i.e., hashes), but they may also be arrays, scalar variables, subroutine references, or any other Perl datatype.

C++ objects may be stored directly in statically typed variables or dynamically created and accessed via typed pointers or references. Perl objects may similarly be variables or unnamed values and are always accessed via references[4] stored in dynamically typed variables. Unlike C++, in Perl there is no need for a manual deallocation mechanism like `delete`, since all objects in Perl are automatically garbage-collected.

C++ also permits the definition of static data members that are (conceptually) shared by all objects of a given class. Perl has no equivalent construct, but it is easy to set up such shared attributes using lexical variables of appropriately restricted scope (chapter 3).

C++ objects are created either by static declaration or by dynamic allocation using the `new` operator. Perl objects are almost always created dynamically, in a method that is often called `new`.

B.2.2 Classes

A class in C++ is a specification of the data and function members (i.e., methods) possessed by a particular kind of object. Classes in Perl also define the methods of a type of object, but do not normally directly specify the attributes possessed by such objects.[5] Attribute specification is typically arranged by the constructor method (e.g., `new`).

In C++, a class specifies a local namespace in which data and function members exist, but C++ also has a separate higher-level `namespace` mechanism with which two or more classes can be grouped. Perl's `package` construct does double-duty as both a namespace and a class specification mechanism, so there is no such ability to construct hierarchical namespaces.

Perl provides better resources for run-time type information than does C++. Whereas a C++ program is restricted to the data provided by the standard `typeid` function, and limited to using dynamic casts to verify class compatibility, Perl allows almost every aspect of a class's structure and capabilities to be interrogated at run-time: class name via the `ref` function, hierarchical relationships via the `UNIVERSAL::isa` subroutine, and method compatibility via the `UNIVERSAL::can` subroutine.

Perl does not directly support generic classes such as those provided by C++ templates. In practice, this presents few problems because the combination of Perl's closure mechanism, interface polymorphism (see below), and dynamic-typing makes generic types largely unnecessary (chapter 12).

---

[4] A Perl reference is semantically closer to a C++ pointer than to a C++ reference. In Perl, references are not automatically dereferenced as they are in C++, nor must they be permanently bound to a given variable.

[5] Although there are modules that make it possible to declaratively specify a class's attributes (chapters 4 and 8).

B.2.3 Methods

C++ and Perl are both hybrid languages that allow code to be executed in stand-alone subroutines as well as methods.

In C++, a class's function members are declared as part of the class specification and may be defined at the same point or anywhere else, provided the appropriate class qualifier (i.e., `ClassName::functionName`) is used. Perl is even more liberal in this respect: a class method may be declared *and* defined anywhere, provided it is suitably qualified (using the same qualification syntax as C++).

Every C++ member function has a specific signature determined by its name and the number and types of arguments it takes. C++ methods may be overloaded, may have default argument values, and may also pass arbitrary arguments (using the "..." specifier). Perl methods have no static checking of parameter types, and Perl unifies the many variable argument list mechanisms of C++ by passing arguments as an actual variable-length list. There is no signature-based method selection (like C++ overloading), but the effect can be achieved using multimethod techniques (chapter 13).

C++ member functions are called on an object or object reference using the "dot" operator (`varOrRef.method(args)`). Methods may also be invoked through a pointer using the "arrow" operator (`ptr->method(args)`). In Perl, methods are always invoked through a reference to an object, using the arrow operator (`$ref->method(args)`). Unlike C++, in Perl, if the method takes no arguments, the trailing parentheses indicating a subroutine call may be omitted.

C++ allows pointers or references to member functions to be used to call those functions on specific objects using the `ptr->*funcptr()` syntax. Perl allows references to methods to be used in the same way, using the `$ref->$methodRef()` notation. Unlike C++, Perl also allows methods to be called by name, by storing a suitable character string—rather than a reference—in the `$methodRef` variable.

In both languages, a method may act like a procedure or a function, depending on whether it chooses to return a value. Both languages provide a `return` statement to specify such return values. However, unlike C++, where a member function that does not return a value must have a return type of `void`, Perl methods do not require, nor allow, any form of return-type specification.

C++ provides the special constant `this` within each member function, which is a pointer to the object on which the method was called. In Perl, a reference to the invoking object is instead passed as the first argument to the call. It is typically extracted from the argument list and stored in a variable called `$self`.

Both C++ and Perl allow class methods to be defined within a class. In C++, such member functions are defined with the `static` qualifier and are called using the syntax `ClassName::method(args)`. In Perl, such methods are defined in the same way as all other methods, and differ only in that they expect the class name—rather than an object reference—as their first argument. They are called using the syntax `ClassName->method(args)`.

Both languages also support the definition of class-specific versions of the standard set of operators (i.e., operator overloading), and, as in C++, overloaded operators in Perl may either be regular subroutines or specific object methods (chapter 10).

B.2.4 Constructors and destructors

C++ classes typically provide a special member function—with the same name as the class itself—that may be used to initialize objects when they are created. Perl has no comparable built-in initialization mechanism. Instead, a regular class method, typically called new, is used to both create and initialize objects.

C++ also provides for destructor functions, which are automatically called on an object just before it goes out of scope or is otherwise deallocated. Perl also allows for destructor methods to be defined using the special method name DESTROY.

B.2.5 Encapsulation

Every data and function member of a C++ class has some associated accessibility—public, protected, or private—which determines the scopes from which it can be directly accessed. Perl has no equivalent concept and does not enforce any form of encapsulation on attributes or methods of objects. There are, however, several programming techniques which permit both attributes and methods to be appropriately restricted in accessibility (chapter 11).

B.2.6 Inheritance

Both C++ and Perl support optional multiple inheritance of superclasses, but in quite different ways. In C++, the classes from which a given class inherits are determined at compile-time by the class definition. The classes that a given Perl package inherits are determined at run-time by the contents of that package's @ISA array.

A subclass in C++ does not have access to the private data and function members of its superclasses.[6] Because the attributes and methods of a Perl class are entirely unencapsulated, there is no equivalent restriction in Perl. Likewise, Perl does not support access variations along the lines of C++'s protected or private inheritance.

Perl does not have a mechanism corresponding to virtual inheritance in C++, nor does it need one, since object attributes are determined dynamically by constructors, rather than statically by class definitions. In practice, the most common forms of class implementation all provide implicit virtual inheritance of attributes.[7]

Unlike C++, Perl classes all implicitly inherit from a single common class called UNIVERSAL.

B.2.7 Polymorphism

In C++, methods are implicitly nonpolymorphic unless they are specifically marked as being virtual. All Perl methods are implicitly polymorphic and there is no way to mark them as nonpolymorphic. Unlike C++, in Perl, any method may be redefined in any derived class.

C++ polymorphism is controlled by class hierarchies because virtual functions are called through typed pointers or references. In Perl, all variables are dynamically typed and, therefore,

---

[6] …except in the highly unusual case where the derived class is also a friend of the base class.

[7] …mainly as a consequence of the uniqueness of keys in the hashes on which most classes are based.

may store a reference to any class of object at any time. Thus, Perl provides the more general form of polymorphism—interface polymorphism—in which any object (regardless of its class hierarchy membership) may respond to any method call for which it has a suitably named method.

C++ allows base class member functions to be accessed from derived class member functions, even if the derived class redefines the function in question. This access is achieved by fully qualifying the nested function call with the name of the desired ancestral class. Perl has the same mechanism. However, Perl also provides a special pseudo-class called SUPER that may be used to delegate a method dispatch to an unspecified ancestral class—namely whichever one actually provides the inherited method (chapter 6).

Perl has no method abstraction construct corresponding to C++'s pure virtual member function declaration. Instead, in keeping with Perl's dynamically typed nature and run-time checking philosophy, if an abstract method is required, a normal method is specified and made to immediately throw an exception.

B.2.8 Comparative syntax

Table B.2 shows a translation into Perl of the fundamental object-oriented features of C++.

Table B.2   Selected comparative syntax for C++ and object-oriented Perl

Construct	C++	Perl
Comment	`// Comment to EOL` `/* Delimited comment*/`	`# comment from '#' to eol`
Assignment	`variable = value;`	`$variable = value;`
Temporary variable	`className variable = init;`	`my $variable = init;`
Class definition	`class className` `{ specification };`	`package className;` `specification`

Class derivation	`class subclassName`
	`  : superclassName(s)`
	`{ specification };`
		`package subclassName;`
		`@ISA = qw( superclassName(s) );`
		`specification`

Attribute specification	`class className`
	`{`
	`  type memberName;`
	`};`
		`bless`
		`  { memberName=>type->new() },`
		`  className;`

Class attribute specification	`class className`
	`{`
	`  static type memberName;`
	`};`
	`type className::memberName`
	`  =init;`
		`package className;`
		`{`
		`  my $var = type->new(init);`
		`  sub fieldName`
		`  { $var = $_[1] if @_>; $var}`
		`}`

Object instantiation	`ptr = new className(args);`	`$ref = className->new(args);`

Table B.2 Selected comparative syntax for C++ and object-oriented Perl (continued)

Construct	C++	Perl
Method definition	```class className { returnType methodName(args) { statements return returnValue; } }```	```package className; sub methodName { my @args = @_; statements; return returnValue; }```
Polymorphic method definition	```virtual returnType methodName (args) { statements return returnValue; }```	```sub methodName { my @args = @_; statements; return returnValue; }```
Abstract method definition	```virtual returnType methodName () = 0;```	```sub methodName { die "Abstract method" }```
Constructor definition	```className(args) { statements }```	```sub new { my {$classname, @args) = @_; my $self = bless {}, $classname; statements; return $self; }```
Destructor definition	```~className() { statements }```	```sub DESTROY { statements }```
Method invocation	```objref.methodName(args); objptr->methodName(args);```	```$objref->methodName(args);```
Indirect method invocation	```retType (class::*methptr)(args) = class::methodName; objref.*methptr(args): objptr->*methptr(args);```	```$methref = \&class::methodName; $ref->$methref(args);```
Class method invocation	```classNam::methodName();```	```className->MethodName();```
Access to message target	```this```	```my ($self) = @_```
Access to superclass method	```this->superclass::methodName();```	```$self->SUPER::methodName();```
Class type identification	```classDescriptor = typeid(object);```	```$className = ref($object);```
Exception handlers	```try { statements } catch { handler }```	```unless (eval { statements; 1 }) { handler }```
Raising an exception	```throw exceptionType(args);```	```die "exceptionText:"```

B.2.9 Where to find out more

The two principal textbooks on C++ are Bjarne Stroustrup's *The C++ Programming Language (3rd Edition)*, and Lippmann and Lajoie's *C++ Primer (3rd Edition)*. There are hundreds of others on the market, but none as definitive or comprehensive as these two.

The distributed and fragmentary nature of C++'s development is nowhere more evident than in the lack of a single overarching website devoted to the language. There are, however, many useful sites devoted to specific aspects of C++. A good starting point is Marshall Cline's C++ FAQ at http://www.cerfnet.com/~mpcline/c++-faq-lite/. Full documentation on the extensive C++ standard template library (or "STL") is available from http://www.sgi.com/Technology/STL/.

C++ is more coherently represented by its various newsgroups. The most relevant and useful two are comp.lang.c++.moderated (for general C++-related questions) and comp.std.c++ (for questions specifically related to the interpretation of the new ANSI standard). Don't bother with comp.lang.c++: it provides too little signal in far too much noise.

B.3 PERL AND JAVA

Java is a relative newcomer to the object-oriented world, having been publicly released in 1995, but it has had a meteoric rise due to the strong support it receives from Sun Microsystems and other industry heavyweights. It has also found a niche because it was carefully targeted as a platform-independent implementation language for web applications.

Java was developed (originally as an embedded systems language called Oak) by James Gosling and his team at Sun. It is (almost[8]) a pure object-oriented language, and derives most of its syntax and some of its general semantics from the C/C++ family of languages. It also draws heavily on Smalltalk.

B.3.1 Objects

Objects in both Java and Perl are collections of data associated with a particular class. In both languages, objects are accessed via references stored in variables. However, unlike Java variables, which are strongly typed, Perl variables may contain references to any kind of object. Like Java objects, Perl objects are automatically garbage-collected.

Java objects are all structurally similar in that they are collections of named fields (i.e., record-like structures). Perl objects, on the other hand, can have a range of internal implementations. In fact, any standard Perl datatype can be the basis for an object. Hence, they may be composed of named entries (in a hash), or a sequence of elements (in an array), or a single value (in a scalar), and so forth.

Java also allows the specification of `static` fields which are not attached to any one object, but belong to the object's class as a whole. Perl has no built-in mechanism for defining

---

[8] A few of its basic types—characters, numbers, and Booleans—are not classes, which is enough to make the more strait-laced language lawyers scoff.

such shared data, but a similar effect can be achieved through the use of lexical variables (chapter 3).

In Java, objects are instantiated by applying the `new` keyword to a class name. Perl objects are created by applying the `bless` function to an existing value. (Although this is almost always encapsulated in a constructor method.)

B.3.2 Classes

A Java class is a specification of the fields possessed by a set of objects and of the methods to which such objects may be passed. In Perl, however, a class is just a specification of methods and doesn't define the attributes of its objects. Instead, the task of setting up object attributes is usually delegated to specific constructor methods.

Packages in Perl are much like those in Java, in that they collect related things in a single separate namespace. However, Java packages operate at a higher level than Perl packages: a Java package may contain several classes which share its namespace; a Perl package can contain only one class.[9]

B.3.3 Methods

Whereas Java is purely object-oriented, at least to the extent that all executable statements must be part of a method, in Perl, object-oriented and non-object-oriented constructs can be used together in the same program.

Java methods are specified as subroutines defined within the scope of a particular class declaration. Perl methods are also subroutines and are defined within a particular package (i.e., namespace), though not necessarily all in the same source file. Whereas each Java method takes a fixed number of arguments, Perl methods always take a dynamically sized list of arguments. In Java, method names may be overloaded, but this facility is not available in standard Perl because dynamic argument lists reduce the need for overloading. If it *is* required, overloading can be simulated (chapter 13).

In Java, methods are invoked by passing a variable containing an object reference, plus any arguments, to the method. The syntax is *var.method(args)*. In Perl, the approach is identical and the syntax nearly so: *$var->method(args)* (chapter 3). Both languages provide a `return` statement for returning values from a method, although, in Perl, the return value is not statically typed.

Within each Java method it's possible to access the object on which the method was invoked through the special reference `this`. In Perl, there is no reserved identifier to provide access to the object. Instead, a reference to the invoking object is always passed as the first argument. Typically, though, that reference is immediately assigned to a local variable, which is almost always called `$self`.

Class methods can be defined in both languages: in Java, by using the `static` modifier when defining a method; in Perl, by declaring a normal method in which the first argument is expected to be a string containing the class name (rather than a reference to some object).

---

[9] ...or, to be precise, a Perl package implements a single class, which has the same name as the package.

Java class methods are called using the syntax `Classname.method(args)`. In Perl, the syntax is once again similar:[10] `Classname->method(args)` (chapter 3).

B.3.4 Constructors and finalizers

In Java, a constructor is a special method that has the same name as the class. It is automatically invoked whenever an object is created. In contrast, constructors in Perl are ordinary class methods, used to both create and initialize an object. By convention, Perl constructors are often called `new`. Java also provides static initializers to set up class attributes. Perl requires no explicit facility to do this. Any initialization code included in a class definition is executed in the normal course of program execution.

A finalizer is a Java object method with the special name `finalize`. This method takes no arguments and has no return type. It is called automatically whenever an object is garbage-collected. In Perl, the equivalent feature is known as a destructor, and it too is distinguished by a special name: `DESTROY`. Unlike a Java finalizer, a Perl destructor is treated like a normal method and does not automatically call the destructors of ancestral classes as well (chapter 6).

B.3.5 Encapsulation

Java objects provide various levels of encapsulation to their fields: `public`, `protected`, `private`, and package visibility. Perl, on the other hand, does not normally enforce any kind of encapsulation on object attributes, all of which are universally accessible throughout a program (chapter 3). Encapsulation in Perl is therefore a matter of convention and programmer discipline, rather than semantics and compiler enforcement. It is, however, possible to "manually" enforce visibility constraints in Perl that are equivalent to Java's "four P's" (chapter 11).

B.3.6 Inheritance

Java classes always inherit from exactly one superclass. Perl packages may inherit from more than one class or from no explicit superclass at all (chapter 6). However, like Java's Object class, Perl has a universal class—called UNIVERSAL—from which all classes ultimately derive.

Perl is unusual in that inheritance relationships are determined at run time, rather than being defined as an integral part of the class definition as they are in Java. In Perl, a subclass inherits methods from whatever superclasses appear in the subclass's `@ISA` array when each method is called.

Subclasses in Java only have access to the non-`private` fields and methods of their superclass. In Perl, which provides no encapsulation of attributes or methods, every class has direct access to every component of its each of its ancestors.

B.3.7 Polymorphism

In both Java and Perl, methods are inherently interface polymorphic (chapter 7). In other words, any method may be invoked on any object whose class conforms to a suitable

---

[10] The syntactic similarities of some aspects Java and object-oriented Perl merely reflect their common inheritance of syntactic features of C/C++.

interface. Perl provides no syntactic mechanism like a Java interface specification—although it may be simulated—but relies instead on run-time checking and exceptions to ensure interfaces are respected.

In both languages, any method inherited from a superclass may be overridden in the subclass. However, Perl has nothing like Java's `final` method modifier to prevent a method from being overridden in derived classes, nor an `abstract` modifier to require that a method be overridden.

In both languages, it's possible to access an overridden method directly. In Java, the pseudo-variable `super` is used; in Perl, the overridden method can be accessed by pretending it belongs to a special pseudo-class called SUPER (chapter 6).

Java's recently extended reflection mechanism, implemented by the `java.lang.reflect` module, provides a means of accessing information about the class of a particular object, as well as the methods and fields it provides. Perl also makes it possible to access this type of information: using the `ref` function to determine an object's classification; the inherited UNIVERSAL::isa method to determine its membership in a hierarchy; and the inherited UNIVERSAL::can method to ascertain whether an object provides a certain method (chapter 6).

B.3.8 Exception handling

Java and Perl provide quite similar approaches to non-resumptive exception handling. The major differences are that Perl exceptions are simple character strings—not full objects as in Java—and that Perl provides no built-in construct equivalent to a `finally` block.

In both Java and Perl, exceptions are thrown by standard execution errors (arithmetic overflow, divide by zero, etc.) and may also be manually raised using a `throw` statement in Java and a `die` statement in Perl. In both languages, exceptions are caught by enclosing fallible code in a special block—a `try` block in Java, an `eval` block in Perl. In Java, any exception caught in this way is handled by a `catch` handler associated with the `try` block. In Perl, the `eval` block simply sets a special variable whenever an exception is caught. Subsequent code can test that variable to decide how to respond.

B.3.9 Comparative syntax

Table B.3 shows the Perl equivalents of the basic Java programming constructs.

Table B.3 Selected comparative syntax for Java and object-oriented Perl

Construct	Java	Perl
Comment	`// Comment to EOL` `/* Delimited comment */`	`# comment from '#' to eol`
Undefined literal	`null`	`undef`
Assignment	`variable = value;`	`$variable = value;`
Temporary variable	`className variable = init;`	`my $variable = init;`
Class definition	`class className` `{ specification }`	`package className;` `specification`

Class derivation	`class subclassName`
	`    extends superclassName`
	`{ specification }`
		`package subclassName;`
		`@ISA = qw( superclassName );`
		`specification`

Construct	Java	Perl
Attribute specification	```class className { public type fieldName; }```	```bless { fieldName=>type->new() }, className;```
Class attribute specification	```class className { public static type fieldName = new type(); }```	```package className; { my $var = type->new(); sub fieldName { $var = $_[1] if @_>1; $var} }```
Object instantiation	```var = new className (args);```	```$var = className->new(args);```
Method definition	```class className { public returnType methodName { statements; return returnValue; } }```	```package className; sub methodName { statements; return returnValue; }```
Abstract method definition	```public abstract returnType methodName();```	```sub methodName { die "Abstract method " }```
Constructor definition	```class className { className(args) { statements } }```	```sub new { my ($classname,@args) = @_; my $self = bless {}, $classname; statements; return $self; }```
Finalizer definition	```class className { public void finalize() { statements } }```	```package className; sub DESTROY { statements }```
Method invocation	```var.methodName(args);```	```$var->methodName(args);```
Class method invocation	```className.methodName();```	```className->methodName();```
Access to message target	```this```	```my ($self) = @_```
Access to superclass method	```super.methodname(args);```	```$self->SUPER::methodName(args);```
Class type identification	```className = object.getClass().getName();```	```$className = ref($object);```
Object interface tests	```class = object.getClass(); methodObject = class.getMethod("methodname");```	```$methodReference = $object->can("methodName");```
Exception handlers	```try { statements } catch { handler }```	```unless (eval { statements; 1 }) { handler }```
Raising an exception	```throw new exceptionType;```	```die "exceptionText";```

B.3.10 Where to find out more

The world is awash with books on Java. The definitive text is Arnold and Gosling's *The Java Programming Language*, while the most popular introductions are Ivor Horton's *Beginning Java* and David Flanaghan's *Java in a Nutshell*. If you're after a nontechnical overview of the language, try *Making Sense of Java*, by Simpson, Mitchell, Christeson, Zaidi, and Levine.

The web is similarly saturated with Java-related information, but there's little need to look anywhere other than Sun Microsystem's own Java Technologies Home Page at http://java.sun.com/.

Java is widely discussed in a number of newsgroups, starting with comp.lang.java and its many specialized subgroups (comp.lang.java.databases, comp.lang.java.beans, comp.lang.java.corba, etc.) A good place to start is comp.lang.java.help.

B.4 PERL AND EIFFEL

Eiffel is a pure object-oriented language designed by Bertrand Meyer in 1985 and first released the following year. It is strongly grounded in software development theory and supports a programming-by-contract view of class design. Semantically, it draws most heavily on the Simula/Smalltalk school of object orientation, though syntactically it is much closer to the Algol/Pascal family of languages.

B.4.1 Objects

Perl takes a much less regimented approach to objects than Eiffel. Whereas every object in Eiffel is either atomic (a numeric or Boolean value) or a recordlike composite of specified fields, Perl allows any of its built-in data types to be used as objects (chapters 3 to 5).

In Eiffel, objects may be accessed through entities, which are strongly typed variable-like constructs. They may store a reference to an object or the object itself. Perl objects are almost always stored and accessed as references in dynamically typed scalar variables (chapter 3). Like Eiffel objects, Perl objects are automatically garbage-collected.

Eiffel also provides a built-in mechanism for declaring class attributes (class instance variables). Perl does not provide such a mechanism, but the effect can be achieved by taking advantage of the scoping rules of lexical variables (chapter 3).

In Eiffel objects are either created implicitly—by declaring an entity of an expanded type—or explicitly—by applying the `!!` operator to an entity of an unexpanded type. Usually, a creation feature, conventionally called `make`, is also called to initialize the new object. In Perl, objects are almost always created by invoking a constructor method, which is often called `new`. The actual creation of the object within that method is accomplished by applying the built-in `bless` function to a regular Perl datatype.

B.4.2 Classes

In Eiffel, a class is a specification of the features (routines and attributes) that a certain kind of object possesses, and every object is a direct instance of some class. In Perl, each class is a package, whose subroutines specify the methods that objects of that class may invoke. In both languages, a clear distinction exists between the concepts of class and instance, as opposed to languages such as Smalltalk and Self where everything, including classes, is an object.

Like Eiffel classes, Perl packages have a name and specify the interface of objects. Unlike Eiffel, in Perl, that interface is simply a list of method definitions.[11] Unlike Eiffel classes, Perl packages do not normally specify the attributes of objects of the class. Instead, it is the responsibility of a class's constructor method to set up any necessary attributes within the object's implementation datatype.

Unlike Eiffel, Perl provides no mechanism to specify class invariants. It is, however, possible to transparently overlay such mechanisms through the appropriate use of autoloaded methods (chapters 2 and 3).

B.4.3 Methods

In Eiffel, a class's methods are those of its features that have been implemented as routines. Routines may be specified as named procedures and functions, or prefix and infix operations. In Perl, methods are always named subroutines belonging to a particular package, although prefix, postfix, and infix operators may also be associated with a class (chapter 10).

Eiffel routines enforce static type checking on their parameter lists. Because they are standard Perl subroutines, Perl methods don't enforce parameter types or counts, though they can interrogate these properties at run-time.

Methods are invoked in Eiffel by naming the entity attached to the object in question, followed by a dot, followed by the name of the routine to be invoked on that entity. Perl method calls are conceptually identical: the variable containing a reference to the object in question, followed by a right arrow, followed by the name of the method to be invoked (chapter 3). In both languages, an argument list may be passed to the invoked method, or omitted entirely if no arguments are required.

Eiffel functions return a value by assigning it to the special entity `Result`. Perl methods return values using an explicit `return` statement. Within an Eiffel routine, the object on which the routine was invoked is available through the special entity `Current`. In Perl, there is no reserved symbol for the current object. Instead, a reference to it is passed as the first argument to the method (chapter 3).

Eiffel's `once` construct declares functions that cache their result and never recompute it. This provides a way to implement class attributes using the cached return value of a particular `once` function to store a shared attribute value. Perl does not provide a built-in mechanism for caching subroutine return values,[12] nor does it directly support class attributes. Instead, it uses lexically scoped variables declared within a class's package to implement encapsulated shared data (chapter 3).

Perl has no built-in mechanism for validating pre- or post- assertions on methods, although it is easy to develop mechanisms to do so (chapter 2).

---

[11] Perl objects also inherit the interface of the datatype with which they are implemented, but it is preferable to avoid the unencapsulated use of this implementation interface (chapter 11).

[12] ...although the Memoize module developed by Mark-Jason Dominus makes it easy to achieve the same effect...

B.4.4 Encapsulation

Eiffel objects provide two levels of encapsulation of attribute features: available and unavailable. A given feature may be made available to a specified set of other classes, or to all classes ("fully exported"), or none except the owner class itself ("secret"). Perl has no mechanism to control the accessibility of methods or attributes in this way. It is as if every Perl method, including those which are part of its implementation, were fully exported (chapter 3). To restrict the accessibility of attributes, manually coded mechanisms or a special module must be used (chapter 11).

B.4.5 Inheritance

Like Eiffel, Perl supports single and multiple inheritance of classes, as well as the specification of classes which inherit from no class at all (chapter 6).

The inheritance relationships of an Eiffel class are fixed when classes are defined, but, in Perl, inheritance relationships are determined at run-time, according to the values assigned to a class's @ISA.

In Eiffel, whether a derived class has access to a particular feature is determined by the export list associated with that feature in the inherited class. Because attributes and methods in Perl classes are unencapsulated, derived classes automatically have full access to all features inherited from any class.

Eiffel and Perl provide different mechanisms for resolving the ambiguities that multiple inheritance can produce. Eiffel provides the ability to rename inherited features, undefine them, redefine them, and select between two or more inherited features of the same name. In Perl, by contrast, a method defined in a derived class always supplants one of the same name inherited from a base class. Perl also uses a single rule to resolve conflicts between inherited methods: the method inherited from the left-most parent in a class's inheritance list is always preferred (chapter 6).

Eiffel enables abstract methods and classes to be defined using the `deferred` keyword. Perl has no equivalent built-in mechanism, but the effect of deferred routines is easily achieved by throwing an exception from each (nominally) abstract method.

Both languages provide a mechanism for accessing an inherited method overridden in a derived class. In Eiffel, the `Precursor` identifier may be used to access the overridden routine. In Perl, the overridden method is accessible via the `SUPER` pseudo-class (chapter 6).

B.4.6 Polymorphism

The dynamic attachment of objects to typed entities provides Eiffel with inheritance polymorphism. That is, an object of a derived class may be attached to an attribute, and subsequent accesses to features of that object will be correctly dispatched to the corresponding routine in the derived class. Perl also provides this form of polymorphism, but because the variables which hold object references are untyped, it also provides the more general form of polymorphism: interface polymorphic (chapter 7).

Eiffel provides the conditional assignment operator (`?=`) to test whether a value is type-compatible with a typed entity before assignment. Perl has no such operator because Perl variables have no associated class type. Instead, Perl provides the type-inquiry function `ref` and two interface enquiry methods: `isa` and `can`.

B.4.7 Genericity

Perl provides no built-in mechanism for parameterized classes as Eiffel does. This is rarely a problem, since the dynamically typed nature of Perl variables, combined with Perl's interface polymorphism, eliminates most of the need for genericity. Where generic classes are desirable, they may be implemented easily using closures or run-time code generation (chapter 12).

B.4.8 Comparative syntax

Table B.1 shows the equivalent Perl syntax for a range of key features of the Eiffel language.

B.4.9 Where to find out more

Bertrand Meyer's textbook *Object-Oriented Software Construction (2nd edition)* is generally considered to be one of the best introductions to object orientation available, and is certainly a good introduction to Eiffel as well.

The online home of Eiffel is the Interactive Software Engineering home page at http://www.eiffel.com/. Eiffel's governing body, the Non-profit International Consortium for Eiffel (NICE), has its home page at http://www.eiffel.tm/. A useful source for Eiffel-related links is Geoff Eldridge's Universal Eiffel Resource Locator (the GUERL) available from the "Eiffel Liberty Journal" site at http://www.elj.com/eiffel/.

The Eiffel newsgroup is comp.lang.eiffel.

Table B.4   Selected comparative syntax for Eiffel and object-oriented Perl

Construct	Eiffel	Perl
Comment	`-- comment from dashes to eol`	`# comment from '#' to eol`
Undefined literal	`Void`	`undef`
Assignment	`entity := value`	`$variable = value;`
Temporary variable	`local entity : type`	`my $variable;`

Class definition	`class className`
	`  specification`
	`end`
		`package className;`
		`specification`

Object instantiation	`local entity : className` `!! entity`	`$objref = className->new();`
Object initialization	`local entity : className` `!! entity.make(args)`	`$objref =` `  className->new(@args);`
Method invocation	`entity.methodName(args)`	`$objref->methodName(@args);`

Class derivation	`class subclassName`
	`inherit`
	`  superclass1, superclass2`
	`  subclassSpecification`
	`end`
		`package subclassName;`
		`@ISA = qw( superclass1`
		`            superclass2 );`
		`subclassSpecification`

Table B.4   Selected comparative syntax for Eiffel and object-oriented Perl (continued)

Construct	Eiffel	Perl
Class attribute specification	```class className feature c : C_TYPE is once !! Result end```	```package className; { my $c = C_TYPE->new(); sub c { $c = $_[1] if @_>1; $c } }```
Method definition	```feature methodname (parameters) is do actions Result := returnedValue end```	```sub methodName { my (@parameters) = @_; actions; return returnValue; }```
Abstract method definition	```feature methodname is deferred```	```sub methodName { die "Abstract method " }```
Access to message target	```Current```	```my ($self) = @_;```
Access to superclass method	```Precursor(args)```	```$self->SUPER::methodName(@args)```
Assignment compatability	```local entity : className entity ?= value```	```$objref = $value if $value->isa(className)```
Exception handlers	``` code rescue recover retry end```	```until (eval { code; 1 }) { recover }```
Raising an exception	```local exception : EXCEPTIONS exception.raise```	```die "exception";```

glossary

Abstract base class. A class—normally in the upper tiers of a hierarchy—that is not intended to instantiate objects. Typically, it exists only as a respository for shared code inherited by other classes or as a means of specifying a particular interface. To enforce these roles, abstract classes may often define one or more abstract methods. See *Abstract method.*

Abstract data type. A description of the attributes possessed by objects of a specific class, the relationships between those attributes, and the operations specified for such objects. The description is independent of all implementation issues.

Abstract method. A method that acts as a placeholder in the base class of a hierarchy implementing inheritance polymorphism. The method has no usable implementation of its own, though it may throw a cautionary exception. It exists to force derived classes to redefine that particular method.

Accessor. A method whose purpose is to provide controlled access to an attribute of an object. Accessors typically enforce the read-only status of certain attributes or provide range checking on assigned values. See *Mutator.*

Actual target. The single multimethod variant selected from the list of viable targets by the multimethod's dispatch resolution process. See *Multimethod.*

Affordances. Physical or logical features of a tool or system that passively encourage correct use.

Aggregation. Constructing a system from simpler components. For example, creating an object by binding together two or more simpler objects (as attributes).

Aliasing. When two or more symbols in a program to refer to the same underlying entity. In Perl, aliasing occurs in several contexts. The subroutine arguments $_[0], $_[1], $_[2], and so forth. act as alternate names for the original arguments to a subroutine; typeglob assignment causes two symbols to refer to the same underlying values; and, in a foreach (*list*) statement, the variable $_ becomes another name for each list element in turn.

Ancestor class. A class that provides a description of attributes or methods that the current class uses (in addition to any attributes and methods it may itself define). See *Parent class.*

Attribute. A container for a specific datum belonging to an object (see *Object attribute*) or to a class of objects (see *Class Attribute*).

Attribute value.   Data stored in an attribute.

Autovivification.   The generally useful—but occasionally annoying—feature of Perl arrays, hashes, and references that allows them to automatically create nonexistent elements, entries, or referents when those missing components are modified.

Base class.   In general, a class appearing in a given class's inheritance hierarchy to provide some attributes or methods to that class. In Perl, if B->isa('A'), then class A is a base class of class B. See also *Superclass*, *Parent class*.

Child class.   Some other class that uses the description of attributes or methods provided by the current class.

Class.   A namespace or user-defined type that specifies the attributes and methods used by a certain set of objects. In Perl, a package used for that purpose.

Class attribute.   A named storage location for data associated with, and preferably encapsulated in, the namespace in a given class. Such an attribute is shared by all objects of that class. Compare with *Object attribute*.

Class hierarchy.   The graphlike structure created by the inheritance relationships between parent and child classes. It is a hierarchy because all inheritance relationships are asymmetrical. It is graph-like because any class may have two or more parents and two or more children.

Class method.   A method that may be called directly on a class, rather than on an object. In Perl, such a method is normally invoked using the *Classname->method(@args)* syntax. The typical example is the constructor method *Classname->new()*.

Closure.   A subroutine that has access to, and preserves the values of, all lexical variables in the scope in which it is defined, even when subsequently called from outside that scope. In Perl, any anonymous subroutine has access to all lexical variables from the scope in which it is defined. Thus, all Perl anonymous subroutines are *potentially* closures, although only those which do refer to external lexical variables are *actually* closures).

Composition.   See *Aggregation*.

Constructor.   A class or object method that creates, and often initializes, a new object. In Perl, a regular class or object method—often, but not necessarily, called new—that blesses and initializes the implementation of a new object and returns a reference to it.

Decoupling.   The separation of unrelated parts of a system. Decoupling reduces complexity and limits the propagation of errors.

Delegation.   Implementing a method's complete behavior by calling some other method, typically one belonging to—or referred to by—an attribute.

Derived class.   In general, any class D that directly inherits from a base class B. In Perl, if the package array @D::ISA contains the name of class B, then class D is treated as being derived from class B. See *Child class*, *Subclass*.

Destructor.   An object method that is automatically called when an object ceases to exist. Typically, such methods are used to undo any side-effects of an object's former existence. In Perl, a method with the special name DESTROY, which is invoked just before an object is garbage-collected.

Dispatch resolution.　The procedure that determines which method to invoke in response to a given method call. In Perl, the dispatch resolution algorithm looks for the method in the package, P, into which the invoking object is currently blessed. If no such method exists, the parent classes of the P, as specified in the array `@P::ISA`, are searched for the method in a depth-first, left-to-right, recursive sequence. Finally, the package UNIVERSAL is searched. If a suitable method is still not found, the dispatch process looks for a method called `P::AUTOLOAD` in the class P, its ancestral classes, and, finally, in UNIVERSAL. If that search fails, the dispatch mechanism throws an exception.

Dispatch table.　A multidimensional table storing references to variants of a multimethod. Each dimension of the table is indexed by the names of classes whose objects may be passed as arguments in a particular parameter position of the multimethod.

Emergent system.　A system with little or no centralized control, whose interesting behavior is not explicitly coded, but develops spontaneously as a result of the low level interactions between components of the system.

Encapsulation.　The restriction of an attribute or method to a namespace. Encapsulated members of a class are not directly accessible, except to methods of the same class. This is desirable because it ensures that changes to attribute values can only be made in controlled ways (by calling methods of the class). It also ensures that alterations to a class's implementation do not affect client code.

Encoding.　The process of converting the internal representation of a data structure into an externally storable format—typically, to a linear sequence of characters. Also known as *Serialization*.

Exception.　A mechanism for transfer of control within a program. Typically used to handle unusual or erroneous conditions (hence the name). In Perl, a call to `die` (or `croak`) anywhere in a program. That call causes control to be propagated back to any enclosing `eval` statement. If there is no enclosing `eval` statement, the program terminates.

Flyweight pattern.　An object-oriented idiom in which objects are small, usually holding only a single scalar value. That value is used as an index or key into a separate, larger collection of data that stores the attributes of all objects of the class.

Helper class.　A class whose task is to assist some other class. Often used as a return type for particular methods of the other class or as an internal representation that the other class uses. Compare with *Mixin*.

Identity.　The property of objects that allows them to be distinguished from other objects, which may otherwise be storing exactly the same data.

Idioms.　Techniques or generic code structures peculiar to a particular coding style, programming language, or language paradigm. Also known as "patterns."

Implementation.　The encapsulated members of a class. The implementation of a class provides the actual functionality of the class's objects. It may be changed as necessary, provided that the apparent behavior of the class's publicly accessible methods is not altered. Compare with *Interface*.

Implementation object.　In Perl, a blessed object that provides the implementation—attributes and methods—for a tied variable.

Inheritance.   A relationship between two classes in which one (the *Child class*) assumes all the properties—attributes and methods—of the other (the *Parent class*).

Inheritance distance.   The number of steps in the inheritance chain between two classes—typically from the actual class of an argument to the class of the corresponding formal parameter. By extension, the sum of the inheritance distances from a set of arguments to a corresponding set of parameters. Typically used to compare the merits of the viable targets of a multimethod.

Inheritance polymorphism.   A form of polymorphism that requires an invoking object to belong to a particular class hierarchy. Under inheritance polymorphism, a method can only be invoked on an object if the object belongs to class derived from a specified base class. Compare with *Interface polymorphism.*

Inherited class.   See *Base class.*

Instantiation.   The process of creating an object from the specification provided by a class.

Instance.   An object belonging to a specified class. In Perl, any standard datatype (array, hash, scalar, etc.) that has been blessed into a specific package.

Interface.   The universally accessible members of a class. Normally, the interface provided by a class consists entirely of methods, which may be called to access or modify encapsulated attributes. However, a class may also provide nonencapsulated attributes as part of its interface. By using only its documented interface, code that uses an object insulates itself from changes in that object's implementation. Compare with *Implementation.*

Interface polymorphism.   A form of polymorphism that does not require the invoking object to belong to a particular class hierarchy. Under interface polymorphism, a method may be invoked on an object provided the object's class has a suitably named method. Compare with *Inheritance polymorphism.*

Invoking object.   The object through which an object method is called. In Perl, for a method call such as `$objref->method(@args)`, the invoking object is the one referred to by `$objref`. A reference to the invoking object is always the first argument (i.e. `$_[0]`) passed to a Perl object method.

Is-a.   The relationship between a child and parent class (or objects of such classes). Indicates that the child class provides the same facilities as the parent class.

Lexical analyser (lexer).   An object or function that breaks a character string into a series of labeled substrings, whose labels indicate each substring's grammatical role in the original string.

Member.   An inclusive term for an attribute or a method.

Memoized computed attribute.   An attribute whose value is not (initially) stored in an object. The first time its value is requested, the attribute computes and then stores it for subsequent reuse. The technique is typically used when an attribute value is expensive to compute, does not change once computed, and may not be required.

Message.   The combination of a method name and a list of one or more objects or values on which the method is to operate. In Perl, a message typically looks like: `$objref->method(@args)`.

Method.   A subroutine associated with a given class, designed to operate exclusively on objects of that class. In Perl, a subroutine defined in a package into which objects have been blessed. See *Object Method* and *Class method*.

Method signature.   The combination of the name of a method and the names of the classes of its expected parameters. Used in multiply dispatched systems, or singly dispatched systems with method overloading, to determine which method to invoke in response to a message. A method's signature is normally required to be unique within the namespace of its class. Perl does not support method signatures directly.

Mixin.   A class inherited solely to provide certain behaviors to another class. Typically, a mixin is incomplete by itself. That is, its objects would serve no useful purpose by themselves, if instantiated. Compare with *Helper class*.

Module.   In Perl, a library file containing one or more packages.

Multimethod.   A polymorphic method dispatched according to the types of all its arguments, not just that of its invoking object. Perl does not provide a built-in multimethod mechanism, though multimethods may be implemented using other standard features of the language. See *Multiple dispatch*.

Multimethod variant.   A method or subroutine that a multimethod invokes in response to a specific set of parameter types. Typically, all variants of a multimethod share the same name, but have unique signatures.

Multiple dispatch.   An approach to polymorphic method invocation in which the method invoked in response to a particular call depends on the classes of two or more of its arguments. Perl does not directly support multiple dispatch. Compare with *Single dispatch*.

Multiple inheritance.   The situation where a class directly inherits from two or more classes. In Perl, the situation of having two or more elements in a class's `@ISA` array.

Mutator.   A method or operator that changes the value of the object on which it's invoked. Compare with *Accessor*.

Namespace.   The potential or actual set of unique names in a particular symbolic reference mechanism. In Perl, the set of distinct symbol names in a package's symbol table.

Object.   A means of identifying, encapsulating, and accessing a collection of data. In Perl, any standard datatype (array, hash, scalar, etc.) that has been blessed into a specific package.

Object attribute.   A named storage location for data associated with, and preferably encapsulated within, a single object. Compare with *Class attribute*.

Object method.   A method which can be invoked on an individual object of a given class. Compare with *Class method*.

Operator overloading.   The ability to change the semantics of a language's built-in operators when those operators are applied to objects of user-defined classes. In Perl, the ability to associate a subroutine with a particular operator, and have it called when that operator is applied to objects of a particular class.

Override.   To change in a derived class the behavior of an inherited method.

Package.   A Perl construct that provides a separate namespace for variables and subroutines.

Parent class.   Some other class that provides the description of attributes and/or methods inherited by the current class. See: *Base class, Superclass.*

Persistence.   The property of a system in which data can survive the termination of the program that creates it.

Polymorphism.   A situation in which the method invoked in response to a particular method call depends on the class of one or more of the arguments to that method—typically, on the class of the object on which the method is invoked. In Perl, all method calls are polymorphic. See *Single dispatch* and *Multiple dispatch.*

Private member.   Internal data or functionality. An attribute or method only directly accessible to the methods of the same class and inaccessible from any other scope. In Perl, notionally private attributes and members are conventionally given names beginning with an underscore. Compare with *Protected member* and *Public member.*

Protected member.   Restricted data or functionality. An attribute or method only directly accessible to methods of the same class or of a subclass, but inaccessible from any other scope. Compare with *Private member* and *Public member.*

Proxy.   An object that takes the place of, or emulates, some other object. Compare with *Delegation* and *Helper class.*

Pseudo-hash.   In Perl, an array that can act as a hash because its first element stores a mapping from keys to indices.

Public member.   Externally visible data or functionality. An attribute or method that is directly accessible from scopes outside the class. In Perl, most members are, by their standard semantics, public. By convention, attributes of Perl classes and objects are regarded as private, as are methods whose names begin with an underscore. Compare with *Private member* and *Protected member.*

Referent.   The datatype or object to which a reference refers.

Serialization.   See *Encoding.*

Signature.   See *Method signature.*

Single dispatch.   An approach to polymorphic method invocation in which the method invoked in response to a particular call depends on the class of its first argument alone. Compare with *Multiple dispatch.*

Subclass.   A class that inherits attributes or methods from the class in question. Subclasses are usually created to augment or restrict the behaviour of the inherited class. Also known as *Child class* or *Derived class.* Compare with *Superclass.*

Superclass.   A class from which the class in question directly inherits. Also known as *Parent class* or *Base class.* Compare with *Subclass.*

Symbolic reference.   In Perl, a string containing the name of something in a package's symbol table. Symbolic references can only refer to package variables.

Token.   A string that has been labeled with some semantic information (such as its part-of-speech or its role in a grammatical construction). See *Lexical analyser.*

Typed lexical.   In Perl, a lexical variable that has a class name associated with it. Typed lexicals allow certain compile-time checks and optimizations to be carried out on variables that store references to pseudo-hashes. See *Pseudo-hash.*

Variant.   See *Multimethod variant.*

Viable targets.   The set of multimethod variants whose parameter types are compatible with those of the arguments to a multimethod call. Not directly supported in Perl.

bibliography

Object orientation

Booch, Grady, *Object-Oriented Design with Applications*, Redwood City, Calif.: Benjamin/Cummings, 1991.

Booch, Grady, *Object-Oriented Analysis and Design with Applications*, Redwood City, Calif.: Benjamin/Cummings, 1994.

Gamma, Eric, Richard Helm, Ralph Johnson and John Vlissides, *Design Patterns: Elements of Reusable Object-Oriented Software*, Reading, Mass.: Addison-Wesley, 1995.

Meyer, Bertrand, *Object-Oriented Software Construction*, New York: Prentice-Hall, 1998.

Reenskaug, Trygve, *Working With Objects: The OOram Software Engineering Method*, Greenwich: Manning Publications, 1996.

Taylor, David A., *Object Technology: A Manager's Guide (second edition)*, Reading, Mass.: Addison-Wesley, 1998.

Perl

Brown, Vicki and Chris Nandor, *MacPerl: Power and Ease*, Sunnyvale, Calif.: Prime Time Freeware, 1998.

Christiansen, Tom and Nathan Torkington, *Perl Cookbook*, Sebastopol, Calif.: O'Reilly & Associates, 1997.

Hall, Joseph N. and Randal L. Schwartz, *Effective Perl Programming*, Reading, Mass.: Addison-Wesley, 1998.

Johnson, Eric F., *Cross-Platform Perl*, New York: M&T Books, 1996.

Johnson, Andrew L., *The Elements of Programming with Perl*, Greenwich: Manning Publications, 1999.

Orwant, Jon (ed.), *The Perl Journal*, New York, EarthWeb, Inc.

Schwartz, Randal L. and Tom Christiansen, *Learning Perl (second edition)*, Sebastopol, Calif.: O'Reilly & Associates, 1997.

Schwartz, Randal L., Erik Olson and Tom Christiansen, *Learning Perl on Win32 Systems*, Sebastopol, Calif.: O'Reilly & Associates, 1997.

Srinivasan, Sriram, *Advanced Perl Programming*, Sebastopol, Calif.: O'Reilly & Associates, 1997.

Wall, Larry, Tom Christiansen and Randal L. Schwartz, *Programming Perl (second edition)*, Sebastopol, Calif.: O'Reilly & Associates, 1996.

Other object-oriented languages

C++

Stroustrup, Bjarne, *The C++ Programming Language (third edition)*, Reading, Mass.: Addison-Wesley, 1997.

Lippmann, Stanley and Josée Lajoie, *C++ Primer (third edition)*, Reading, Mass.: Addison-Wesley, 1998.

Eiffel

Meyer, Bertrand, *Eiffel: The Language*, New York: Prentice-Hall, 1992.

Java

Arnold, Ken and James Gosling, *The Java Programming Language*, Reading, Mass.: Addison-Wesley, 1997.

Horton, Ivor, *Beginning Java 2*, Chicago: Wrox Press, 1999.

Flanaghan, David, *Java in a Nutshell (second edition)*, Sebastopol, Calif.: O'Reilly & Associates, 1997.

Simpson, Bruce, John Mitchell, Brian Christeson, Rehan Zaidi and Jonathan Levine, *Making Sense of Java: A Guide for Managers and the Rest of Us,* Greenwich: Manning Publications, 1996.

Smalltalk

Budd, Timothy, *A Little Smalltalk*, Reading, Mass.: Addison-Wesley, 1987.

Goldberg, Adele and David Robson, *Smalltalk-80: The Language*, Reading, Mass.: Addison-Wesley, 1989.

Liu, Chamond, *Smalltalk, Objects, and Design*, Greenwich: Manning Publications, 1996.

Miscellaneous

Friedl, Jeffrey, *Mastering Regular Expressions*, Sebastopol, Calif.: O'Reilly & Associates, 1997.

Norman, Donald, *The Psychology of Everyday Things*, New York: Basic Books, 1988.

Norman, Donald, *The Design of Everyday Things*, New York: Doubleday, 1990.

index

expectation 293
expediency 280, 293
explicit method definition vs
&AUTOLOAD 92
explosion, disarming 340
exponentiation 279
Exporter module 55, 89, 408
exporting from object-oriented
modules 89
external representation 17
extraction
of persistent data 394
of variable names 403

F

factoring out shared code 12
fallability 248
fall-back
for polymorphism failure 11
strategy 204
fallback pseudo-operator 281
familiarity 136
fascism
compile-time errors 344
linguistic 236
fastidiousness 96
fatal signals 405
Fates 46
Fcntl module 393, 402
feature 18
feature set 18
feedback to pager 163
field 18, 130
donation 191
of a pseudo-hash 132
fields.pm module 130, 190,
309, 439
file
as object 413
flat 393, 408
mapping 416
name 408
permissions 414
filehandle 60, 159, 253, 414
memory mapping 417
object-oriented 268
tied 256, 268

fileno function 257
fill in the blanks 16
fine-grained persistence 17,
388, 412
FinePersistence module 423
finite state machine 108
FireTruck class 5
flag
indicating reversed
operands 279
persistent bit-strings 414
flag-like attributes 226
flat files 393
flattening for data
serialization 389
flattening of lists 24
flexibility 118, 296, 321, 330,
400
floating-point
constants 288
numbers 276
flock of birds 349
flyweight pattern 302, 435, 461
foresight 195
fork 162
forking open 162
format 60
formatting code 157
forward-compatibility 196
forwarded method 229
fragmentation of generic
class 334
freeze 388, 390, 391, 394
FreezeThaw module 391, 418
and UNIVERSAL
package 400
Freidl, Jeffrey 69
friendly warning 249
frugality 391
fully-qualified
method name 173
package variable names 45
functionality, inherited vs
defined 183
functions 24
future-proof code 88

G

garbage-collection
in other languages 439,
444, 449, 454
gcc 153
GDBM_File module 394
GDP, China vs USA 276
genealogy 204
generation
code 329
of code 214, 392
of consistent unique
identity 388
of dispatch table 368
generator subroutine 57
generic
"maximum" function 29
behaviour of abstract
method 12
handler 368
method 16, 18, 418
name of parent class 183
peristence 412
persistence 424
subroutine 327, 426
type 327
generic class 16, 330
fragmentation of 334
other terms for 18
generic module 18
generic package 18
genericity 15, 327, 436
in other languages 444, 457
the point of 339
vs abstraction 327
genes, dominant 372
genetic information 250
Genome::Array class 414
gensym 162, 253, 260, 268, 415
getc function 257
get-or-set accessor 224
gigabytes of data 250
global accessibility, badness of 4
glossary 459
glue 21
gods, Ancient Greek 46
good